The Structure of
International Society

Second Edition

D1405115

THE STRUCTURE OF INTERNATIONAL SOCIETY

An Introduction to the Study of International Relations

Second Edition

GEOFFREY STERN

continuum
LONDON • NEW YORK

T&T Clark
A Continuum imprint

The Tower Building
11 York Road
London SE1 7NX

80 Maiden Lane
Suite 704
New York, NY 10038

www.continuumbooks.com

First Published in 1995. Paperback reprinted 199, 1998.
Second edition published in 2000.
Reprinted 2003, 2006

British Library Cataloguing - in-Publication Data
A catalogue record for this book is available from the British Library.

ISBN 1-85567-646-X (hardback)
ISBN 0-8264-6823-3 (paperback)

Library of Congress Cataloging - in Publication Data
Stern, Geoffrey
     The structure of international society: an introduction to the
study of international relations / by Geoffrey Stern - - 2nd ed.
          p.   cm
          Includes bibliographical references and index.
          1. International relations.   I. Title
     JZ1305.S74 2000
     327 - - dc21   99-44176
                                                              CIP

Typeset by ensystems, Saffron Walden, Essex
Printed and bound in Great Britain by MPG Digital Solutions, Bodmin, Cornwall

CONTENTS

Part VI The international political economy

Part VII World society?

Part VIII Postscript

PREFACE TO THE SECOND EDITION

At one time it might have appeared either an extravagance or a tacit admission of error to have produced a second and substantially revised edition of a book on International Relations within five years of the first. But in fact so swift is the pace of kaleidoscopic change in the contemporary international landscape that not even the most seasoned analysis of world politics can survive intact for long without considerable modification. This is not to say that the fundamentals or the core concepts necessarily change. It is to say, however, that in our media-conscious age the news of the day before yesterday is already stale today and that a book such as this that attempts to capture and retain the interest of the first-year student cannot rely on the historical record alone, but must attempt to keep as up-to-date as possible. And, of course, in a second edition the writer has an opportunity to remedy some of the defects and omissions of the first.

In the meantime I have had the advantage of a further five years of intellectual interchange with students, academic colleagues and fellow broadcasters which have helped to broaden and deepen my comprehension and communication of the subject as, I hope, will be evident to those able to contrast the second edition of *The Structure of International Society* with the first. I have also had the good fortune in being able to benefit from the wise and perceptive comments of my colleague, Michael Donelan, who scrutinised the draft text with an eagle eye and a sympathetic understanding. To him and to all the others who have greatly enriched my understanding I am eternally grateful. I would also like to express my thanks to Mark White for the thought-provoking back cover motif, to my son Jonty for an imaginative and comprehensive index, to my secretary, Martina Langer, who gave far more time to processing the various drafts than she needed to have done, and to Caroline Wintersgill of Continuum, my publisher, for her encouragement and good humour.

Once again, I alone bear responsibility for errors of fact, judgement and taste and, regardless of whether or not there is to be a third edition at some stage in the future, I should be glad to hear from readers with suggestions as to how the text might be improved.

Geoffrey Stern
London School of Economics
June 1999

PREFACE TO THE FIRST EDITION

Having taught International Relations for more than thirty years and published a series of books and articles on subjects somewhat tangential to the central core, I decided it was high time to produce a text addressing IR's chief concerns. Since, however, the field is already overburdened with volumes assuming familiarity with the subject, but is somewhat deficient in readable and reliable introductions, I thought it best to offer a book for the beginner. Though students new to the subject may find the first five chapters rather daunting, I hope they persevere since once they have mastered the opening theoretical and historical sections the rest will be much easier to grasp.

If *The Structure of International Society* represents in a sense nearly four decades of study and reflection, it is also a product of the distinctive grounding in the subject I received at LSE first as a student, then as a colleague of such luminaries as Charles Manning, Martin Wight, Hedley Bull, Fred Northedge, Geoffrey Goodwin and Alan James (which, I suppose, places me in the 'English School' of International Relations). In addition, it owes something to the countless hours spent over coffees or Carlsbergs in discussion with students many of whom taught me as much as I like to think I taught them. And in its presentation and content I hope it bears the imprint of my moonlighting activities as a freelance broadcaster. For thanks to the BBC I have been able not only to keep abreast of a wide range of international developments but also to question at close quarters some of the people named in the text and whose thoughts and actions may well have affected the course of history. I would also like to feel that prolonged exposure to a medium which puts a premium on clarity of exposition may have had a positive effect on my writing, so that even if what follows is not profound, at least the reader may be spared the ordeal of having to plough through the kind of dense and opaque verbiage that sometimes passes for scholarship in the social sciences.

To all those colleagues, students and friends, past and present, who have enlightened and encouraged me and passed on their enthusiasm for the study, I should like to express my sincere gratitude. I should also like to thank my current colleagues Christopher Coker, Michael Donelan and Justin Rosenberg for their invaluable comments on the draft text and my secretary Judy Weedon whose labours on it were, as always, uncomplaining and undertaken with far more good humour than I deserved. Needless to say the responsibility for errors of fact and of judgement are mine alone.

Finally, to my current students attending my lectures on the Structure of International Society my apologies for retracing what may appear to be rather familiar ground. On the other hand the book does include material not in the lectures and, as ever, any constructive comments, critical or otherwise, and from whatever source, will be gratefully received.

Geoffrey Stern
London School of Economics
June 1994

To Joy, with love and in gratitude for her encouragement, understanding and patience

PART I

CONTENDING THEORIES

CHAPTER 1

REALISM, RATIONALISM AND REVOLUTIONISM

We are, by common consent, living in an era of almost unparalleled change, and not just in the field of technology and communications, but in virtually every other sphere as well. To try to convey the kaleidoscopic transformation in the global political, economic, technological, environmental and cultural landscape, terms such as 'complex interdependence', 'globalisation' and 'transnationalism' have entered the vocabulary of the social sciences, while many contemporary sages speak of our world as 'a global village', 'planet earth' or even 'spaceship earth'.

On the other hand, for all the innovations which leave their imprint on world politics, economics and society, there are features of the global landscape that remain stubbornly resistant to change. Institutions such as states, nations, tribes, classes, churches and so forth which have been around for centuries are still as capable as ever of exacting and receiving devotion, loyalty, even deference, despite what more trendy scholars might say about their imminent demise. People are still, that is, prepared to fight and die for Serbia, for an independent Kosovo, for Turkey, for a Kurdish Republic, for a Palestinian state, for the Israel of the Bible, for the defence of Islam, for a united Ireland, for or against a communist revolution.

But which are the more significant in international affairs, the forces of continuity or the elements of change? Much depends on the focus – whether, that is, the angle of concentration is more broadly or more narrowly based. Some look at international relations against a background of technological and economic developments, others centre on the state or on particular states, others highlight actors on the world stage other than states, while yet others examine the forms, patterns and rules of interaction among the participants in international society. There is also, of course, the question as to what is regarded as 'significant'. Because the criteria of significance will tend to differ from individual to individual, from group to group and society to society, perceptions of the balance between continuity and change will also tend to be disparate and diverse. Those of conservative disposition will tend to stress the degree to which little of fundamental importance has altered, if they are optimistic, and to exaggerate the changes if they are more alarmist. In the case of the more radically inclined, it is the pessimists who will stress the continuities, the optimists who emphasise the innovations and the capacity for further transformation.

Since the way in which the balance between continuity and change is perceived and interpreted can affect behaviour patterns as well as judgements, it would seem appropriate to begin a study of the structure of international society with a brief résumé of the recent shifts in the international landscape which have caused some to review and others to reconfirm their understanding of international relations.

The last decade of the twentieth century witnessed in rapid succession the collapse of Communist power in Eastern Europe and beyond, the reunification of Germany, the end of the cold war, the end of white minority rule in South Africa, the violent fragmentation of the Soviet Union and Yugoslavia, the Gulf War, the 'velvet divorce' of the Czechs and Slovaks, the ultimately bloody divorce between Ethiopians and Eritreans, the horrors of 'ethnic cleansing' in places as far apart as Rwanda, Bosnia and Kosovo, the cycles of war- and peace-making in the Middle East and, of course, the ambiguous legacy of the UN's manifold and underfunded peacekeeping activities which have strained its resources and credibility almost to breaking point and dispelled much of the optimism at the end of the cold war. As the new millennium begins, a world supposedly safe from war has to some degree become a world safe for war.

In the meantime a number of other issues have appeared on the international agenda – some for the first time. For example, the dramatic political and economic decline of Russia, the growing assertiveness of China, the turmoil in the world's money markets and the question marks it poses for the free market system, the dialectics of integration and fragmentation in the European Union, the reinvention of NATO's mission as it mobilises and expands, the creation of virtual protectorates in the Balkans and the uncertain impact of what is called Islamic Fundamentalism. Other issues currently under discussion have long been deserving of concern, but are only now receiving popular scrutiny – ethnic and religious intolerance (symptoms of what Samuel Huntingdon identifies as a 'clash of civilisations'),[1] forced migration, child labour, the status of women, third world debt, the trade in narcotics, international terrorism, nuclear proliferation, resource depletion, environmental degradation and the socio-economic impact of natural disasters.

Whether or not such changes are regarded as fundamental, they are clearly sufficient to make any agreed categorisation of our era difficult. To some, we are living in a new world order: others characterise it as a new world disorder. For some, it is an era of globalisation: for others it is a period marked by increasing regionalisation. Some view this as a post-

modern age – an era devoid of universal values; for others the Enlightenment project is still with us and ours is an epoch in which modernity
finds its highest expression. And for many the role of the United States
presents one of the most intriguing puzzles of all. While the talk is often
of American hegemony, the US is the world's largest debtor, and for far
too long Congress seemed more preoccupied with the sexual and other
foibles of the US President than with foreign policy. And as the country
contemplated its own and its President's navel, some political or religious
extremists were as likely to turn their guns on fellow citizens as in the
service of external policy.

If there is no agreement on how to characterise our era, is there any
accord on the dilemmas recent changes pose for scholars, statesmen and
ordinary citizens? Again, this is disputed territory, but readers who
manage to get to the end of this volume should have a better idea of what
the discussion entails and the range of possible perspectives; but as this is
an introductory text to a subject that can be approached in diverse ways,
it would be as well to clarify at the outset what *The Structure of International Society* as expounded below embraces.

1.1 THE STRUCTURE OF INTERNATIONAL SOCIETY

Subject matter

In essence it is a kind of melange. It has a theoretical as well as a practical
component, draws on a wide range of sources, non-Western as well as
Western, and requires some familiarity with history as well as with
current affairs. But since there are frequent references throughout the text
to contending theories, the key conceptual conundrums are set out in the
first three chapters. Readers unfamiliar with such ways of thinking may
find them hard going at first and it may require some re-reading before
the essential elements are properly digested and understood. On the other
hand, once the basic ideas essayed in Part I have been grasped, the rest of
the text should hold few terrors.

Though the term 'international society' can be used in different ways,
in this text it is generally employed to suggest a network of international
relationships that are reasonably orderly and predictable, despite the
absence of world government or global sense of solidarity. In this sense it
conforms to the usage of the so-called English School of International
Relations, of which Hedley Bull was a pioneer, and whose expression
'anarchical society'[2] to depict the context in which international relations
occur more or less captures the essence of the approach. Accordingly, the
analysis below will attempt to define international society more precisely,

to examine who belongs and on what basis, detail the various local, regional and global configurations it can take, outline the types and patterns of interaction, the institutions making for orderly international intercourse and the effect of changing ideologies and technologies. In addition, it tries to deal with some of the central dilemmas of statecraft and in particular with how, if at all, order and justice, a concern for power and a concern for morality may be reconciled.

Though *Structure of International Society* is an introductory text to the study of International Relations, it can also be of interest to the general reader wishing to make sense of a world that is increasingly complex and in some ways paradoxical – with its propensities for both interdependence and independence, as in the European Union, cooperation and also conflict, as in NATO, internationalism and nationalism, as at the United Nations, globalisation and fragmentation, order and anarchy, altruism and egoism, idealism and cynicism, reality and make-believe and, as suggested earlier, continuity and change.

Philosophy

If there is a philosophy underlying the text it is the reverse of Karl Marx's famous dictum: 'hitherto philosophers have attempted to understand the world. The point, however, is to change it.'[3] All too often civilised life is imperilled by opinionated, insensitive and fundamentally ignorant ideologues who without any proper appreciation of social norms and political cultures would try to reshape society in the name of 'God', 'progress', 'freedom', 'morality', 'the market', 'socialism' or whatever. Here the assumption is that knowledge, empathy and understanding are essential prerequisites for action and that those who would attempt to improve the health of the international body politic require a thorough grounding in the complexities of international politics, economics and law. This volume is about fostering the requisite comprehension.

Methodology

Unlike the historian, the student of international society tends to deal with the general rather than the unique – with, for example, wars rather than a particular war, revolutions rather than a specific revolution, sanctions rather than an individual embargo or boycott, the problems of peacekeeping rather than any particular example. Moreover, the methodology tends to be analytical and comparative rather than chronological and sequential. And for documentation, the student has to rely on whatever is available – archival material if possible, personal interviews, eyewitness reports, specialist articles and the like in the absence of authentic records.

Shortcomings

The scientifically-inclined hoping to derive from the study testable hypotheses which can be validated or falsified by experiment may be disappointed since it suffers from two separate, if related handicaps. In the first place, most of its key concepts are essentially ambiguous. When a natural scientist proposes to test the boiling point of water, there are few, if any semantic problems involved. The words 'test', 'boiling point' and 'water' present no conceptual conundrums. When, however, the International Relations scholar decides to investigate the causes of 'revolution' or the effects of 'imperialism', regardless of whether or not such propositions are testable, we have here formidable semantic and conceptual problems *ab initio*. Like 'the state', 'nation', 'sovereignty' and 'interdependence', such key terms as 'revolution' and 'imperialism' which are the subject's stock in trade, can be conceptualised in different ways – meaning different things to different people, sometimes meaning different things to the same people, depending on the context. The term 'power', for example, is central not only to International Relations discourse but also to post-modernist, feminist, Marxist and critical theory, and yet can be used in almost a dozen different senses: as a means to an end, as an end in itself, as the capacity to produce intended effects, as the attainment of those effects, as a synonym for force, for control, as a relationship, as being empowered to do something, and more besides.[4]

A second shortcoming stems from the abstract nature of the key concepts in the study. The state, for example, is a shorthand term for a complex of notions involving decision-making, authority, allegiance, citizenship, territory and so forth. Though we have never seen, felt or touched a sovereign state, we are apt to speak of it as if we had. Just as we can talk of banks being generous or universities as over-ambitious, so we might refer to the state as, say, being under pressure, showing resolve, making threats or preparing for war. In other words, we personify, that is, speak of the state as if it were a person. But, even if the state can be as real to us as a table and a chair, to which there is, in the jargon, a concrete referent, it 'exists' on a totally different plane of reality. Its existence is notional only. The state is what social scientists like to call 'a social construct'. On the other hand even if it is not to be found in the realm of the 'in fact', its presence can be felt in the world of the 'in effect,'[5] for it is a concept in terms of which people act. The problem is that each of those imputing personality to the state entertains a different idea of what it is. For some it connotes an organised political community – a territory or a government associated with a particular society or a people. For others it is a coercive, executive authority, what the Soviets used to call an *apparat*, which may speak in the name of but is distinct from society. But no matter what it is deemed to be, large numbers of people continue to believe in the reality of the sovereign state and to play roles in its service, even sacrificing their lives. Thus, the way in which reality is conceived, imagined, understood becomes part of reality itself, and the student of International Relations has to consider the situation as perceived at least as much as the situation itself.

The need for 'linguistic analysis'

Such conceptual difficulties make it imperative to subject such ambiguous and personified expressions to what is called 'linguistic analysis', as elaborated in *Language, Truth and Logic* by A.J. Ayer.[6] For Ayer, who once dominated the philosophy faculty at Oxford, as for the eccentric Cambridge don, Ludwig Wittgenstein, words do not have intrinsic meanings. They have uses, and our task with words like 'power', 'sovereignty' or 'imperialism' is to deconstruct or 'unpackage' them, discover from the context how they are being employed and what they are intended to convey.

1.2 'SOCIETY', 'COMMUNITY' AND 'ANARCHY'

When 'the Structure of International Society' emerged on to the LSE syllabus in the late 1940s its architect, Professor C.A.W. Manning, intended to convey that the study was concerned with the implications for the real world of the widely shared notion that there exists an international society, and that while it now comprised several kinds of politically significant legal persons – international, transnational, subnational and supranational – its oldest and most durable members were states. Furthermore, that this conceived-of, socially constructed or postulated international society now encompassed the globe, making impossible the kind of total isolation once exercised by Japan and China.

But why the term 'society'? When 'Structure' first appeared, the more scientific-sounding expression 'international system' was not yet fashionable, while the terms 'international community' and 'international anarchy' both seemed unsuitable, the former suggesting solidarity and cohesiveness, the latter implying disorder and chaos. People generally conceived of international relations as being to a degree orderly and subject to mutual constraint, stemming from a shared interest in co-existence, which is what the word 'society' was meant to convey. As a society it was, of course, unusual both because it comprised states and other politically significant entities and because it lacked government, even though it was not without rules and regulations. But the term 'society' had a further advantage. For societies could be studied at several different levels of analysis – at a psychological level, as individuals thinking and behaving; at a sociological level, in terms of group behaviour; and at a macro- or systemic level when society is understood holistically, as a socio-political unit – as an orchestra, as it were, rather than as a group of individual players. 'International society', thus, could be investigated at the level of individuals entertaining ideas; at the level of the state or other politically significant entities on behalf of which individuals operated or at the global level, conceptualised as an interactive collective or social whole with its own history, traditions and watershed periods. And because it rested on changing concepts as to what precisely international society amounted to, a dynamic element was built into the study. If concepts changed, then what was understood as 'international society' would change accordingly.[7]

Today the expression is probably used rather less frequently than when the subject was introduced and its underlying significance is in any case dismissed by ultra-Realists who can detect no common interests, shared values or modicum of order,[8] by idealists for whom the state is outmoded and who see only the individual in a global setting as the appropriate unit of study,[9] and by residual Marxists for whom class not state is paramount in a world polarised between the dominant and the dependent.[10] Nonetheless, the idea that international relations are best conceived of as reasonably orderly and predictable and that investigating its perceived structure is worthwhile would probably command more general assent than the ultra-Realist, idealist or classical Marxist position. It does mean, however, that in the study the linguistic precision of the physical and biological sciences is lacking, and though most of the social sciences face much the same problem, few economists or sociologists dare to admit it.

1.3 CLASSICAL THEORIES

In one sense the phenomenon of international relations, of a kind, has been a subject of study for well over two thousand years. In about 400 BC an Athenian general, Thucydides, detailed the conflict that had polarised Greece for over 30 years, and in what became known as his *History of the Peloponnesian War* he developed a theory of inter-state conflict which still bears examination, even today.[11] In trying to account for war he suggested that a mixture of factors – geographical, demographic, economic, technological, political as well as psychological (he thought that human actions were motivated by greed, pride and fear) – would cause the power of one state to grow, in turn inducing perceptions of threat in other states, leading to war and the establishment of a new international system by the victor. In effect Thucydides had pioneered what was to become known as the Realist approach to international relations in his emphasis on human fallibility, the state, power balances and international anarchy.

But classical Realism was not confined to Western thinkers. About 100 years after Thucydides had written his epic, the Indian statesman Kautilya in similar vein produced his *Arthashastra* or *Book of the State*, in the course of which he examined, amongst other things, the reasoning behind the time-honoured maxim: 'my enemy's enemy is my friend'.[12] And sometime between Thucydides and Kautilya, the Chinese thinker Sun Tzu addressed one of Realism's central concerns, warfare, providing a practical manual on strategy and tactics.[13] In it he stressed the importance of intelligence, planning and flexibility in any campaign – tactics which were to prove an inspiration to Mao Zedong in his struggle for power some two millennia later.

It was, however, at the beginning of the Renaissance that Realism acquired one of its most notorious, yet durable texts. In *The Prince*, written in 1513, the Florentine diplomat, Niccolò Machiavelli, produced a treatise responding to the secular humanism then emerging and calling on his aristocratic employer, and, by implication, other leaders, to abandon medieval religious and moral constraint and pursue unambiguously his own political interests and those of his state.[14] Focusing on the problem of achieving security in an increasingly anarchic world, he suggests various strategies for survival and success in a fractious arena of political intrigue, assassination and diplomatic treachery.

But not all the classical writers were Realists. Indeed, since biblical times there had been optimists who had dreamed dreams of a much more harmonious world, and in the seventeenth century – a century of almost incessant warfare, at least in Europe – several distinguished visionaries set out their agenda. The jurist Hugo Grotius in *De Jure Belli ac Pacis* (*On the Law of War and Peace*), written in 1625, outlined a project for a workable society of sovereign states, which he rooted firmly in law.[15] This was the first major text in what Martin Wight called the Rationalist tradition[16] – which will be explored later in the chapter.

But the seventeenth-century religious wars together with the civil war in England also spawned a further spate of Realist texts, of which Thomas Hobbes's *Leviathan* is one of the best known. Writing in the 1650s, the English philosopher, who had translated Thucydides, returns to the theme of anarchy, both domestic and international, which in his view reigns in the absence of strong government.[17] A century later, the Scottish thinker and diplomat David Hume produced his formula for reducing international anarchy. In his treatise *The Balance of Power* he both analyses and recommends use of this time-honoured diplomatic device in which one country's inventory of mobilisable assets is counterbalanced against those of its rival, producing at least for a time a measure of order and stability.[18]

But neither Realist nor Rationalist perspectives could satisfy those who wanted to see a total transformation of society and a much more lasting global fellowship, and in his celebrated essay on *Perpetual Peace*, written at the end of the eighteenth century, the German philosopher Immanuel Kant laid the groundwork for many an idealistic treatise on international relations. For in it he envisaged a harmonious world federation of republics bound by the rule of law and built upon the destruction of artificial barriers dividing humankind, such as empires, dynasties and autocracies.[19] For Martin Wight, referred to above, this is the first major Revolutionist text.

By the end of the eighteenth century, therefore, and long before anyone had taken up the systematic study of international relations, there existed three different frameworks, conceptual maps or paradigms, as Martin Wight calls them, for analysing inter-state relations: Realism, with an emphasis on power; Rationalism, stressing cooperation; and Revolutionism, with an agenda for global transformation. If we study them today it is because, like the maps of the London tube network at the back of many a British diary, they may help us to find our way around a complicated landscape. Unlike the tube map, however, they may also suggest ways of evaluating and improving that landscape. In the jargon, they have normative and prescriptive as well as empirical components.

Though the various classical approaches will be elaborated below, the reader should treat the following outlines with a degree of caution since any such typology can only be rather rough and ready, and there is always a danger of misrepresentation. After all, many thinkers straddle the fence as between one tradition and another. For example, anyone glancing at his works other than *The Prince* will observe that Machiavelli was not, after all, a thoroughgoing Machiavellian, while an equally famous theorist, Karl Marx, even made a point of saying that he was no Marxist.

Realism

Classical Realism as expounded by Thucydides, Kautilya, Machiavelli and Hobbes rests on a pessimistic analysis of human nature. Humankind, in this view, is deeply flawed – driven by self-interest, pride, ambition, anger and other passions. For Realists in the Christian tradition, such as St Augustine, humankind has the added affliction of being tainted by original sin, which affliction will remain until the final redemption.[20] If there is to be any kind of social order, therefore, the baser instincts must be controlled, and this can only be done by men with the power to command and the authority to make their dictates effective. That is, only where there exist stratified, hierarchical societies in which the elites relish their responsibilities and the masses are assured of a secure and predictable existence and a sense of identity, can there be order. By extension the classical Realists hold that in a world of sovereign states, humanity's continued existence depends on the maintenance of such orderly state structures, and society is best served where the state is regarded as the highest focus of loyalty from which all notions of law and morality derive. In such a perspective there is, therefore, no room for concepts such as equality, individuality, innovation or human rights, which challenge existing hierarchies and disrupt what Edmund Burke called 'the partnership between those who are living, those who are dead, and those who are to be born'.[21]

Thus, what is initially a theory of human nature becomes a theory of the state – the state being regarded here as a political and diplomatic agency which uses military power either as an end in itself or as a means to an end – the end being the survival and success of the state through which a community's life is safeguarded.

From such assumptions, several conclusions follow. First, that international relations are characterised by neither community nor society, if 'community' means a collectivity whose members share a sense of solidarity and kinship, and 'society' suggests an association organised for a specific common purpose, as in the case of a music or a dramatic society. In classical Realism, as distinct from more modern Realist views, international relationships entail neither common sentiment nor common purpose. They are, therefore, anarchic, and typified by conflict and strife as each state attempts to secure its objectives often at the expense of others. Secondly, that in such international anarchy, the possibility of war always exists and peace, therefore, has to be seen as impermanent. Thirdly, that legal or moral rules make little practical difference since rights and duties arise only in the context of society, and no international society exists. To put it another way: international relations can be neither moral nor immoral for the international arena is not a milieu in which moral criteria apply. Fourthly, that anything going by the name of international law or morality must be a form of 'power politics in disguise'[22] since any moral or legal goals pursued internationally can only be those of the state itself. And fifthly, that in deference to the powerful, domestically and internationally, lies the best hope of checking the incidence of international conflict. This is because in a world of disciplined societies in which passions are kept under control, the strongest powers generally have an interest in maintaining the status quo and the weaker powers have little incentive to change things.

Thus, the classical Realist prescription for national conduct in such conditions consists in pursuing policies to preserve internal order and to protect and promote the interests and values the ruling elite deem important. In the celebrated words of Hobbes, often regarded as the embodiment of classical Realism: 'covenants without the sword are but words and of little strength', and superior force, prudence or expediency are the only possible constraints on international activity.

Rationalism

Such a view of international relationships has tended to find favour in a time of international turbulence and rapid social change when values are in flux. But, of course, international conflict can also be the catalyst for a different type of theorising – for people of a Rationalist disposition, such as Grotius, Locke, Bentham and John Stuart Mill – who would have been far more tolerant of radical ideas than the classical Realists.[23] After all, they shared with the French Revolutionaries the notion of man as the possessor of natural rights, possibly but not necessarily divine in origin, and of law as based on consent rather than command. As they saw it, any valid legal system depended on notions of equality before the law and of law as guarantor of individual liberties. They also conceived of law as a body of rules which evolve as society changes, Grotius himself having formulated a new theory to fit a rapidly changing world – a world in which Western Christendom was rapidly disintegrating.

So what did these Rationalists or Grotians have to say about the nature of man and the state? Because of their belief in reason, they saw human beings as rule-creating and rule-obeying persons ready to accept limitations on their immediate desires, for the long-term good of themselves and of their societies. Sociable behaviour was, for them, the product of rational thought rather than of coercion, and wherever social institutions were perceived as just and reasonable, there was a harmony of interests between self and society. But this implied that those who make laws must seek to serve society, since people cannot indefinitely tolerate laws that are despotic or arbitrary.

From such a conception of man in relation to law, the Rationalists derived their understanding of international society. Unlike the Hobbesians who regarded the international arena as one of constant struggle, the Grotians held that – at least between Christian (that is, European) nations – controversies and disputes could be mediated or resolved through the application of generally recognised rules and procedures. But how was this possible without an accepted world sovereign or judiciary? As against the Hobbesians, the Grotians argued that society does not depend on government and that, despite periodic wars, there was sufficient order internationally to merit the ascription of society. By society they meant some kind of collectivity – not as close-knit as a community, perhaps – but whose members did have significant contacts, some common interests and orderly procedures and rules to manage their interrelations.

What was it that for the Grotians constituted evidence of international society? First, increasing acceptance of the body of binding rules understood as international law – recognition of sovereign status, sovereign equality, non-intervention, the right of national self-defence and so forth. Secondly, the development of the institutions of diplomacy, with resident ambassadors and the evolution of diplomatic methods, immunities, procedures and rank. Thirdly, the growth of world trade on a regular and regulated basis. Fourthly, the residual sense of international moral obligation, presumably stemming from their common Christian ancestry. Fifthly, the periodic meetings of Great Powers which together acted as self-appointed guarantors of international law and order. Sixthly, the role of prudence in constraining the activities of states especially when there was a perceived balance of power. And seventhly, the manifest capacity of international intercourse to survive wars, ideological disputes and acts of international barbarism.

Yet if all these were characteristic of international society, how did the Grotians explain the brutalities of, say, the Spanish *conquistadores* or the colonisers of North America and Australia in their dealings with the indigenous peoples? Though they adhered to the medieval Christian idea of the 'just war', which required a just cause – i.e. in response to a wrong inflicted – and just or proportionate means in prosecuting hostilities, many, though by no means all, Grotians regarded membership of international society as being confined largely to those of Christian ancestry – that is, to the countries of Europe. Whatever the latter's obligations to non-Europeans, these were not of the same order as their obligations to members of their own international 'club', and until the non-Europeans were ready to join the family of civilised (i.e. Christian) nations – a matter, incidentally, which would be determined by the Europeans themselves – the latter had the rights and duties of tutelage over them.[24] But, of course, we can all have our own theories as to whether those who set such appalling examples in far-off lands are morally entitled to set standards about anything.

Since international society for the Grotians was confined largely to the European sphere, how did they account for war within and between European states? In fact, as against the Hobbesians they came to see war as an abnormality, not a norm, that is, as a breakdown rather than a continuation of policy.

What, then, is the Grotian prescription for national conduct in international society? Clearly, anything making for good neighbourliness:

mutual respect, willingness to compromise and to honour pledges, pacts and commitments, and, as a guide to policy, the principle of the lesser evil. Do that which entails the least sacrifice of value!

Revolutionism

If compromise and accommodation were the essence of the Grotian approach, they were the very opposite of the Revolutionist or Kantian position. For the Kantians – who in Wight's interpretation included not just Rousseau but also Robespierre, Marx, Lenin and a host of religious fundamentalists – were so zealous in their pursuit of the ideal society that they held any accommodation with existing domestic or international orders to be a betrayal of principle, unless undertaken for strictly tactical reasons.[25] For since all existing structures deflected humankind from its true potential, any compromise with them was tantamount to an acceptance of injustice, and hence corrupt.

What then was humanity's true potential? Each Revolutionist had his own view of that destiny. It was one thing for the Protestant at odds with a Catholic world; another for the bourgeois idealist struggling against feudal rule and privilege. It was one thing for the patriot or religious zealot whose country is under foreign domination; another for the Marxist estranged from capitalist society, yet another for the eco-warrior prepared to go to extremes to save a planet believed to be at serious risk.

But for all their differences, they shared a common conception of the brotherhood (and sisterhood) of humanity, i.e. of a global or cosmopolitan community in which the true interests of all are realised, and perpetual peace and justice are established. They also held that existing socio-political structures condition perceptions and expectations and impose artificial barriers between people, preventing humankind from achieving its destiny. It followed that such structures had to be destroyed by revolution or else transformed through constant pressure.

Yet for all their principled intolerance, the Kantians nonetheless had to have some means of coping with an as yet unreformed world. So what did they offer? Their prescriptions follow from the broad ideological screen through which they filtered events. First, they made a clear distinction between those of the true faith and those not of their fraternity. Theirs was, so to speak, a polarised, dialectical view, with the 'righteous' trustees of the potential community of humankind on one side and their 'wicked' adversaries on the other. Secondly, they believed themselves to be in a permanent state of war, if not physical then at least psychological, against those who for whatever reason impeded progress to the inevitable goal. Thirdly, they believed that the ends justified the means and that there was no room for compassion, sentiment or notions of moderation when there was so much at stake.

Behind this way of thinking lay the tradition of the Crusade, of the *Jihad* or Holy War, even though Kant himself was an advocate of disarmament. This points to a paradox – that a doctrine aimed at ultimate harmony and integration, in practice tended to worsen existing divisions, and to create a few more, and not just between but also within the nations, since the basic conflict which the Revolutionists diagnosed and promoted was one cutting across state boundaries. For to them, existing state structures were irrelevant. The real struggle was transnational, horizontal, across the nations.

Thus, if for the Hobbesian Realists 'power' was the main consideration in an international context they deemed anarchic, and if for the Grotian Rationalists 'order' was paramount in what they took to be an international society, for the Kantian Revolutionists the pursuit of 'true justice' took priority in a polarised world destined ultimately to become a single global community. And, of course, their descendants are to be found in many of today's religious or political guerrilla groups.

1.4 ORIGINS OF THE SUBJECT

It is ironic that though men of letters had mused on inter-state relations for some two thousand years, the term 'international' was not coined until the philosopher Jeremy Bentham used it in a text on inter-state law of 1780,[26] and that as an academic discipline, International Relations did not appear until the beginning of the twentieth century. Nor was it regarded as a subject in its own right, since in its first few years it was confined to a handful of US universities and led a shadowy existence as a sub-branch of History or Political Science. What had prompted its appearance was a characteristic American concern for solving problems. As the ancient Greeks had invented the study of Politics to deal with the problem of order in a world of revolutionary change, so a few pioneering Americans early in the twentieth century embarked on the study of what they termed 'World Politics' to find a formula for an end to war, which they feared to be on the horizon. Their apprehensions were, of course, justified by the cataclysm of 1914, and that they clearly failed in their self-imposed task was to undermine the subject's credibility in the eyes of some scholars. For others, however, the motivation was itself suspect, the argument being that an academic study is about acquiring knowledge and understanding and enlarging the capacity to reason and does not concern itself with immediate practical pay-offs. As the following chapters indicate, scholars today are still divided on the question as to whether or not a study has to be 'useful'. What is clear is that the formula sought by the pioneers of the subject which was to lead to the eradication of war, sadly, has proved as elusive as ever.

NOTES

1. Huntingdon, S., *The Clash of Civilisations and the Remaking of World Order*, London, Simon & Schuster, 1997.
2. See Bull, H., *The Anarchical Society*, London, Macmillan, 1977.
3. 'Theses on Feuerbach' in Marx, K., *Selected Writings*, ed. Mclellan, D., Oxford, Oxford University Press, 1977, p. 156.
4. At least a dozen separate meanings of the term are teased out in Minogue, K., 'Power in politics', *Political Studies*, October 1959, pp. 269–89.
5. The distinction between the 'in fact' and the 'in effect' is to be found in Manning, C.A.W., *The Nature of International Society*, London, Bell, 1962, p. 15.
6. Ayer, A.J., *Language, Truth and Logic*, Harmondsworth, Penguin, 1990.
7. The argument is detailed in Manning, op. cit.
8. It is ironic that one of the exemplars of ultra-Realism was a Professor of International Law. See, for example, Schwarzenberger, G., *Power Politics*, London, Stevenson, 1964.
9. See, for example, Burton, J., *World Society*, Cambridge, Cambridge University Press, 1972.
10. See, for example, Wallerstein, I., *The Modern World System*, London, Academic, 1974.
11. Thucydides, *History of the Peloponnesian War*, trans. Rex Warner, Harmondsworth, Penguin, 1976.
12. Kautilya, *Arthashastra*, trans. Shamasastry, A., Mysore, Wesleyan Mission Press, 1929.
13. Sun Tzu, *The Art of War*, Oxford, Oxford University Press, 1963.
14. Machiavelli, *The Prince and The Discourses*, New York, Random House, 1940.
15. Grotius, *Prologomena to the Law of War and Peace*, New York, Liberal Arts Press, 1957.
16. In *International Theory: The Three Traditions*, Wight, M., elaborates what he calls the three classical paradigms of explanation – Realism (Hobbesianism), Rationalism (Grotianism) and Revolutionism (Kantianism).
17. Hobbes, *Leviathan*, Harmondsworth, Penguin, 1968.
18. Hume, 'Of the Balance of Power', in *Essays Moral, Political and Literary*, vol. 1, Longmans, Green and Co., 1898.
19. Kant, *Perpetual Peace*, New York, Bobbs-Merrill, 1957.
20. See, for example, St. Augustine, 'Confessions' and 'City of God' in *Great Books of the Western World*, vol. 18, Chicago, Encyclopaedia Britannica, 1986.
21. Burke, *Reflections on the Revolution in France*, New York, Dolphin Books, 1961.
22. The phrase is taken from the heading to Part II of the three-part volume, Schwarzenberger, G., *Power Politics*, London, Stevenson, 1964.
23. See, for example, Locke, *Two Treatises on Government*, Cambridge, Cambridge University Press, 1960; Bentham, J., *Theory of Legislation*, Oxford, Oxford

University Press, 1914; and Mill, J.S., *On Liberty and other writings*, Cambridge, Cambridge University Press, 1989.

24. On the 'just war' tradition see, for example, Russell, F.H., *The Just War in the Middle Ages*, Cambridge, Cambridge University Press, 1975.

25. See, for example, Rousseau, *The Social Contract and other writings*, London, Nelson, 1953; Marx and Engels, *The German Ideology*, London, Lawrence & Wishart, 1989; and Lenin, *Imperialism, the Highest Stage of Capitalism*, Moscow, Progress Publishers, 1982.

26. Wright, Q., *The Study of International Relations*, New York, Appleton-Century-Crofts, 1955, p. 3.

CHAPTER 2

BEHAVIOURALISM VERSUS TRADITIONALISM

The previous chapter detailed some of the contending theories or conceptual maps concerning international society developed long before anyone had taken up the systematic study of International Relations. In the terms used by Martin Wight, they were paradigms which could be classified as Realist or Hobbesian, Rationalist or Grotian, Revolutionist or Kantian. This chapter examines some of the paradigms of international relations that have gained currency especially in academic circles since the study of International Relations (or World Politics, as it is sometimes called) came out of the closet from its isolated outposts secreted in the History or Political Science department of a handful of American universities.

2.1 WHY STUDY INTERNATIONAL RELATIONS?

The rapid expansion of the study in recent years may well have been due not just to the burgeoning interest in the subject matter, but also to the variety of purposes IR appears to serve – academic, personal and political. For those with a scholarly interest in acquiring knowledge and understanding for its own sake, a relatively new subject that appears to encompass as broad a prospectus as the great globe itself and yet seems manageable must represent an exciting intellectual challenge. But International Relations is not just a formidable mental discipline. In its focus on the world as perceived as well as on the world as it is, it also provides an avenue for increased self-awareness and self-knowledge. At the same time it can be a vehicle for self-advancement, as good and sometimes not-so-good graduates in the subject may find themselves in diplomatic posts, international organisations, international business corporations, the media or, if they have nothing better to do, in teaching and research. Others may take to the subject for political reasons, hoping that a more sophisticated understanding of the ways of the world may enhance their chances of furthering some particular cause or of finding a formula for remedying some of the ills facing world society.

2.2 A DISTINCT ACADEMIC DISCIPLINE?

Since the subject has often been taught as a byproduct of some other study, is International Relations, in fact, an academic discipline at all? Here we need to bring linguistic analysis to our aid. For if by academic discipline is meant a separate field of study wholly distinct from any other, it clearly does not merit that ascription. Some grasp of history, geography, political theory, sociology, economics and so forth is essential if one is to get a sense of the many-layered dimensions of international relationships, and in this sense the subject may be described as 'inter-disciplinary'. For some scholars, moreover, IR is merely a branch of the social sciences and should not be studied in isolation from the rest of the field. On the other hand, if by academic discipline is meant disciplined study of a particular field, with a recognisable focus of interest and body of theory, then International Relations is, and always has been a discipline, albeit one which has tended to move with the times.

2.3 THREE POST-1919 PARADIGMS

The idealist/utopian

Though the study first appeared in the US, the first two Chairs in the subject were established in Britain and in the shadow of the First World War. At the time, many scholars, especially among the victorious powers, were persuaded by liberal internationalists such as the American President Woodrow Wilson that war could be avoided in future if its causes were sufficiently understood and the appropriate lessons learned. And they were in no doubt as to its roots. For since they believed in the essential 'goodness' of humankind, violent behaviour had to be a product of flawed institutions: elitist politics, secret diplomacy, imperialism, armaments, weak and inadequate intergovernmental institutions and widespread ignorance of world affairs. Their proffered remedy, accordingly, was to reform both international institutions and domestic political structures. In the international arena they sought open diplomacy (President Wilson spoke of 'open covenants . . . openly arrived at'),[1] national self-determination (at least in Europe: they still had qualms about letting go their Asian and African possessions), disarmament, legislation to outlaw war and new international institutions to encourage cooperation and collective security – a system according to which any aggression by any state would meet a collective response. Their domestic agenda included 'democratic control of politics', on the dubious grounds that people never want war, and a more educated and enlightened public, so that it could make informed choices. To spread that kind of intellectual illumination, Aberystwyth in 1919 and the LSE in 1923 established a department of International Relations and Alfred Zimmern and Philip Noel-Baker, both Wilsonian idealists, were appointed to head them.

Both men were, however, to have their academic careers cut short. At Aberystwyth, Zimmern soon felt the wrath of both the Welsh nationalist and the Welsh religious establishment when his private life came under critical scrutiny.[2] And after a few years at LSE, Noel-Baker decided to take his brand of oratory to Geneva to become a disarmament lobbyist for the League.[3] Nevertheless their kind of idealism more or less infused the teaching of the subject for a couple of decades. Till the late 1930s, that is, IR scholars in Britain, Europe and North America laboriously ploughed through lengthy volumes on international law and institutions, drawing up blueprints for a better world and pinning their hopes on the League of Nations and the Kellogg–Briand Pact, which in theory outlawed war as an instrument of policy as of 1928.

If the pioneers of the study were a product of their time, so were their successors. For just as post-cold war hopes of a new world order were to be dashed by a spate of regional conflicts, so the tide of events would rudely shatter the idealism after the First World War.[4] True, in its first decade the League had been moderately successful. It had helped defuse tensions in the Baltic, the Balkans, East Central Europe and beyond. But the Wall Street Crash, the Great Depression, the drive to protectionism and the rise of Fascism changed the picture. And when in 1931 Japan successfully defied the League by invading and occupying Manchuria and making further incursions into China with impunity, the precedent was set for a spate of brutal foreign conquests. Among them, the Italian seizure of Abyssinia and of Albania, and the German occupation of first Austria, then the Sudetenland, then the rest of Czechoslovakia and finally of western Poland. Though this last invasion in September 1939 triggered the Second World War proper, the opening salvos had in effect been fired in Manchuria in 1931. But the Fascist powers were not the only predators. For following the Nazi–Soviet pact of August 1939, the Soviet Union occupied eastern Poland, invaded Finland, annexed the independent Baltic states of Latvia, Lithuania and Estonia and seized Bessarabia and Northern Bukovina from Romania.

By the late 1930s it was becoming increasingly obvious, even to teachers of International Relations, that the Wilsonian aspirations of 1919 had been misplaced and that for people such as Japan's General Tojo, Mussolini, Hitler or Stalin the rule of law, international or otherwise, meant little or nothing. Not for the first time had exaggerated hopes turned to despair, and in academic circles, as outside it, there occurred what has been called a paradigm shift, the earlier, rather idealistic paradigm now being regarded as inadequate. The radical American theologian, Reinhold Niebuhr, sounded the alarm in his influential text of 1932, *Moral Man and Immoral Society* – which, as its title implies, muses on the selfish behaviour of human groups and the problems caused by collective egoism.[5] But the watershed came with the publication in 1939 – significantly just before the outbreak of war – of E.H. Carr's seminal work *The Twenty Years' Crisis*.[6] Who, then, was Carr, and why did this particular book make such a stir?

The modern Realist

Edward Hallett Carr was one of the most accomplished British scholars ever to teach the subject. A former Foreign Office official and leader writer for *The Times*, he had already published the first of a score or more of distinguished books on contemporary history and had the Chair of International Politics in, of all places, Aberystwyth. In *The Twenty Years' Crisis* – a work somewhat influenced by Marxist ideas of class conflict and a belief in the planned economy – he ridiculed the previous generation of IR scholars, including his predecessor at Aberystwyth, Alfred Zimmern, believing them to be 'utopian' in their thinking. First, as to their objectives, Carr held them to be far more concerned with the 'ought' than with the 'is' and with the desirable rather than the feasible. Second, as to their perceptions, to Carr they were culture-bound intellectuals often oblivious to the collective self-interest behind their ideals. Of course Britain, the US and the other victorious powers of 1918 were interested in peace, disarmament and the status quo. Their objectives had more or less been achieved. But why should the dispossessed and the despoiled – in particular Austria, Germany and Italy – aggrieved by the post-war settlement at Versailles, be expected to share the enthusiasms of the satisfied powers? Third, as to their dispositions, Carr saw them as far too judgemental. They would ignore the degree to which necessity, contingency, determinism and chance constrained political choice, and appeared to assume that statesmen had almost unlimited freedom of action. Fourth, as regards their understanding, Carr felt that in their emphasis on cooperation as against conflict, on solidarity as against self-interest and on harmony as against discord they showed little understanding of either history or human nature.

Carr's epoch-making study spawned the first of many major theoretical debates in the subject,[7] though the terms under which it was conducted – that of 'Realists' versus 'Utopians' – reflected, of course, the thinking of the former. In claiming to be Realists, Carr and his supporters were implying not merely that they had a monopoly on the understanding of reality, but that, in a world in which people resorted all too easily to myth and fantasy, having a grip on reality was a virtue in itself. Further, that Realism was able to provide a much needed corrective to the kind of wishful thinking on the nature of man, the state and of world order that in their view had permeated the international politics of the 1920s and 1930s. Not that Carr himself altogether excludes ideals, ethics or morality from his analysis, for like so many Realists, both classical and modern, he seems to have been, according to his biographer Jonathan Haslam, something of a disillusioned idealist.[8] Carr does, however, believe that the political context determines what is morally attainable and accuses the Wilsonian generation of being either myopic, hypocritical or else entirely impractical in the pursuit of their ideals.

So what was the new paradigm suggested by Carr and later championed by Georg Schwarzenberger at London's University College, Raymond Aron in Paris, Hans Morgenthau in Chicago, Henry Kissinger at Harvard, and others?[9] First, it assumes that the environment within which international relations take place is anarchic, since there is no world government, global moral consensus or sense of solidarity. Secondly, that despite the existence of various non-governmental entities, the state remains the main actor on the international stage, and recognition of its sovereignty the cornerstone of the international political process. Thirdly, that the operating procedure of international relations has to be one of self-help, which means that in decision-making the national interest, self-reliance, and, if necessary, self-assertion have to take priority. Fourthly, that the state is rational in the sense that its policy-makers make a cost/benefit analysis of different options and try to choose the most cost-effective means of attaining its objectives. Fifthly, that in a world of power-hungry dictators the politics of not being overpowered is the only feasible course. But any viable strategy for security and survival has to depend in turn on analysis of the uses, abuses and distribution of power capabilities and with a view to accumulating sufficient military capacity alone or in concert to deter or defeat potential aggressors. Here, an accurate perception of the distribution of mobilisable assets which sustain the dynamics of the balance of power is essential. Sixthly, that in an insecure world, foreign rather than domestic policy considerations have to take precedence in decision-making and that no matter how numerous the inputs into it, the state is best regarded, once policy is agreed, as a unitary actor, speaking with a single voice. Seventhly, that though there may be a role for ideals, in international politics these have to be tempered by considerations of power; the desirable, in other words, has to be sought within the framework of the possible.

In the select British and American academies that taught IR in the 1940s and 1950s, Realism became and remained till recently the dominant paradigm. After all, the Western powers had come to see themselves as having merely exchanged one set of enemies for another, and the 'power political' approach still seemed relevant in cold war conditions, even if the development of nuclear weapons and the manifest erosion of the state's ability to maintain exclusive control might call for certain adjustments in the concept of power. The modern Realist, that is, shared the state-centredness of classical Realism. They regarded all other political, economic and social forces as a function of the state in interaction, and saw the quest for national security and prosperity as factors leading to intense competition between the powers, tempered only by considerations of reciprocal advantage, prudence and enlightened self-interest. On the other hand, modern Realists were prepared to respond, if sometimes begrudgingly, to changes in the international landscape, and many could not endorse Hobbes's thoroughly pessimistic understanding of human nature, his justification of authoritarian rule or his denial of an ethical dimension. Nor did they necessarily take any delight in the state-centred approach. For example, both the American theologian Reinhold Niebuhr, who had written *Moral Man and Immoral Society*, and Martin Wight, who wrote one of the standard texts on *Power Politics* were pacifists.[10] They were describing not commending: analysing not advocating.

The Stalinist/Marxist

Meanwhile, from the late 1940s, a very different paradigm was being expounded in the countries of the Soviet bloc. Deriving from a peculiarly Stalinist version of Marxism, it owed at least as much to the Soviet Union's recent history as to the notion lying at the base of Marxist dialectics, that is, of progress through conflict. In this view, the Soviet state, like Russia before it, had been much abused by foreign powers. On the state's being invaded and blockaded by a dozen or more powers supporting the anti-Bolshevik forces in the civil war after the 1917 Revolution, the Red Army had at one time been forced to defend several different fronts simultaneously.[11] And between the end of the intervention in 1921 and the Nazi assault on the Soviet Union two decades later, Poland had invaded the Ukraine, several Eastern European countries had established an anti-Soviet 'cordon sanitaire', Washington had diplomatically isolated Moscow, while Fascism had risen unchecked as Britain appeased Hitler. Then, following Germany's second onslaught on Russia in less than 30 years, the West's lengthy delay in opening up a second front in Europe had left a much-pressed Red Army to fight the Germans largely unaided, with a loss of 1 in 9 of the Soviet population by the end of the war. Meanwhile, the West had excluded Moscow from the project to develop the A-Bomb, and after using two such bombs against Japan, Washington had been willing to shelter leading Nazi technologists in return for their services to the US. And finally there had been the West's covert support for anti-Communist militants in the Ukraine and other parts of the Soviet Union after the war.[12] Naturally all this received the appropriate ideological treatment when the Stalinist paradigm emerged.

Basically it emphasised not the state, but class solidarity across frontiers and dismissed national boundaries as comparatively unimportant. Wars, hot and cold, were not the product of competing alliances but of conflicting ideologies. They were a function of capitalist imperialism and a consequence of domestic class struggle and would persist until the Communist millennium was achieved – a classless stateless world of altruistic and versatile atheists.[13] If it sounds familiar it is because it was a twentieth-century variant of the Kantian revolutionary theme.

Although these three post-First World War paradigms – the idealist/ utopian, the Realist and the Stalinist/Marxist – were by no means carbon copies of the Grotian, Hobbesian and Kantian models, some of the more recent controversies relating to the study can be readily understood in terms of both earlier and later paradigms. What then of these debates and contentions?

2.4 THE BEHAVIOURAL REVOLUTION

They were an almost inevitable byproduct of the sudden influx into the field of scholars from other disciplines at a time – the 1950s – when people were both curious and fearful about international politics. Some had migrated from mathematics, others from the natural sciences, others yet again had been seduced from the other social sciences and had brought with them the very latest techniques of analysis – some more comprehensible than others. But with so many novices taking to the discipline, there were bound to be new modes of explanation, new concepts, new ways of defining the subject. Equally there were almost bound to be exaggerated claims for some of those novel approaches, and also resistance and hostility from traditionalists who put a premium on clarity of exposition and saw some of the 'new' techniques and methodologies as obscurantist, pretentious or misconceived.

The first post-Realists offered not so much a new paradigm as more rigorous methods of enquiry. For Realism's basic assumptions could not, in their view, be substantiated. They lacked both proof and means of verification. Further, Realism was flawed conceptually, since 'power' and 'national interest' were far too ambiguous and vague to be useful indicators of behaviour. What's more, as a prescriptive theory it was deficient in that too many contradictory policies could be derived from it. After all, considerations of national interest had led one Realist, Morgenthau – to oppose and another – Kissinger – to support US involvement in Vietnam. Moreover, as a description of international relationships it was likewise inadequate, since in its stress on the role of the state it underplayed the extent to which territoriality and sovereignty had been penetrated by inter-, trans-, sub- and supranational actors, movements and processes. Equally in an age of nuclear 'overkill', 'spy-in-the-sky' satellites, common markets, debt crises, information explosions, population explosions, depleting ozone layers and Great Power humiliations at the hands of small powers, as at Suez, in Vietnam and Afghanistan, the Realist emphasis on national security and power balances seemed in need of drastic overhaul.

On the other hand, many of those challenging Realism in the 1950s and early 1960s were less concerned with its state-centricity than with its methodology. Whereas the Realists relied mainly on historical analysis and political theory and were more interested in explanation than prediction, the newcomers offered what they liked to call a behavioural scientific approach of the kind then fashionable in the social sciences.[14] What, then, was behaviouralism?

Behaviouralists assumed that people and the institutions they created acted in patterned ways and that therefore those patterned interactions could be studied according to the methods of science. Basing themselves on the observable, the tangible and the measurable, they sought quantifiable data, testable hypotheses and verifiable knowledge on a range of conduct types. Above all they prized objectivity, and claimed their 'science' to be value-free. In theory this would mean their suspending judgement on a matter under investigation until sufficient evidence was forthcoming. In addition, they offered a new kind of theorising based on computer simulation, systems analysis, game and bargaining theories, etc. borrowed from other disciplines so as to give more rigour and precision to the study. On the other hand, the net effect was to stimulate yet another Great Debate in the subject, with the self-styled 'scientists' accusing the self-styled Realists of, among other things, failing to give precise answers to many of the questions they raised about the nature of the state, power, national interest, security and the like; the Realists in turn accused the 'scientists' of a contempt for history, of a penchant for the incomprehensible and of dealing in measurable trivia.[15]

2.5 REALISM RECONSTRUCTED

As it happens, many Realists were already beginning to review their ideas even before the scientific 'onslaught'. In the first place, Realists were themselves expressing dissatisfaction with a conceptual framework from whose assumptions several contradictory conclusions could be drawn. For example, even if the national interest was of critical concern, precisely whose interest was involved and by what criteria was it to be determined? How did ideology and interest relate? What were the characteristics of international stability, how could power balances be accurately assessed and was a bipolar or multipolar global balance of power most conducive to world peace? Did an accumulation of arms contribute to national security or undermine it by encouraging opponents to follow suit? Clearly, to such questions the Realists could offer no agreed answers.

In any case changing realities had seemed to require at least a review if not the replacement of traditional Realism – the spread of nuclear weapons; the proliferation of new and often unviable states following the collapse of empire; the effect on state structures of transnational, supranational and subnational forces; the globalisation of the international economy; the North/South divide; the problem of environmental degradation; the trend towards integration in Western Europe; the revolution in communications; the growing relevance of moral criteria in international discourse, and so on.

Such developments caused many Realists to abandon their more crude power political calculations according to which security is defined almost exclusively in military terms and most outcomes are determined by relative strengths, and to allot greater weight to economic and environmental factors and to the role of non-governmental organisations and subnational groups, such as secessionist movements. Anyone picking up, say, *The Anarchical Society* by Hedley Bull, setting out the case for what has become known as the English School,[16] or *The International Political System* by F.S. Northedge, which essays the essentials for peace as well as war and for conflict resolution as well as conflict,[17] will readily discover how far the 'traddies' had moved towards the 'trendies'.

On the other hand, for the 'traditionalists' IR was still primarily a study of government-to-government relations. As Fred Northedge put it: 'The political level of international relations is in itself an intellectual concern of heroic dimensions ... If the entire social world of sovereign states is included, we run the risk of being defeated by the subject's sheer dimensions.'[18] But, of course, for the 'scientists' such a definition of the study was far too narrow and restrictive.

2.6 FOREIGN POLICY ANALYSIS

The first critiques of 'traditionalism' came, naturally enough, from the US. For with America beginning to experience the ups and downs of superpowerdom and what has been called 'the pulling and hauling' process of decision-making, many of its scholars had grown impatient with what they saw as an oversimplified conception of international politics in which states were seen as hard-shell 'billiard balls'. In the late 1950s and 1960s, therefore, the so-called 'scientists' turned to foreign policy analysis, in the process grafting a host of theories derived from other social science disciplines.[19] As a supposedly scientific endeavour, however, foreign policy analysis was somewhat discredited when some 'analysts', especially those connected with American defence and foreign policy 'think tanks' such as the Rand Corporation and the Hudson Institute, abandoned 'objectivity', using the study as a rationalisation for US strategy and a tool to 'beat' the Soviets. In any case, in focusing on particular states it tended to reinforce the state-centric view of International Relations. On the other hand it made a useful contribution by indicating that decisions can stem as much from personal or party preoccupations as from considerations of national advantage and are often in any case less the product of rational choice than the chance result of a complex bargaining process, in which the outcome represents, as it were, the lowest common denominator.[20] Never again would the testimony of those statesmen and women who claim to have masterminded virtually everything done in the name of their country be accepted without considerable reserve.

2.7 POST-BEHAVIOURAL PLURALISM

Hardly had they disposed of the 'billiard ball' model when some of the self-styled 'scientists' concluded that the new decision-making approach was itself inadequate to explain the complexities of 'world politics'. 'World politics' or 'world society', as some called it, encompassed a far broader framework than inter-state relations, for it comprised several layers of analysis simultaneously, i.e. the human, the state, the transnational, the subnational, the supranational and the international systemic or global level, and in turn required study of the various environments – economic, technological, ideological, etc. – within which international relations occurred.

Such a perception was to lead to a new kind of paradigm or conceptual map. Associated with scholars such as Robert Keohane, Joseph Nye, James Rosenau and John Burton,[21] it was to be known by various names – liberal, pluralist, internationalist, transnationalist, globalist. Its central assumption, as essayed in John Burton's *World Society*, was that contemporary international relations differed fundamentally from earlier networks of relationships in that they comprised multiple highly complex interdependent structures and were best represented not as billiard balls in collision but as a 'cobweb' with diverse interlinkages.

More specifically, the pluralists held, first of all, that in an age in which the level of communication and interaction was low, the idea of the self-contained, impenetrable sovereign state may have had some validity. But that now in an age of rapidly developing military, industrial and communications technology, the notions of sovereign equality and independence were increasingly at odds with reality. Governments could no longer exercise full control over the flow of information, ideas, funds, goods and people across frontiers or protect their civilians against new and subtle forms of hostility, subversion or aggression from within or outside the state. It was also the pluralist claim that a profusion of new regional and functionalist organisations, which offered the potential for much greater cross-frontier cooperation than in the past, and of non-governmental actors such as the multinational corporation (MNC), many of which disposed of more financial resources than most governments, were eroding the competence of the state, and deserved study in their own right.

Secondly, the pluralists claimed that the various members of the international system were now interdependent to an unprecedented extent. And by interdependent they meant both sensitive and vulnerable to one another and in many different dimensions, involving various sectors of society. Interdependence was to be found at global, continental, regional or local levels. It was, moreover, both a physical reality which could be measured objectively and a condition that governments subjectively recognised as a fact, modifying their policies accordingly. It also applied to all international actors and not just states and was to be observed in at least six clearly identifiable areas.

Economic interdependence

First in the economic field – in international trade, investment and finance. There was now, pluralists argued, a globalised market place involving a complex international division of labour as a result of which a sudden rise or fall in the price of oil, fluctuations in American, German or South Korean interest rates, a sudden fall in the value of the yen or the rouble, the decision of an individual like George Soros to speculate against sterling or of a Latin American country to default on its debts and so forth have 'knock on' spillover effects throughout the international system.

Political interdependence

Second, in the political arena, in the sense of multiple linkages between various governments and societies, of which James Rosenau highlights three.[22] What he calls Reactive linkages, as, for example, when domestic considerations make a strike against so-called terrorist installations in Afghanistan and Sudan or a modest American diversion in Iraq attractive options for a beleagured President Clinton; when mounting unpopularity at home and abroad encourages Indonesia's former President Suharto to commission and dedicate an outsize statue to Christ in East Timor, which his country has raped and pillaged, or when reports of his loss of effective power or creeping Alzheimer's stirs Russia's President Yeltsin into sacking successive governments. Then there are Emulative linkages, where governments and social groups copy one another's policies or actions, as when there is a spate of incidents of 'ethnic cleansing', racist violence or air piracy. Finally, Penetrative linkages, as when criminal gangs, such as the Mafia, in one country spread their tentacles to other countries, undermining their social and economic order. One has only to look at post-Communist Eastern Europe to see how, as the unregulated market has replaced government control, the main beneficiaries are often those who best understand the notion of corporate greed – former Communist bosses now seemingly recruited to serve the international Mafia.

Strategic/institutional/ecological interdependence

A third area of interdependence, pluralists argue, operates in the military/strategic field, with the proliferation of collective defence organisations on the one hand and the interest of all, especially in the aftermath of the 1962 Cuban Missile crisis, in avoiding a nuclear conflict on the other. In the process of institutionalisation lies a fourth arena of interdependence. The growth of intergovernmental organisations, such as the International Monetary Fund (IMF), they claim, imposes constraints on government action, while the rise of international non-government organisations, such as the MNC or Amnesty International, undermines the role of governments altogether. In the threats to the environment caused by developments both natural and man-made, and in particular the insatiable desire of people to consume more and more of the earth's resources, lies a fifth arena of interdependence – the ecological.

Policy-making

A final domain for interdependence is perhaps the most basic – policy-making. Traditionally, domestic policy was sharply differentiated from foreign policy. The former had to do with decisions affecting behaviour within the state's borders, the latter with the arena beyond a state's jurisdiction. However, according to the pluralists, the traditional distinction can no longer be maintained. Domestic policies have repercussions abroad: external policy can markedly affect a state's internal circumstance. And since the domestic and the international dimensions of policy are now so closely interwoven, there is little point in treating them as separate entities.

Global awareness

So much for mainstream pluralism. But some adherents – John Burton, for example – took behaviouralism even further, believing their 'science' to be progressing from 'islands of theory' in an ocean of ignorance towards a general theory of behaviour. Such a theory, they held, would revolutionise our understanding of both human relationships and human needs, making it easier to curb or control conflict at all levels. With this new understanding, they claimed, people's residual attachment to sovereignty, territory, ethnicity and the like would dissolve and we human beings would become conscious of our solidarity with every member of this 'spaceship earth' or 'global village'. At that stage, of course, there is no more war because no one has an interest in promoting it.[23] By bringing ethics back in to the study, such behaviouralists had moved beyond the objectivity they had formerly commended and might be said to have become 'post-behaviouralists'.

Cooperation, not conflict

But the pluralists' assertion that the Realist paradigm was now outdated had two further components in addition to the argument about the penetration of the state, the growth of interdependence, and the potential for a general theory of behaviour. Like the idealists after the First World War they stressed the potential for cooperative action in world politics and derided the notion that conflict was the norm. They were also disdainful of the idea that force could still be an effective tool of foreign policy or that security necessarily topped the list of government priorities. In their view, military issues had largely lost their salience, and as an option war was no longer viable.[24] Clearly these particular 'scientists' had failed to notice that millions had been killed as a direct or indirect consequence of the 250 or more inter- and intrastate wars since 1945.[25] On the other hand, they were right to point out that superior strength did not necessarily determine outcomes nowadays, as France had learned to its cost in IndoChina and Algeria, Britain at Suez, the US in Vietnam and the Soviet Union in Afghanistan.

2.8 THE NEW AGENDA

So what were the issues that in the perspective of the post-behaviouralists now topped the agenda? Clearly matters calling for and, in their view, producing cooperation rather than conflict, and not necessarily because of innate goodness but, echoing Grotius, because of human rationality. In a mode of thinking some call 'neo-liberalist',[26] they called for an investigation into the kinds of conditions under which convergent interests might produce international cooperation, bringing mutual if not necessarily equal benefits. But they also claimed that international cooperation was already being increasingly attained in matters of 'low' politics – i.e. socio-economic policy – as distinct from 'high' or diplomatic/strategic politics. Such concerns as food allocation, population growth, the debt crisis, the problems of pollution and the depletion of scarce resources – problems far too large to be solved by the traditional state – were now the province of inter- and transgovernmental agencies, making the state if not obsolescent, then somewhat inadequate to meet modern needs. To which the Realists would respond: if the state has had its day, why have the Latvians, Lithuanians, Estonians, Slovenes, Croats, Bosnians, Kosovars, Kurds, Palestinians, Kashmiris, Eritreans, Chechens and the like have been so anxious to acquire sovereign statehood? Why does Umberto Bossi receive an enthusiastic response to his demand for what he calls Padania to secede from Italy? And why in any case should not new issues be accommodated in the old way – through diplomatic accords between the Powers? For modern Realists the state was not about to wither away and deprive their theory of its foundations.

But Realism's major counter-criticism was that the methodologies and measuring techniques of the natural sciences so favoured by the behaviouralists contained hazards of which they often seemed blissfully unaware.

2.9 HAZARDS OF THE 'SCIENTIFIC' APPROACH

1. Complexifying the obvious, as when one well-known pluralist produces a lengthy tome based on a questionnaire distributed among what he calls opinion-formers, only to discover the earth-shattering truth that if you ask a group of people about foreign policy they will agree on some things and disagree on others.[27]

2. The misleading measurement, as when inferences are drawn from statistical observations that are either unwarranted or else trivial in relation to the cost and effort of producing the figures. One celebrated behaviouralist appeared to believe that the nature of the changing relations between the US and Britain could be measured by comparing mail flows between them at the turn of and in the middle of the twentieth century. He seemed not to have realised that the volume of correspondence might be affected by other forms of communication, and that, in any case, the number and direction of letters exchanged between peoples often bear little relationship to the state of relations between governments.

3. Being conned by the computer into thinking that it can always improve on the data. The fact is: if you feed garbage into a computer, garbage is what you get out of it.

4. Gambling on gaming and being seduced by simulation. Computer simulation exercises, war games and the like may make good teaching devices and from them one can learn much about the states of mind of those who have to make crucial decisions at critical times. But games and simulations are not real-life situations and it is a mistake to confuse them with empirical reality – which is, sadly, what many American intelligence and strategic advisers tended to do at the height of the cold war, often with what were, arguably, dangerous consequences.

5. Generalising from insufficient instances. That rather speaks for itself.

6. Claiming as of 'scientific' validity some conceptual scheme that is no more than a rationalisation of political prejudice. All too often pseudo-scientific verbiage serves to conceal partisan views, complete with unwarranted assumption and preconceived conclusion. This last hazard is, of course, an ever-present danger in the social sciences, and can apply to any approach. For this reason, whether facing the purveyors of 'science', of 'realism' or of some other seductive credential, students are well advised to be on their guard!

NOTES

1. Quoted in Padover, S.F. (ed.), *Wilson's Ideals*, Washington, 1940, p. 70.
2. See, for example, Appendix I to Porter, B. (ed.), *The Aberystwyth Papers: International Politics 1919–69*, London, Oxford University Press, 1972, p. 362.
3. Lloyd, L., 'Philip Noel-Baker and peace through law' in Long, D. and Wilson, P. (eds), *Thinkers of the Twenty Years' Crisis*, Oxford, Oxford University Press, 1995.
4. See Bartlett, C.J., *The Global Conflict: 1880–1970*, London, Longman, 1984, pp. 148–226.

5. Niebuhr R., *Moral Man and Immoral Society*, New York, Scribner, 1932.
6. Carr, E.H., *The Twenty Years' Crisis 1919–1939*, London, Macmillan, 1939.
7. For a résumé of the contentions between IR scholars see Banks, M., 'The Inter-paradigm debate', in Light, M. and Groom, A.J.R. (eds), *International Relations: A Handbook of Current Theory*, London, Pinter, 1985, pp. 7–26.
8. *The Vices of Integrity: E.H. Carr, 1892–1982*, London, Verso, 1999.
9. See, for example, Schwarzenberger, G., *Power Politics*, London, Stevens, 1964; Morgenthau, H.J., *Politics Among Nations*, New York, Knopf, 1948; Kissinger, H., *A World Restored*, Boston, Houghton Mifflin, 1957; and Aron, R., *Peace and War*, London, Weidenfeld & Nicolson, 1966.
10. Wight, M., *Power Politics*, Leicester, Leicester University Press, 1972.
11. Treadgold, D., *Twentieth Century Russia*, Chicago, Rand McNally, 1959 pp. 165–87.
12. This is implicit in a radio discussion between Fred Halliday and the veteran US State Department official and diplomat George Kennan on 7 April 1995. It was part of a series of interviews between Professor Halliday and other veteran American statesmen and published by the BBC under the title *From Potsdam to Perestroika*.
13. It is interesting that even as late as the Brezhnev era such analyses were to be found in Soviet literature. See for example Alexandrov, V., *A Contemporary World History 1917–1945*, Moscow, Progress Publishers, 1986.
14. See, for example, Kaplan, M., *System and Process in International Politics*, New York, Wiles, 1957, and Rosenau, J., *The Scientific Study of Foreign Policy*, London, Pinter, 1980.
15. For a representative sample, see Bull, H., 'International theory: the case for a classical approach' in *World Politics*, vol. 18, April 1966, pp. 361–77 and Kaplan, M., 'The new great debate: traditionalism versus science in international politics' in *World Politics*, vol. 19, October 1966, pp. 1–20.
16. Bull, H., op. cit., London, Macmillan, 1977.
17. Northedge, F.S., *The International Political System*, London, Faber, 1976.
18. Ibid., pp. 22–3.
19. See, for example, Olson, W. and Groom, A.J.R., *International Relations: then and now*, London, HarperCollins, 1991, pp. 165–70.
20. The studies of Braybrooke, D. and Lindblom, C., *The Strategy of Decision*, New York, Free Press, 1970 and Allison, G., *The Essence of Decision*, Boston, Little, Brown, 1971 were especially valuable.
21. See, for example, Keohane, R. and Nye, J.S. (eds), *Transnational Relations and World Politics*, Cambridge, Mass., Harvard University Press, 1971; Rosenau, J.R. (ed.), *In Search of Global Patterns*, London, Collier-Macmillan, 1976; Burton, J., *World Society*, London, Cambridge University Press, 1972.
22. Rosenau, J., *Linkage Politics*, New York, Free Press, 1969.
23. Burton, J., op. cit., pp. 35–45.
24. See, for example, Keohane, R. and Nye, J., *Power and Interdependence: World Politics in Transition*, Boston, Little, Brown, 1977, pp. 23–37.
25. Three invaluable statistical compendiums on war since 1945 are Kidron, M. and Smith, D., *The War Atlas*, London, Pan, 1983, a revised edition published in 1991, and Smith, D., *The State of War and Peace Atlas*, London, Penguin, 1997.

26. The book by Baldwin, D. (ed.), *Neorealism and Neoliberalism: The Contemporary Debate*, New York, Columbia University Press, 1983, contains some valuable contributions on the strengths and weaknesses of neoliberalist theory.
27. See for example Rosenau, J., *National Leadership and Foreign Policy*, Princeton, Princeton University Press, 1963, especially p. 359.

CHAPTER 3

STRUCTURALISM

In the previous chapter reference was made to a paradigm reflecting a peculiarly Stalinist version of Marxism, in which the dialectical view of history was filtered, as it were, through the eyes of the man who had led post-revolutionary Russia for thirty years. But Marxism was also to spawn other perspectives on international relations, and in this chapter the focus is on a Marxist-derived paradigm which entered the IR textbooks long after Stalin's departure for the 'Great Politburo in the sky'. Known alternatively as 'structuralism' or 'world-system theory', it characterises the world as a single, if complex system, but whose nature determines significant divisions as between its interacting units. But like earlier analytical frameworks, structuralism arose out of dissatisfaction with the approaches to international relations then on offer.

3.1 PARADIGMS AND METHODOLOGIES REVIEWED

First, there had been the paradigm stemming from the mood encapsulated by President Woodrow Wilson at the end of the First World War behind which lay a complex of notions derided by E.H. Carr as 'utopian' – that human nature was fundamentally good and capable of unselfish action, that there was an essential harmony of interests between the states of international society and that the morality or otherwise of foreign policy could be objectively assessed.

The advent of Fascism, economic nationalism and the approach of war in the 1930s had led people like Niebuhr and Carr to counterpose another paradigm – what they called 'Realism' – to the 'idealism' of the earlier generation of IR specialists. Taking conflict as the norm in a world of independent sovereign states and of peoples whose sense of solidarity scarcely extended beyond state boundaries, the 'Realists' had assumed 'power politics', that is, the politics of not being overpowered, to be the essence of statecraft. Though they would not altogether exclude economics, morality or law from their analyses, they had viewed as of much greater significance the threat, display or use of force in a world of countervailing military pressure. But at the end of the 1950s as the so-called 'behavioural' revolution swept through the social sciences, Realism had come under challenge.

The behaviouralists had found Realism lacking in scientific rigour – conceptually flawed, deficient as a guide to policy, inadequate as a description of international relations and too narrow in scope since, in concentrating on international conflict, it had underestimated the degree of cooperation and, in portraying the state system of the past 350 years as virtually unchangeable, had taken a misleadingly conservative view of international relations. However, the early behaviouralists had offered not so much a new paradigm as a set of new tools and methodologies. Their concern was with the observable, testable and measurable: what they sought was 'objective' value-free data.

Soon, however, the behaviouralists had fashioned a paradigm of their own, based loosely on the concepts of 'transnationalism' and 'interdependence'. Significant interactions were occurring in ways which, they held, were transnational (i.e. across frontiers rather than inter-state), and such interlinkages – multinational enterprise, business cycles, drug-trafficking, mass migrations, contagious epidemics, trans-border tribal conflicts or whatever – were in turn affecting both policy and the capacity to make it. In consequence, groups, societies and states had become both sensitive and vulnerable to the various forces, processes and movements which shaped their existence. In the meantime, new issues were dominating the international agenda, with new possibilities for cooperation between and beyond governments.

Each successive approach had been shaped by the changing climate of international events – 'structuralism' being no exception. For it permeated the mainstream social sciences books in the 1960s – a decade of exceptional social, cultural and political turbulence. The US was in serious trouble – at home, with the mounting unrest of the urban blacks; abroad in Vietnam, a war beginning to look increasingly brutal, costly and unwinnable – and the revolt among potential conscripts on the American campuses had had repercussions throughout the Western world and beyond. In 1968, in one of those Emulative linkages referred to in the previous chapter, students in North America and in Europe, East as well as West, had turned their campuses into theatres of protest. It was at this time that the LSE, though by no means the most turbulent of the British universities, had briefly regained its ill-deserved reputation as a hotbed of revolution, its proximity to Fleet Street (where most of the national dailies were then printed), Thames TV and BBC Bush House, ensuring that it would be constantly in the headlines.[1]

But the Soviet Union was at that time also under pressure. Warsaw Pact troops had been used to suppress the 'Prague Spring', following Czechoslovakia's repudiation of the Soviet model, and in consequence Moscow's relations with independent-minded Communist states like China, Romania, Yugoslavia and Albania had plummeted, as had the Soviet reputation further afield among Communist and non-Communist alike. There were even dissensions within the Warsaw Pact countries that had intervened, and in Poland these soon took a violent turn.[2]

While both Superpowers tried to come to terms with their new vulnerability, the international focus increasingly shifted to economic factors. With the growing success of the European Community and Japan, the rise of the multinational corporation (MNC), the decline of the post-war international monetary system and the appearance of a large number of recently decolonised states, development issues began to loom large on the international agenda. And when in both North America and Europe a new generation of scholars decided to place their 'science' once again in the service of humankind, they sparked off what was to become known as the 'post-behavioural revolution'. In 1969 at a conference of the American Political Science Association, Professor David Easton set out the agenda. In a world of violence, oppression, poverty and hunger, it was 'more important to be relevant and meaningful for contemporary urgent social problems than to be sophisticated in the tools of investigation'.[3]

3.2 PLURALISM AND ITS CRITICS

In effect, post-behaviouralism broke with mere number-crunching and marked a return to ethics and ideals, but this time, so its advocates hoped, with analyses grounded in science. There then appeared a surfeit of theories, loosely derived from pluralism's 'interdependence' paradigm – integration theory, functionalism and neo-functionalism, regime theory, peace research, conflict theory, needs theory and world order modelling – all supposedly concerned with the creation of a better world.[4]

But the interdependence paradigm and its derivatives were not without their critics. From a Realist perspective, Kenneth Waltz suggested that domestic markets were growing even faster than world trade and that in that peculiarly economic sense interdependence was in decline.[5] Others, such as Hedley Bull, pointing to the fact that many governments were intervening to an unprecedented degree in matters relating to development and welfare, the environment and ideological orientation as well as to security and prestige, contended that the erosion of state sovereignty was less palpable than the pluralists imagined.[6] Indeed, had the Realists of the time then known, say, how far the East German authorities had been prepared to interfere with the genetic programming of their female athletes, how far American officialdom had gone in using mind-altering drugs or of life-threatening medical experiments against poor blacks at home and abroad or how many Scandinavian Social Democratic governments were sanctioning the sterilisation, incarceration or lobotemisation of the handicapped, the poor and the illegitimate, they would have been further strengthened in their view.

There were, however, Realists who could accept the claim that interdependence was growing. On the other hand they did not see this as necessarily inconsistent with the formal independence of states, nor as necessarily something to be welcomed. Their fear was that greater interdependence would engender greater friction within and between political communities in the form of increased transnational terrorism and other kinds of turbulence, drug-trafficking, organised crime and the like.[7] At the same time they could detect little evidence to indicate that military power was losing its salience. Even if the incidence of international war was declining, civil war was all too frequent, producing spillover effects in neighbouring countries.

But criticisms of the pluralists came not just from die-hard Realists but from a very different source – from those who accepted interdependence as a fact but claimed that it was asymmetrical. That is, that it applied to and benefited only a comparatively small group of developed, mainly Western capitalist societies, but that with the developed countries increasingly trading with one another, the trade-dependent lesser-developed countries (LDCs), which they had exploited, were at their mercy. Given the serious imbalances in power and wealth between developed and developing countries, for the latter there was not interdependence but one-way dependence. In short, the world economy was characterised by inequalities of benefits and liabilities and, hence, a structure of dominance and dependency.[8] And since, in the view of these radical critics of the interdependence paradigm, the nature of the whole determined the kinds of segments into which the world was structured or divided, the term 'structuralist', borrowed from linguistics and anthropology, was applied to the kinds of theories they elaborated.

3.3 STRUCTURALIST THINKING

Holism versus individualism

The rudiments of structuralism can be traced to Aristotle, but it is to German philosophy especially of the eighteenth and nineteenth centuries one must turn to understand its peculiar mode of discourse. From the ethical imperatives of Kant to the somewhat grandiloquent methodology of Hegel and Marx, who claimed to have divined the logic of history, 'structuralism' takes its cue. What distinguishes its methodology is what is called its holism. Holism is probably best understood in terms of its opposite – individualism. An individualistic approach rests on a study of individual psychology and reduces group behaviour to the level of individual interests and subjective motivations. Holism, in contrast, denies that social interaction can be reduced to mere individual psychology, for such an approach could not explain conditions such as, say, the traffic jam or a sudden rise in inflation or unemployment, though it might provide some useful clues. In any case, for the holist no proper comprehension of changing social norms and circumstances is possible without an understanding of the historical process that shapes our lives; and even if holists disagree on the nature of that process – for Hegel it was essentially spiritual and for Marx basically material in character – they agree that our behaviour is moulded by the kinds of social and other systems in which we find ourselves: the family, the tribe, the neighbourhood, the social class, the church, the economy, etc. The main premise of holism is that patterns of social conduct are constantly being reproduced, creating a framework of constraints and allowances to which people adjust, largely without thinking.[9]

Though most recurrent patterns of social interaction have a history, new ones can appear, producing similar outcomes. For example, one person crosses a cornfield and makes a path which others follow as if it had been there for all time. One person decides to wear a baseball cap back to front, and then others do likewise without bothering to ask why. Some people take a bunch of flowers or a teddy bear to London's Kensington Palace in memory of a dead princess, and soon many others follow suit, to considerable emotion but not necessarily much thought.

In their holistic approach, structuralists perceive as a single system the network of interactions that some call international relations. For whereas Realists and pluralists focus on actors in international society, structuralists consider what they regard as the 'big picture'. Theirs is a world rather than an inter-state perspective, and as such they study the global system in terms of its units, norms, forms of interaction, patterns of interaction as well as the environment – economic, technological, ideological, geographical and so forth – within which the interactions occur. And since structuralists also tend to believe that the overall characteristics and properties of the system more or less determine the structural divisions within it, they see little room for individual initiative. A Hitler, Saddam Hussein or Milosevic is merely a product of economic, social or political circumstance rather than an individual, independent mover or shaker of history.

The global system

Since structuralists talk of a global system, what do they understand by a system? In a sense anything that can be construed as an intelligible whole made up of a web of interacting units.[10] The planets, the electrical circuits in a house, the brain, the administration of justice in a particular country, the mores of a football crowd or the process of government can be conceived as systems. In this sense, a global system is for structuralists merely another network of interaction deserving of study. However, unlike systems analysts in business, industry or medicine, structuralists find in their perception of the global system the key to an understanding of world economics, politics and geopolitics since it provides the context conditioning the inter-penetration of individuals and all other systems, classes, societies and states.[11]

3.4 TYPES OF STRUCTURALIST THINKING

Economic – Marxist, Marxist/Leninist and neo-Marxist

Structuralists that are also Marxists – as most are – hold that to understand the crucial divisions within a social system, domestic or international, one needs to analyse social relationships as a function of a particular socio-economic system. For such a system, whether feudal, capitalist or socialist, forms the material base on which every other relationship depends. From it stem political, legal, ethical and religious ideas and institutions (Marxists use the word 'superstructure') which justify and perpetuate the socio-economic system in question.[12] For example, the ideas and institutions in a capitalist system structure the relations between the advantaged and the disadvantaged, empowering the rich and subjugating the poor, while promoting international institutions of domination, such as the MNC, which sustain world capitalism. But such ideas and institutions eventually antagonise those who feel oppressed by them, causing them ultimately, when the social stratification is at its most extreme, to seek to overthrow the system. In this sense such systems contain the seeds of their own destruction. When, for example, the stock market can see-saw from crash to recovery and back again in a matter of days it alienates people from finance capitalism, merely encouraging the search for a better system.

Where, then, does the state fit in to this kind of analysis? For a Marxist, the state is but an artificial construct – part of that superstructure of concepts and institutions the ruling class devises to secure its domi-nance. As such, it is a mere projection of the class struggle and can last no longer than the social order it is designed to serve. In time, when a revolution from world capitalism to world socialism sweeps away the economic base, the state will disappear. In the meantime, however, international politics do not, in this view, comprise politics between states; in the words of Fred Halliday they constitute 'civil war within one international social system'.[13] Accordingly, the foreign policies that governments pursue are no more than rationalisations of the interests of the ruling class.

One Marxist, Vladimir Ilyich Lenin, used the standard Marxist argument as a peg for a theory specifically to account for imperialism.[14] The unequal distribution of wealth within the capitalist system had brought it to crisis point. A few owners and controllers of capital amassed great wealth, but the workers lacked enough purchasing power to keep the domestic market in profit. As a result private entrepreneurs were driven to combine into monopoly cartels and to reinvest surplus capital abroad. But the search for profitable foreign outlets, overseas sources of raw materials and strategically important real estate, could only lead to fierce inter-state rivalry, to imperialism and eventually war – which is how Lenin explained 1914. Yet the impulse towards imperialism and war was not so much psychological as structural in origin. It was as independent of will and conscious choice as any other form of socially conditioned conduct. Following a kind of structuralist imperative, imperialism was best described as a term for a structural relationship of dominance and dependency generated by the system of world capitalism. Nonetheless from it would emerge the very forces which could be harnessed to a global revolution.

Lenin's theory was to have as many Marxist detractors as admirers, but one contemporary disciple, the American Immanuel Wallerstein, developed it into a historically based theory of global development, which he terms 'world-system theory'.[15] Though like the Realists his starting point is the existence of political anarchy, his conclusions are very different. For it becomes the setting for a far-reaching analysis of economic dynamics. His argument is that although no state can exercise global political or economic control in the absence of world empire, the lack of a central political structure facilitates the development of world capitalism. Capitalism, in this view, provides the critical environment in which the behaviour of states, markets and classes are shaped and constrained. It also determines the contours of the three broad economic arenas into which the world system is partitioned – core, periphery and semi-periphery. The core areas are the most advanced economically and are to be found mainly in the West; the periphery regions are the most underdeveloped, in part because the developed core impedes their development, and are to be found in the South, while the semi-periphery are neither fully developed nor especially backward but, like the former Fascist states of Italy, Germany and Japan and the former Communist countries of Eastern Europe as well as the newly industrialising countries (NICs) of Asia and the Middle East, pursue economic avenues which defy established modes of capitalist development. And though Wallerstein maintains that the standing of particular actors within the world capitalist economy may change over time, the system itself would remain hierarchical and exploit-ative unless transformed by revolutionary 'anti-systemic' forces, capable of bringing down the whole edifice of capitalism.

On the other hand, while more orthodox Marxists had seen capitalism as progressive – 'an engine of growth' – in that it was anti-feudal and created the kinds of industrial conditions at home and abroad that would enlarge the working class and eventually produce a socialist order, Wallerstein had serious doubts, which were shared by several other Marxist scholars, many from the LDCs. And in the 1950s a group of Latin American neo-Marxists, foremost among them Raul Prebisch, formulated a theory to explain why a century and a half of formal independence had failed to produce in the region effective political or economic indepen-dence and why, for all Latin America's indigenous wealth (many, after all, had gold, silver, oil, fertile soil and abundant forests), their economies were generally backward and their peoples poor.[16] In their attempt at explanation, the Latin American neo-Marxists disparaged the assumptions of economists left and right.

Both orthodox liberals and mainstream Marxists had tended to equate development with industrialisation and to advocate Western-style indus-trialisation for the LDCs. In addition, traditional Marxists had sought protectionism for infant industries as well as import substitution, but in the view of the Latin American theorists – collectively known as *dependen-distas*, dependency theorists – these were mistaken policies. Why?[17]

1. Because the internal market for consumer goods was too small;
2. Because import substitution rested on capital-intensive enterprises which required little labour and, therefore, did little to stimulate demand;
3. Because such a strategy generally needed imports which would rein-force dependence on multinational capital and foreign technology, and enlarge the debts so crippling to the region;
4. Because such a policy did nothing to break the chain of capitalism worldwide.

In any case, for the dependency theorists, development did not necessarily mean Western-style industrialisation. After all, a number of successful Western economies had managed largely to do without it – Denmark and New Zealand, for example, whose development was based on agriculture; Iceland which had a thriving economy based on fish; and, of course, Switzerland, whose development was based on service industries, insur-ance and banking practices with no questions asked. And, even if West-ern-style industrialisation were desirable, was it not, claimed the *dependendistas*, unfeasible given Latin America's lowly position in the international division of labour?

In their analyses they shared many of Wallerstein's conjectures. They argued that capitalism had been around since the fifteenth century, producing a world economic system characterised by unequal relations as between the economies of the dominant 'centre' and those of the dependent 'periphery'. In other words, they located the source of underdevelopment not within a particular country but in the system as a whole, and believed that for the 'periphery' economic specialisation and the division of labour were disastrous, since their economies were either plundered or neglected and all were dependent on the whims and fancies of international finance capital. Furthermore, international capital had developed novel instruments of LDC subjection of which the MNCs and the international banks were among the most pernicious. These were not the benign agents of progress, as liberal pluralists might characterise them, nor the marginal actors as portrayed by the Realists. They were key players in the attempt to maintain the hegemony of world capitalism, and their corrupting influence needed to be exposed and resisted. Since, moreover, capitalism had also developed indirect means of penetrating the LDCs through its close ties with the 'centre of the periphery', i.e. the elites of the LDCs (witness the number of Western-educated Third World leaders with second or third homes in the United States, Britain or France and an evident penchant for the lifestyle that goes with them), it had to be fought as much at home as abroad. Capitalism everywhere was the enemy.

More specifically, the dependency theorists claimed that the structures generated by world capitalism put the LDC at the mercy of adverse terms of trade; their independence compromised by their creditors; their elites bribed into serving the interests of foreign enterprise; their cultures sapped by creeping 'cocacolonialism' and 'pepsicology', and their dependency reinforced by lack of regional cooperation. Where there had been a degree of development in the region, the *dependendistas* claim it was merely 'dependent development', dependent, that is, on world economic trends rather than independently determined and that many who began the process of development, say, when cut off from the world economy, as in a world war, found that growth checked as they rejoined, so to speak, the world economic system. There followed what A. Gundar Frank calls 'the development of underdevelopment'[18] – in some ways a worse affliction than that of undevelopment, which was their condition prior to capitalist penetration.

Whether these are serious arguments or merely alibis for corruption and mismanagement, such theories have enjoyed considerable appeal not only in Latin America but throughout the LDCs and especially in Africa, where they were once widely held to explain the growing impoverishment, to supply an intellectual focus for resistance to Western economic policy and to serve as a basis for the adoption of more socialist strategies. For the traditional Marxist this meant preparing for the world revolution; for the card-carrying Communist, in the days when there *were* card-carrying Communists, it meant identifying with the policies of either Moscow, Peking, Tirana, Hanoi or Havana; for the neo-Marxist, despairing of there being Marxist-style revolutions in the foreseeable future, it meant decoupling the economies of the LDCs partly or wholly from the international division of labour, possibly aligning with other like-minded peripheral states.[19]

While the more radical theories were at least coherent and clear and offered some explanation of both the economic backwardness and the enormous gulf between rich and poor in some of the LDCs, they rested on some dubious assumptions and led to some even more dubious conclusions.

First, the starting point for most world systems and dependency theorists – that the world capitalist system had been in operation for some 500 years – requires some nifty verbal juggling. True, they define capitalism, rather unusually for Marxists, as a mode not so much of production as of exchange, characterised by the search through trade for profits. But it is still rather an eccentric notion. Secondly, in tending to treat dependency and development as mutually exclusive they seemed to virtually rule out the possibility of sustained economic development in the LDCs. But what of the rise of Japan and the so-called Newly Industrialising Countries (NICs) of Asia such as Taiwan, South Korea, Singapore, Malaysia, Indonesia and some of the oil-rich Sheikhdoms of the Middle East which, for all their current problems, have made spectacular economic progress? And what of China, whose development suffered greatly during the years of the Great Leap Forward and the Cultural Revolution, when the People's Republic more or less decoupled itself from the world economy, and has been at its most impressive since becoming firmly linked to the world system? Thirdly, in stressing structural economic factors, dependency theorists have tended to underplay the extent to which internal factors, and in particular indigenous culture, can affect development. For example, that the Japanese having received their culture more or less from China have no sense of shame in adopting and adapting ideas from foreigners has served their economic development well since, unlike their neighbours, they were never embarrassed to borrow Western technology and managerial techniques. Fourthly, as regards trade terms, the polarities of the systems and dependency theorists were too stark, for there were primary producers in the North and industrialised states in the South, while in any case the prices of commodities rise as well as fall – sometimes favouring the primary producer at the expense of the importer of manufactures.[20]

Economic – reformist

However, among such theorists there were advocates of a less radical solution, people who saw the way ahead, possibly somewhat illogically in view of their premises, in terms of reform and redistribution. In 1974, for example, at the UN, leaders representing the so-called Group of 77 LDCs in a quest for revision of the global economy grouped together in one package a series of demands regarding assistance, trade and representation that they had issued at various times before. Though their programme for a New International Economic Order received the enthusiastic support of a few Western statesmen, notably the late Willy Brandt of West Germany and Britain's Edward Heath, who viewed its agenda as a relatively painless method of serving the interests of both rich and poor in what they took to be an interdependent world,[21] most were sceptical. Portraying it as a largely socialist scheme to undermine free enterprise, the majority of Western governments dismissed the demands for a NIEO and the so-called North/South dialogue became largely a dialogue of the deaf.[22]

Political – structural Realism

Not all structuralist theories have a Marxist- or neo-Marxist-derived base or have to do with economics. Some view the global system in political terms, and one of the most celebrated is Kenneth Waltz's *Theory of International Politics*.[23] Though Waltz is in the Realist tradition, unlike classical Realists he acknowledges the importance of the international economy, yet in true Realist style sees the state as the main actor and the economy as subordinate. At the same time, however, he accuses more traditional Realists of 'reductionism' for failing to recognise the structural conditions that determine state behaviour. For, as a Structural Realist or 'neo-Realist', he accounts for the policy of the state in terms not of its internal composition or the particular qualities of leaders but of situational determinants, i.e. the location of the state in the global power configuration. His is a macro- not a micro- approach. States behave as they do not because of the brilliance or cunning of decision-makers or even because of some defect in man's psyche or soul but as a result of systemic imperatives stemming from the anarchic nature of the international political process. In a world of competing sovereign states lacking government or moral consensus and in which power is dispersed, survival is always at stake. And because of the resultant fear, apprehension and lack of trust, every government faces a security dilemma which preoccupies so much of its time and resources that the capacity for inter-state cooperation becomes effectively limited. It is this concern for survival and not, as Morgenthau would have it, the desire to dominate,[24] that explains the power struggle between states. In the meantime, the balance of power has to be the central organising mechanism in the international system and 'force ... the ultimate arbiter of disputes'.

Political – global systems

Another influential structuralist theory is George Modelski's *Long Cycles in World Politics.*[25] Like the dependency theorists he claims that a single world system has existed for the last five centuries or so, but sees as fundamental not a single world economy but a global political system of sovereign states whose frequent conflicts create cycles in the incidence of war which then change the structure of the system. Like other structuralists, he divides the world into the dominant and the dependent, but in his theory the composition of the dominant changes as does the pattern of what he calls world leadership. By world leadership he does not necessarily mean the exercise of hegemony – a term suggesting a desire to dominate – because in his view not all world leaders seek power for its own sake. Some try to act in the common interest through clarifying and defining global problems and priorities; recruiting support for the existing global system and charting a more desirable future; securing the economic and other resources necessary to promote the desired change in the global system, and disseminating new technologies and ideas.

In the long cycle the balance in each system shifts as between the exercise of world leadership and the maintenance of hegemony, and Modelski identifies within the present world system five such periods – the first led by Portugal in the sixteenth century; the latest by the US in the twentieth century. For Modelski each system contains a similar sequence of events: 'a global war; a world wide struggle of major proportions and consequences; an era of political and economic consolidation (world power), a mid course of political unsettlement ... and a final sequence of rivalry and competitive disruption ... setting the stage for another global conflict,' which eventually produces a new hegemonic power, and the cycle begins again.[26] It is an intriguing argument, but like most structural analyses it involves a good deal of selection of evidence.

Geopolitical

A further set of structural arguments stems not so much from political as from geopolitical assumptions. Here the world system is perceived in terms of the strategic imperatives posed by geography. Though geopolitics was somewhat discredited when Hitler used the theories of German geographer Karl Haushofer to justify Nazi Germany's eastwards expansion, it does have fairly respectable forebears and descendants. For example, at the turn of the twentieth century when an American admiral, Alfred Mahan, was testifying to the political potentialities of sea power and impressing the German Kaiser with the need for a sizeable navy, the British geographer and former Director of LSE, Sir Halford Mackinder, was developing a land-based strategic theory, which was to permeate the British Foreign Office mentality for more than half a century. For Mackinder 'the geographical pivot of history', which was the title of his influential paper of 1904, lay in the huge island land mass stretching from Ostend to Okhotsk, from Spitzbergen to Singapore and from Kamchatka to Cape Town. He was, in other words, viewing Europe, Asia and Africa as one continent since he could see no clear-cut frontier between them, and because of its size and geopolitical importance he dubbed it 'The World Island'. His chief concern, however, was the centre of that World Island, which he called 'the Heartland' – roughly from the Rhineland through the Central and East European plane to the Urals and beyond. As he put it: 'Who rules East Europe commands the Heartland; who rules the Heartland commands the World Island; who rules the World Island commands the world.'[27]

It was this kind of analysis that prompted Britain to declare war against Germany in 1939 – for though Berlin had not threatened Britain, Hitler had annexed Austria and Czechoslovakia and invaded Poland, after making it clear in *Mein Kampf* that he intended to subjugate the Soviet Union, that is, take over the Heartland. And, no doubt, a similar consideration lay behind Britain's attempt, as early as 1945 and under a Labour government, at an anti-Soviet alliance after Moscow was perceived as threatening the Heartland, as it were, from the reverse direction.[28]

The major weakness in geopolitical theorising is the problem of determining criteria of significance. For Mahan sea power was critical, for Mackinder a particular land mass. More recent geopoliticians have seen air power, the availability and location of resources, industrial capacity or of populations as crucial. Another weakness in geopolitical analysis is the extent to which technological innovations – the plane, the rocket, the A-Bomb, the H-Bomb, the chemical weapon, etc. – can make a nonsense of earlier geopolitical assumptions and priorities. For example, a large but indisciplined army equipped with obsolete weapons is likely to be no match for a much smaller but highly motivated and technologically advanced force.

3.5 THE ROLE OF CONTENTION IN THE STUDY

The theories surveyed in these first three chapters by no means exhaust the list available to the student of International Relations. There is, for example, a growing body of literature which approaches the study from a critical theory perspective, strongly normative in orientation, and calling in question the basic institutions upholding existing social and inter-national systems and the theories which purport to explain and justify them. There are also post-modernist approaches which deny the existence of a single objective reality and would view international society as a social construct to be interpreted, as all social constructs have to be interpreted, in different ways by different 'narrators'.[29]

Having ascertained the degree of division in the field of IR, some readers by this time may have begun to wonder what is the point of studying the Structure of International Society at all. The schools in contention cannot all be right, and who is to say which is nearest to the truth? The short answer is that people have to decide this for themselves. On the other hand, the lack of certainty does not make the study any more problematic than most others, for in almost any respectable study there is contention, controversy and doubt.

After all, if one asks a group of philosophers or scientists about the proper subject of philosophical or scientific enquiry or, indeed, the origins of the universe, one will tend to get more answers than there are philosophers or scientists. And none of the social sciences is free from dissension and dispute. In economics there are the Keynesians, the Free Trade merchants, the Marxists, the neo-Marxists and an array of others. In psychology there are the residual devotees of Freud, of Jung, of Adler, of Melanie Klein, of Skinner, of a galaxy of other great names. In the arts, too, contention is king. The English faculty is as divided on key issues at Cambridge as it is at Oxford, while the faculties of music and the graphic arts appear in most institutes of learning to generate more discord than harmony. Indeed, it could be argued that controversy is the life blood of scholarship, and that where the questioning of ideas including one's own ceases, so in effect does the academic enterprise. It is for this reason that the writer deplores those academics on both sides of the Atlantic who seem to prefer cyphers to scholars and are delighted when their tutees merely regurgitate the ideas of their professors. How can merely memor-ising the ideas of others, no matter how celebrated, be said to constitute an education?

Surely a university should provide a kind of intellectual hothouse within which the student mind can grow, and where vigorous debate between academics is taken as a sign of strength not weakness. On the other hand if students are going to criticise a particular mode of thought in this or any other study they need to ensure, first, that they understand it; secondly, that they do not misrepresent it; and, thirdly, that they at least give it due respect since in the course of time they may come to regard it as no less valid than their current critique of it.

NOTES

1. See Dahrendorf, R., *LSE: A History of the London School of Economics and Political Science*, Oxford, Oxford University Press, 1995.
2. Stern, G., *The Rise and Decline of International Communism*, Aldershot, Elgar, 1990, pp. 205–9.
3. Easton, D., 'The new revolution in political science', in *The American Political Science Review*, December 1969, p. 1051.
4. Such theories are elaborated in Olson, W. and Groom, A.J.R., *International Relations: Then and Now*, London, HarperCollins, 1991, pp. 171–6 and 190–217.
5. Waltz, K., 'The myth of national interdependence' in Kindleberger, K. (ed.), *The International Corporation*, Cambridge, Mass., MIT Press, 1970.
6. Bull, H., 'The state's positive role in world affairs', *Daedalus*, no. 108, Fall 1979, pp. 60–73.
7. See for example Morse, E., *Modernization and the Transformation of International Relations*, New York, The Free Press, 1976, p. 14.
8. For a characteristic exposition see, for example, Wallerstein, I., 'The rise and future demise of the world capitalist system' in *Comparative Studies in Society and History*, vol. 16, no. 4, 1974, pp. 387–415.
9. An idiosyncratic but revealing elucidation of 'holistic' as distinct from 'individualistic' forms of thinking is to be found in Manning, C.A.W., *The Nature of International Society*, London, Bell, 1962, pp. 38–41 and 47–53. For a more conventional but lucid exposition see Little, R., 'Structuralism and Neo-Realism', in Light, M. and Groom, A.J.R., *International Relations: A Handbook of Current Theory*, London, Pinter, 1985, pp. 74–89.
10. The 'systems approach' is elaborated clearly in Young, O., *Systems of Political Science*, Englewood Cliffs, New Jersey, Prentice-Hall, 1968, Chapter 2.
11. For a more detailed exposition of 'structuralism' see for example Pettman, R., *State and Class: A Sociology of International Affairs*, London, Croom Helm, 1979, pp. 53–63, and Braudel, F., *Afterthoughts on Material Civilisation and Capitalism*, Baltimore, Johns Hopkins Press, 1977.
12. Marx's materialist conception of history and its relevance for the study of IR are elaborated in Halliday, F., *Rethinking International Relations*, London Macmillan, 1994, pp. 47–73.
13. Halliday, F., ibid., p. 145.
14. Lenin, *Imperialism, the Highest Stage of Capitalism*, Moscow, Progress Publishers, 1982.
15. Wallerstein, I., *The Modern World-System*, vols. I, II and III, New York, Academic Press, 1974, 1980 and 1989.

16. Prebisch, R., *The Economic Development of Latin America and its Principle Problems*, New York, UN, 1950.
17. Their analyses are encapsulated in Harris, N., *The End of the Third World*, London, Penguin, 1986, pp. 11–29.
18. Frank, A.G., 'The development of underdevelopment', in *Monthly Review*, Sept. 1966, pp. 17–30.
19. The arguments are essayed in Cardoso, F. and Faletto, E., *Dependency and Development in Latin America*, Berkeley, University of California Press, 1979.
20. For a more comprehensive rebuttal of dependency theory see for example Fukayama, F., *The End of History and the Last Man*, London, Penguin, 1992, pp. 98–108.
21. See the Brandt Commission's Report: *North–South: A Programme for Survival*, London, Pan, 1981.
22. See for example Krasner, S., *Structural Conflict: The Third World against Global Liberalism*, Berkeley, University of California Press, 1984.
23. Waltz, K., *A Theory of International Politics*, Reading, Mass., Addison-Wesley, 1979.
24. See his *Politics Among Nations*, New York, Knopf, 1985.
25. Modelski, G., *Long Cycles in World Politics*, London, Macmillan, 1987.
26. Modelski, G., 'Long Cycles and the Strategy of US International Economic Policy', in Avery, W.P. and Rabkin, D.P. (eds), *America in a Changing World Economy*, New York, Longman, 1980, p. 100.
27. Mackinder, H., *Democratic Ideals and Reality*, New York, Henry Holt, 1919, p. 150.
28. See Bell, C., *Negotiation from Strength*, London, Chatto & Windus, 1962.
29. For a comprehensive survey of critical theory and postmodernist thought see Brown, C., *International Relations Theory: New Normative Approaches*, Hemel Hempstead, Harvester, Wheatsheaf, pp. 195–233.

PART II

THE EVOLUTION OF INTERNATIONAL SOCIETY

CHAPTER 4

PRE-MODERN INTERNATIONAL SOCIETIES

4.1 THE VALUE OF HISTORY

In this chapter we move from theory to history, attempting to trace the evolution of international society from the earliest times. But why this excursion into the distant past? How can what happened a long time ago be relevant now? In the first place, political or international events – a war, perhaps, a revolution or a global recession – do not usually come out of the blue, and in order to assess their significance we need to place them in context, tracing not just the elements of continuity connecting them to what had gone before but also the novel factors distinguishing them from the past. Secondly, though we cannot extrapolate the future from the past since tomorrow may well be different from yesterday, the historical record can reveal how societies, including international societies, evolve. In this way we might be able to assess whether the international order as we know it is likely to be the last or is destined to be superseded. Thirdly, though history cannot provide proof of an idea or theory, it can give us the evidence, patterns and precedents we need to make out a case or to cast doubt on one.

Unfortunately, history is a study resting in part on subjective judgement, which means that there can be contradictory interpretations as to both the facts and their exact significance. On the problems of disputed evidence one has only to consider such questions as: who or what caused the First World War? Did as many as six million Jews die in the Holocaust? Was there only one assassin of President Kennedy? As to the thorny question of interpretation: was it a revolution or a coup that propelled Lenin to power in Russia in 1917? Was Communism defeated, or was it never tried? What precipitated the 'ethnic cleansing' of the Kosovars – a Milosevic plan or NATO's bombing of Belgrade? Highlighting the problems of interpretation: when asked to give an assessment of the French revolution, the former Chinese Premier Zhou Enlai refused on the grounds that, since it had occurred only some two hundred years previously, it was far too soon for a verdict.

One such question, 'when did modern international society originate?' may appear simple enough, but in fact it conceals several conceptual conundrums. For instance, what in this context are 'international society' and 'modern' intended to convey? Once again, some linguistic analysis is called for. Suffice it to say that, like many other expressions in the political vocabulary, the term 'international society' was coined long after the appearance of the political phenomena it purports to designate, and thus that giving definition to the notion of 'modern international society' must require an examination of earlier networks of relationships. Yet such an enquiry suggests a further question: 'why this penchant for packaging the past into specific epochs and eras?' A possible answer is that it helps us to locate ourselves and our social circumstance in relation to the past. But since there is no general agreement as regards the appropriate criteria for determining what constitutes a historical watershed, we are again in the realm of subjective speculation.

4.2 WHAT IS AN INTERNATIONAL SOCIETY?

If we are to highlight the distinctive features of modern international society, how far back into history must we go to find relevant comparisons? Do we need to go back to the dawn of history – to primitive men and their womenfolk, to their families and extended families, to the clans and tribes emerging from the various forms of intercourse in which they engaged? Do we start with the more complex social arrangements that evolved subsequently, when nomadic hunters and gatherers stopped their wanderings to become cultivators of a fixed territory and to rely on one another for the tasks that needed to be performed for the benefit of the whole? Not in this analysis, since here the starting point is not the organisation of society as such but of relations *between* societies, and not just random or haphazard interaction, but something more sustained and continuous.

For students of the subject, especially of the English School, international society exists where there are separate and autonomous political units, significant interactions between them to an extent conditioning their behaviour, and a dominant culture shaping such norms, codes of behaviour and institutions as exist between the political units.[1] Our concern, moreover, is with 1. the types of political community comprising those units; 2. their forms of interaction, from cooperation through compliance to conflict; 3. their rules of conduct, explicit or implicit; 4. their patterns of relations, whether hierarchical, in rough balance, multi-polar or whatever; and 5. the environment – geographical, political, economic, technological, etc. – in which the web of interaction operates and where significant changes could affect the society's structure and functioning.[2] Here, of course, we are using the term 'international' very loosely since nowadays it connotes a network of relations in which a key role is played by the sovereign state, while the following analysis includes networks of relations long predating the use of that term.

4.3 PRE-MODERN INTERNATIONAL SOCIETIES

In terms of the criteria identified here – i.e. separate and autonomous units, significant interactions between them and a dominant culture – it is possible to classify at least seven international societies prior to that with which we are familiar. Their forms of organisation, however, are diverse. At the one extreme there is the web of relations with a manifestly dominant state or group of states that tries to unify the known world under a single command or set of political ideas. At the other is the loose association of kindred independent communities each with a degree of self-government and interacting in terms of diplomacy, trade, the migration of peoples and, of course, war.

Ancient empires of the Near and Middle East

If we take as our first set of examples the ancient empires grouped around the fertile crescent of the Tigris, Euphrates and Nile – the Sumerian, Egyptian, Babylonian, Assyrian and Persian, i.e. from roughly 4000 to about 400 BC – we find a kind of dialectic or contradiction not unknown in our own day between the desire of the city states of these regions to preserve their independence and the largely economic imperatives towards amalgamation and integration. In fact, many such states were too small and too weak to be able to survive on their own and, as they were dependent on scarce water supplies for agriculture, government became increasingly concentrated into the hands of the strong and the wealthy who could finance and supervise the much-needed irrigation projects. In the process these powerful individuals would add to their growing authority by mediating conflicts between neighbours over trade, land and water. From such socio-economic conditions emerged the many dynasties in the region at whose head was a figure who governed as either god-king (occasionally god-queen) or the custodian of a divine mission and whose word was law, at least while he (or she) retained power. But not all attempted to secure direct control over territory. For some it was enough to attain dominion over other rulers, in effect establishing satellite or vassal states.

In maintaining and consolidating their supremacy, the god-kings used a variety of methods. For example, the Assyrian monarchs imposed a common religion and transported their more rebellious subject peoples from one part of the empire to another. On the other hand, they governed an inner core of city states far more tightly than more distant polities. The ancient Egyptians planted garrisons among their subject peoples, and though generally leaving them a semblance of self-government, often compelled them to pay tribute and to work in the service of the god-ruler, which is probably how the pyramids came to be built. The Persians would also plant garrisons in more remote areas, but developed a much looser system of control than that of the Egyptians, in effect giving rewards to rulers who would work with them. Nonetheless, those governing these massive ancient empires had little notion of either legal equality or the right to independence. Though they might interact with other empires and civilisations, engaging in diplomatic dialogue and trade with them and sometimes concluding alliances, such relations were seen as essentially temporary. The ancient empires were primarily ventures in domination, and their rulers tended to regard those not yet under their sway as potential vassals or enemies.[3] The idea of permanent coexistence was as yet unknown.

The Chinese system

In the case of the second of our pre-modern international societies, i.e. the Chinese empire, the impetus to consolidate central power was not dissimilar. There was, however, a crucial difference. For though China was a country of some twenty different cultures and divided by two enormous rivers and a series of mountain chains, once it had gradually coalesced into a single entity, it was able to preserve a continued existence from the eighteenth century BC right down to AD 1911. On the other hand, fear of disintegration has been a constant feature of national life, perhaps not surprisingly since the country experienced prolonged bouts of civil war, local rebellions, hostile blocs and partition. Even so, the idea of China as a unique civilisation with deeply embedded rituals and ceremonials was so well entrenched that for much of its early existence even its brutal internecine wars were conducted according to generally accepted rules. For example, hostilities were prohibited during the planting and harvesting periods, and also during months of mourning following the death of a feudal lord, while in battle it was forbidden to strike at the elderly or the already wounded.

On the other hand, the pattern in China was established largely in isolation and ignorance of the empires of the Near and Middle East. And if successive Chinese regimes shared with other imperial systems a sense of superiority toward their neighbours, unlike, say, the Egyptians, this was based not on wealth, power or race but on culture, and was bred of centuries of continuous settlement and civilisation. China was the Zhung

Guo, the Central Land, an island of elegance located in the middle of the world and surrounded by political barbarians, who were as yet outside the Chinese orbit, or tributaries, who were within it. Moreover, vast, populous and for a time technologically innovative, China had no need to deal with what it saw as uncouth neighbours, unless forced to by invasion. And as the peoples farther afield usually came to China as pirates or adventurers, the Chinese were merely reinforced in their view of the inferiority of the non-Chinese.

Significantly, the Chinese emperors, claiming to have 'the Mandate of Heaven' and buttressed by an extensive network of Mandarins or civil servants, also assumed exclusive sovereignty not only over China proper and what became known as Outer China – Manchuria, Mongolia, Sinkiang and Tibet – but, in theory at least, over the rest of the world as well. They talked not of acquiring but of recovering territory, and of other nations as tributaries. They were thus quite unable to accept other peoples as equals. Significantly, when Buddhism penetrated China in the sixth century BC, like Christianity and Communism in later years, it had to be sinicised, i.e. made Chinese. Until comparatively recently therefore Peking could have no conception of a world of sovereign states grounded in equality before the law.[4]

The Indian system

As in Imperial China, so in and as between the kingdoms of ancient India there was no conception of legal equality, even though the Aryans, who had migrated from Persia and established dominion over much of the subcontinent in about 1000 BC, had imposed certain uniformities. They had brought a common language, Sanskrit, a religion and a set of customs which blended into earlier ways of life to form a common Hindu civilisation. Yet rather like classical Greece, to be discussed below, or medieval Germany, the region was divided into a large number of independent and often warring units, even though there existed a common culture. What was, however, unique about the Indian subcontinent at the time was that though local rulers sought to expand their territory, they also accepted that they should not disturb the laws, customs and economic life of a subject people. As a result, of course, the ancient caste system by which the various Indian states had been stratified survived almost intact.

However, the introduction of Buddhism together with renewed interventions from the Persians and from the Greeks shook the value system of the subcontinent. From this ferment of ideas emerged two men who were to shape the political destiny of the region for nearly a century and to leave an imprint on international politics to this day. The first was Chandragupta Maurya who in 300 BC was able to fashion in Northern

India an empire based on an amalgam of Indian and Persian values; the second was his Prime Minister and mentor, Kautilya, whose volume *Arthashastra, Book of the State* had contained the blueprint for the establishment of the Mauryan empire.[5] Though in many ways his recommendations foreshadow those of Machiavelli's *The Prince*, written some 1800 years later, his proposed strategy – to aim at dominion, but always allowing some autonomy in the hope of winning over the subject peoples – proved more immediately successful. The Mauryan empire, built on Kautilyan principles, lasted from 300 BC until the death in 231 BC of Chandragupta's grandson, Ashoka, when the desire for independence was reasserted and India reverted to the anarchy described and deplored in the *Arthashastra*.[6]

Anyone reviewing the *Arthashastra* today would be struck by its remarkable foresight. In a chapter entitled 'The decay, stabilisation and progress of states' Kautilya details practices many of which are utterly familiar to those born in the twentieth century – for example, treating one's enemy's enemy as a friend, seeking expansion in time of superiority and support at times of weakness. Another striking feature is its stark, if brutal, realism in which the political arena is portrayed as a merciless jungle, lacking effective law, order or scruple and in which security is understood, as by many strategists today, in terms of the deterrence, containment or defeat of rivalry – potential or actual.

The Greek city states system

It is only when we come to the fourth international society – that of the Greek city states of the fifth century BC – that the pattern of the ancient world seems to be broken. For though the Greeks were as scornful of foreigners as their predecessors – calling non-Greeks 'barbarians' because their speech was unintelligible and sounded like 'bar bar bar' – they were a fiercely competitive people often at war with each other. And yet, linked by bonds of language, religion, descent and culture, their city states were, as in China, to develop a code of honour towards one another from which we could well learn today. For example, they held that treaties sealed under oath should be observed, that Greeks should never enslave other Greeks, that in wartime olive groves should never be destroyed and that after battle armies should leave the people in peace to bury their dead. Such a code, moreover, offered mutual benefits, making it easier to turn today's enemies into tomorrow's allies. But, unlike the Chinese, the Greeks were not virtually self-sufficient and, being an island people, travelled and enjoyed extensive trade links with the non-Hellenic world, which gave them access to foreign ideas and technologies and led to the development of an early form of maritime law.

What, then, of their polities? The Hellenic world comprised about 1500 intensely independent city states throughout mainland and insular Greece as well as in what was called Greater Greece, i.e. Greek settlements in Sicily and Southern Italy, most governed by corporations of citizens rather than by monarchs. However, about a dozen states became important, what we today would call Great Powers, including Athens, Sparta, and Corinth on the mainland. Moreover, they maintained an intricate web of relations with one another, their envoys offering in the name of their patrons alliances, trade agreements or their 'good offices' in mediating disputes and generally enjoying what would we would now term diplomatic immunity. But all this was before the conflict which shattered the Hellenic world rather as the First World War was to shatter Europe. The Hellenic 1914 came in 431 BC. Called the Peloponnesian war by Thucydides, the Athenian general who wrote a masterly treatise on it,[7] it became a titanic struggle between the two Superpowers of the time – Athens and Sparta – and was to last, with brief peace interludes, for twenty-seven years. During that time, however, civilised inter-state standards went into serious decline.

Yet the pattern of inter- and intra-Greek politics during this period has several contemporary resonances. First, the Peloponnesian war was an outcome of tensions arising during the previous cold war between ideological rivals Athens – democratic, prosperous, and expansionist – and Sparta – authoritarian, militarised but wedded to the international status quo. Meanwhile, prior to hostilities, each had acquired a host of client states and satellites, Athens heading the Delian League of mainly island states, on which it hoped to impose a common currency; Sparta presiding over the Peloponnesian League of states fearing Athenian domination. As in today's international society, its various members were as much divided within as between, such divisions frequently leading to revolutions (which is, perhaps, why Greek society so fascinated Karl Marx). And when a state in a roughly bipolar world is in turmoil, then as now outside powers are tempted to intervene to try to secure a more favourable power balance. Given the bipolar tension in the Hellenic world of the fifth century BC there was always the possibility that, as in 1914 or 1939, a sudden increase or decrease in power by one side might trigger hostilities, and that is precisely what happened in 431 BC. So what was the immediate as distinct from the long-term cause?

A revolt in a Corinthian colony, Corcyra (modern Corfu), was the catalyst. Corinth was, in fact, Sparta's major ally, and so Athens, eager to side with an enemy's enemy, decided to support the rebels. Naturally Corinth called on Sparta to help contain the uprising, and soon the rival alliance systems were locked in combat, the theatre of operations gradually widening to include most of the Hellenic world. It had become a struggle between those supporting Athens, which was bent on reshaping that world, and those determined to resist, and for some time the former had the advantage. Athens, after all, had command of the oceans. But the Persian decision to intervene with gold and military equipment to check Athenian power tipped the balance at sea, and Sparta was eventually to emerge victorious. The Peloponnesian war had demonstrated what was to become all too familiar, that a power aiming at hegemony will tend sooner or later to face a hostile coalition which will ultimately defeat it. Later historians were to call this recurrent pattern 'the balance of power'.

However, the Athenian defeat in 404 BC did not quell the impetus to unite the Hellenic world, and subsequently the independence of the Greek city states was to be frequently endangered. When Sparta somewhat uncharacteristically sought its own hegemony in the region, the Persians, whose assistance had once been so vital to it, threw their considerable weight behind the Athenians. Later, however, as the Aegean appeared again to be at risk from Athenian power, the Persians switched back again in support of Sparta. Here, then, was Persia acting as power balancer, 'holding the ring' between rival states, as Britain was so frequently to do more than 1500 years later.

The situation was unstable, however, and in the fourth century BC when Persia was in retreat, the Greek multi-state system was to be virtually destroyed by two powerful and ambitious men. Both came from Macedonia – the part-Greek, part-Persian kingdom to the north. For all his heavy drinking and womanising, Philip II, King of Macedonia from 359 to 336 BC, was a shrewd judge of character. Well aware of the political and military weaknesses of both the Hellenic city states and the Persian empire, he used both diplomacy and force to establish his dominion over all Greece. But when an assassin's bullet prevented him from completing his self-imposed mission to add the Persian empire to his domain, his son, Alexander the Great, took up the challenge. Having forged an impressive coalition of Macedonians and Greeks, he was able to fulfil his father's dream, in 330 BC proclaiming himself the legal successor of the Kings of Persia, succeeding in addition to the throne of the Egyptian Pharaohs and ruling as suzerain in India. In conquering the known world Alexander abandoned the liberal principles he had once imbibed as a pupil of the Greek philosopher Aristotle. Yet despite the brutalities of his rule he broke down the barriers which until his days had separated Greek from 'barbarism' and introduced a high degree of civilisation into what before his time had been a disordered world.[8]

His achievement transformed the eastern Mediterranean lands from a number of relatively small competing sovereignties to an empire stretching from Macedonia to the borders of India. It was, however, short-lived, for, aged only 33, Alexander died of fever in 323 BC, to be buried in the

Egyptian city, Alexandria, that bears his name. Nonetheless, the old Greek multi-state system was gone, and henceforth the city states were submerged in one or other of the large kingdoms in Asia Minor, Macedonia and Egypt into which Alexander's imperium was now divided. And between these vast kingdoms a new kind of balance of power system was to be played out until the first century BC – in which the few great powers of the day combined and recombined without the emergence of any major alliance system or dominant power.[9]

The Roman system

The Roman system – the fifth to be discussed – put an end to the uncertainties of the previous two centuries, and with it the Near Eastern and Mediterranean worlds were again impelled towards the imperial end of the international spectrum. Yet Rome had originally been no more than just another city state on the western fringe of Hellenism. So how had this often unstable central Italian state been able to rise to become the greatest power in all Italy between the eighth and third centuries BC, and then to head the world's largest and most enduring empire? How had it been able to bring under one order peoples and lands from Scotland to the North of Africa, from Spain to Iraq and beyond? How was it that Roman law, administration, communications, architecture, sculpture, poetry, philosophy and Roman-inflected Christianity became, as it were, the property of the world?

First, it had a geographical advantage. Located mid-way up the western coast of Italy, with its long-settled communities, good harbours and high vantage points, Rome was strategically well placed. Second, its rulers were politically astute and devised an effective formula for orderly government – strong, centralised and popular – in which the masses, i.e. non-slave males, were allowed the vote and their own tribune to monitor the work of administration. Its success encouraged the Romans to export a modified version to their colonies, extending to them Roman citizenship as well as law and order. The stratagem on the whole worked and served to defuse hostility to colonial rule. Third, Rome excelled in political intrigue. Despite periods of political turbulence, its many rivals were prone to even greater instability, and the Romans cleverly exploited their divisions to establish control. However, the process of attaining dominion was piecemeal, the political dominoes, so to speak, falling one by one. First the Romans secured the city states of central Italy, then the Etruscan communities to the north and, finally, the Greek city states to the south. It was a technique of political control which later generations of imperialists, including the British and the Russians, were to use to advantage – *divide et impera* – divide and rule!

But none of this would have succeeded without a fourth and crucial ingredient, military superiority. The Romans of those days had a talent for organisation as well as for engineering, giving their army a critical advantage over its rivals. In most of the military arts it had the edge over its opponents, and by the time of its epic struggle against Carthage toward the end of the third century BC, Rome had at its disposal the manpower of virtually all Italy. In the end not even the Carthaginians with their North African reserves could match Rome's resources, and with the defeat of Carthage in 202 BC, Rome could add North Africa to its growing list of provinces, and was well on the way to what we would now call Super-power status. By the end of the second century BC Rome had taken in turn the territories in Greece, Asia Minor and Egypt once under Alexander the Great, and no power was strong enough to stop it. Thus, it was already virtually an empire even before Augustus Caesar formally proclaimed it in 27 BC, with each province run by a governor, often a general, appointed by the Senate in Rome.

From 27 BC, central control was tightened still further. Imperial law was made in Rome and administered by Roman judges, while the Emperor presided over the system as commander-in-chief, the provincial governors now being known as the Emperor's lieutenants. But to give the inhabitants of the provinces a stake in the system some were allowed to hold positions of authority in Rome, even on occasion becoming Emperors themselves. The current French practice of giving their overseas colonies representation in the National Assembly closely resembles Roman procedure, but with one critical difference. No one ever suggested that the French President was divine, not even de Gaulle, whereas the Roman imperial system rested on the divine authority of the Emperor.

But if Rome bestowed comparative peace and prosperity upon the Mediterranean world and beyond for upwards of four centuries, increasingly its rulers became the creatures of contending warlords. And though the period from AD 96 to 180 was the high noon of the *Pax Romana*, its intricate interrelated structures came under increasing strain, not least because of the mounting burden of defence and the growing boredom of troops for whom building walls and roads was far less exciting than slaughter, rape and pillage. When regional interests reasserted themselves, the centre could not hold – and the folk memory of that disintegration haunts the current government in Rome, always sensitive to secessionist threats from north and south.[10]

In the one and a half centuries following the death in AD 337 of the Emperor Constantine, the Roman Empire split into a Latin Western and a Greek Eastern realm, the former still based on Rome, the latter on Constantinople (named after Constantine), which is modern Istanbul. By this time Christianity had become the official religion of the Empire, but with the decline and eventual fall of the Western Empire in 476, following a series of military defeats inflicted by an array of Germanic invaders, the only surviving institution standing for the unity now lost was the Church. However, soon that, too, was fragmented. In the Eastern so-called Graeco-Byzantine Empire, which was more centralised than that of Rome and survived the Western Empire for a further thousand years, Christianity began to take on an oriental hue. Other rifts within the Church followed, and there was to be an additional major schism not long after AD 800 when Western Christendom acquired, ironically with papal blessing, a temporal head, the Holy Roman Emperor, in addition to its spiritual leader. The battle for supremacy between Pope and Emperor, at its fiercest from 1076 to 1268, enfeebled both and, together with the mounting rivalry between Roman and Byzantine Chritianity, helped to destroy the political and religious fabric of medieval European society.

In the meantime, in devising new strategies to deal with the rising tide of Islam, which from the seventh century had been spreading over the southern and easternmost parts of the empire, Byzantium appeared to take the *Arthashastra* as a model for its ethics and political vocabulary. Abba Bozeman has written of Byzantine statecraft: 'As the paramount manifestation of the Byzantine state in the realm of competitive power politics, diplomacy was as amoral as the state itself. The chief purpose was to protect the state, ensure its survival and promote its power by any method which promised success.'[11] After all, it was now making a friend of its enemy's enemies, and attempting to win converts, while at the same time sowing dissension among them, by encouraging the translation of the Orthodox litany into local languages and the establishment of national Churches within the Orthodox tradition. It is during this period that, in what was centuries later to become Greece, Russia, Serbia, Bulgaria and Romania, religion came to be identified with a particularly lethal form of national self-consciousness.[12] What of the international system – our sixth – which was to destroy the Byzantine Empire having seized its capital, Constantinople, in 1453 – Islam?

The Islamic system

The Islamic era can be said to have begun in 622, when Muhammed, a reasonably successful Arab trader, and his followers, devotees of Islam – the word means submission to one uniquely powerful, merciful and compassionate God – were forced by idolators in his native Mecca to flee to Medina some 300 miles to the north. Having begun as a religious and social movement, Islam soon took on a military as well as a political dimension and its advance was remarkably swift. By the time of Muhammed's death in 632, Islam already commanded the whole of the Arabian peninsula, and within a further two decades had wrested Jerusalem, Damascus, Alexandria and the rest of Syria and Egypt from Byzantium. It had also pushed north-eastward to the heartlands of the old Persian empire as far as the Afghan marshlands and the borders of China. Within a few more years it held sway from Tripoli all the way to the frontiers of India and from the Nile as far as Armenia. And in a second wave of conquests and conversions in the eighth and ninth centuries it had reached down into Morocco, swept through Spain to the borders of France, and penetrated further into Asia as far as the Indus valley and into Sind, now part of Pakistan. But how did Mecca – a somewhat obscure Arabian trading centre – come to spawn the world's fastest-growing faith and become a place of pilgrimage for millions of people?

Certainly the dedication and commitment of its leaders inspired those looking for a God-centred creed that, unlike Judaism, which is not a proselytising religion, was apparently open to all. More importantly, because of its geographical origins, it had a special resonance to those speaking a Semitic language, as in much of the Near East, where there was considerable irritation at the intrusions of Byzantine or Persian imperial politics. In addition, its message of universal brotherhood and equality under God had an especial appeal wherever people felt oppressed by divisive heirarchical or caste systems. Moreover the conception of a single community – *umma* – of the faithful had an obvious appeal (ironic when one considers today's divisions in Afghanistan, Algeria, Somalia or Yemen) wherever tribal and inter-tribal squabbles, blood feuds, vendettas and the like made life insufferable for those not wishing to get involved. In addition, of course, nothing succeeds like success, and the Islamic warriors were able to add to their armoury an array of military hardware, including ships, acquired from their conquests.

It is possible that had not the existing empires already been in decline, the spread of Islam might have been slower. Nonetheless, its rapid expansion also presaged a cultural as well as spiritual reawakening for, having emerged from the desert, the Islamic conquerors were quick to assimilate the ideas and skills of those whose civilisations they overran. From Damascus and then Baghdad, they encouraged translations of Greek, Persian and Indian philosophy, mathematics, science and literature, passing them on to Europe where they provided the intellectual leavening for the Renaissance. This is when, for example, the Roman numerical system with its cumbersome X's, V's, I's, M's and C's are replaced by simpler Arabic numbers and algebra (*Al Gebr*) arrives. So, too, do a number of Arabic ideas on medicine, chemistry and astronomy, making a major contribution to modern science.

At the same time, and contrary to the somewhat distorted depiction in the West where we tend to hear only the Christian view on the Crusades, the Muslims, though prepared to use the sword in the service of the faith, came to learn the value of tolerance, and developed a formula for dealing with people of other creeds. Though they believed in the superiority of Islam, they allowed Christians and Jews to maintain their religious traditions and most of their laws, provided they lived in autonomous communities and paid extra taxes. In consequence, the three monotheistic religions were able to coexist perfectly satisfactorily in medieval Spain until the Church turned both Moslem and Jew into bogeymen and began its forcible conversions, the Crusades and the Inquisition.

Like the Revolutionists portrayed by Martin Wight, the Muslim conquerors divided the world into two: the *dar al Islam*, an arena of peace and harmony where the faithful lived and which in time would encompass the planet, and the *dar al harb*, an arena of war, where conflict with non-Muslims was always a possibility. With the authorities in the *dar al harb* there could be, if expedient, temporary accords, but Islam drew a distinction between different kinds of infidel negotiating partners. For most of Islam's existence, the Jews in its midst never suffered like the Jews of Christendom, as Judaism was a religion of people with whom Mohammed had at one time been socially and spiritually close. And both Jews and, until the Crusades, Christians, being people of the Book, i.e. of the Bible, were accorded much greater respect than what Islam regarded as idolatrous heathens – which would explain in part why relations between Hindus and Muslims have often been so troubled.

In practice, however, there was considerable dissension within the *dar al Islam*, since the death of Muhammed had left a problem of succession that had led to rival claims to the caliphate, the political centre of the movement. From this rivalry was derived the great schism between the Sunni and the Shi'a, and it widened still further when the distribution of the vast wealth acquired in the course of Islam's expansion failed to accord with the equalitarian precepts of the faith. Such rivalries generated further rifts and divisions, opening up a wide chasm between the theory and practice of the *dar al Islam*, which the Muslim community has never properly bridged. But there were to be further sources of instability – the fact, for example, that in its Bedouin origins Islam was hostile to political power structures and settled government, yet was unable to do without them.[13] And even where there was Islamic solidarity, it tended to be undermined, as Ibn Khaldun, the great fourteenth-century Islamic scholar, pointed out, in the ease and luxury of city life, while in the Courts of Damascus, Baghdad and Istanbul the rulers of Islam tended to disregard their moral and religious principles.[14] Substitute the word 'governments' for the word 'Courts' and it becomes a remarkably prophetic utterance!

Paradoxically, though Islam embodies probably the most total and unified way of life ever devised, because it was fragmented politically almost from the start it was never in practice to secure the cohesion or status of, say, the Roman or Chinese Empires. Though it was able to attain something more regulated and ordered than the Greek city states system, even today there are rival conceptions of what, say, Islamic justice requires. The beheading of murderers, the flogging and stoning to death of adulterers, the circumcision of women? Many Muslims claim there is no Koranic justification for any of these practices and vehemently oppose them. No doubt it was Islam's many strengths that contributed to its rising fortunes until the seventeenth century. It was, however, its weaknesses that account in large measure for its more recent setbacks, partly at the hands of Western colonialism, partly self-engendered.

The medieval European system

Reference has already been made to medieval Europe, and since it was a kind of socio-cultural womb from which more modern notions of an international society emerged, it will be analysed in greater detail in the following chapter. Suffice it to say here that although earlier religious institutions and ideas still permeated European society – the Papacy, after all, still insisted on being regarded as the fount of Christian orthodoxy and on treating local rulers as viceroys of the Pope – theory and reality increasingly diverged. Moreover, from the rivalry between Byzantium and Rome and between Pope and Holy Roman Emperor, which generated additional rifts and divisions, evolved the prerequisites for a conception of an international society more familiar to us today. Pre-eminent among them, the secularisation of politics, and the creation of sovereign and legally equal states acknowledging no political superior and with their own *raisons d'être* and *raisons d'état*. Yet in attempting to establish and legitimise a new order in Europe, the emerging powers were to find inspiration in an earlier age – in the accumulation of laws and codes that had served as a basis for coexistence and had helped to contain violence within and between the states of ancient Greece and Rome. At the same time, they were to find in late medieval Italy diplomatic practices that would leave their imprint on the international societies of the future, in effect shaping first European, then global diplomacy.

NOTES

1. See Bull, H., *The Anarchical Society*, London, Macmillan, 1977, pp. 13–16.
2. This framework of analysis is adapted from Holsti, K.J., *International Politics*, Englewood Cliffs, New Jersey, Prentice Hall, 1967, pp. 27–9. The following text owes much to Bozeman, A.B., *Politics and Culture in International History*,

Princeton, Princeton University Press, 1960; Wight, M., *Systems of States*, Leicester, Leicester University Press, 1977; and Watson, A., *The Evolution of International Society*, London, Routledge, 1992.

3. For detailed analyses of such ancient societies, see for example, Garnsey, P. and Whittaker, C.R. (eds), *Imperialism in the Ancient World*, Cambridge, Cambridge University Press, 1976; Kramer, S.N., *History Begins at Sumer*, New York, Doubleday, 1959; and Oppenheim, A.L., *Ancient Mesopotamia*, Chicago, University of Chicago Press, 1977.

4. For detailed analyses of the Chinese system, see, for example, Hirth, F., *The Ancient History of China*, New York, Columbia University Press, 1923; Rubin, V.A., *Individual and State in Ancient China*, New York, Columbia University Press, 1976; and Fitzgerald, C.P., *The Chinese View of their Place in the World*, London, Oxford University Press, 1964.

5. Kautilya, *Arthashastra*, trans. Shamasastry, A., Mysore, Wesleyan Mission Press, 1929.

6. See, for example, Majumdar, R., Raychandhuri, H. and Datta, K. (eds), *An Advanced History of India*, London, Macmillan, 1964; and Thapar, R., *The Penguin History of India*, Volume I, Harmondsworth, Penguin, 1966.

7. Thucydides, *History of the Peloponnesian War*, trans. Rex Warner, Harmondsworth, Penguin 1976.

8. Nicolson, N., *Monarchy*, London, Weidenfeld & Nicolson, 1962, pp. 56–7.

9. For analysis of the Hellenic era see for example Boardman, J., *The Greeks Overseas*, London, Thames and Hudson, 1980; Burn, R., *Persia and the Greeks*, London, Arnold, 1972; and Meiggs, R., *The Athenian Empire*, Oxford, Oxford University Press, 1972.

10. Badian, E., *Roman Imperialism*, Oxford, Blackwell, 1968; Luttwak, E., *The Grand Strategy of the Roman Empire*, Baltimore, Johns Hopkins University Press, 1976; and Millar, F., *The Emperor in the Roman World*, London, Duckworth, 1977.

11. Bozeman, A.B., op. cit., p. 338.

12. Obolensky, D., *The Byzantine Commonwealth*, New York, Praeger, 1971; Ostrogorsky, G., *History of the Byzantine State*, Princeton, Princeton University Press, 1969; and Urbanski, A.B., *Byzantium and the Danube Frontier*, New York, 1968.

13. See for example Gibb, H.A.R., *Mohammedanism*, London, 1950; and Arnold, T., *The Caliphate*, London, Routledge, 1965.

14. See Schmidt, N., *Ibn Khaldun: Historian, Sociologist and Philosopher*, New York, Columbia University Press, 1930.

CHAPTER 5

MODERN INTERNATIONAL SOCIETIES

5.1 THE MEDIEVAL EUROPEAN ORDER

In the previous chapter it was argued that the European medieval order was, so to speak, the womb or chrysalis from which the modern conception of an international society emerged. But what constituted the medieval system and when and how did it originate? It may be said to have materialised following a kind of collective European nervous breakdown on the death, after a long illness, of the Roman empire in AD 476. It is, in fact, not uncommon for a period of turbulence to accompany and then follow the disintegration of a political personality such as an empire, a state or a system of states. We saw it early in the twentieth century with the disintegration of the Ottoman, Russian and Austro-Hungarian empires and more recently with the strife and unrest in much of Asia and Africa associated with the decline of the British Raj. And we are still living with the dire effects on the European body politic of the collapse of the Soviet state and the disintegration of what was Yugoslavia. What tends to happen is that, as centralised administration begins to break down, old grievances surface as do new rivalries over who or what should succeed. Meanwhile living conditions often worsen, aggravated by the collapse of an integrated economy and communications infrastructure and the problem of establishing stable successor governments in face of resistance from supporters of the old order.

In the case of medieval Europe the period of nervous collapse probably lasted until the eleventh century as the religious and political successors to the now divided Roman empire further fragmented and international trade and communications almost dried up.[1] There were, nonetheless, several vain attempts to restore the Roman body politic and return to the imperial womb, while other efforts by Papacy, Church, missionaries and monks to keep alive the idea of a Christian Empire found a kind of perverted expression in the Crusades against Islam. But it was a forlorn hope since, though in theory Europe represented in some sense one Christian civilisation, in reality the Christian body – spiritual as well as temporal – was hopelessly divided.

Changing political obligations

As to the political as distinct from the religious reality, by the end of the tenth century Europe had been parcelled into clusters of feudal entities centred around castles and towns, within which peasants offered their services in exchange for their chieftain, lord or warlord's protection. Yet the wars, conquests and migrations that had destroyed the old order had also produced that kind of receptiveness to new ideas that, as the psychologist William Sargent reminds us, can accompany the process of recovery following a nervous breakdown.[2] And as the small feudal units sought greater security by amalgamating into larger units, notions of political obligation – what duties, in other words, were owed to which political authorities – were thrown into the melting pot.

Changing religious obligations

The nature of religious obligation was also beginning to be rethought, as Christian kings wrestled with bishops and as local merchants took on the abbots, while Pope and Emperor, and Western and Eastern Christendom struggled for supremacy, leading to a formal divorce in 1054. According to Norman Davies: 'Three hundred years earlier, the principal line of division in Europe lay between the Christian lands of the south and the heathen lands of the north. From now on it lay between the Catholic lands of the West and the Orthodox lands of the East.'[3] The conflict was to become especially notorious when in 1204 troops in the service of Western Christendom launched a bloody campaign against Christian Byzantium, robbing, burning, pillaging and raping their way through Constantinople. The effect was, of course, to widen still further the growing rift between the two wings of Christianity which has never even to this day been truly healed[4] – witness the growing tensions between the Catholic and Orthodox Church in the Ukraine and the savagery that characterised the bloody struggle in what was Yugoslavia between the Croats, supported by the Vatican and Catholic co-religionists from Italy, Germany, Austria and Hungary, and the Serbs with the assistance of their sanctions-busting Orthodox friends in Russia, Greece and Romania. Meanwhile, a century after the Latin assault on Byzantium, religious sensitivities were to be tested to almost breaking point, as the Papacy became divided against itself and two, then three Popes appeared simultaneously. If too many cooks spoil the broth, too many Popes tarnish the faith!

A revolution in loyalties

The Renaissance at the end of the fifteenth century indicated that a revolution in loyalties was already in prospect. For by then both the social and the material conditions of European life were being transformed – in part a consequence of ideas and inventions imported from Arabia, China, classical Greece and Rome given currency by the Islamic invaders and the more literate monks. In particular, the newly invented printing press served to shape or reshape both language and literature and in turn political organisation, while the introduction of the mariner's compass and improvements in ship-building ensured that the spread of ideas went ever faster and farther. Fifteenth-century Europe was on the verge of the great voyages of discovery that would lead to a vast expansion of international trade and commerce and the colonisation of whole continents.[5]

The revolution in loyalties referred to earlier was to result in the gradual transfer of allegiance from religious to secular authorities and from local to something like central government. Facilitating the process was the spread throughout Europe of the mystique of monarchy, of the idea that kings and queens, even if brigands and pirates themselves or the descendants of brigands and pirates, had a divine right to rule. And as political expediency began to displace religious authority, the political units to which Europeans were increasingly expected to owe allegiance were states. But being royal realms under sovereign rule, these self-same states were eventually themselves to be accorded sovereign status, the implications of which will be discussed in the next chapter, taking as their model the wealthy Italian city states of Venice, Milan, Florence and Naples.

5.2 THE ITALIAN CITY STATES SYSTEM

In contrast to the part-religious, part-secular hierarchies of authority elsewhere in Europe, by the late fifteenth century the Italian city states had broken altogether with the global aspirations of Christendom and developed systems of government under rulers with unashamedly secular ambitions. For them policy was to do not with religious principle but with material advantage, and what was to become known as *raison d'état*, reason of state. Nor was their acquisition of power to be moderated by moral scruple. And yet it was not a licence for unbridled brutality, so characteristic of conflicts between peoples claiming to have God on their side, as in the Crusades, in the religious wars that were to come or, for that matter, in many of the conflicts of our own day. For the casualties in wars involving conflicts of principle, i.e. so-called 'just wars', are generally far higher than in wars arising from conflicts of interest, which is in part why Hans Morgenthau sees a moral dimension to the idea of 'national interest'.[6] In fact precisely because the Italian rulers were unconstrained by dogma, they saw nothing wrong in making compromises, exercising caution or doing deals with the enemy. And since by the time of the Renaissance each Italian city state had more or less accepted the existence of the others, they developed novel techniques for managing their inter-relations. In fact we owe to them our diplomatic system with its embassies, procedures, privileges and immunities.[7]

Though the Assyrians, Egyptians, Greeks and Romans had also employed envoys and ambassadors, these were for particular assignments, to be withdrawn when the mission had been completed. What the Italians had invented was the permanent embassy and the career diplomat to man it, charged with many, if not most of the functions we associate with diplomacy today – communication, representation, negotiation, accommodation, ingratiation (i.e. winning friends and influencing people), and, above all, extracting information, not least after a bottle or two or a romp in the hay with some well-placed woman of easy virtue.

If, however, diplomacy failed, the Italian rulers had a whole arsenal of alternative pressures and inducements, including bribes, threats, subversion, assassination and, ultimately, war – as Machiavelli, one-time secretary to the republican regime in Florence, points out in *The Prince*. As to Italy's internecine wars, these were waged not between individual citizens; nor by the princes who declared them. They were fought between mercenaries in receipt of *soldi* – the word means money or pay, and is the origin of our word soldier – led by professional officers under contract to conduct a given campaign, which is why they generally did not last long. Nor was the aim ever to destroy an opponent since this might draw neutral states into a hostile coalition. The objective, as befits those whose main concern was banking, was to establish a favourable balance but not at the cost of destabilising the states system. Again, the Italians had taken an arrangement used ad hoc by the Persians and the Greeks, among others, and turned it into a permanent institution – to be known as the balance of power.

Unfortunately the intervention in 1494 of France in the affairs of the peninsula hastened the collapse of the cosy, if cynical relationship between the Italian states, and for the next four centuries they would become mere objects of the rivalries between the new dynastic states of France, Spain and Austria. On the other hand the Italian break with tradition and the writings of Machiavelli encapsulating the new approach were to prove infectious, and in this way the Italian system forms a crucial link between the medieval and the modern conceptions of an international society. For scholars such as Martin Wight, the roots of modern international society lie in fifteenth-century Italy.[8] Others, however, trace its source to the time when the concepts of sovereign equality and territorial integrity formally entered the European political vocabulary, i.e. about a century later.

What the rest of Europe derived from the Italian experience was a clear alternative to the complex layers of authority, spiritual and temporal, local, provincial and central, territorial and extra-territorial that had characterised European politics. The Italian city states were governed by rulers with the power to command, and their example proved attractive wherever religious doubt, pride in secular languages and literature and budding capitalist activity called in question the Pope's intrusive authority. It was, however, the Protestant Reformation – in effect a religious rebellion triggered by the Renaissance – that put the final nail into the medieval coffin. For by the mid-sixteenth century both Protestant and Catholic rulers were insisting on determining the religious affiliations of their subjects, thereby adding to both their political power and their legitimacy. On the other hand, before a society of independent secular states could emerge, Reformation bred Counter-Reformation and Europe was to experience a lengthy and exceptionally bloody struggle culminating in the Thirty Years war of religion that virtually tore the continent apart. At the end of hostilities both the Netherlands and Germany, each riven by religious dissent, were partitioned, a factor which, while it eventually brought prosperity to the former, wrought utter devastation in the latter, leaving physical, social and psychological scars still not entirely healed at the end of the twentieth century.

5.3 THE WESTPHALIAN SYSTEM

The Thirty Years war ended in 1648 with the Treaties of Westphalia – a negotiated settlement based for the first time outside of Italy on the principle of *raison d'état* and which helped crystallise a framework enabling states in conflict and enclosed within a hard shell of sovereignty to enjoy tolerable relations with one another. For many scholars, including F.S. Northedge and Hedley Bull, Westphalia marks the formal beginning of the European states system, and hence of modern international society.[9] For others, Westphalia is more a convenient reference point than the source of a new system, merely ratifying, as it were, a state of affairs already in existence.[10] Ironically Westphalia did not bring an end to war, and throughout the century the European states knew only seven years completely free of bloodshed. Indeed, believing that Westphalia had changed very little, Thomas Hobbes had published his famous *Leviathan* three years after the settlement. To him international relations were characterised by anarchy, and peace was, in his words, 'a breathing time'

– a mere interlude between wars. Yet soon it was apparent that Westphalia had marked some kind of watershed, given definition to the political shape of Europe, embodied a rudimentary community of interests among its rulers and provided for a modicum of order in an inter-state system in which power is dispersed.[11] In what way was Westphalia a turning point?

Sovereign statehood

First and foremost, it formally broke with many of the medieval restrictions on government and with the universal laws which were supposed to regulate the behaviour of rulers. Henceforth Pope and Emperor were reduced legally to the same status as other rulers and neither could oblige a king or prince to do anything he had not consented to. In other words, Westphalia symbolised the fragmentation of authority and gave official currency to the principle of sovereign statehood. A state recognised as sovereign would be self-contained, legally free of outside interference, accorded equality before the law and having the sole right to enter into treaties. By implication this meant that a state not so recognised was not entitled, so to speak, to membership of the European 'club'. Like a colony, protectorate or province today, a state whose ruler lacked supreme authority or whose country was not constitutionally or juridically self-contained, such as a duchy within France or Spain, had no legal standing in European international society. But how could the sovereignty principle provide the basis for an international society and be conducive to orderly relations?

In the first place, since a sovereign state was one which could not permit other political entities to apply their rules on its territory without its approval, it had the corresponding duty not to intervene in other states or compromise their integrity. Admittedly the principle of non-intervention may well have meant turning a blind eye not just to the religious affiliations of others but also to the most blatant abuses of power. After all, if the medieval Church was a kind of state, the new states were taking on some of the characteristics of a Church – demanding loyalty, trust and deference. But Westphalia put orderly relations first, and internal developments within another state, including considerations of justice for individual citizens and groups, was no longer to be of concern. Secondly, despite divergencies in size, location, population or military capability between the sovereign members of international society, all were to be regarded as equal as regards legal rights and duties, which included the right of self-defence. Meanwhile developments in military technology and the ability of monarchs to raise mercenary or conscript armies helped to increase the viability of even small states, so that henceforth a sovereign violated the territory of another at his peril. Thirdly, all sovereign states were pledged to respect their treaty and other obligations under international law. But this raises the question: how could a state be sovereign and yet subject to law?

International law

To this conundrum there were to be at least three alternative answers. Those looking back to classical Greece and Rome held that the relationship between states was governed by rules binding on all individuals and social institutions according to what they called natural law, a kind of ultimate reservoir of ethical precepts.[12] Most such theorists argued that natural law was of divine origin and discoverable through the exercise of what they called 'right reason' (a question-begging phrase, if ever there was one!).

Others, the 'positivists', claimed that states were subject to law because in seeking sovereign status for their respective countries, their rulers had borne implicit testimony to the validity of an international legal system. For the accord of sovereign status only made sense within a framework of law. Recognition was, after all, a legal act from which duties as well as rights flowed, and among those duties was respect for international law – a body of rules not imposed on but established between sovereigns for their mutual benefit. But were those legal rules binding? C.A.W. Manning maintains that law is a body of rules deemed to be binding and in that sense that international law is binding by definition. It obliges us to do something or to refrain from doing something. To speak of a non-binding law would be as absurd as to speak of a four-sided circle or triangle – that is, it would be to use the term in a highly eccentric fashion.[13] The operative question is not whether or not it is binding, which it is by definition, but whether it functions effectively in an international context – an inquiry to be investigated further in chapter 9.

One other school of thought, associated with Hugo Grotius – a systematiser rather than an originator, even though widely regarded as the founding figure of international law – occupied the middle ground between the Naturalists and the Positivists. Drawing on the legal heritage of both Greece and Rome, on the rules of medieval commerce as well as on the recent writings of jurists both religious and secular, Grotius held that sovereign states were subject to law both because they were composed of human beings who were bound by natural law and because their rulers, preferring order to chaos, consent to it. Ironically, in order to make that point in his treatise *De Juri Belli ac Pacis* (*The Law of War and Peace*) of 1625, Grotius had to hide in a trunk and escape his native Holland to avoid the horrors of the Thirty Years War.

Given that international law had to function between sovereign authorities, its implementation clearly had to be different from the application of law in a domestic context. For example, as there is no international arbiter, agreements between sovereigns have to be self-regulated. Yet, as any player of a rule-governed enterprise such as bridge, snooker or table tennis will know, the idea of a self-enforced body of rules is not so unusual. For such contests, though not necessarily free of controversy, do not usually appear to require a referee, umpire or police intervention. And like a game of bridge, the international legal 'game' tends to proceed more or less satisfactorily, since having a generally agreed body of rules to govern international conduct appears to serve the interests of all the players. If one competitor constantly breaks the rules, the others eventually refuse to play. Applied to international relations, the habitual law-breaker becomes a pariah, and the others break off diplomatic ties, generally to its disadvantage.

Diplomacy

Diplomacy was the second Westphalian instrument for minimising international disorder. Once a periodic and fitful endeavour, European diplomacy, following Italian practice, became a permanent fixture, tending to continue even in time of war when the negotiating and intelligence functions of a diplomat were perhaps more vital than ever. To this end diplomacy began to be organised as a profession, diplomatic despatches being viewed as state property and not the personal possession of the envoy, and the diplomat and his embassy being regarded as legally sacrosanct and bound by rules of procedure, styled largely on French diplomatic etiquette. By the beginning of the eighteenth century the profession appeared to be developing a corporate identity, and this was to be much in evidence at the various congresses called to settle outstanding issues at the end of a war.

Balance of power

A third mechanism for managing the affairs of the European system, post-Westphalia, was the balance of power. Though its precise meaning is disputed, it clearly had to do with strategies – military, political or economic – for preserving and if possible enhancing the standing or influence of one state relative to its rivals. Though balance-of-power strategies were not unknown to the ancient Indian, the Greek, the Roman and other pre-modern cultures, in its post-Westphalian sense, balance-of-power became a conscious and continuous policy to secure political advantage at the least possible cost to self or society. Indeed, in the eighteenth century it was widely regarded as an indispensable prop to international law, and at the Treaty of Utrecht ending the War of Spanish Succession in 1713, express reference was made to the balance as a principle of foreign policy. What, then, did the balance connote?

Like the solar system as portrayed by Isaac Newton, states were understood to exercise attraction and pressure in proportion to their mass and the distance they kept from one another. If one power in this complex, fluid and dynamic system was perceived to be growing or declining in strength, in order to achieve equilibrium the others would have to adjust, either within or outside the European arena. In this sense the idea of the power balance resembled the laws of supply and demand which form the basis of classical economics.[14] In practice, however, where the requisite adjustment to the European balance was made outside of Europe, imperialism was generally the outcome – in effect denying non-Europeans the sovereignty the Europeans claimed for themselves. The objective of the balance was to prevent the domination of Europe by any one power or group of powers, and though war was not necessarily excluded, it was generally a last resort and to be fought by limited means. Accordingly, the human and material costs of combat in the years between 1648 and the end of the eighteenth century were as nothing compared to the religious wars preceding Westphalia or the national wars following the French Revolution. In this so-called 'Age of Enlightenment' warfare had become a demonstration of strength rather than an orgy of destruction.

Cultural ties

In addition to international law, diplomacy and the balance of power, the framework of order established in the wake of Westphalia had an additional prop. Despite their insistence on sovereign independence, the rulers of eighteenth-century Europe and their courtiers and servants were linked to one another by ties of blood and a common culture. They generally spoke French, continued to identify themselves as Christians and accepted the principles of royal legitimacy and dynastic succession. That eighteenth-century Europe still possessed a common culture can be attested by the numbers of Germans serving in the Russian court, of Italians in the French court, of Englishmen, Irishmen and Germans in Spanish diplomatic and military service and the fact that in 1688 a Dutchman and in 1714 a Hanoverian became king of England – one, moreover, who spoke almost no English and loathed the country of which he was the sovereign head.

Forces of disorder

On the other hand for all the factors making for order there were, as usual, countervailing forces which would undermine and eventually destroy the dynastic system sanctioned by Westphalia. For those dynasties often treated populations, their own included, like commodities, and would transfer territory and peoples from one area to another regardless of heritage or the wishes of inhabitants. For example, the fragmented domains of Germany and Italy were constantly being sold, swapped or reallocated from one dynasty to another as if pieces on a chessboard. It was a process which eventually led at the end of the eighteenth century to the partitions of Poland by Prussia and Austria as well as Russia to prevent it from falling wholly under Russian control. The idea that the sovereigns were in charge and that the will of their subjects did not matter much bred increasing resentment, especially among those peasants and townspeople under despotic, corrupt or alien rulers. The time bomb ticking away under the Westphalian order that would eventually destroy it was, of course, nationalism – a movement which in its initial liberal phase set out to shift the locus of sovereignty from ruler to people.[15]

5.4 THE NATIONALIST REVOLT

The American revolution

In North America in the third quarter of the eighteenth century there was an indication of what was to come. Europeans had settled in the Americas at least since the fifteenth century, but the rulers of their country of origin had tended to regard such settlers and the lands they colonised as sources of revenue, and continued to do so long after the settlers had spread inland, out of reach of any effective rule from the mother country. By the mid-1770s the British-Americans began to question their subservience to Britain. Heavily taxed, but denied a say in how those taxes were to be spent, with their trade, including their export potential in tea, sacrificed to the interests of the British Crown, they insisted on 'no taxation without representation'. To show they meant business they threw cargoes of tea imported from the London-based East India Company into Boston harbour. And when the British government tried to arrest two of the protesters near Boston in 1775, fighting erupted. In effect, the first shots had been fired in what was to become America's War of Independence, and in 1783 at the Peace of Paris, the Thirteen Colonies, from Maine to Georgia, were to become a union of sovereign states.

The French revolution

The significance of the 1783 agreement had not been lost on the heavily taxed Parisians themselves, especially those who had long resented the fact that the wealthy nobility and clergy paid no taxes at all.[16] And among those familiar with the ideas of philosophers such as Rousseau, who had challenged the whole system of dynastic privilege and patronage on which the eighteenth-century idea of 'legitimacy' rested, resentment developed political overtones. The first chapter of Rousseau's *Social Contract*, written in 1762, had contained virtually a clarion call to revolution: 'Man is born free, yet everywhere he is in chains',[17] and many a literate middle-class Frenchman began to feel that even if a state were recognised as sovereign, it could not be regarded as truly 'legitimate' if it oppressed the mass of the population. Matters came to a head in 1789 when the growing financial embarrassment of a spendthrift monarch who had squandered much of the taxpayers' money was compounded by a sudden bread shortage in the capital. The effect was to trigger off a largely middle-class uprising designed to break the chains hampering economic growth and professional advancement. In the name of 'liberty, equality and fraternity' they expounded a doctrine with profound implications for the European system. For they sought to replace tradition by consent and dynastic rule by popular sovereignty. In the process, however, they reintroduced a fanaticism into inter-European relations not seen for a century and a half. For, in accordance with the Revolutionist tradition Martin Wight talks about, their ideas knew no frontiers. They sought to spread them throughout Europe and beyond, and any power opposing them was likely to be the target of France's new citizen army.

It was at this time that a new word entered the political vocabulary – ideology – to describe the new political creeds displacing the old religious dogmas. For Cambridge historian F.H. Hinsley, it is when France tried and finally failed to force the states of Europe into a common mould that the European states system was completed.[18] For Hinsley there was now a Europe of the nations rather than a Europe of the states – yet another conception as to the genesis of modern international society.

As it happens, the violence of the French Revolution was rather less than legend suggests. After all, the suppression of the Paris commune in 1871 claimed more lives than were lost in the worst months of the Terror, and in fact fewer people fled abroad to escape the turmoil in France than had emigrated from the American colonies during the American Revolution.[19] Nonetheless its psychological impact was immediate, widespread and profound. Executing a monarch in the name of the nation and expressly breaking with Christianity conveyed abroad the possibility of massive social change. In the broadest sense political debate was now about a single issue – stability or change, conservatism or liberalism, immobility or innovation. In the French National Assembly of 1789, those opposing reform sat on the right of the President, those for reform sat on his left, and the terms 'right' and 'left' entered the political lexicon as indicators of political orientation. Like all such expressions, however, these were over-simplifications; for where, for example, would one put a radical Conservative such as Margaret Thatcher or a conservative Radical such as Fidel Castro?[20] Suffice it to say, even if the distinction is somewhat blurred today, when many politicians claim to be searching for the 'third way', the terms 'left' and 'right' have left their imprint on history, and most of us know what they are intended to convey.

More problematic, however, were the claims of the revolutionaries regarding fundamental rights. For though they sought 'liberty, equality and fraternity', they held the right of a people to sovereignty to be paramount; but what if the people, or at least their spokesmen, wanted to 'cleanse' ethnic or religious minorities, to promote demagogues, to participate in public executions and so forth, which, as it happens, they frequently did? Were they to be accorded such rights? As we know, in the name of the people of France in 1789, of Russia in 1917, of Germany in 1933, of China in 1949 and elsewhere, the most terrible deeds have been done, while the Americans in the cause of 'freeing' or 'rescuing' the people of other countries such as Vietnam, Nicaragua or Panama seemed to kill a great many of them. In any case were 'liberty' and 'equality' compatible? After all, if an equalitarian society was what was required, then surely those who outclassed their fellow citizens in one capacity or another would have to be held back in some way, which would be an infringement of liberty: if the emphasis was on individual freedom, then some would do better than others and an inequalitarian society would result.

Having challenged the Westphalian international order, the French revolutionaries were eventually to alienate by their over-zealous militancy those intended to be their strongest supporters. The effect of the coups and counter coups in Paris, the promiscuous use of the guillotine and the behaviour of republican troops in looting the lands they were supposed to be liberating was to turn allies into enemies. But not before Napoleon had virtually crushed the various foreign coalitions ranged against him and reshaped the map of Europe, establishing French dominion directly or indirectly in all but Britain, Scandinavia, Russia and the Ottoman domains at the extremities of the continent, and giving the final *coup de grâce* to the already virtually moribund Holy Roman Empire.

5.5 THE CONCERT SYSTEM

In the aftermath of Napoleon's defeat at Waterloo in 1815, the victors, having failed to check French ambitions for some two decades, reaffirmed in Vienna their commitment to balance-of-power diplomacy and vowed to restore the pre-Napoleonic configuration of Europe. And since Napoleon had eventually been crushed by concerted action of the Great Powers, their leaders decided to constitute a more formal directorate – the Concert of Europe – to hold periodic conferences whenever international developments called for Great-Power action or threatened to destabilise the continent. Though the Concert system was intended to restore the Westphalian order, it also aimed to provide a modicum of central management hitherto lacking. In the event, however, the rival pulls of sovereignty and a complex range of diverse interests and capabilities prevented the Concert from turning itself into a form of world government.[21]

Nonetheless, through the multilateral action of the Concert, which came to include France, its monarchy restored thanks to its fellow members, the Turks were forced to grant Greek independence and the Dutch to surrender the Belgian provinces, which were to be given independence and neutralised, and in contrast to much of Africa which was partitioned, Serbia, Romania and Bulgaria received sovereign recognition. On the other hand no 'management', domestic or international, can function properly when the principles are in conflict, as in the Crimea in the 1850s or in Central Europe a decade later. Still less can there be effective management where there is, in addition, a serious conflict of principle, as in relation to nationalism, which threatened the European domains of at least two members of the Concert – Austria and Prussia – and received some encouragement from a third – Britain.

In fact nationalist sentiment had been on the rise throughout the century, and according to Evan Luard at least three-quarters of the wars between 1815 and 1914 stemmed from nationalist attempts to secure an independence which some or all of the Concert powers were determined to resist.[22] And among the smaller European Powers there was, in addition, mounting resentment at the way their sovereign rights would often be disregarded by members of the Concert. The so-called century of peace was, thus, built on flimsy foundations;[23] and though tensions within Europe would sometimes be relieved by expansion outside it – with whole continents falling to Western imperialism – in the end the rise of Germany combined with the decline of Ottoman, Russian and Austrian power was sufficient in 1914 to bring down the whole diplomatic structure erected a century before. Though balance-of-power politics had worked to the extent that alliance commitments entered into prior to hostilities were kept, they had failed to secure that mutual deterrence on which peace depended. At the same time, the invention of the tank, torpedo, heavy artillery and aircraft ensured that the fatalities would be the worst on record for such a comparatively short conflict.

5.6 THE VERSAILLES SYSTEM

Many hailed as a 'new world order' the international system inaugurated at the Versailles Peace Conference following the devastation of the First World War. It was to be built, in the words of President Woodrow Wilson, not on 'a balance ... but a community of power', and the notion of collective security, in which each Power pledges to deter or defeat aggression, was enshrined in the League of Nations. A further corner-stone, supposedly, of the post-Versailles settlements and suggested by the recent collapse of Empires was the creation of new states in accordance with the principle of national self-determination. This says that peoples with a sense of nationhood should be permitted to give political expression to their feelings – a comparatively modern doctrine, leading Evan Luard to identify 1918 as the source of contemporary international society.[24] But in fact the pleas of many nationalists at Versailles, including Ho Chi Minh, who was much later to found Communist Vietnam, were ignored, while some of the new states created after Versailles were hardly exemplars of the nationalist principle. As is only too obvious today, Yugoslavia and Czechoslovakia incorporated an ill-assortment of peoples, as did the newly revived Poland, which was less than sixty per cent Polish. Meanwhile, the League's lack of enforcement provisions and the absence from the Concert in Geneva of the composer who was to have conducted the proceedings – the US – only made things worse. And with the world economy in severe and progressive decline and resentments welling up in Germany, Italy, Japan and wherever people felt deprived of their rights to full self-determination, the hopes of the League's founders lay in ruins, and another world war was in prospect scarcely more than twenty years after the end of the first.

5.7 WORLD POLITICS

If international society is characterised in terms of its basic political units or their forms of interaction, then the post-1945 period may not necessarily be regarded as fundamentally different from its predecessor. After all, though the borders of the sovereign state may now be more porous and its economy to a degree more interdependent, sovereign status still tends to be prized, even by those enmeshed in military alliances and economic unions. And while modern governments are supposed to respect and reflect the wishes of their citizens in a way never envisioned at Westphalia, their concern for national preservation and enhancement will have scarcely diminished over the years. In this sense, though there have been perceptible changes since 1648, these have, arguably, not been such as to suggest the emergence of an entirely new international society in 1945.

On the other hand many contemporary scholars have other criteria by which to characterise an international society and most would tend to identify 1945 as a watershed. For the typical American scholar, what constituted 'modern' international society was a particular form of balance of power in which the United States took the leading role. It was one involving a cold war between two sets of hostile powers, each espousing a different ideology and seeking to gain for itself worldwide sympathy and support. But with the cold war now over, and a different kind of international society in prospect – potentially more unified but in practice even more diverse than before – such scholars are struggling to find an appropriate tag by which to label it. Are we now in a 'post-modern' as distinct from a 'modern' international order? To identify an international society simply in terms of a particular configuration of power is to focus on merely one dynamic of international political interchange.

If the spotlight is on the technological environment within which international interactions take place, then it could be argued that international society has been virtually transformed in recent years. For the political and economic potential of nations can be said to have been revolutionised by developments in communications, military, industrial and agricultural technology, which pose new hazards while presenting fresh opportunities to those engaged in international intercourse.

Yet another way of characterising international society has to do with the issues on the international agenda, and in recent years, as was pointed out in Chapter 1, these have also recently been considerably recast.[25] The preoccupations, that is, of those who exercise influence on world politics have been steadily broadening since the end of the Second World War, and at the start of the twenty-first century they include many environmental, health, educational, social, economic and human rights concerns which could never have been in contemplation even half a century ago.

Generally speaking, in their attempt to identify the nature of international society, Realists, both structuralist and state-centred, tend to focus on changing power configurations, pluralists on the erosion of state autonomy and on changing agendas, Marxists on world economic systems and structural divisions.

It would, however, be difficult to deny the existence of at least one fundamental shift since 1945, and that is the tendency towards political, economic and socio-cultural globalisation, by which is meant the expansion, following decolonisation, of a largely European-based international order with its values, norms and institutions to encompass every continent of the globe. Fundamental to that process has been the development of instant global communication, dramatised in 1969 when among the few people not in a position to eavesdrop on the Apollo moon landings were the astronauts involved.

In sum, when precisely modern international society originated depends on one's definition and characterisation both of 'international society' and of 'modern'. It is, of course, possible to avoid the question altogether by speaking of the emergence of modern international society as a continuous and gradual evolutionary process from the disintegration of unified Christendom to today's complex global society comprising non-state actors as well as states, with their norms and complex patterns of interaction. In this sense, it begins somewhere around Westphalia, takes on a new dimension after the Napoleonic wars, is enlarged after Versailles and is completed around the mid-twentieth century. Clearly, however, the notions of 'modern' and of 'international society' are bound up with a third concept – 'sovereignty' – to which we turn in the following chapter.

NOTES

1. See for example Talbot Rice, D. (ed.), *The Dark Ages*, London, 1965.
2. Sargent, W., *Battle for the Mind*, London, Heinemann, 1957.
3. Davies, N., *Europe: A History*, London, Pimlico, 1997, p. 332.
4. On relations between medieval Rome and Byzantium, see for example Roberts, J.M., *The Triumph of the West*, London, BBC, 1985, pp. 149–74 and Obolensky, D., *The Byzantine Commonwealth*, New York, Praeger, 1971.
5. See for example Roberts, op. cit., pp. 175–202.
6. Morgenthau, H., *In Defence of the National Interest*, New York, Knopf, 1951. See also Taylor, A.J.P., *Rumours of War*, London, Hamish Hamilton, 1952, p. 44.
7. See Mattingley, G., *Renaissance Diplomacy*, London, Cape, 1955.
8. Wight, M., *Systems of States*, Leicester, Leicester University Press, 1977, pp. 110–13.
9. Northedge, F.S., *The International Political System*, London, Faber, 1976, pp. 53–9 and Bull, H., *The Anarchical Society*, London, Macmillan, 1977, chapters 1 and 2, pp. 3–52.
10. See Wight, M., op. cit., pp. 129–52.
11. See for example Keens-Soper, M., 'The practice of a states system' in Donelan, M. (ed.), *The Reason of States*, London, Allen & Unwin, 1978, pp. 25–44.
12. For a discussion of natural law and its origins in classical Greece, see for example De Burgh, W.G., *The Legacy of the Ancient World*, Vol. II, Harmondsworth, Penguin, 1953, pp. 468–81.

13. Manning, C.A.W., *The Nature of International Society*, London, Bell, 1962, pp. 103–6 and 160–1.
14. Since the architect of classical economics, Adam Smith, and the author of a leading text on the balance of power, David Hume, were close friends, each may well have influenced the other's ideas.
15. Hobsbawm, E., *Nations and Nationalism since 1780*, Cambridge, Cambridge University Press, 1990, pp. 18–24.
16. Davies, N., op. cit., traces the connection between the American and French revolutions, pp. 678–9.
17. Rousseau, *The Social Contract*, London, Dent, 1933.
18. Hinsley, F.H., *Power and the Pursuit of Peace*, Cambridge, Cambridge University Press, 1967.
19. Roberts, op. cit., p. 284.
20. Davies, op. cit., examines the conceptual problems arising out of the notion of a Left/Right divide, pp. 696–7.
21. For a range of conflicting views about the origins and effects of the Concert see for example Holbraad, C., *The Concert of Europe*, London, Longmans, 1970.
22. Luard, E., *Conflict and Peace in the Modern International System*, London, University of London Press, 1970, pp. 10–11.
23. See for example Northedge, op. cit., pp. 81–106.
24. Luard, op. cit., p. 11.
25. See for example Halliday, F., 'International relations: is there a new agenda?', *Millennium*, vol. 20, no. 1, 1991.

PART III

THE STATE

CHAPTER 6

SOVEREIGNTY: LEGAL AND POLITICAL

What do Nauru, Vanuatu, the Vatican and Malta have that Kashmir, Kurdistan, California and Queensland do not, and that Quebec has several times narrowly failed to establish? The answer is sovereign status. Each of the former is recognised in international law as a sovereign state, even though most of the latter, which are not so recognised, are far larger and more cohesive. This chapter seeks to analyse the significance of such anomalies and to explain how and why they occur.

6.1 STATE SOVEREIGNTY: PREREQUISITES

Given the hierarchical nature of medieval society, discussed in the previous chapter, the very notion of sovereignty as a legal status involving recognition of a state's claim to territorial integrity, independence and equality of status with other such entities could only have surfaced with the disintegration of medieval feudalism and the collapse of unified Christendom. For as feudal barons and warlords reinvented themselves as dukes, princes or kings and acquired vast territories, they also greatly enhanced their authority as against the claims of Pope, Emperor and rival warlords. In Machiavelli's *The Prince*, written in the fifteenth century, ambitious monarchs had a practical manual on how to rid themselves of medieval constraints, and in *De Republica* of 1576, the Frenchman Jean Bodin provided a theory to validate that sovereign independence.[1]

6.2 SOVEREIGNTY AS A POLITICAL CONCEPT

Bodin believed that the often bloody medieval confusion of political authorities with residual ties to a distant Pope or Emperor was outdated and that the hierarchical conception of world order needed to be replaced. Henceforth, he argued, each state should have a single focus of authority – a temporal ruler who would represent the *summa potestas*, the supreme or sovereign power in the realm. In effect, this gave the sovereign the exclusive right to make ultimate decisions regarding his subjects and to act on any matter within the confines of his realm to the exclusion of any other authority. Attempting to justify the centralisation of royal power since the time of Louis XI in the fifteenth century, Bodin claimed that it had divine authority. The sovereign, in other words, was God's representative, and though subject to divine law, natural law or the laws of the realm, including those he had himself promulgated, he could not otherwise be called to account. Since he ruled by 'divine right' any challenge to his power was effectively a challenge to God. On the other hand since the world embraced actually or potentially many such sovereigns, Bodin's theory implied that in their interactions all sovereigns had to be considered as having equal rights.

Though the notion of 'divine right' which was often used to justify absolutism clearly appealed to the new regal families and crowned heads of Europe, it was also to enjoy broader support. In a strife-torn continent Bodin's theory attracted the rising commercial classes who sought order and predictability, and gained adherents wherever a sense of political community was beginning to emerge of the kind later to develop into the phenomenon of nationalism. On the other hand, by the eighteenth century when Enlightenment philosophers such as Locke, Rousseau and Kant were defying the principles of absolutism, Bodin's conception of sovereignty came increasingly under challenge.

Because it commended a particular kind of rule as a recipe for effective government, Bodin's theory had been essentially political. But it had legal implications – and not just in respect of relations between rulers and ruled, but also as regards the state in relation to other states. For if a sovereign ruler acknowledged no political superior, was this not also true of the state he governed? Bodin's theory seemed to suggest that a state with internal sovereignty – that is, being under the effective control of an identifiable supreme authority – must also have external sovereignty – that is, having sovereign status in the world at large. In practice, however, this does not necessarily follow, for states under exclusive internal control are not always free from outside interference, nor are they necessarily accorded legal recognition. For example, though Tibet claimed sovereign status after the collapse of the Chinese empire early in the twentieth century, its assertion never received diplomatic support. Nor did that of Ian Smith's Rhodesia in the 1960s and 1970s, while Turkey alone recognises the so-called Republic of Northern Cyprus. Yet conversely, some states lacking in effective control, such as Angola, Congo, Sierra Leone and Somalia continue to be regarded as sovereign. They retain, that is, membership of the society of sovereign states while others, far more disciplined and controlled, are excluded. How come?

6.3 SOVEREIGNTY AS A LEGAL CONCEPT

First we must examine how sovereign status is acquired in international society.[2] Since the origin of the international legal system in the seventeenth century, there have been legal criteria for achieving sovereign statehood, though never clearly articulated till the 1933 Treaty of Montevideo. Surprisingly, these do not prescribe a minimum of size or population. They do, however, include the existence of clearly demarcated boundaries defining the territorial area of the state, a permanent population inhabiting the territory, an effective government commanding loyalty and deemed capable of respecting international obligations. There is, however, a further test before admission to the 'club', as it were, of sovereign states. A state must have sovereign status ascribed to it by those capable of conferring it. That is, it must be recognised as sovereign by the governments of other sovereign states. On the other hand governments are free agents and are not obliged to confer recognition even on a state fulfilling all the necessary criteria.

This is why some apparently independent states go unrecognised, while countries such as Israel and North Korea can be recognised by some governments and not others. This does not mean that such states are semi-sovereign, for in the eyes of international law, sovereignty is like virginity: you either have it or you don't. Israel and North Korea are wholly sovereign to those recognising them as such. So, too, was Taiwan when it was recognised as the seat of the government of China, which it claimed to be. But there cannot be two Chinas, and almost all governments have withdrawn recognition from Taiwan and transferred it to the People's Republic, thereby identifying Beijing as the legal capital of China. To them Taiwan can now have only a *de facto* not a *de jure* status, which means that recognition is provisional, subject to withdrawal when one government succeeds another, and does not involve the exchange of diplomats or other legal responsibilities and benefits. Taiwan, in other words, cannot enjoy the full rights and duties of a sovereign state.

Why such micro-states as Nauru, Vanuatu or the Vatican, shambolic states such as Sierra Leone or Somalia, or states under virtual foreign occupation, such as Lebanon today or some of the Eastern European countries in Stalin's time, have continued to enjoy recognition is a political question which need not concern us at this stage. On the other hand the tragic fate of states such as Bosnia indicates the folly of disregarding the criteria for recognition drawn up by international lawyers long ago. For the European Community's decision to recognise Bosnia and, indeed, Croatia a few months before when their governments were clearly not in effective control of key regions can only have widened existing ethnic and religious divisions in both countries, giving the Serbs a pretext for their intervention.

But legal theory, which is what has been discussed, and political and economic reality, to be considered below, may be two different things, and the possibility of a contradiction between theory and practice may apply as much to the internal as to the external dimensions of sovereignty. For in many countries the actual initiation, formulation, approval and implementation of policy are often far removed from what the constitution prescribes. Though the British parliament, for example, which in theory can make or unmake any law, is not overridden or ignored to the same extent as, say, the old Supreme Soviet, cabals of cabinet officials and civil servants and the operations of big business, of political and other pressure groups and of the media, to say nothing of the machinations of international bankers, of the EU and of the new assemblies in Scotland and Wales, can seriously undermine the legislative powers of the parliament at Westminster. And though Mao Zedong's China tended to be regarded in the West as 'totalitarian', implying that the administration exercised total control over its people, not even the ultra-radicalism of The Cultural Revolution could stamp out the corruption, nepotism, racism, drug abuse, prostitution and female infanticide declared illegal after the Communist takeover of 1949. Thus a government's degree of effective authority may be rather more limited than it appears.

6.4 LEGAL IMPLICATIONS OF STATE SOVEREIGNTY

When we come to the external dimensions of legal sovereignty, that is, the state in respect of other states, the relations between theory and practice, i.e. between sovereign status and the capacity to exercise it, can be even more remote. But first, what does the status of external sovereignty imply? In an international context it does not connote 'supremacy' as in the domestic setting, for a sovereign state does not have unlimited freedom of action in either theory or practice. It has to honour its legal obligations and is therefore not above the law, and in practice its activities are constrained by the actions of others. In fact external sovereignty betokens, as even Bodin's theory suggested, equality in terms of the law. States may vary in size, capabilities and vulnerability, but once accorded sovereign status they have an equal entitlement to a number of rights, powers and privileges.[3] What are these?

1. First and foremost, the exclusive power to control its own domestic affairs, to make ultimate decisions concerning the lives of its citizens;
2. the right of self-defence;

3. freedom from outside intervention, unless requested or else sanctioned by some legally constituted body, such as the UN, in response to a threat to the peace or a gross breach of international law;
4. the right to make and amend treaties;
5. the right to participate as a full member in the work of international organisations;
6. the right to create or amend international laws;
7. the right to all the traditional diplomatic privileges and immunities;
8. the sole jurisdiction of crimes committed within its territory;
9. the right to sue in the international courts;
10. the right to admit and expel aliens, and so forth.

But rights imply responsibilities, and states are duty-bound by virtue of their sovereign status not to perform acts of sovereignty on or to intervene in the territory of other states save under exceptional circumstances, to be detailed below. On the other hand, whereas the principle of sovereignty used to provide legal protection to intolerable regimes, whether they can continue to shield behind it in the light of recent international legislation remains to be seen.

Legal equality and inequality

While there are obvious discrepancies between theory and practice, the notion of sovereign equality seems to be belied even in theory.[4] For example, at the UN there are the special prerogatives of the members of the Security Council and of the veto powers of the five permanent members. At the other end of the political scale are the micro-states such as the Vatican, Vanuatu and Liechtenstein whose foreign and defence policies are determined by others, despite their sovereign status. Yet such violations of sovereign equality are more apparent than real, since in their sovereign capacity the relevant states expressly agreed to these inequalities in the first place. The Great Power veto was accepted by all the Powers at the inaugural meeting of the UN in San Francisco in 1945, even if somewhat under duress, since both Moscow and Washington had hinted that they might not join the world body without the veto. As for the micro-states, since they could only afford to take part in international politics if other states managed their defence and foreign affairs, again they may be said to have opted for second-class status.

But this does not exhaust the list of seeming legal inequalities which appear at first sight incompatible with the notion of sovereignty. For even though one of the most fundamental attributes of sovereignty is supposed to be a state's freedom from the juridical or constitutional authority of outside bodies, many states clearly lack full control of their legislative, executive or judicial functions. With regard to the question of law-making capacity, the decisions of the European Council of Ministers now have to be effected by the members of the EU, who must also give access to Community officials to investigate any matter of common concern. And as Britain has found often to her cost, the judgments both of the European Court and of the European Court of Human Rights can overrule decisions of parliament and overturn long-established procedures (some might say perversions), such as birching, i.e. a peculiar kind of beating for male offenders much-championed by the courts of the Isle of Man, and corporal punishment, much-enjoyed by certain kinds of schoolteachers, particularly in the private sector.

Even more fundamental infringements of sovereign status would appear to occur when one state is granted the right of armed intervention in another – as was Britain as a guarantor of the independence of Cyprus in 1960. Ironically it was Britain's failure to take action in response to the Greek-inspired crypto-Fascist coup in Cyprus in 1974 that led to the Turkish intervention and the continued presence of Turkish troops on the island. Meanwhile, during the cold war several states allowed part of their territory to be used by Soviet or US troops, and since the Superpower bases were often granted certain immunities from the authority of the local courts, Moscow and Washington effectively exercised the right of jurisdiction. Britain, too, was granted certain immunities in connection with its base in Valletta which was maintained several years after Malta had achieved its independence in 1964. Perhaps the most glaring example of an apparent infringement of sovereign status is the continued use by the US of the Guantánamo base on Cuba. Called into service in the 1994–5 American intervention in Haiti, it is a legacy of the days when Cuba served as an American playground, casino and vice den.

Furthermore, the dispatch of UN forces, whether to Korea, Kashmir, Egypt, the Congo, Cyprus, Cambodia, Croatia, Bosnia, Macedonia or wherever can also entail privileges making them immune from local jurisdiction. Finally, there are instances, though declining in number, when the judicial authorities in one country are empowered to make decisions affecting another. For example, the British House of Lords sitting in a juridical capacity retains the right to commute death sentences in a handful of former colonial countries, now members of the Commonwealth.

Sovereign inequality?

In most of the cases just outlined, the apparent inequalities can be explained as consistent with sovereign equality in that in their sovereign capacity, and for whatever reason, the powers whose rights have ostensibly been infringed specifically agree to such intrusions. Nor should this cause any surprise, since 'sovereignty' has a much more restricted meaning than in the days when few limits on state autonomy were acknowledged, and even the greatest power will agree to limitations on its freedom of action if it believes it stands to benefit. After all, that is what happens whenever a state joins a multilateral alliance or economic community.

Non-intervention eroded

Nonetheless the question of intervention, which has been defined as 'forcible interference in the affairs of a state',[5] primarily of a military nature, does involve something of a legal anomaly. For though non-intervention is regarded as a fundamental norm, international law, paradoxically, has long made provision for the intrusion of foreign forces into a state in exceptional circumstances.[6] It permits such interventions, for example, at the invitation of a sovereign government, for self-defence, to protect its nationals abroad or to counter an illegal intervention already undertaken. The trouble is that the law in these matters is somewhat unclear and full of loopholes, which states will exploit to their advantage. What, for example, if the 'invitation' to intervene is issued by a government itself lacking legitimate authority, as it is claimed was the Hungarian government who invited in the Red Army in 1956 or the South Vietnamese administration who 'sent for Uncle Sam' in the 1960s? Can self-defence include the right to make pre-emptive strikes against foreign guerrilla bases housed in densely populated civilian areas, as was the claim of the Israelis in the 1950s and 1960s? Does counter-intervention have to be proportionate to the original intervention?

If legal ambiguities remain in these areas, the fact that the UN, while reaffirming the norm of non-intervention in article 2 (7) of the Charter, has added to the list of permissible interventions has merely increased the confusion. For it has sanctioned collective interventions in answer to international aggression, as in the Gulf in 1990, where civil order appears to have collapsed, as in Somalia in 1992, and in response to what is seen as a gross violation of human rights, as in Bosnia 1993–5. It has also, as it were, contracted out to UN members the task of peace enforcement either where its initial endeavours falter, as in Bosnia, or when it is reluctant to get directly involved, as in Haiti, Georgia and Sierra Leone. But using force 'to save lives' implies a contradiction; and because such interventions can be seen as conflicting with the norm of non-intervention, as representing in the eyes of many a non-Western administration a form of Western cultural imperialism, as risking aggravation of the situation it is designed to remedy, and as threatening international as well as domestic order, they are always controversial.[7]

But with a raft of new human rights conventions designed to protect oppressed peoples, the creation of war crimes tribunals and the proposed introduction of an International Criminal Court, the balance might well shift in favour of what are called 'humanitarian interventions', in effect setting aside the right of a sovereign government to do as it pleases within its own territory.[8] Yet when in 1999 NATO, a supposedly defensive alliance, took it upon itself to bombard Serbia and Montenegro on behalf of what it saw as the oppressed and brutalised Albanians of Kosovo, its action was legally questionable since, even though recent international legislation of the kind to be discussed in chapter 9 can be cited in justification, its action had not been expressly sanctioned by the UN. What NATO regarded as 'humanitarian intervention' its critics saw as 'coercive diplomacy' and an example of state-sponsored international terrorism. It seems, therefore, that while there is as yet no unambiguous and generally agreed duty of 'humanitarian intervention', the principle of non-intervention remains the norm – if only for the time being.

Constitutional self-containment

What, then, in law is this sovereignty which is not necessarily infringed, eroded, violated or compromised by the kind of examples cited above? It would seem that the irreducible minimum is what Alan James calls 'constitutional self-containment'; that is, not being part of another's domain.[9] For example, even if, as is often said, California has the world's eighth-largest economy, it cannot sign treaties, exchange Ambassadors, join international organisations and the like because it is a part of the constitutional structure of the US. By contrast Vanuatu and Nauru can do these things because they are constitutionally self-contained. They are not part of another's territory.

Here, then, is a possible answer to the British 'Eurosceptics' who claim that EU membership means a loss of sovereignty. For no state is forced to join the organisation. But, of course, in joining that or, indeed, any other kind of 'club', one agrees to abide by the rules, and in the case of the EU, members agree to delegate certain sovereign powers to international civil servants and adjudicators. If the rules of membership are not acceptable or the bureaucrats betray their trust, its members can always try to get them changed, as when they sacked the EU Commission in 1999 and had its President, Jacques Santer, replaced. A more drastic alternative is to leave, though the political and economic costs of relinquishing membership of the European Union would be far greater than that of leaving the National Union of Teachers or the Mothers' Union. Nor, without an effective political, defence or broader economic union does the creation of the European Monetary Union (EMU) necessarily alter the picture. After all, for years Britain and Ireland had a common currency; yet they were separate countries with quite different and sometimes opposed foreign and defence policies. Nor did the post-war monetary union between Belgium and Luxembourg make them identical in either policy or interest. And, of course, monetary unions, of the kind that bound the Roman empire in the third century and the Scandinavian states in the mid-nineteenth century, can ultimately fail and be wound up.

So far, we have examined the kinds of inequalities that are arguably compatible with legal equality. But there are many inequalities that cannot be so regarded, which is why states equal in law may not be equal in diplomatic esteem. That is to say, a country which is constitutionally self-contained may in practice be hard put to exercise its sovereign power, so that its standing (as distinct from its status) suffers accordingly. Since some states are better placed than others to exert their sovereignty, it is necessary to consider the concept in a more broadly political context. Here the question is one of substance rather than form – in particular, regarding how far the sovereign authorities within the state are free to define and implement what they consider to be that state's interests. How independent, in other words, is the state? Though in law a state either has or does not have sovereignty, in any other sense – political, economic, cultural or whatever – some states can be more sovereign than others, and ever since the emergence of the modern states system structural inequalities between the various states have produced a kind of international hierarchy.

6.5 CONSTRAINTS ON THE EXERCISE OF SOVEREIGNTY

Given that the various powers comprising international society are so diverse, their capacity to exercise sovereignty can be affected by a variety of factors. As such they can be classified and graded in many different ways, each illuminating one of the structural factors constraining state behaviour,[10] the first being the relatively changeless factor of geography.

Geography

Though one should be as wary of geographical as of psychological or social determinism, it is undeniable that a country's size as well as its place on the world map can affect its perceptions and international actions. The priorities of a land-based, land-locked continental power such as the Czech Republic, Congo (Zaire) and Mongolia are likely to be different from those of a maritime or oceanic state such as Britain, Sri

Lanka, Japan or New Zealand, or, indeed, from those like France, Germany, Canada and the US with both continental and maritime outlooks.

Evidence suggests that being a small offshore island off a politically restless continent has had a distinct impact on the history, national attitudes and policy options of a Britain or a Japan. Both have pursued strategies to prevent the domination of their respective continents by any state that could threaten their security. At the same time, their perception of geography impelled both into overseas adventures, the acquisition of empire, formal or informal, and a naval strategy for protecting trade and supply routes. They can also react with unexpected violence to a perceived threat to their freedom of action – as in the case of Washington's oil embargo against Japan in the late 1930s or Nasser's nationalisation of the Suez Canal Company in 1956. Meanwhile their insular positions have generated in both countries a kind of insular mentality which expresses itself in resistance to continental labels ('We are British, not European: Japanese, not Asian!'), and, to the irritation of their neighbours, encourages them to move simultaneously in different political and strategic spheres but without any strong sense of commitment or allegiance.

By contrast, if a country occupies a land mass lacking any clear geographical boundaries with its neighbours – as for example Germany or Poland – its preoccupations are likely to be different. Germany became an overseas colonist reluctantly. Its opportunities for expansion were mainly over land, and since Poland stood in the way, the two countries were often fiercely at odds. At the end of the eighteenth century Prussia helped engineer Poland's disappearance from the map for a century and a quarter, and in 1939 Berlin joined Russia in yet another carve-up of its Eastern neighbour. Not even their shared experience of Communist rule could eradicate that legacy of animosity and, since the collapse of Communism in both countries, Polish refugees have been among the prime targets of neo-Nazi violence in Eastern Germany.

But a history of repeated conflict induced by lack of clear boundaries can in time also encourage the creation of new institutions to keep antagonisms within bounds, and it is in that context that Franco-German efforts to make a success of the European Union must be seen.

Among other geographical variations there are states in the vicinity of the traditional epicentres of international conflict on the one hand and those in much more remote areas on the other. Countries contiguous to the great trade routes, strategic waterways or sources of raw materials where the ambitions of the powerful tend to cut across one another are at a double disadvantage. They are in constant danger of getting caught in the crossfire between antagonists and of being drawn into a war not of their own choosing. Alternatively they risk becoming the client state of one or other adversary in a high-risk tension area. For example, many a state in the Balkans, Central Asia and the Middle East has been caught up against its will in the disputes of others, and being a foreign policy decision-maker in, say, Albania, Macedonia, Jordan, Azerbaijan or, for that matter, Kuwait is no sinecure.[11]

The social matrix

A second method of classification, which also has a basis in geography, relates to what might be called the social matrix. Clearly, states with a high degree of ethnic and cultural homogeneity such as Japan, the Scandinavian countries, Hungary and Portugal may be spared some of the secessionist problems of heterogeneous states where a sense of national identity is lacking. Sadly, many of the LDCs tend to suffer not only from poverty, but also from a lack of coherence. Being accidents of colonial rule and often the hapless offspring of a system in which the imperialist powers, ignoring tribal boundaries, literally drew straight lines in the sand to demarcate one state from another, such countries as Chad, Sudan and Zaire (Congo) have often been too prone to separatist rebellions to be able to pursue rational and effective policy. There are also states where a combination of geography and history have left a legacy of political schizophrenia, and are torn, as it were, between competing cultures, which can only complicate the process of policy-making. For example, the recently revived conflict in Russia between the Slavophiles and the Westernisers as well as the current contention in Turkey between the Islamicists and the secularisers reflect the geopolitical dilemmas of countries with mixed European and Asiatic roots. But the resulting instability can affect not only neighbours but also minorities, such as the Chechens and, of course, the Kurds, who seem destined to become scapegoats whenever central government is under pressure.

Political values and orientations

A further and related method of classifying states is in terms of political culture, value systems and behaviour patterns. For these can shape not only a state's policies, but also the process – democratic, oligarchic, autocratic or whatever – by which they are deliberated. In addition they can affect the way the country presents itself, in terms of its diplomatic style, whether combative or conciliatory, inflexible or flexible, uncertain or assured. And from the time of the Peloponnesian war onwards ideological factors, and in particular the entrenched perceptions and misperceptions of ruling elites, have tended to heighten existing inter-state conflicts as governments position themselves in relation to the ideological fray.[12] Frequently, however, as indicated in the previous chapter, ideological disagreements break down into a simple contention – between those broadly favouring the current status quo in the international system and the 'revisionists' craving radical change. However, some governments may be satisfied as regards the world balance overall but dissatisfied with the situation in a particular region, and vice versa. By the same token, a state may appear 'revisionist' in relation to some countries, status quo in relation to others. It may also give different impressions to friend and to foe. While, for example, the Soviet Union appeared to many in the West as a radically dissatisfied power whose ambition to secure a Communist world was virtually unstoppable, the Marxist–Leninist governments of China, Albania and North Korea came to see Moscow as a broadly conservative force, and were probably right in so doing.[13]

While there exist competing claims, interests and idea systems few governments can ever be entirely content with the international order they face. Yet there is always the thorny question as to how far contending value systems cause and how far they reflect and rationalise conflicts of interest. To this a Realist, a pluralist or a structuralist would doubtless give different answers.

Position in the world economy

A fourth great point of divergence among the states concerns their position in the world economy. Till recently the existence of economic inequality within and between states was more or less taken for granted – regarded as a God-given fact of life. But with decolonisation and the sudden arrival of a large number of scarcely viable new states came the plea for an economic status measuring up to the sovereignty newly acquired. In this way reform of the world economy was thrust on the international agenda, and in the meetings of the Non-aligned movement and of UNCTAD – the UN Conference on Trade and Development – representatives of the LDCs called for a New International Economic Order. What they had in mind was: 1. a transfer of resources from richer to poorer states by means of development assistance; 2. easy access to Western markets and a preferential position in trade; and 3. greater say in the administration of international economic institutions such as the IMF and World Bank.

If the LDCs anticipated a meaningful dialogue with the developed countries (DCs), they were to be sadly disillusioned. As far as the free-marketeers who had the ear of most of the Western delegates were concerned, if the LDCs were in trouble they had only themselves to blame. Their plight had nothing to do with the colonial legacy: everything to do with corrupt and inefficient administration and an addiction to central planning, and there was no point in furnishing government to government grants or subsidised loans.[14] As Peter Bauer wryly observed: such patronage amounted to 'poor people in rich countries subsidising rich people in poor countries'[15] – a view widely shared among the rich man's club known as G7, which accounts for their resistance to the idea of an NIEO.

True, in the 1970s and early 1980s when petrodollars earned from the sale of oil flooded into Western banks, the latter were not just willing but eager to lend to almost any potential customer and at low rates of interest. But later when interest rates soared and the burden of repayment was too much for many LDCs, Western financial institutions proved less than generous, and many low-income countries found themselves, like many a mortgage-holder, with negative equity, i.e. facing interest payments far larger than the capital originally borrowed. As regards access to Western markets, the Western powers have conceded less than was promised under The General Agreement on Tariffs and Trade (GATT) and The World Trade Organisation (WTO), and though they encourage the LDCs to step up their exports, they are often less than wholehearted in honouring their commitments to removing trade barriers which restrict imports from the LDCs.

In fact, many recent developments have served to widen the gap between North and South. Naturally the richer countries have more capital to invest in new technologies, such as the production of synthetic fibres and rubber, which reduces their need for the raw materials of the LDCs and causes a corresponding fall in world prices. Thus, in many an LDC, technical inferiority often combined with political, religious or ethnic turbulence and the existence of corrupt and inept government can produce spectacular falls in living standards, exacting in the case of countries such as Somalia, Sudan, Rwanda and Congo a heavy daily tally of lives. And though aid agencies may try to fill the breach, often their help is insufficient to provide first aid, let alone aid for development.

Disappointed by the West's response to what they saw as comparatively modest reformist demands, some LDC economists and political scientists have proposed more radical solutions. These range from selective delinking from the world economy, self-help among the LDCs, self-sufficiency and, at the extreme, world revolution. In fact, both liberal/conservative and radical panaceas have often proved woefully defective in practice. Neither Socialism in the Third World nor the free market in the post-Communist states of Eastern Europe has been a conspicuous success. On the other hand the experience of the NICs such as Singapore, South Korea, Taiwan, Indonesia and Malaysia, as well as that of the oil-rich states of the Middle East, indicate that, even if they have been through troubled times, change is possible and that the old North/South division can be bridged if pragmatism replaces dogmatism.

There is, however, an interesting paradox about the world distribution of economic wealth. Ironically, many so-called poor countries – Angola and Congo, for instance – are far more rich in resources than many of the so-called rich countries. In terms of raw materials Japan, Taiwan and Singapore are far less well endowed than China; Germany has far less mineral wealth than Russia and it is hard to see what Switzerland produces in abundance other than magnificent scenery, 'yummy' chocolate, cuckoo clocks and the occasional dubious bank practice. Yet since these largely under-resourced countries are among the world's leading economies, the sum total of a country's resources would appear to matter far less than its skill in utilising them.

6.6 THE GRADING OF THE POWERS

Perhaps the most dramatic evidence of the gulf between the theory and the practice of sovereign equality lies in the ascription of rank to the powers – from small, to medium, to great to Superpower status. Such classifications represent a kind of international consensus as to the range of interests of a particular power, whether local, regional, intercontinental or global, its ability to defend those interests, its influence among the nations and the extent to which its concerns have to be respected by others. Estimates of rank tend to be based in part on some of the classifications to which reference has already been made – geography, sociology, ideology and economics – but in part also on a calculation of potential military capacity in the light of past achievements.[16] The so-called 'great power' is generally a state with a reputation enhanced through war, expansionism or the absorption of neighbours, with global interests and influence, a perceived ability to protect them and a claim to be heard in key diplomatic discussions. In this sense 'greatness' is not necessarily related to size, since some of the powers that have merited that title – Portugal, Holland and Britain, for example – have been comparatively small in area. By the same token, those regarded as small states (i.e. with a limited range of interests they are able to defend) might be quite sizeable – for example, Libya, Chad or the Sudan. Nowadays, however, with the imputation of 'greatness' clearly goes the responsibility for maintaining what is called 'world order', though their rivalries often hinder, for good or ill, their exercise of what Ian Clark calls joint 'tutelage' over the international system.[17]

Since international politics are a dynamic process, the pecking order tends to change with changing circumstances. It is no secret that the standing of at least three of the permanent members of the Security Council – Britain, France and Russia – has much diminished in recent years, raising the question as to whether they should be allowed to retain the veto, when countries such as Japan and Germany have interests and influence probably no less than theirs. Conceivably, we may now be moving into a world in which a country's esteem depends not so much on its military as on its economic potential, and in this sense there could be many a new Great Power on the horizon, though doubtless the older powers will strive to cling on to the privileges as well as the responsibilities of imputed greatness.

6.7 THE CONTINUING RELEVANCE OF SOVEREIGNTY

Though sovereignty has been the cornerstone of the international system since Westphalia, is it still relevant? Few today would hold any brief for a theory, such as Bodin's, serving to justify absolutism. Though governments still have to demonstrate their effective control if they are to merit sovereign status, most Western and many non-Western critics would argue that the authorities must also answer to the people they are supposed to administer. Sovereignty, in other words, must no longer be a licence for abuse of power. It needs to be exercised responsibly, and a Saddam Hussein, Milosevic or, for that matter, Pinochet, Mobutu or Hitler can no longer shield behind the principle of sovereignty in riding roughshod over what are considered elementary human rights.

There are, on the other hand, pluralists such as John Burton who would claim that sovereignty, whether democratically grounded or not, has little or no meaning in an interdependent world, since modern military, technological and economic developments have destroyed the notion of sovereign self-reliance. Realists, structuralists and not a few pluralists, however, would disagree. For while it is evident that nowadays the state is neither invulnerable nor impermeable, it is questionable that it ever was, and if the principle of sovereignty could withstand centuries of penetration from international, transnational, subnational and supranational forces, the so-called 'globalisation' trends in the world economy are not necessarily going to bring it to an end now. But on what, in this view, does the continued relevance of sovereignty depend?

First, recent developments in military and communications technology have, if anything, enhanced the ability of medium and small states to exercise their sovereign powers.[18] The very strength of the Soviet Union and the US tended to make them somewhat musclebound, and in the end Moscow proved unable to prevail over its recalcitrant neighbours to its East, West and South, while the US failed to humble Vietnam, Cambodia, Laos, Iran, Iraq, Lebanon, Libya and Cuba.

Second, while secessionism poses a very real danger to the political contours of many existing states, it represents no threat to the state system as such. Secessionists, whether in Spain, Yugoslavia, Indonesia, India or Congo do not want to destroy international society. They want to join it.

Third, the fact that the number of sovereign states is well over three times that of 1945 and rising suggests that the sovereignty principle is as much sought-after today as ever. Kashmiris and Kosovars, Palestinians, Abhazians and the people of East Timor have a sense of separateness to which they wish to give political expression. Who are we to tell them that sovereignty is an illusion and to deny them the opportunity to run their own show?

Fourth, if many whose countries lack sovereign status wish to have it, it is increasingly clear that some, say, in western Europe, afraid that they might lose sovereignty to the bureaucrats in Brussels, wish to reassert it. That, surely, is the real message of the recent rows over the composition of the European Commission, the management of the European bank and the question posed in Britain, Sweden and Denmark of whether or not to join the Euro.

NOTES

1. Bodin, J., *Six Books of the Commonwealth*, Oxford, Blackwell, 1967.
2. On the establishment of sovereign statehood see Brierly, J.L., *The Law of Nations*, New York, 1949, pp. 122–35.
3. Goodwin, G.L., 'The erosion of external sovereignty', in *Government and Opposition*, vol. 9, no. 1, Winter 1974.
4. See Duchacek, I., *Nations and Men: An Introduction to International Politics*, New York, Holt, Rinehart and Winston, 1971, pp. 146–8.
5. Rosas, A., 'Towards some international law and order', in *Journal of Peace Research*, vol. 31, no. 2, 1994, p. 134.
6. Grotius himself argued that intervention is sometimes justifiable, acccording to Beitz, C., *Political Theory and International Relations*, Princeton, Princeton University Press, 1979, p. 71.
7. For a sample of the different views on the legality of intervention, see, for example, Falk, R., *Human Rights and State Sovereignty*, New York, Holmes & Meier, 1981; Bull, H. (ed.), *Intervention in World Politics*, Oxford, Clarendon Press, 1984; Nardin, T., *Law, Morality and the Relations of States*, Princeton, Princeton University Press, 1983; and Mayall, J., *The New Interventionism 1991–1994: The UN Experience in Cambodia, former Yugoslavia and Somalia*, Cambridge, Cambridge University Press, 1996.
8. See for example Roberts, A., 'Humanitarian war: military intervention and human rights', *International Affairs*, vol. 69, no. 3, July 1993, pp. 429–49.
9. James, A., *Sovereign Statehood*, London, Allen & Unwin, 1986.
10. For a thoroughgoing taxonomy see Northedge, F.S., *The International Political System*, London, Faber, 1976, pp. 154–76.

11. For a lucid analysis of the relations between geography and international politics see Sprout, H. and M., 'Environmental Factors in the Study of International Politics', in Rosenau, J. (ed.), *International Politics and Foreign Policy*, 2nd edn., New York, Free Press, 1969, pp. 41–56.

12. On the relationship between perception, misperception and conflict see for example Jervis, R., *Perception and Misperception in International Politics*, Princeton, NJ, Princeton University Press, 1976. Also Booth, K., *Strategy and Ethnocentrism*, London, Croom Helm, 1979.

13. Northedge, F.S., op. cit., pp. 173–5.

14. See for example Krasner, S., *Structural Conflict: The Third World against Global Liberalism*, Berkeley, University of California Press, 1985.

15. Bauer, P., 'The case against aid', in *Millennium*, vol. 2, no. 2, 1973, p. 13.

16. On the grading of the powers see for example Purnell, R., *The Society of States*, London, Weidenfeld & Nicolson, 1973, pp. 66–107 and Wight, M., *Power Politics*, London, Penguin, 1979, pp. 61–7 and 295–301.

17. *The Hierarchy of States: Reform and Resistance in the International Order*, Cambridge, Cambridge University Press, 1989.

18. A point noted by Herz, J. who, in an article, 'The territorial state revisited' *Polity*, 1, 1968, pp. 11–34 revised the main thrust of his argument on 'The rise and demise of the territorial state', in *World Politics*, 9, 1957, pp. 473–93.

CHAPTER 7

NATIONALISM – THE NATION AND THE IMAGINATION

When a therapist succeeds in wringing from a patient vivid memories of sexual, physical or emotional abuse that bear no relation to reality and possibly never even happened, we speak of 'false memory syndrome'. But there is a kind of socio-political equivalent to 'false memory syndrome', when nations come to believe things about their history that are largely fabrications.

The origins of the 'traditional' British Christmas, with its carols, Christmas trees, yule logs and 'Santa' are not to be found in the mists of time, as many believe, but largely in the nineteenth century, and in which Prince Albert, with his memories of Christmas in Germany, and Charles Dickens with his book *A Christmas Carol* played a key part. Likewise, the Scottish kilt, which many even north of the border regard as a relic of the distant past, was invented in the 1730s by an English cloth merchant, while the tartan whose colour and pattern is supposed to indicate clan allegiance was designed for an early nineteenth-century pageant – both innovations, of course, being lucrative money spinners. Again, much of the 'pomp and circumstance' associated with Britain's royals are either inventions or reinventions devised in the 1870s to boost the flagging popularity of Queen Victoria. Only since then did monarchs indulge in public relations spectaculars, engaging in colourful public ceremonials, such as the state opening of parliament – itself a largely nineteenth-century reconstruction in medieval style – parading every so often in ornate state coaches, being anointed at coronations, assisted by clergy now dressed in designer-coloured vestments, and lying-in-state after they depart for the 'Great Palace in the Sky'.

One of the latest of these invented British traditions is the reconstructed 'Shakespearean' theatre recently opened in Southwark on the bank of the Thames. In fact the 'Globe' is no reconstruction. It is in the wrong place, is built with the wrong materials and has the kinds of safety and amplifying devices inconceivable in Shakespeare's day.[1] Yet already this edifice, built yards from the original site, is known as 'Shakespeare's Globe'.

7.1 THE 'NATION' AND THE IMAGINATION

According to the Marxist historian Eric Hobsbawm, in a compilation *The Invention of Tradition* of which he was joint editor, nationalism and the nation, like the 'traditional' Christmas, the 'traditional' tartan and kilt, the 'traditional' royal ceremonials and the 'traditional' Shakespearean theatre, are of comparatively recent origin – in its modern sense probably no older than the eighteenth century. A nation, according to Hobsbawm, can be sited, planted and tended to a conscious design. Its continuous history, that is, is often in part a fabrication, sustained with the aid of semi-mythical figures, forged documents, symbols, such as the national flag, and images – Marianne, Germania, John Bull and 'Uncle Sam' – designed to foster the kind of sentiment we call nationalistic.[2] As he puts it: 'The history which [becomes] part of a fund of knowledge or the ideology of nation, state or movement is not what has actually been preserved in popular memory, but what has been selected, written, pictured, popularised and institutionalised by those whose function it is to do so.' Though it does not feature in Hobsbawm's text, he might have cited as an interesting example the Serbian pretext for trying to hang on to Kosovo. Belgrade's main claim is that it was in the battle of Kosovo of 1389 when the Serbs lost to the Turks that Serbian nationalism was forged. In fact the battle was not decisive. It was more or less a draw, and Serbs and Albanians were to be found in support of both sides. That the 1389 conflict sealed the fate of the Serbs for centuries was a later invention designed to foster Serbian national self-consciousness.[3]

7.2 THE EVOLUTION OF THE NATIONAL IDEA

The idea of the nation as essentially a construct built on myth is the theme of another volume also written by a Marxist, Benedict Anderson, and with another intriguing and evocative title, *Imagined Communities*.[4] For Anderson the nation is imagined, since its members will never know most of their fellow members, a community because it is conceived as a fellowship of the like-minded and limited because it has finite boundaries beyond which lie other conceived-of nations. In detailing its historical origins, he argues that five major factors encouraged its rise: the growth of separate national or state Churches after the collapse of medieval Christendom; the invention of the printing press which made possible the wide dissemination of novel ideas; the increasing use in official communications of indigenous local languages; the gradual weakening of dynasticism and monarchy in the eighteenth century; and changing conceptions of time in which a concept such as the nation could, rather like the New Testament, be made to appear simultaneously as both radically new and yet encompassing the best or even the fulfilment of some earlier tradition.

The most original part of Anderson's thesis relates to the geographical origins of nationalism. Most scholars trace its source either to Europe or to Europeans. For example, in his *Nations and Nationalism*, Ernest Gellner links nationalism to the process known as 'modernisation' on the breakdown of traditional agrarian society.[5] To create an industrialised, secular and integrated nation out of ethnically diverse peoples, Gellner argues, the elites would manufacture a new identity for their citizens using mythical as well as real events from the past and transmitting them through texts, speeches, songs and sermons. Since modernisation occurred first in Europe, Gellner locates the origins of nationalism there. Not so, says Anderson, who traces the concept to the Creoles of central and Latin America in the latter half of the eighteenth century, as Enlightenment ideas spread while Spanish control was being tightened. As for the political and territorial contours of Latin American nationalism, Anderson argues: 'The very vastness of the Spanish-American empire' ensured that any sense of nationhood would be based on 'the original . . . American administrative units marking the spatial limits of particular military conquests.' How such units came to be conceived of as fatherlands was, in Anderson's view, the work largely of disaffected Creole bureaucrats who were discriminated against, despite their invaluable service to the administration and resemblance to the thoroughbred Spaniards who received preferential treatment.

Yet it might be objected, even if nationalism is an invention and its origins are to be found between the Gulf of Mexico and Tierra del Fuego, what of the Egyptians, Ethiopians, Chinese, Celts, Greeks or Jews, among others, who believe they can trace their national ancestry back thousands of years? Are they not entitled to assert an unbroken sense of nationhood? Well, yes and no.

7.3 PRE-NATIONAL SOCIAL GROUPS

First, no one suggests that the national idea emerges in a vacuum. Before nations were 'invented' there were, as there still are, social groups such as extended families, clans and tribes as well as societies with some sense of a common ethnic, cultural or religious identity; there were also sociopolitical entities such as city states, provinces and principalities which generated local loyalties. At the same time, some of the sentiments we associate with modern nationalism were not unknown in earlier times. In Shakespeare's evocation of England in *Richard II*, for example, such emotions are given powerful expression: 'This precious stone set in the silver sea . . . ; this blessed plot, this earth, this realm, this England'. In *Nations and Nationalism since 1780*, Eric Hobsbawm calls such sentiments proto-nationalism, suggesting a kind of nationalism that is ill-formed and immature.[6] Perhaps 'patriotism', derived from the Latin word for 'fatherland' and meaning civic loyalty, love of country and of service to the state would be a better word. In fact, humans have always needed to feel a part of some sort of community or imagined community which appears to enshrine their hopes and to serve their interests. Yet though the desire for fellowship has existed throughout history, the national idea does represent something new.

7.4 THE NOVELTY OF 'NATIONALISM'

Though the ancient Greeks may have had a sense of cultural identity, their political loyalty was to the city state. In Roman times, allegiance was to the imperial order. In medieval Europe people identified themselves in terms of their religion and occupation. Thus, the nationalism of the eighteenth century and after was novel in that its advocates sought to give the concept of the nation specifically political, geographical and generally secular dimensions. Though the precise origins and political contours of the nation might be debated, most nationalists assumed that nations could be identified objectively, that they had interests, that those interests were discoverable by those entitled to act as interpreters, and that those interests should be accorded priority and given appropriate political expression, which generally though not always implied sovereign statehood. Nationalism had become, in Gellner's words, 'a political principle which holds that the political and the national unit should be congruent'. That, in brief, is the doctrine of national self-determination – a logical development of the politicisation of the national idea.

7.5 CRITICAL DISTINCTIONS

There remained, however, the problem of the precise definition of the nation and of how to distinguish it from other kinds of socio-political organisation. Perhaps the first distinction that must be made, since the two are often used interchangeably, is between 'state' and 'nation'. Though the term 'state' has many different connotations, in discourse concerning world politics it generally refers to an administrative unit based on territoriality. If, moreover, the unit in question receives widespread legal recognition, we call it a sovereign state. But the 'nation' as such is not an administrative unit, nor does it ever have sovereign status. It comprises a group of politically aware, like-minded and sometimes kindred people, but it is rare for any state to encompass all and only the people who wish to identify with it – and in this sense 'nation' and 'state' rarely coincide. And it only confuses matters when the term 'nation state' is used as a synonym for 'sovereign state', when the expression 'inter-national relations' is used to refer to 'inter-state relations' and when we talk of the League of Nations and the United Nations when we are really speaking of associations of states. In fact, the idea of the state emerged long before the modern notion of the nation, and in this sense the sentiment of patriotism – of love of country and of loyalty to the state – was around well before the rise of modern nationalism.

Another important set of distinctions is between 'tribe' and 'nation'. A 'tribe' comprises a group of people with characteristics in common – physical as well as cultural. Its basis, therefore, is ethnic. Ethnicity, cultural and physical kinship and tradition is what differentiates one tribe from another – the Hutu, say, from the Tutsi. The 'nation', too, refers to a group of people, but is a much more elastic concept, and attempts to give it precise definition usually fail, not least because nationalist writers are often more interested in propaganda than in description.

7.6 THE 'NATION': OBJECTIVE CRITERIA

Language

In the nineteenth century, many nationalists, especially in central, eastern and south-eastern Europe, claimed that 'language' was 'the badge of nationhood', that which distinguished 'us' from 'them', the advanced civilisations from the barbarians. In reality, however, national languages were generally the opposite of what nationalist propagandists supposed them to be. They were not natural but artificial constructs – the creation of those who wanted to devise a standard idiom out of a variety of spoken dialects, using grammarians, orthographers, who created a written language and lexicographers, who compiled dictionaries for the purpose. For example, Shakespeare wrote before any standard English had been devised and his own manuscripts had virtually no punctuation or settled spelling. He even spelt his own name in several different ways, and there was no linguistic authority to correct him.[7] Yet as if oblivious to this point, nineteenth-century Polish, Czech, Croat and other nationalists encouraged the development and analysis of what they called indigenous literature, while other nationalists took to the study of languages that had seemed in terminal decay, such as Irish, Welsh and Hebrew. Yet if language was the decisive factor, what of the Swiss with their several languages, the Canadians and Belgians with their two official languages, what of the English-, French-, Spanish- or Arabic-speaking peoples, so divided in their national loyalties?

Religion

Others sought to root the nation in religion, which for the Poles, the Irish, the Greeks or even the Jews might have had some plausibility since their religious identity was frequently imperilled. On the other hand, such a conception would have had little relevance for the Americans, Canadians, Germans or British with their several religious denominations. Nor is there much evidence that a common religious heritage, say, as between Iraq, Iran and Afghanistan or between Pakistan and Bangladesh makes for a common sense of identity.

Ethnicity

Others, notably Anthony Smith, claimed to see in ethnic identity the key, suggesting that the nation is based on the rediscovery and reinterpretation of an ethnic past.[8] And while such an analysis has more in common with 'the sleeping beauty' than the malign racial theories of the nineteenth century,[9] it is easy to see how it could be misappropriated. In any case both kinds of theories are open to similar objections. First, with the depopulation and resettlement of large areas of the world in face of the ravages of man and of nature, common descent is difficult to establish. Peoples tend to have diverse origins and there is more than an element of myth in the accounts they give of their past. In any case, though ethnicity as a basis for the nation might have a certain appeal to the Japanese, Armenians, Greeks, Bulgars or Basques, it would hardly strike a chord among the polyglot Americans or among those trying to weld a nation in South Africa or, for that matter, in Israel. And recent experience in Somalia indicates that even perceived common descent is no guarantee of national solidarity. Conversely, often the most ardent champions of a particular nation are people who have little or no ethnic claim to it. Napoleon, for example, was not a Frenchman, but a Corsican, Hitler was not German but Austrian and probably part Jewish, Stalin was not a Russian but a Georgian, while the Cossacks who fought so valiantly for Russia throughout the ages were ethnically mixed.

7.7 THE 'NATION': SUBJECTIVE APPROACH

If none of the objective tests is entirely satisfactory, perhaps one should look for the key in subjective factors – in collective consciousness, in a sense of national identity and of attachment to a people and a homeland distinct from any other. According to the philosopher J.S. Mill, the nation comprised people 'united among themselves by common sympathies . . . which make them . . . desire to be under the same government and desire that it should be government by themselves or a portion of themselves exclusively'.[10] The nineteenth-century historian Ernest Renan located the nation in 'a great solidarity . . . It supposes a past, but it is contained in the present in a tangible fact: the common feeling, the clearly expressed desire to continue life in common'.[11] And W.S. Pillsbury, an American psychologist writing after the First World War, summed up what the nation meant for each member. 'He identifies himself with it as a part of himself, he suffers pain when it is diminished, he rejoices with it as it thrives.'[12] By this test, then, the nation can arouse the kinds of partisan sentiment we usually feel when *our* team, *our* tribe or *our* faith are under pressure.

But these sentiments can be fostered as much by a sudden shared misfortune or predicament as by perceived deprivation at the hands of an oppressor. Years after the founding of Israel, the displaced and dispossessed Arabs in the country still considered themselves to be part of the wider Arab family. But the Six Day War of 1967, which brought them little practical help from their Arab brethren and saw the Israelis in occupation of the West Bank and Gaza, changed all that, helping to solidify among the indigenous peoples a sense of Palestinian self-consciousness. In the case of the even swifter rise of Bangladeshi nationalism, the catalyst was the failure of the government in West Pakistan to disburse to the East the massive aid donated in response to a series of calamitous floods in 1970. The effect was to deepen the sense of alienation growing in the East since the creation of Pakistan, and to strengthen the desire to be rid of the now thoroughly alien government in Islamabad.

Anomalies

Yet even if the nation is best discussed in subjective rather than objective terms, here, too there may be anomalies, especially when membership of a particular nation is claimed on behalf of people who do not wish to be so considered – for example, of assimilated children of immigrants whom others categorise as belonging to a national group with which they no longer wish to identify. If the nub of the nation lies in collective sentiment the obvious question is how does this collective consciousness arise?

Prerequisites

While the earliest manifestations of national self-consciousness may well have occurred within the sovereign states of Western Europe, such sentiments could not have evolved until a kind of cultural fusion had occurred. After all, each state comprised an often lethal cocktail of peoples. In medieval England there were Saxons, Celts of Cornish or Welsh origin and people who spoke French, the English language emerging eventually from a synthesis largely of Saxon and French. In France there were Bretons, Normans, Provençaux, Burgundians, Flemings, Germans, Basques and Catalans, in addition to the French, themselves largely a combination of Gauls and Romans. In Spain the mix comprised people of Roman, Visigothic, Arab and Basque origin as well as peoples of an even older heritage, the Spanish language emerging from Castile. Yet not until well after the various monarchies of these countries had consolidated power could national consciousness develop to any degree, as people's physical horizons were largely confined to a few miles from their place of birth and their intellectual horizons circumscribed by both their inability to read or write and the pervasive teachings of church or mosque.

However, once developments in commerce and communications had made travel easier, at least for Europe's rising middle class, and provincial loyalties were supplanted by a broader sense of obligation to central authority, the potential was there for at least patriotic sentiment, especially in time of inter-state war. After all, as suggested earlier, people do like to support their team, and by the end of the eighteenth century many writers and composers, priests and prelates, traders and merchants had become partners, wittingly or unwittingly, in an effort by officials and administrators to convince fellow citizens that the state and its inhabitants constituted just such a team. Though the process of forging a national identity may have been semi-spontaneous, it was assisted in the eighteenth century by the circulation of political, religious and artistic materials designed to emphasise the differences between 'them' and 'us' and dwelling on 'our' virtues in contrast to 'their' failings. In addition, there was a growing litany of national saints, heroes and martyrs for our emulation, of sinners, villains and reprobates for our censure, as well as anthems, emblems, flags, monuments, shrines and other symbols designed to arouse feelings of solidarity.

The role of the adversary

On the other hand the existence of a suitable adversary which can be portrayed as the national enemy has probably contributed most to the rapid growth of national sentiment. Indeed, nationalism, rather like Communism, with which it has a number of common characteristics, has tended to be a creation of its enemies. That is, it has often arisen in a context of perceived deprivation in which power-holders are unresponsive to pleas for changes in the structure of political or economic power. In this sense national movements – Chechen, Palestinian, Kashmiri, Kosovar, East Timorese, Ogoni or whatever – come to serve as repositories of discontent and instruments for securing what their adherents conceive as their rights, even if based on a highly selective understanding of history. But, of course, in resisting such secessionist movements and in asserting their rights to national sovereignty and territorial integrity, the existing authorities tend to draw on another kind of nationalist sentiment. It is partly because so many national movements define themselves primarily in terms of what they are against that nationalism has come to be associated with so many apparently contradictory political platforms, from extreme left to extreme right, from popular sovereignty to 'ethnic cleansing' and 'the final solution', from the ballot to the bullet, from a policy for political integration and state-making to an agenda for fragmentation and state-breaking.[13]

The Latin American experience

If Anderson is right in his view that modern nationalism first surfaced in Latin America, then he is equating nationalism here with anti-imperialism, anti-colonialism and anti-racism in the form of resistance to discriminatory practices by colonial administrators. But to classify such sentiments as nationalism poses a problem. For these are purely negative manifestations. They are about eliminating something. But removal of the source of the discontent, as when Spain finally relinquished its American colonies and the expatriates lost some of their privileges, does not necessarily produce national solidarity, and in Latin America as in much of Africa, Asia and Eastern Europe narrow parochial or tribal loyalties often prove stronger than loyalty to the nation. And, of course, in many countries – Aghanistan, Sudan, Congo and Yugoslavia, for example – lack of national solidarity can engender bitter and protracted civil conflict.

The revolt of the American colonies

If anti-imperialism was the mainspring for the political turmoil in eighteenth-century Latin America, it was also the rationale for the revolt of the thirteen American colonies. For though many of the complainants were British expatriates, they now saw the British Crown as unrepresentative, exploitative and oppressive. However, once again a successful anti-imperialist strategy failed to produce any feeling of nationhood for some considerable time, what with slave revolts, skirmishes between settlers and Indians, the bloody civil war of the 1860s and the vast cultural and geographical distances and differences between the republics. And when a sense of American nationhood eventually emerged, it required the education system, the media, the manipulation of symbols and rituals and, above all, the existence of perceived adversaries to promote it. First there were the 'heartless' Spanish and British imperialists, then the 'Godless' Nazis followed by the 'Godless' Communists (the most dangerous of them, apparently, Fidel Castro) . . . and now what? Could some prominent Americans be desperately searching for an enemy to try to hold together a Union in danger of falling apart? And if so, could they have found the answer in Islamic fundamentalism?

The French revolution

When it comes to the 'nationalism' of the French revolution, here the adversary was not foreign but domestic. Armed with the ideas of the Enlightenment, the revolutionaries declared war on patronage and privilege in the name of the French 'nation', by which they appear to have meant anyone entitled to French citizenship. Basically their nationalism was an ideology closely bound up with the idea of popular sovereignty. It was an assertion that government should be by consent and that the locus of sovereignty should be transferred from monarch to people. Two problems, however, arose with this formulation, which were to produce unintended political consequences. First, as indicated in chapter 5, 'equality' and 'fraternity', which were also sought by the French revolutionaries, were not easily reconciled with liberty; and, secondly, France was far too large to be run like the Swiss cantons Rousseau so admired and in whose governance theoretically every adult male had a voice. In any case, Rousseau's 'general will' needed interpretation and, as can happen with any philosophical legacy, the self-appointed interpreters tended to be at odds with one another. In fact, the attempt to effect an apparently liberal doctrine met unexpected obstacles and, after lurching from one kind of rule to another, France ended up with the Napoleonic dictatorship.

The Western European experience

But the greater the discord between France's new rulers, the greater their tendency to want to internationalise the struggle against the old order, and thanks to that peculiar institution of revolutionary nationalism, the *levée en masse* (conscription), France could command a formidable array of armed might, as it were, to force the rest of Europe to be free. On the other hand when the peoples who came under French hegemony began to be treated as subordinates, not equals, they sought liberation from their somewhat oppressive liberators and played their part in the final defeat of Napoleon in 1815.[14] Here, however, what had begun as anti-imperialism was to give rise to more positive feelings, and to a sense, ultimately, of national self-consciousness. On the other hand the long-term effects were contradictory. In Western Europe the national idea continued to mean what it had meant for the architects of the French revolution – individual liberties and constitutional guarantees against arbitrary power. Generally speaking that is what they got, and the peoples of Western Europe came to see their states as an expression of their nationhood. However, in Central and Eastern Europe it was different.[15]

Central and Eastern European nationalism

Within the vast empires of the Ottomans, Russians and Austrians as well as in the politically fragmented regions of Italian and German civilisation, the civic virtues of liberal democracy were not the priority for nationalists. What they wanted above all was the removal of all barriers to cultural and linguistic self-expression. It was intolerable that Greeks should have to speak Turkish in official communications, that Poles should have to speak Russian or German, and Czechs to speak German or Hungarian. Equally unacceptable was the idea that Italian- and German-speaking peoples should be parcelled out like pieces on a chessboard among different states – and so the nationalist emphasis shifted from a political/ territorial to a cultural/linguistic concept. In Central and Eastern Europe, nationalist movements sought to redraw the political map along linguistic and cultural lines, and in the century between the 1820s and the 1920s they were on the whole successful. But at a price, to be discussed below.

The Asian/African experience

Though the Japanese victory over Russia in the war of 1904–5, the revolutions in Turkey (1908), Persia (1909) and China (1911) and the anti-colonial revolts in the wake of the outbreak of war in 1914 had boosted the fledgling nationalist movements in Asia and Africa, it was not until after the Second World War that they had any chance of success. It had taken the retreat of Western imperialism in face of Japanese power in the early stages of the war, the West's physical and economic exhaustion at the end of it and the UN Charter's commitment to 'self-determination' to translate what was becoming known as Third World nationalism into political reality. The 1940s saw the first transfers of power in Asia: the 1960s the first transfers in Africa. But the largely arbitrary boundaries drawn when the European colonialists carved out their empires in the eighteenth and nineteenth centuries were to leave a bitter legacy. For many of the new countries were too fragmented in their ethnic, religious or linguistic composition to develop strong nationalist movements after the initial triumph of anti-colonialism, and many succumbed to factionalism, fragmentation and civil war. For many of their leaders, therefore, 'nationalism' was to become associated with the process of nation-building, i.e. of trying to create through myths and symbols a sense of solidarity and of common purpose among diverse and often hostile peoples.[16]

Eastern Europe – post-Communism

Since cultural and linguistic nationalism had flourished in Eastern Europe throughout the nineteenth and early twentieth centuries, it should have come as no surprise that nationalism would again dominate the political agenda with the decline of Moscow's hold over the states of the Communist Warsaw Pact and over the Soviet Union. And as Soviet and Eastern European Communism collapsed, the diverse peoples of the region naturally sought an alternative creed as a basis for solidarity and to provide meaning in a world fraught with doubt. They found it in nationalism, but as in much of Africa and Asia, the patchwork quilt of confessions and ethnic identities in the area threatened to tear apart some of the successor states, and in the case of Yugoslavia the effect was to be especially brutal and bloody.[17]

7.7 IMPLICATIONS FOR WORLD POLITICS

In the first place, national liberation did not necessarily bring about individual liberty, and many people were probably to have less personal, political and economic freedom after independence than before. Secondly, far from resting content with their countries' newly acquired independence, some leaders were hell bent on seizing territory from their neighbours, while depriving their own national minorities of the kinds of right they had claimed for themselves. Such behaviour discredited nationalism in the eyes of many liberals who had originally embraced it, and in turn generated a multiplicity of destabilising claims from so-called suppressed and submerged nationalities. The national principle may have united nineteenth-century Italy and Germany, but has caused the disintegration of far more states and injected fresh uncertainties into the workings of international society. Thirdly, ever since the end of the nineteenth century, ideologues of left and right have hijacked nationalism to suit their various purposes, having capitalised on popular discontents and resentments. In the Communist-ruled states where the leaders, forsaking Marx, paraded themselves as heirs to a nationalist tradition, capitalism and Western imperialism were the proclaimed enemies. In Nazi Germany where nationalism tended to become the ideology of the right, the foes included Socialist as well as Communist, the Jew, the pacifist, the gipsy or the socially inadequate who could be portrayed as having sapped the country of its vitality. In much of post-war Asia and Africa, nationalism served left- and right-wing ideologues, first in the cause of colonial liberation and then against a host of domestic or foreign targets which could be blamed for all or most of the new country's problems. And in the Western democracies, the economic nationalism of protectionism has tended to become fashionable in time of recession.[18]

7.9 THE MANY MEANINGS OF NATIONALISM

To summarise: nationalism is a sufficiently plastic notion to be equated with contradictory phenomena and has at least five different connotations. It is a collective sentiment focusing on and celebrating the political aspirations of a particular people; it is a theory relating to such political aspirations – an exclusive doctrine in the hands of the racist Right, an inclusive concept in the hands of the liberals and democratic Left; it is a political movement – subversive of the state when the aim is secession, supportive when the objective is enhancement or expansion; it is a process, that of nation-building by governments of states attempting to create a unified political entity out of a host of tribal, ethnic and linguistic groupings; and, finally, it is a tool used by governments to justify whatever political or economic policy they choose to identify as being in the national interest.

7.10 'BLOOD' AND BELONGING

Earlier in the chapter the question was posed: cannot many modern nations claim their ancestry from peoples of ancient times? Possibly, which is presumably why Anthony Smith speaks of nation-builders as political archaeologists rediscovering and reinterpreting the past – selectively forgetting as well as remembering in order to regenerate the national community.[19] But clearly, not all modern nations can claim to have had a distant collective ancestry, which is why Michael Ignatieff in a book called *Blood and Belonging* distinguishes between what nowadays is called civic nationalism which maintains that 'the nation should be composed of all those – regardless of . . . gender, language, or ethnicity – who subscribe to the nation's political creed' and ethnic nationalism, which claims that an individual's deepest attachments are inherited, not chosen and that the only people deserving of trust are those of the same culture and blood.[20]

On the other hand, perhaps ethnic nationalism is a misleading term given the degree of inter-marriage, of miscegenation and of illegitimacy throughout the ages, and this is precisely where the element of myth and make-believe comes in. Yugoslav Serbs, Croats and Moslems may have been encouraged to think that they are ethnically distinct, but their differences, exaggerated by self-serving politicians, are slight and to an ethnographer they are all South Slavs, their blood a cocktail of Slav, Turkish, Hungarian, Albanian and Latin. And could it really be that Mussolini, that obese narcissistic little man with the loud voice who created Fascism in Italy, was a true descendant of those Romans that conquered and civilised whole continents? Was Hitler, the little man with a black moustache and an ill-fitting raincoat who invented National Socialism, really a product of Aryan culture and race? And can the Aryans be considered a race at all? And do some of the agnostics who chart Israel's fortunes today have much in common with the twelve desert tribes of biblical times wandering in search of a theocracy? More importantly, perhaps, could any so-called ancestor have thought in terms of the secular territorial state, a standard national language, representative government and some of the other notions contemporary nationalists appear to value?

7.11 THE IMPACT OF NATIONALISM

The impact of nationalism, whether in the form of anti-imperialism, secessionism, irredentism or in its emphasis on national solidarity and pride, has of course been immense. First, as a source of conflict and fragmentation within the state it can invite intervention from outside – either in defence of the status quo or in support of nationalists seeking fundamental change. Second, since cementing a sense of nationhood is often bound up with the existence of an enemy, real or imagined, nationalism has tended to engender new rifts and divisions in international relations. Third, it has been instrumental in redrawing the world political map, especially since 1945 during which time the number of states has more than trebled. Fourth, the nationalism the new states have conveyed to the UN and other international forums has significantly affected the international agenda, bringing LDC economic and political concerns to the fore. Fifth, as nationalism has brought into being several scarcely viable states, the distinction between legal sovereignty and the capacity to exercise it has grown ever wider. In the process the traditional criteria for sovereign recognition have been further undermined.

7.12 THE PERSISTENCE OF NATIONALISM

The persistence of nationalism into the age of interdependence, instant communication and the global market place will have dismayed many liberals for whom nationalism was not only discreditable but also increasingly irrelevant. That it may even have been strengthened by globalisation will have come as an even greater shock. Why, then, does it endure? To this there are two possible sets of answers. One socio-historical and essayed in the writings of Carr, Hobsbawm and Gellner. It holds, broadly, that nationalism is more shallow than the great mass political and religious movements of the past, has produced no grand thinkers and is essentially a short-term phenomenon – the creation of powerful elites who use myths and symbols to rally the masses behind their various purposes. In this view, the elites capitalise on popular discontent arising out of the economic and social insecurities induced by modernisation, but are likely to find their message losing force as we move to an age of supra- and trans-national structures. Indeed, somewhat optimistically, Carr calls his slim volume on the subject, *Nationalism and After*.[21]

A second school stresses psycho-social factors. Anthony Giddens, Walker Connor, John Gray [22] and Anthony Smith suggest that nationalism is no passing fancy but a product of the modern imagination, as much a 'bottom up' as a 'top down' phenomenon, in which people react to the breakdown of traditional communal structures and belief systems by seeking a new kind of community grounded in a sort of secular religion. Further, that like many religions, nationalism can satisfy a range of needs, including the need to belong, transplant itself into different terrains and align itself with diverse political constellations. Moreover, that the need for 'identity', which preceded modernity, will outlive modernity, and that interdependence, technology and the globalised market place far from outdating nationalism make it even more relevant. This is because they all serve to highlight ethnic, cultural and economic difference, while the intrusion of foreign ideas and the homogenising effects of modern industry – people throughout the world are 'popping' similar pills, watching similar movies, eating similar convenience foods, and being dwarfed by similar architectural monstrosities – are often so resented that they create a demand for the distinctive, the local and the specific. Nationalism, in other words, is a vehicle for resisting homogenisation and the growing influence of trans-, supra- and international institutions and processes. In this regard, the internet has the potential for raising national awareness. It is, after all, a potent means by which groups of people with a narrow range of interests and concerns can communicate with each other and imagine a sense of intimacy with or alienation from people whom they have never met.

Thus, as a repository of discontent, a secular religion, an indication of difference and a guarantee of cultural integrity against the threat from the world of the Big Mac and Coca-colonialism, nationalism continues to offer a vision of the good life, secured through the attainment of certain political objectives. In particular, it contests the very interdependence that is sometimes seen to threaten group identity – though for how long is debatable.

NOTES

1. I am indebted to my daughter Tiffany for these observations, which are to be found in her forthcoming article for the *Shakespearean Quarterly*, '"You that walk i'th Galleries": Standing and walking in the Galleries of the Globe Theatre.'
2. Hobsbawm, E., 'Introduction: Inventing Traditions', in Hobsbawm, E. and Ranger, T. (eds), *The Invention of Tradition*, Cambridge, Cambridge University Press, 1983, pp. 1–14.
3. Vickers, M., *Between Serb and Albanian: A History of Kosovo*, London, Hurst, 1998, pp. 12–16.
4. London, Verso, 1991, pp. 47–58.
5. Gellner, E., *Nations and Nationalism*, Oxford, Blackwell, 1992.
6. Cambridge, Cambridge University Press, 1990, p. 75.
7. Petti, A.E., *English Literary Hands from Chaucer to Dryden*, Cambridge, Mass., Harvard University Press, 1977, p. 87.
8. See for example Smith, A.D., *The Ethnic Origins of Nations*, Oxford, Blackwell, 1986 and his essay on 'The origins of nations' in *Ethnic and Racial Studies*, vol. 12, no. 3, pp. 340–67.
9. See for example Poliakov, L., *The Aryan Myth: A History of Racist and Nationalist Ideas in Europe*, New York, 1974.
10. Mill, J.S., *Utilitarianism, Liberty and Representative Government*, London, Dent, 1910, pp. 365–6.
11. Quoted in Zimmern, A., *Modern Political Doctrines*, New York, Oxford University Press, 1939, pp. 202–5.
12. Pillsbury, W.D., *Psychology of Nations*, London, Macmillan, 1919, p. 59.

13. Hobsbawm, E., op. cit., especially pp. 163–72.
14. On the nationalist ramifications of the attempt to spread the French revolutionary idea see for example Davies, N., *Europe: A History*, London, Pimlico, 1997, pp. 725–57.
15. The contrast between Western and Eastern European conceptions of nationalism are elaborated in Davies, N., op. cit., pp. 812–35.
16. See for example Kedourie, E. (ed.), *Nationalism in Asia and Africa*, London, Weidenfeld & Nicolson, 1971.
17. See for example Kemp, W., *Nationalism and Communism in Eastern Europe and the Soviet Union: A Basic Contradiction?*, Basingstoke, Macmillan, 1999, pp. 208–20, and also Duncan, R.W. and Holman, P.G. (eds), *Ethnic Nationalism and Regional Conflict: The Former Soviet Union and Yugoslavia*, Oxford, Westview Press, 1994.
18. See for example Keynes, J.M., 'National Self-sufficiency', *Yale Review*, vol. 22, 1933, pp. 755–67, and also Mayall, J., *Nationalism and International Society*, Cambridge, Cambridge University Press, 1990.
19. Smith, A.D., 'Gastronomy or geology? The role of nationalism in the reconstruction of nations', in *Nations and Nationalism*, vol. 1, part 1, March 1995.
20. London, Oxford University Press, 1995.
21. London, Macmillan, 1945.
22. See for example Giddens, A., *The Nation-State and Violence*, Cambridge, Polity Press, 1985; Connor, W., *Ethno-Nationalism: The Quest for Understanding*, Princeton, New Jersey, Princeton University Press, 1994, and Gray J., 'The end of History – or of Liberalism?', in *The National Review*, 27 October 1989, pp. 33–5.

CHAPTER 8

THE MAKING OF FOREIGN POLICY

It is the fashion among the the more 'trendy' teachers of International Relations to claim that domestic and foreign policy are so closely intertwined that there is little point in attempting to differentiate between them. And yet almost anyone familiar with the layout of a newspaper or of a radio or television bulletin will know the difference between a foreign and a domestic news story. The fact, moreover, that most countries have a Foreign Office to deal with some kinds of issues and a Home Office to consider others in itself suggests a significant differentiation of function. The irony is that though the 'trendies' may regard domestic and foreign policy as one, the American electorate in the presidential elections of 1992 and 1996 were able to draw a distinction, for in voting for Clinton many understood that they were backing a man who, unlike former President George Bush, had promised to put domestic affairs first (though perhaps they did not appreciate at the time just what kinds of affairs he might have had in mind).

If lay persons can tell the difference, why not some of those with a claim to expertise on these matters? Part of the problem, as so often in this subject, is linguistic. Clearly, foreign policy is one of those tantalising concepts with multiple meanings and whose very existence seems designed only to torment the student of IR. It would seem, however, to contain a core notion, that is, of an activity of government directed at and largely implemented in an environment external to the state in question.

8.1 FOREIGN POLICY: DIVERSE MEANINGS

But what kind of endeavour is foreign policy-making? Is it like creating and implementing a Grand Design, as in architecture? Is it similar to navigation, in which the ship of state has to be manoeuvred towards some given destination? Are its major concerns diagnosis and prescription, as in medicine? Or is it more akin to mechanics whereby a given stimulus produces an automatic response? In fact, as a process it would appear to encompass planning, analysis, steering and reaction. But foreign policy-making is more than a process. And this is where linguistic analysis can be of assistance. For foreign policy can connote one of a number of different things.

Objectives

It can refer to the objectives sought by political authorities in the arena beyond a country's national jurisdiction. Such purposes can be of different degrees of precision – ranging from the abstract, such as prestige and national honour, to the concrete, as for example the retention or restoration of territory belonging to another power; positive, by way of seeking to attain something, or negative, designed to deprive another of something; long-term, relating to some distant aspiration, or short-term, concerned with the more immediate; conservative, attached to the status quo, or revisionist, working for a more favourable balance of world power.

Principles

Secondly, foreign policy can mean the norms and principles from which such goals are derived, ranging from the fundamental precepts of national self-preservation and enhancement to the more congenial canons of respect for international law, peaceful coexistence between ideological rivals, care for the environment, assistance for the needy and so on. Such norms may be explicit – for example, Imperial Preference (the economic orthodoxy of the British Empire), Manifest Destiny (the political orthodoxy of nineteenth- and early twentieth-century America), Lebensraum ('living space' – the basis of Nazi expansionism), Islamic Fundamentalism, Zionism, Marxism–Leninism. Alternatively, they may be encapsulated in some strategic or geopolitical theory, as for example the Monroe Doctrine, whereby Washington insisted on the Europeans keeping out of Latin American affairs in return for an American commitment not to intervene in Europe; 'containment', according to which the US sought to counteract Soviet influence after the Second World War, or the 'domino theory' by which Washington was persuaded that once North Vietnam succumbed to Communism, the rest of South-east Asia and beyond would be bound to follow, falling like dominoes. A significant strand, moreover, in NATO's concerns for the Kosovars which led to its bombardment in 1999 of Yugoslav targets was the fear that if Kosovo were 'ethnically cleansed', its neighbours would feel a 'domino effect', possibly leading to a much wider Balkan conflagration. NATO's critics, of course, argued that the bombardment itself produced the much feared 'domino effect'.

Means

Thirdly, foreign policy can refer to the inventory of methods, measures, stratagems, tactics and devices by which political authorities seek to obtain their goals in the international arena. These can range from coercive, such as the threat, display or use of force to the gently persuasive – a plea for support, an appeal to sentiment based on ideological or religious affinity, kith and kin and so forth.

Positions/decisions/reactions

Fourthly, foreign policy can refer to a sequence of positions or courses of action in pursuit of a goal or goals or with reference to a particular area. Britain's policy, say, in respect of the European Monetary Union would come into this category. Fifthly, it can refer to a particular decision or action undertaken in pursuit of a particular objective, for example the British decision to respond to General Abacha's brutal and corrupt activities in Nigeria by banning arms sales to but not oil imports from the country to hasten a return to democracy. Sixthly, it can refer to an accumulation of piecemeal and pragmatic day-to-day reactions to situations, events and pressures emanating from the international arena. Nor does this list exhaust the possible meanings of the term 'foreign policy'.

8.2 A DISTINCT FOREIGN POLICY ARENA?

Is the notion of a distinct foreign policy arena as obsolete as it is ambiguous? Pluralists like James Rosenau and John Burton claim that it is.[1] And on two broad grounds. First, that the very idea of foreign policy suggests a rational and considered activity of government when increasingly policy instigations come from outside government, through what Andrew Scott calls 'informal access' or 'informal penetration', when an administration's ability to determine its own destiny is undermined, accidentally or deliberately, by forces beyond its control.[2] In other words, that sub-, trans-, inter- or supranational bodies set the agenda, bypassing government and subverting the traditional centres of political authority. Secondly, that in an age of increasing cross-frontier ties, multilateral diplomacy, globalised markets, information systems and environmental concerns, all policy, whatever its source, has internal as well as external dimensions and thus any attempt at a rigid distinction is misconceived.

They would point out, for example, that the failure of a nation's bankers and businessmen to put their economic houses in order has profound international ramifications; that a country's lax attitude to feeding and slaughtering possibly infected cattle can have serious repercussions on export sales and consumption patterns; that 'ethnic cleansing' whether in Rwanda, Bosnia or Kosovo has enormous consequences abroad, not least in terms of forced migration and military responses, and that the question of 'global warming' has domestic as well as international implications.

They would claim, moreover, that this interweaving of domestic and foreign policy is by no means new and that the distinction between the two dimensions of policy has long been artificial and unreal.

For did not sudden changes in domestic economic policy often have foreign repercussions even before the removal of Britain's Corn Laws in the 1840s? Was there not a close connection between Washington's decision to levy high tariffs in the 1920s and the ensuing world depression and perhaps fascism, too; and was there not some correlation between the removal of American price controls in 1946 and the widening of the 'dollar gap', which created a world economic crisis requiring in turn massive aid to Washington's Western allies? At the same time, pluralists would contend, what begins as a domestic obsession, for example, Hitler's hatred of the Jews, Netenyahu's apparent indifference to the fate of the Palestinians or Milosevic's contempt for the Albanian Kosovars can produce serious and profound international consequences.

In similar vein they would hold that a policy pursued in the arena beyond a state's jurisdiction can have serious effects within it, say, on its currency reserves or balance of trade, even on the popularity or perceived legitimacy of its government. For example, President Carter's decision to embargo grain sales to the Soviet Union following that country's intervention in Afghanistan in 1979 so alienated the farmers of the American mid-West that it may have cost him the Presidency when he stood for re-election the following year. By the same token, whenever a country is in conflict with its neighbours, the tourist trade suffers, which can mean a serious loss of revenue, as India and Pakistan, Ethiopia and Eritrea, to say nothing of the countries in the vicinity of former Yugoslavia have learned to their cost. But, of course, a successful war or some other decisive action overseas can boost a government's approval rating, and leaders will often pursue foreign adventures or diversions in the hope of obtaining domestic advantage.

As for EU directives on such subjects as beef cattle exports, food hygiene, the conservation of fish stocks, working hours, Sunday trading, employment law, weights and measures, seat belts: these, the pluralists would claim, defy conventional categories. Are these not simultaneously external and domestic policies?

Certainly, the pluralists have a point. Many governments tend to react to events rather than initiating policy, and as the actors, concerns and instruments of foreign policy greatly expand, it is probably unwise to separate totally a government's domestic from its foreign policy. Clearly, there are more and more grey areas as 'low' politics – i.e. economic, social and culural issues – increasingly intrude on an agenda once monopolised by 'high' politics – i.e. militarily related matters. On the other hand, the pluralists probably take their point a little too far. For rather like knowledge, which is a unity, but tends to be segmented into various subject specialisms, so policy, which might similarly be regarded as one, is probably best charted and understood if compartmentalised.

8.3 FOREIGN POLICY FORMULATION

But even if the distinction between domestic and foreign policy is today less clear-cut than it once was, the formulation and reporting of the latter still tends to be in a class by itself. Often it has to be devised under the pressure of events at great speed, yet with insufficient information for a considered assessment, which can occasion serious errors of judgement and a failure to think things through. Moreover, because of the security implications, foreign policy tends to be drafted in greater secrecy and by fewer people than for domestic policy.[3] Meanwhile, the various specialised Departments associated with it generally ensure that information which might prove useful to a potential enemy is concealed from popular scrutiny, which is no doubt why governments are generally anxious to muzzle, prosecute or extradite intelligence agents who 'spill too many beans'.

But if there still is such a thing as foreign policy-making, must a country always have one? Until the Western powers forced their attentions on Japan and China in the mid-nineteenth century, these countries had been able to isolate themselves from world affairs. And in 1917 immediately after the Bolshevik Revolution, Soviet Foreign Commissar (Minister) Trotsky was preparing to, in his words, 'shut up shop', assuming that in a post-revolutionary Communist world no foreign policy would be necessary.[4] But within days he was forced to admit that his country would after all need a foreign policy. Why? Not only because the 'inevitable' world revolution had failed to materialise but because, with the international system now encompassing the planet, a state was no longer able to escape its neighbours, near or far. It had to continually conserve, adjust or change the balance vis-à-vis friend and foe, if only to find some basis for interaction, and this calls for precisely the kinds of undertakings that go under the name of foreign policy.

Yet given that policy-makers have only finite resources and limited control over the international environment, how do they attempt to arrive at an appropriate policy? Clearly this depends in part on personalities, their degree of competence and frame of reference, and these are broadly determined by the nature of the political system.[5] The way foreign policy is formulated depends in part on whether a country is a democracy, under a Party dictatorship or ruled by monarch, sheikh, General or civilian despot.

On the other hand a country's political structure can only be a rough guide to decision-making responsibility, not least because formal positions and titles are not always reliable indicators of effective power. When, for instance, in the late 1950s Andrei Gromyko became Soviet Foreign Minister, he was not expected to have a mind of his own. As Party leader Khrushchev revealed, Gromyko 'does exactly what we [i.e. the Politburo] tell him and if he doesn't we get a new foreign minister'.[6] Later Gromyko was to acquire much greater responsibility, but his initial role in decision-making was clearly miniscule. And when Washington took the decision to bomb Cambodia during the Vietnam War, Secretary of State William Rogers was not in the know. Moreover, the Prime Ministers, Presidents, monarchs and miscellaneous rulers who nominally give the orders may also have rather less say than is commonly assumed. For instance, until the final surrender to the Americans, Japan's Emperor Hirohito seems to have had comparatively little impact on foreign policy, despite his semi-divine status, whereas the rather less divine Margaret Thatcher and her friend Lee Kuan Yew in Singapore usually got the compliant cabinet they wanted and their views would tend to prevail.

But who makes the operative decisions is not just a matter of constitutional structures and personalities. It is also a product of systems, pressures and institutions. As issues become more complex, foreign policy is seen to require, in virtually every political system, a host of organisations and agencies to gather relevant information, to find the necessary expertise to interpret and assess the evidence and to advise the decision-makers. In the process the political agenda or the policies which emerge may be markedly affected by people working behind the scenes.

8.4 THE NATIONAL INTEREST

Yet whether or not the outcome of many or comparatively few hands, foreign policy formulation is a product of a particular political culture and set of beliefs and generally centres around yet another ambiguous concept – the national interest. This is a term fraught with all manner of conceptual booby traps, and it is not entirely certain that most of those who have held the highest office could give a coherent account of what the term is supposed to mean. It does, however, serve as a kind of intellectual core around which policy is framed and suggests the existence of objectives which can be identified and promoted by enlightened statesmen and rational observers.[7] And since its concern is generally with both what we want and what we are prepared to settle for, it has 'aspirational' as well as 'operational' dimensions. As the concept is also rather nebulous, it tends to be framed according to its user's intent – employed by

governments to give legitimacy to their external purposes and by opposi-
tions to imply an objective standard from which the government has
fallen short. After all, since the claim to be acting in the nation's interest
plays into the widespread notion that the nation should be the citizen's
ultimate concern, its exponents often use the term to try to place their
chosen policy, as it were, beyond scrutiny. It thus has a 'polemical' as well
as an 'aspirational' and 'operational' application.[8] But can so elastic a
concept have any settled meaning at all?

At the very least it must have two separate if related connotations,
stemming from the ambiguity of the word 'national'. Does it pertain to
the state or to the people of the state? Here there is ample room for myth-
making as well as semantic sophistry. As for interests, is their existence
'objective' – i.e. relating to ultimate goals independent of but discoverable
by policy-makers through systematic enquiry – or 'subjective' – i.e.
dependent on the preferences and prejudices of each administration?
Realists tend to be 'objectivists', pluralists 'subjectivists'. Certainly in the
world of personified abstractions in which states are presumed to exist
legally, diplomatically and politically, the 'national interest' is generally
deemed to have objective reality. In fact, however, it is what is perceived
as the relevant interests which count, and, of course, in their perceptions,
policy-makers are informed, misinformed, influenced or prejudiced by all
kinds of considerations. Marxists, believing that all perceptions are class-
based, claim that what is presented as the national interest is in fact the
interest of the ruling class. And even non-Marxists might agree that too
many governments equate the administration's interest with that of the
state. For yet others, conceptions of national interest are bound up with
personal preoccupations, regional bias, religious fanaticism, ideological
zeal or gender-based considerations – in particular the idea that a woman
Prime Minister or President has, if anything, to be as tough as if not
tougher than a man, and if Mmes Thatcher, Meir, Gandhi, Bhutto,
Hassina, Bandaranaike, Cumaratunga, Campbell, Ciller, Plavsic and Co.
are anything to go by, it could well be true.

On the other hand, if the national interest is merely what politicians say
it is, and subject to the vagaries of political circumstance, the concept can
offer no practical guidelines or prescriptions for the policy-maker and
provide little or no basis for academic analysis. Indeed, on this understanding, neither statesman nor scholar would be profitably engaged in
attempting to study it.

8.5 SHAPING NATIONAL INTEREST

History and geography

In fact, of course, politicians are not by and large unconstrained actors on a level playing field, and foreign policy-making does not arise in a vacuum. In the first place, its formulation tends to reflect changes in both domestic and international military, political or economic circumstance – the advent, say, of a new government with a radical agenda, the end of a cold war, plunging stock markets, a series of natural disasters, a rise in international terrorism, etc. Secondly, the interplay between the enduring features of the international system and the geopolitical circumstance of a particular country tends to give foreign policy a degree of continuity, regardless of belief systems and personalities. For instance, the people of a particular land mass with relatively unchanging neighbours, near and far, will often inherit a framework of perceptions, aspirations, apprehensions and expectations about the world,[9] and in this sense the process of defining national interest acquires an historical dimension.

In illustration of this last point, a couple of examples can be taken from recent and current events. First, in a country like Iran, recent interpretations of the national interest have to be seen against the background of centuries of interference by the British, the Russians and, latterly, the Americans. In short, Teheran since the Shah's overthrow could afford to be neither pro-Western nor pro-Communist, and the emphasis on Islam was a way of disengaging the country from its often humiliating past and providing a new leadership role for itself. Then, as for the international implications regarding the conflict over Kosovo, this cannot really be understood without reference to the semi-mythical defeat of the Serbs by the Ottoman Turks in 1389, the favoured position in the Ottoman Empire of the Albanians, who converted to Islam, and the decision of the Powers who determined the contours of the Albanian state after both world wars to exclude the Albanian Kosovars from it. Thus both history and geography affect perceptions of national interest.

Influential individuals, lobbies and pressure groups

Particular formulations of the national interest can also be shaped or reshaped by influential individuals within government, and in particular by strategically placed civil servants. Britain's policy in turning a blind eye to the activities of those illegally ferrying arms to Sierra Leone during its recent civil war seems to have been fashioned by diplomats or Foreign Office officials, and it is not even clear if Foreign Secretary Robin Cook knew what was being done in Britain's name. They can also be moulded by people outside of government – by close relatives such as Hillary Clinton and Mark Thatcher, by personal private secretaries who can set the agenda and even, on occasion, by lovers (often the same thing as personal private secretaries). They can also be fashioned by pressure groups and lobbies (even authoritarian regimes have their military or industrial complexes), and increasingly, too, the media can set the agenda. Successive French governments would hardly have been so wedded to the Common Agricultural Tariff had not the French farmers been such an influential lobby, with powerful backing from the press. And, of course, successive US governments have bowed to pressures from Zionist, cotton and oil lobbyists in pursuit of Middle Eastern policy. All three lobbies were influential in Washington's decision to deny funding for Nasser's Aswan Dam electrification and irrigation project in 1956.

8.6 PRIORITIES

To give meaning to the concept of the national interest, governments sooner or later have to sort out the 'vital' interests for which in the final analysis they may well be prepared to use force from the 'secondary', those deemed to be of lesser importance and from which ultimately they could retreat. Though priorities can alter over time, in accordance with changing conditions and perceptions, they are shaped by the various demands placed on governments by constituencies, both external and internal.

Security: military and political

Despite Keohane and Nye's claim about the disappearance of a hierarchy of issues,[10] generally speaking, most governments continue to place a high value on sovereignty and territorial integrity. What has changed is the interpretation of 'security'. Till recently it was understood as a function largely of military strength. Today, however, given that security can be jeopardised from within as well as between states, many understand the maintenance of physical integrity in political, economic and diplomatic terms. For example, awesome military strength alone could not preserve the Soviet state, while countries with but a fraction of the armed might of the former Communist power survive and prosper, in large part because of the judicious diplomatic, economic and other policies of their governments. In any case, for a small country, such as Honduras or Nicaragua, vulnerable to the ravages of nature as well as of man, the guarantee of ample clear water supplies may well be as much a security as an economic priority.

Independence

Also high on the list of most interpretations of national interest is the notion of independence, or rather of as much freedom from outside interference as is possible in an interdependent world in which networks of mutual obligations and commitments tend to constrain political action. If we imagine a critically self-aware child growing up in a rather restricted household, the paradox of an existence both independent and interdependent becomes clear. Britain, for instance, is able to retain its sovereign independence for certain purposes, even though it is interlinked in a complex web of interconnections with its partners in the European Union, NATO, the Commonwealth and a host of other inter- and transnational bodies. Independence and interdependence need not be mutually exclusive.

Prestige

A further perceived interest relates to the esteem in which a country is held. At one time prestige was equated with power, authority, status and, above all, military repute, and governments would go to great lengths to preserve or restore their military reputation. The surrender of the French army in 1940 proved so humiliating as to inspire its much more brutal, though equally unavailing, tactics in Indochina and Algeria in the 1950s and 1960s in a vain attempt to restore its good standing.[11] President Kennedy's willingness to go to the brink of nuclear war to rid Cuba of Soviet missiles in 1962 is said to have been influenced by the mishandling and failure of the abortive American landing in Cuba's Bay of Pigs the previous year.[12] Today, however, in an age of mass communications and literacy, the question of credibility seems, if anything, even more important than military repute. For many a developing country the mere fact of participation in the UN General Assembly, where its vote carries as much weight as that of the US, Russia or China, is an indication of esteem. But for those powers with a global reach, the credibility of commitments is critical, for if they make threats which they fail to follow up in the short- or long-term or commitments which they then renege on, their integrity is thrown in doubt and their reputation suffers accordingly. It was partly out of concern for its credibility that NATO, having issued repeated 'last warnings' to Milosevic, embarked on its controversial bombing campaign to try to end 'ethnic cleansing' in Kosovo.

But what happens when a country makes a commitment which turns out to be excessively costly and manifestly unsuccessful? While at Harvard in the mid-1960s, the author discussed the question of Washington's support of South Vietnam with Henry Kissinger, then a professor of International Politics, before becoming US National Security advisor and Secretary of State. Originally strongly opposed to the commitment to Saigon on the grounds that it was very unpromising terrain from which to resist Communism, he was then of the opinion that Washington had to live with the consequences and to 'soldier on' with a flawed policy. 'To give in now,' he said, 'would ... suggest that American commitments aren't worth anything', and the country would 'be seen as yielding to pressure from campus militants and left-wing ideologues'. To my suggestion that Vietnam was a war the US could not win Kissinger said, 'if you can tell me how we can get out of it with honour, I'd be delighted to pass your recommendation on to the White House'; but to the contention that Washington was unlikely to get out of Vietnam with honour, that the later the withdrawal the greater the dishonour, he had no answer. In fact, by continuing the conflict, losing it and then having to abandon its Vietnamese allies, the US was humiliated (even if Kissinger collected a Nobel peace prize shortly before America's withdrawal), with long-lasting consequences. Thus, prestige, credibility, esteem and self-esteem matter, and an unwise commitment raised to the status of a vital interest can end in ignominious defeat.

Preserving a stake in the international system

Somewhat less abstract than prestige is the concern for national welfare, including the maintainance of internal order, a guarantee of the requisite essentials of social life – food, water and shelter – and the preservation of whatever stake a state may have in the international system, that is to say, the rights, privileges, assets and amenities they enjoy beyond their frontiers. These would include, first, their strategic interests – the security of allies and alliances, overseas possessions, bases and staging posts, communications with overseas markets and sources of supply, and the maintenance of a favourable perceived global or regional balance. Secondly, their political interests, in particular the maintenance of a type of international order consistent with their political ideals and structures. Thirdly, their economic interests, and in particular the maintenance and enhancement of the country's share in world trade and investment. And in time of religious or ideological polarisation they would also include the projection and protection of a value system against alien intrusions.

8.7 A RATIONAL ENDEAVOUR?

In practice, the ordering and interpretation of national interests are matters for argument. Whether guns take precedence over butter, conflict over cooperation, confrontation over appeasement, and whether security is to be sought through strength, negotiation, cajolery or non-involvement has to be thrashed out by the decision-makers. It used to be assumed that such discussion proceeded from a cost/benefit calculus and a serious evaluation of possible options after a thoroughgoing assessment of relative capabilities and intentions. Often this does happen, but by no means always.

The unforeseen

Sometimes there just is not time to consider all available options. An unforeseen crisis – the bombing of Pearl Harbor, say, the North Korean incursion into the South, the Argentinian landing in the Falklands or Iraq's invasion of Kuwait – can occur overnight requiring an immediate reaction, often taken under stress and in ignorance of the full facts.

The mistaken

At other times rational decision-making may be hampered by the cumulative effects of previous mistaken policies, from which a state might find it difficult to extricate itself. For example, Washington's erroneous belief that the Communist world was somehow monolithic and united was to lead to a foolhardy and ultimately futile policy in Vietnam. Again, in redefining Israel's security needs, the Likud government under Prime Minister Netenyahu was merely to compound the very security problems his tough policies were designed to alleviate. And, of course, NATO's decision to incorporate into its membership former Soviet allies only two weeks before launching its offensive against Yugoslavia could only weaken ties between the NATO countries and Russia, Serbia's traditional protector, and complicate NATO's military and political campaign.

The contradictory

A further impediment to rational policy can stem from the attempt to implement contradictory and incompatible goals. Though this might result from a failure of proper coordination, more often than not it proceeds from loose thinking. 'Peace' and 'security', for instance, are not necessarily compatible, even if governments claim to be pursuing both. When, for example, Britain's Prime Minister Chamberlain returned from a meeting with Hitler in September 1938, the 'peace in our time' he claimed to have secured at Munich was bought at the expense of Europe's security in that it allowed Germany to annexe that part of Czechoslovakia containing one of Europe's most important arsenals, one of its best equipped air forces and 35 military divisions – all of which contributed greatly to the Nazi war machine. By the same token, going to war may be a way of safeguarding security in the long run. That, at least, is what the Israelis felt after joining battle against Egypt in 1956.

'Pulling and hauling'

The desire for consensus may introduce other irrationalities into the decision-making process. For example, Graham Allison in his *Essence of Decision*, which deals with the Cuban missile crisis,[13] stresses the degree to which policy outcomes can be more a matter of chance than of serious deliberation. For where policy is devised by what he terms 'organisational process', and here would appear to have the US particularly in mind, decisions are the product not of choice but of a complex bargaining process involving 'pulling and hauling' between the representatives of different government departments each functioning according to standard operating procedures. What results is a policy which may satisfy no one but, in the jargon, 'satisfices'.[14] That is, it represents the lowest common denominator – a policy which no one is especially happy with but to which no one strongly objects. And where decision-making proceeds from what Allison dubs 'bureaucratic politics', where the various, possibly contradictory personal, professional and political objectives of key individuals in administration enter into the relevant discussions, the policy which ultimately emerges may well be one in which individual preferences and prejudices, including those of the leader and the foreign minister, are entirely submerged. US Presidents, in other words, do not always get their way in foreign policy.

Fragmented responsibilities and processes

In another study, *Understanding Foreign Policy*,[15] one of the editors, Michael Clarke, suggests that the process of decision-making can sometimes be even less rational than that depicted by Allison. He argues that in a world in which the foreign affairs arena has broadened to encompass a host of political, economic, military, diplomatic, legal, scientific, technological, cultural and even sporting activities, few decisions of consequence can be traceable to particular personalities. For foreign policy-making now can involve so many different hands – informants, advisors, envoys, negotiators as well as official decision-makers – that it is sometimes difficult for even the participants to discover who precisely is responsible for what policy.

Moreover, says Clarke, what appears to be a 'decision' may in fact lack that element of conscious choice and selectivity normally conveyed by that term. It may be the effect of habit, of inertia or of mindless routines and standard practices, as when a given aid programme is maintained regardless of significant changes in economic circumstance and bilateral relations. It may be the product of a fragmented process in which minor officials make a series of minor decisions the cumulative effect of which is to produce a momentum in favour of a particular course of action, but which no one in particular has willed. For example, the unplanned and unwelcome chill in East–West relations in the mid-1970s appears to have been the product of a combination of actions, no one of which was particularly significant in itself, taken in the wake of the fall of Nixon after the Watergate break-in.

Tunnel visions and overseas temptations

Even where particular foreign policy outcomes can be easily traced to particular individuals, it cannot be assumed, according to Clarke, that either rationality or 'the national interest', in some sense, have necessarily prevailed. All too frequently rational decision-making is impaired, as indicated earlier, by false reports and further marred by misperception, prejudice, lack of understanding or empathy, wishful thinking and the kind of intellectual short-sightedness that goes under the name of 'tunnel vision'. Here one thinks, for instance, of Stalin's dogged conviction after his quarrel with Tito in 1948 that Yugoslavia must return to the Soviet fold because he believed it was quite impossible for a Communist-ruled state to be anti-Soviet; of Prime Minister Anthony Eden's dogmatic insistence that Egypt's President Nasser was another Hitler in the making – a delusion which led in 1956 to Britain's counter-productive invasion of Suez, or of the dogma of successive US administrations that Castro was far more brutal than Pinochet, 'Papa Doc' Duvalier, 'Baby Doc', Rios Montt, Somoza and all the other Central and Latin American dictators put together. Nor should one overlook the impact on policy of domestic electoral considerations. The desire to be seen as 'doing something' so as to enhance personal or party fortunes or to placate a particular interest group may be the mainspring, say, for a foreign policy pronouncement, overseas trip or adventure. Bill Clinton is only the latest leader whose enthusiasm for overseas initiatives seems to grow whenever he is in trouble at home.

8.8 THE ROLE OF LEADERS

Even though leaders tend to exaggerate their own role in getting things done and to take the credit for popular and successful policies instigated by others, their room for manoeuvre is, in fact, rather more limited in external than in domestic policy. A variety of geopolitical, technical, military, economic and psychosocial factors act as physical constraints, affecting their capabilities as well as their proficiency in mobilising them. There are, in addition, legal and perceived moral obligations, to be discussed in the next chapter, which circumscribe actions and affect political will and intentions. As F.S. Northedge puts it: 'Effective freedom in foreign affairs ... is the capacity to choose between relatively few options'.[16] Accordingly, after an initial attempt at setting the foreign policy agenda, many leaders settle into the role of pragmatic operator rather than grand strategist, adjusting commitments to capabilities and aspirations to practicalities. Here short-term expedients to buy time, to sow confusion among enemies and reassure friends or simply to avoid having to make a decision at all are substituted for principle, even if the official rhetoric suggests purposeful activity.

This is not to say that the age of the Great Leader has entirely disappeared. After all, Yasser Arafat was able to devise and implement a plan for creating the Palestinian nation; in Serbia, Milosevic, and in Croatia, Tudjman, in their ruthless way succeeded in uniting their ethnic and religious kinsfolk across frontiers; the Ayatollah Khomeini was able to spread a highly politicised version of Islam well beyond the confines of his country. And, of course, there are still visionaries, like Maurice Schumann, who dreamed up the European Coal and Steel Community, thereby laying the groundwork for a host of novel European institutions.

In a world, moreover, in which the forces of international integration are constantly vying with the factors of national disintegration, opportunities for high-profile political activity are not lacking, even if they are not always seized. And in crisis situations when there are heightened threat perceptions and serious time constraints, leaders are often well placed to, as it were, impose their particular stamp on history, as, for example, Gorbachev in the Soviet Union, Lee Kuan Yew in Singapore, Nelson Mandela in South Africa, and, in his own way, Augusto Pinochet in Chile.

On the other hand, the complexities of modern statecraft and the fact that a post-colonial, post-Communist era leaves comparatively little scope for political messiahs and charismatic rulers seem recently to have produced a shift away from the kind of high-profile, adventurous leadership once so common. Moreover, as time seems to have dented the reputations of many of the 'giants' of recent times, and idols from Kennedy to Gorbachev and Gandhi to Mao – of all of whom so much was expected – crumble under scrutiny, there is not perhaps the same incentive as before for political heroics.

What, then, are we to conclude? Are 'great men' the motive force behind history, as the nineteenth-century literary historian Thomas Carlyle suggested, or was the late Harold Macmillan nearer the mark when he claimed that the most difficult things an administration has to face are 'events'? Did Chamberlain mould or reflect British opinion in appeasing Hitler? Was Churchill's role in Britain's war effort critical or did he merely, as he claimed with unaccustomed modesty, give the 'roar' to 'the British lion'? Did Gorbachev kill European Communism and with it the cold war or was he the instrument of an historical process already underway? Such thorny issues will doubtless long continue to be hotly debated, and though John Garnett has suggested that 'policy-makers are never as free as their critics think they are'[17] they will always be expected to seek that precarious balance between freedom and constraint, even if they never quite find it.

NOTES

1. See for example Burton, J., *World Society*, London, Cambridge University Press, 1972; and Rosenau, J. (ed.), *The Scientific Study of Foreign Policy*, New York, Free Press, 1971.
2. *The Revolution in Statecraft*, New York, Random House, 1965.
3. Franck, T. and Weisband, E. (eds), *Secrecy and Foreign Policy*, New York, Oxford University Press, 1974.
4. Quoted in Carr, E.H., *The Bolshevik Revolution, Vol. III*, Harmondsworth, Penguin, 1966, p. 28.
5. For a critical review of the literature on the role of personality in politics, see Rosenau, J. (ed.), op. cit., pp. 239–49.
6. Quoted in Kissinger, H., *The White House Years*, Boston, 1979, p. 788.
7. See for example Stern, G., *Leaders and Leadership*, London, LSE/BBC World Service, 1993, pp. 185–91.
8. The terms are from Frankel, J., *The National Interest*, London, Pall Mall, 1970.
9. Northedge, F.S., 'The Nature of Foreign Policy' in Northedge, F.S. (ed.), *The Foreign Policies of the Powers*, London, Faber, 1974, pp. 13–14.
10. *Power and Interdependence: World Politics in Transition*, Boston, Little, Brown, 1977.
11. Thornton, A. P., *Imperialism in the Twentieth Century*, London, Macmillan, 1980, pp. 290–3.
12. See, for example, Allison, G., *Essence of Decision*, Boston, Little, Brown, 1971.
13. Ibid.
14. The phrase was coined by Herbert Simon. See his *Administrative Behaviour*, New York, Macmillan, 1959.

15. Clarke, M. and White, B. (eds), *Understanding Foreign Policy*, Aldershot, Elgar, 1989.

16. Northedge, F.S. (ed.), op. cit., p. 16.

17. Garnett, J., *Commonsense and the Theory of International Relations*, London, Macmillan, 1984, p. 61.

PART IV

INTER-STATE BEHAVIOUR

CHAPTER 9

CONSTRAINTS AND RULES OF INTERNATIONAL BEHAVIOUR

In this chapter we come to the paradox at the heart of what is sometimes called 'the English School' approach – the notion of 'ordered anarchy' or 'anarchical society'.[1] While not necessarily breaking with Realism, in that it still places the state, national interest and balance of power at the centre of the study, it nonetheless subjects all three concepts to critical scrutiny, stresses the importance of reciprocity in international affairs and challenges the notion that the international arena must necessarily be more conflict-prone than the domestic.

From the late 1930s to the late 1950s when the world lurched from one political or economic crisis to another, the specialised literature on IR was prone to a kind of Hobbesian pessimism, highlighting imbroglios, hostilities and conflagrations. At least two of the major texts were entitled *Power Politics*[2] – a term widely used to depict both the ends and the means of international activity and to distinguish the international from other theatres of politics. But was 'power politics' an appropriate expression and does it pinpoint the distinction between international and domestic politics?

9.1 'POWER POLITICS': THE HALLMARK OF INTERNATIONAL RELATIONS?

The various connotations of 'power'

The problem with 'power' is that it has so many different connotations that no single and agreed meaning to suit all contexts and occasions is possible.[3] For 'power' can refer to the sum total of a country's capabilities, to the various means by which a government can attempt to secure an international objective and to one set of means in particular – the coercive. Here power becomes a synonym for 'force', 'muscle', 'strength' or, alternatively, for the type of behaviour we associate with such activity – 'assertive', 'aggressive', 'forceful'. But 'power' can connote not simply means but also ends – 'ascendancy', 'control', 'dominance', 'supremacy', 'hegemony', 'sovereignty'. In addition, the term might indicate a relationship involving some kind of legitimised or accepted structure of command inviting a degree of deference. Here the emphasis is on such notions as 'leadership', 'authority' or 'competence'.

The various connotations of 'politics'

If 'power' is a slippery concept, so is 'politics', though, mercifully, its range of possible meanings is somewhat more narrow.[4] One way to delimit the general area of interpretation is to consider the antithesis of the word 'political'. Since 'apolitical' suggests 'apathy', 'disinterestedness', 'non-involvement', 'unconcern', 'not taking sides', the word 'political' must have to do with commitment, interest, involvement, concern, partisanship and in a context concerning government, rule, regulation or authority, since it is derived from the Greek word for the governance of the city state. In short, a political arena is a social framework characterised by disagreement about either the structure of authority or about purposes, procedures or priorities and in which such contentions are mediated according to recognised procedures – a vote, a consensus, an administrative act or a decree. In this sense political activity has to do with non-violent contention within an ordered framework. In its most narrow interpretation, it is a process under formal government, as in a cabinet meeting, parliament or local council. In its broader connotations politics can occur in any social situation.

Clearly, then, the notions of 'politics' and of 'power' are closely connected, and to suggest that international politics are unique in being 'power politics' would be mistaken since the contest for attention, authority, influence or decision-making power is of the very essence of politics in any social framework, including, say, the family, the classroom, or the mothers' meeting.

9.2 'POWER POLITICS' AS APPLIED TO INTERNATIONAL RELATIONS

What, then, did Realists such as Carr, Wight and Morgenthau intend to convey in suggesting that international politics were uniquely power politics? Frankly, it is not always clear, but if they meant that the international arena is one in which states are the main actors and the politics of not being overpowered are a major consideration, in which the actions of the Great Powers form the backdrop against which international relations occur and in which violence is all too frequent, they had a case. If, however, they meant that the parties to the political process have an excessive 'lust for power', that all inter-state relations are governed by ratios of physical strength and determined by threat, display or use of military power, they were clearly overstating the case.

9.3 DOMESTIC CONSTRAINTS ON THE USE OF FORCE

If there were such ready resort to violence, sustained international relations would surely be virtually impossible, and the state system validated at Westphalia in 1648 would hardly have lasted 35 years, let alone more than 350. For to maintain relations between human groups a degree of regulation is always necessary, and such constraints have never been entirely absent from the international relations of the past three centuries and a half. In the early days of the Westphalian system there was still an ethos of common Christian obligation, buttressed by international law, diplomatic procedure and Great Power management, and though such a bond could not survive when international society expanded to include states which repudiated Christianity or lacked a Christian background, the governments in an enlarged international society did at least share a number of common interests, and these found expression in the elaboration of rules and institutions for constraining behaviour.[5]

The idea of constraint suggests an activity, thought process or passion in need of restraint, but perhaps human behaviour is not so unbridled in the first place. For even if we subscribed to the most pessimistic theories of Hobbes, Darwin or even Freud, it still would not follow that we are all potential murderers. For aggressive individuals are not necessarily violent individuals, and even violent people do not necessarily have the urge to kill. It is significant that during military training men have to be taught to kill by sticking bayonets through sandbags, as if to counteract those years of conditioning by which we learn to live and socialise in society.[6]

Nor is there automatic resort to coercion whenever there are conflicts of interest or of principle between states. Indeed, far from spoiling for a fight, governments will often shy away from a fray for as long as possible, and it was because others preferred not to get involved that empire-builders from Alexander the Great and Attila the Hun down to Hitler and Mussolini could make their considerable conquests, dealing with their victims one by one.

Whether or not a government contemplates the threat or use of force depends on at least five factors: first, the importance of the matter at issue. Clearly, if it is perceived as of comparatively minor concern, few countries would risk making a military riposte. Secondly, the overall state of relations between the parties involved. If they are long-standing allies, as, for example, the US and Canada, or Norway and Denmark, force will not be a relevant consideration, no matter how thorny the issue between them.

Thirdly, the country's orientation. A respected, somewhat conservative power with a substantial stake in international law and order is likely to be more reluctant to instigate hostilities than a radical power with unfulfilled ambitions and little interest in the status quo. Fourthly, the degree to which a country enjoys the substance as well as the status of sovereignty. The greater its dependence on others, the less its ability to issue credible threats or to mobilise for sustained hostilities. Finally, the available alternatives to the military option. Coercive measures lose priority when there are alternative pressures and inducements.

ALTERNATIVES TO FORCE

Moral suasion

There is, first of all, the kind of pressure most likely to be used by small states and as between long-standing allies – moral suasion: an appeal to sentiment based on the existence of a common religious, ideological, historical, ethnic or some other bond. When, for instance, Britain neglected New Zealand's economic interests in applying for entry into the EEC, the New Zealand Prime Minister of the day flew to Britain to remind his opposite number, Macmillan, that New Zealanders had fought and died for Britain in two world wars and were, in any case, kith and kin. How could Whitehall let Wellington down? The appeal was successful in that Britain then asked for New Zealand lamb and butter to be specially exempted from EEC tariffs and received a favourable response. A similar sort of pressure seems to have been used by US President Clinton in encouraging both London and Dublin to sink their differences over Ulster prior to his first trip to Ireland in 1997.

Diplomatic pressure

There are, secondly, a range of diplomatic pressures – official and unofficial: public and private – which can be exercised by states great and small. For membership of international institutions gives small states a much-sought-after platform for their concerns and enables them to exercise a degree of diplomatic leverage they might not otherwise possess. Countries such as Luxembourg and Ireland have benefited greatly from membership of the European Union, which is no doubt why Malta and the former Communist states of Eastern Europe are anxious to join, while for vulnerable countries such as Belize and Guyana, the Commonwealth tie greatly adds to their security as Britain can warn off potential invaders. And in joining the UN, small states not only project a symbol of sovereignty but also obtain diplomatic access to countries in which they cannot afford to have missions. In such organisations their chief weapon is reasoned argument, and many smaller states can, like their larger neighbours, call on the services of expensive lawyers and spin Doctors with the gift of the gab.

When states prove unable to resolve their differences directly, officials of a country in good standing with both parties to a dispute or from an institution like the UN or the Organisation of African Unity (OAU) can use their good offices to act as sounding boards or mediators: as when Pakistan put its services at the disposal of both the United States and Communist China to engineer their rapprochement in the early 1970s, or when Romanian, Moroccan and US diplomats prepared the ground for Egypt's President Sadat to make his historic visit to Israel in 1977. And had not the Norwegians put their good offices at the disposal of the Israelis and the Palestine Liberation Organisation (PLO), the Middle Eastern peace process, such as it is, might scarcely have begun.

But third parties need not necessarily be serving politicians, international civil servants or diplomats. They can be individuals of repute, such as former Australian Prime Minister Malcolm Fraser and former Nigerian President Olusegun Obasanjo,[7], who in the mid-1980s as part of the Eminent Person's group on South Africa, prepared the ground for the white minority government to share power; the American Senator George Mitchell, who helped devise a formula to heal Northern Ireland's sectarian divisions; South Africa's President Nelson Mandela, who facilitated a compromise between Libya, Britain and the US over the trial of two alleged saboteurs of a *Pan Am* plane; and the former US President Jimmy Carter, whose mediation skills have been used to some effect in both Korea and the Middle East.

Though the mediation efforts of the above were much publicised, many such attempts never hit the headlines and are done through unofficial channels. During what was called 'the second cold war', when the West would dismiss even the most reasonable suggestion from Moscow, the writer was approached by Soviet foreign office officials to convey to their British opposite numbers that the Soviet Union would be prepared to release many well-known dissidents if only the Western powers would negotiate with Moscow on terms of equality and cease its relentless and patronising lectures on Soviet behaviour. But with President Reagan in the ascendant, the West's anti-Soviet diatribes continued unabated, and the failure of Moscow's initiative to soften the West's rhetoric may have sealed the fate of many an incarcerated dissident for a further four or five years.

When such diplomatic pressures fail there are more formal compellants, such as mobilising critical or hostile resolutions in international forums (especially favoured by smaller states, for obvious reasons), recalling Ambassadors, withdrawing Embassy staff and ultimately total diplomatic rupture – as between the US and Cuba and the Soviet Union and Albania, both occurring in 1961. There is also, though somewhat less common, the possibility of a multilateral breach of ties, sometimes coordinated through an international organisation – as when the UN sanctioned the boycott of Franco's Spain and, later, the diplomatic isolation of South Africa following its withdrawal from the Commonwealth in 1961, or more recently when Nigeria was temporarily suspended from the Commonwealth. Meanwhile, many countries, including the Soviet Union, China, Libya, Iraq, Haiti and Yugoslavia, have discovered at some time in their history what it is to be an international pariah and others, among them North Korea, East Germany (the GDR), Israel, Rhodesia and the Republic of Northern Cyprus have suffered the indignity of widespread non-recognition.

Judicial pressure

There are, thirdly, judicial pressures. These would include resort to an international court or tribunal, either where both parties to a dispute agree to submit their case or where one party seeks a judicial ruling in the hope of obtaining a favourable judgment which it can use in a political campaign to win support and discredit an opponent. This happened, for example, in the Corfu Channel case in the 1940s when the Albanians were ordered by the International Court to pay compensation for the mining of a British warship off the Albanian coast – a claim only recently settled after more than 40 years of wrangling. Meanwhile, the recent House of Lords adjudications regarding the possible extradition of Chile's former dictator General Pinochet offers up new possibilities of judicial pressure against authoritarian and brutal regimes.

Political pressure: propaganda of word and deed

Fourthly, there are a host of pressures that could be classified as political. These differ from diplomatic pressures in that their immediate targets are influential interest groups and lobbies as well as the general public in the state in view; though, of course, the ultimate objective is to secure a change of policy, government or social system.[8] Before the internet and the fax the principle instruments for conveying the requisite messages were external broadcasts, syndicated articles, books, leaflets, films, TV productions and videos. And in commissioning a vast and expensive array of propaganda materials during the cold war, both Moscow and Washington would generally attempt to disguise their source. Even the

British got into the act. Ampersand, the publisher that commissioned the author's first book *Fifty Years of Communism* in the 1960s, turned out unbeknownst to the writer to have been a front for the Foreign Office.

Another form of political pressure is what has become known as the media event, as when shortly after the Iraqi attack on Kuwait in 1990, a tearful Kuwaiti appeared before the UN General Assembly with a heart-rending eyewitness account of how Iraqi troops had killed dozens of Kuwaiti babies by removing their incubators from the hospitals. Her narrative, broadcast on coast-to-coast TV, helped to intensify American support for the Allied intervention. We now know, however, that the so-called 'eyewitness' was the daughter of the Kuwaiti Ambassador to the UN and her account a complete fabrication – but it did produce the desired result. The First World War's British propaganda machine, with its stories of Germans cutting off the hands of Belgian babies and using priests as clappers in church bells, could not have done it better![9]

Another kind of political lever is what has been called 'propaganda of the deed', from which it is hoped that appropriate inferences will be drawn abroad. At its most benign it would include such manifestations as a Reagan 'walkabout' in Moscow or a Gorbachev 'walkabout' in Washing-ton, to suggest that neither Superpower had anything to fear from the other; or Yasser Arafat's much-photographed teatime visit to Yitzhak Rabin's widow immediately after the assassination of the Israeli Premier in 1996, to demonstrate Palestinian sympathy and concern. More contro-versial would be the recent spate of French nuclear tests – a reminder that the country is still to be regarded as a Great Power. Rather more menacing would be the psycho-political 'war of nerves' in which the language of gesture takes on an unmistakably threatening dimension. In addition to weapons-testing, examples would include manoeuvres, overflights, put-ting forces on the alert, mobilisation – all of which occurred on the Soviet side of the Polish border prior to the establishment in Poland in December 1981 of martial law, and many see a direct connection between these events.

At its most extreme, propaganda of the deed can take the form of infiltration into the target state of so-called 'sleepers'. These are people, such as the IRA bomber who accidentally blew himself up with his own bomb while on a London bus, who stay in a foreign country for some time and then when ordered into action undertake whatever subversive acts their masters require. These might include sabotage, seizing key installations, kidnapping or assassinating prominent personalities and so on – though such actions can be counter-productive – stiffening rather than stemming resistance.

Economic pressures and inducements

Finally, governments can employ a variety of economic inducements as well as pressures. Inducements would include the pledge or grant of assistance, financial or technical, of commercial investment or most-favoured-nation trading status; pressures can range from the revocation of aid, the rescinding of trade advantages, dis-investment, the threat or imposition of discriminatory tariffs and quotas, and the freezing of assets to, ultimately, economic boycott (a refusal to buy) and embargo (a refusal to sell). The distinction between threat and imposition of economic pressure is important since the threat can sometimes be sufficient to secure compliance. In 1925, for example, both Greece and Bulgaria stopped short of hostilities when the League of Nations threatened sanctions against both sides. In 1956 Britain withdrew its troops from Egypt thus ending the Suez Crisis following Washington's threat to deny Britain an IMF loan, which contributed to a run on sterling, and in 1958 Finland revamped its government following a Soviet threat to boycott the country's exports. More recently US economic threats led the Croatian government to hand over to the International War Crimes Court in The Hague people alleged to have been involved in the massacres during the conflict in Bosnia, and persuaded the Chinese to close a few pirate publication, video and record companies and the Japanese to ease some protectionist tariffs.

On the other hand, where the primary objective is either compliance, deterrence or subversion, the implementation of economic pressure will tend to fail unless there is widespread international support for it.[10] For example, the Soviet Union's curtailment of trade with China in 1960, its severing of economic links with Albania in 1961, and the US cut-off of commerce with Cuba, also in 1961, may have caused severe economic disruption, but badly misfired politically. Indeed, they were counter-productive, merely encouraging the target states to make alternative domestic and international arrangements.

If unilateral economic sanctions have a somewhat dismal record of success, the chronicle of multilateral sanctions – so strongly commended by Woodrow Wilson as an alternative to force – is scarcely more encouraging. The Soviet bloc's measures against Tito's Yugoslavia in 1948 merely propelled Belgrade first into the Western orbit then into the non-aligned camp. By the same token the Western Powers' strategic embargo against the Soviet bloc in the 1940s and 1950s merely served to solidify it, as the embargoed Eastern European countries became increasingly dependent on the Soviet Union as a market and source of supply. And while the threat of League sanctions may have helped avert a Greco-Bulgarian war in 1925, when it and its successor, the UN, were obliged to implement sanctions, the results were generally disappointing. They failed to end Italy's occupation of Abyssinia in 1935, and the jury is still out on the role of UN sanctions in ending white-minority rule in Rhodesia in 1980, in bringing South West Africa to independence as the state of Namibia, in virtually ending Apartheid in South Africa and in persuading Milosevic to reduce his support of the Bosnian Serb forces he had originally promoted and financed. For in all these cases military and other pressures were also involved, and if the economic weapon was the most decisive, which is arguable, the desired effect was a long time in coming.

Sadly, one all too frequent effect of economic sanctions is the infliction of massive hardship on the people of the country targeted while their rulers insulate themselves from the adversities endured by others, retreat to their bunkers and become even more entrenched in their policies. For years, for example, Saddam Hussein and Slobodan Milosevic not only remained impassive in face of the untold suffering of their peoples, they became, if anything, even more intransigent in their defiance, wreaking a terrible vengeance on minorities such as the Kurds and Kosovars.

When, as so often, economic pressures fail to secure the requisite compliance, deterrence or subversion, the sanctioning governments can at least congratulate themselves on having demonstrated resolve and concern for principle. To be seen as having 'done something' can be considered a form, so to speak, of propaganda of the deed and may conceivably bring its own reward.

But what enables a state to resist the effects of economic sanctions? Naturally, countries such as the former Soviet Union or Communist China could withstand sanctions because they were not trade-dependent and could produce most things for themselves. Again, a state such as Albania could survive because it did comparatively little trade with the outside world, while its people, though poor, were used to low living standards. As for trade-dependent countries, if they know that sanctions are in prospect they can stockpile goods in advance, alter domestic production and consumption patterns, recruit countries or corporations willing to act as sanctions-busters (which can be a lucrative business), and apply counter-sanctions against the sanctioning states, some of whom are considerably worse off economically than they are. For example, during the lengthy period of sanctions against Apartheid in South Africa, Pretoria successfully employed counter-sanctions against the vulnerable economies of Northern and sub-Saharan Africa. In any case, governments of target states are often fortified in their defiance as their people rally round the flag, accept whatever hardships are necessary and blame their current misfortunes on the sanctioning states. Thanks to sanctions, the governments of Fidel Castro, Saddam Hussein and Slobodan Milosevic have probably lasted longer than they might otherwise have done.

Under President Reagan a further weapon seems to have been added to the arsenal of economic pressure. In advocating the immensely costly Star Wars defence project (SDI), a major objective seems to have been to force Moscow to follow suit and in the process bankrupt the Soviet Union and hence win the cold war. Readers must use their own judgement as to whether or not as a pressure it proved effective.

Lack of capacity, opportunity and fear of consequences

With so many moral, diplomatic, judicial, political and economic instruments at the disposal of governments, clearly they do not have to react to a perceived injury with force or threat of force. And even if a government faces a severe test of its resolve on an issue it deems vital, it may still rule out coercion, and on one of three grounds. First, lack of capability. It may feel it lacks the means to guarantee success and that a military enterprise would be too risky. Secondly, lack of opportunity. It may have the means, but be unwilling or unable to bring them into play at a particular time. Thirdly, fear of the consequences. Even a successful military operation can have unforeseen adverse effects. For instance, though the Soviet-led intervention in Czechoslovakia in 1968 effectively suppressed the Prague Spring, it also cemented an anti-Soviet alignment among Communists, created serious rifts within the Communist Warsaw Pact, propelled the Americans and the Communist Chinese into an entente and aroused resentment within the intervening countries as well as within Czechoslovakia. To try to stabilise the situation, Moscow was obliged to furnish generous assistance to Prague which the Soviet treasury could ill afford, and the widespread disillusionment this caused all round was in the end to destroy both the bloc and its creator, the Soviet Union – a high price to be paid for a temporary success.

9.4 INTERNATIONAL CONSTRAINTS

So far the analysis has focused on the constraints within the discretion of a state. However, the entire international system is permeated with rules, norms and general principles of conduct, providing at least modest mechanisms for regular interchange, for containing hostilities, resolving conflict or increasing solidarity. What, then, are these mechanisms and how effective are they?

International law

Clearly, in an international society lacking government or common culture and in which power is dispersed, the framing and operation of rules will be different from those in an orderly civil society. On the other hand, by comparison with countries such as Afghanistan, Somalia, Rwanda or Sierra Leone, international society would seem to be reasonably well ordered. And a critical element in this 'ordered anarchy' is international law, even though its relevance has been queried by both classical Realists and civil lawyers. Like all law, it comprises a body of rules deemed to be binding which prescribe and proscribe certain methods of conduct. That the rules, which are based on custom, treaties and what are called 'the general principles of law', inferred from legal writings and previous legal rulings, are not always in a form similar to those of domestic law, that there is no international legislature, no international central police force and only an imperfect international judiciary does not mean that law is irrelevant to international relations. For if it were irrelevant, why would governments crave legal recognition, why would they be so anxious to seek legal justification for their actions, be so keen to participate in creating new law, and why would those who expressly repudiate the international system – as did the Soviet Union in 1917 or Communist China in 1966 – so soon opt back in again?

In any case, despite the lack of a central legislature, there are nonetheless recognised rules of international conduct and also the rudiments of a judicial structure. At the same time international war crimes tribunals have been established – along the lines of the Nuremberg and Tokyo courts – in connection with the atrocities in Rwanda, Bosnia and Kosovo, an international criminal court is about to come into existence in Rome, while regional courts, such as the European Court or the European Court on Human Rights, are increasingly resorted to (often to the embarrassment of governments such as that of Great Britain, whose decisions are increasingly challenged). Meanwhile, the International Court of Justice and other international tribunals are frequently asked for an adjudication or advisory opinion. On the other hand, no state can be forced to submit its disputes to or give evidence before the courts and there is no enforcement machinery to ensure that their judgments are respected.

If lack of an international legislature, compulsory adjudication and enforcement procedures are serious weaknesses, so, some argue, is the lack of precision in the law relating to war and peace. The term 'aggression' still lacks exact legal definition, which makes it possible for any country instigating hostilities, as did Japan against China in 1931 or Iraq against Iran in 1979, to claim that it is a reprisal for a wrong already inflicted – which is perfectly justified in law – or that the appearance of one country's troops in the territory of another is in answer to a government invitation. This, after all, is what Moscow claimed in entering Hungary in 1956 and Afghanistan in 1979 – which, if true, would have made both Red Army interventions legally valid. And the growth of humanitarian law, dealing with questions of human rights, provided NATO with a pretext for its encroachment on Yugoslav sovereignty and its bombardment of the country in 1999.[11] On the other hand, perhaps the very vagueness of international law on matters of war and peace is the price we have to pay for a legal system which is more precise in other respects.

In fact, international law is both more pervasive and more effectual than we generally realise. At any large port, for example, the passage of ships, freight, passengers and letters through territorial waters, the use of ship-to-shore radio transmissions, the exploitation and transportation of fish and other undersea resources, the use of harbour facilities and so forth are all matters for legal regulation. What may come as a surprise is the degree to which international law is respected, even though governments may object to particular laws. For because it is a system between and not above states, its existence appears to serve the interests of most, and they will hesitate before bending or breaking the rules. After all, international law offers reciprocal benefits in terms of sovereign recognition, non-intervention, diplomatic immunity, regulations on trade, commerce and communications, the status of belligerency and non-belligerency, and so on. It provides a framework for order, which even the most revolutionary states prefer to chaos, and while some governments are law-abiding out of moral conviction, habit or inertia, others will obey the rules out of concern for their reputation at home and abroad, possibly in the hope of rewards for good behaviour, often out of fear of sanctions.[12]

International organisations

The strengths and weaknesses of international law in constraining international activity are to be found in almost equal measure in international organisations – global, regional or functional. Since the role of such organisations will be explored in a subsequent chapter, suffice it to say here that there are broadly two views as to their function in regard to international order – one being the rationalist or pluralist view that they are, as it were, the harbingers and custodians of a potential community of humankind: the other being the Realist view that they are the instruments of their members, generally of their leading members, which in the case of the UN today would be the US. Undoubtedly the UN today can do comparatively little in face of strong US opposition, and without Washington's support it is doubtful if Kofi Annan would have been elevated to Secretary General. On the other hand, in providing a meeting place and a forum for specialists as well as diplomats and politicians who might not otherwise get together, the UN may facilitate the kind of cooperation and regulation between the nations that might not otherwise occur. In addition, the UN has played a role in peacemaking as well as peacekeeping, speeding the process of decolonisation, in transmitting the concerns of the 'have-nots' to the 'haves' and in the creation of new law. Meanwhile bodies such as NATO, the EU, the Association of South East Asian Nations (ASEAN) and the North American Free Trade Area (NAFTA) have helped to moderate the claims of narrow national interest, though not without protest.[13]

'Rules of the game'

In addition to the kinds of formal rules attaining the status of law and the decisions or recommendations of international institutions, there are informal understandings, tacit agreements, what might be termed 'rules of the game' between governments, where considerations of prudence and discretion rather than legal obligation demarcate what is permitted from the forbidden. The existence of such 'rules' may be inferred from such things as the willingness of hostile states to keep confidential any secret discussions between them, the ability of rival powers to exchange prisoners of war and spies and to preserve unchallenged for lengthy periods of time spheres of influence. A good illustration of the importance of 'rules of the game' would be the lack of any Western move against the flimsy wall the East Germans erected in August 1961 and which could at the time have been knocked down by a few West German bulldozers.[14]

Regimes

Both legal formality and the informality of the prudential 'rules of the game' play their part in the establishment and maintenence of what are called 'regimes'. By regime we generally mean a body of regulations laying down norms of conduct and prescriptions for the management and control of actions in specific issue areas – trade, commerce, navigation, fishing, energy conservation, space exploration, arms control and so forth.[15] What distinguishes a regime from the body of legal ordinances and the rules of the game is not just its combination of formal and informal but also the fact that its framework of allowances, prescriptions, and prohibitions owes as much to international and non-government organisations and specialised agencies as to governments. Among examples of regimes may be cited the two US–Soviet strategic arms treaties

(SALTs I and II), the Strategic Arms Reduction Treaty (START), the EU's Common Agricultural Policy (CAP), the Exchange Rate Mechanism (ERM), the General Agreement on Tariffs and Trade (GATT) and the World Trade Organisation (WTO).

International morality

If international law and institutions, 'rules of the game' and regimes contribute to international order, should what is termed international morality also be included in the list? The problem is that even if one begs a host of questions by defining 'international morality' as a concern with certain kinds of obligations, duties and rights, identifying the moral agent as the state and the object of its moral endeavours as other states, some other state, group, individual or even humankind, two other thorny questions arise. First, do states in fact have moral obligations? Secondly, if they do and they are honoured, does this enhance or undermine international order?

There are, of course, conflicting opinions. Classical Realists like Machiavelli and Hobbes would have dismissed the idea entirely. In their view serving the state was the highest moral duty and no state had external obligations. However, philosophers of a cosmopolitan outlook, from the Roman Cicero through the natural law theorists and Kant down to Charles Beitz, who put individuals not states at the centre of things, would hold that there is a universal law with a moral dimension binding on all individuals, peoples and states.[16] But then ideologues and revolutionaries from Marx to the Ayatollah Khomeini would take a dialectical, polarised approach, arguing that those representing states had moral obligations only to those of like mind, not to the reactionary, class enemy or infidel who stands in the way of a just order. Finally there are the communitarians, as it were: modern Realists in the English School tradition, such as E.H. Carr, Hedley Bull and Herbert Butterfield, who argue that morality cannot be a static concept but that it arises in context and that the moral requirements of a state which must survive in a context of potentially hostile states, and above which there is no political superior to enforce law and order, must be different from those of an individual in an orderly civil society.[17]

Yet for the student of International Relations the question is not so much whether states in fact incur such obligations, since the state is only an artificial construct, a personified abstraction. The operative question is whether in the realm of discourse in which states are deemed to exist they are also deemed to incur such obligations. Where, as in many Western democracies, what Michael Ignatieff has called the 'moral imagination'[18] of the articulate and influential expands and enlarges, the obvious answer is 'yes'. Discussions about the recent turmoil in Rwanda, Bosnia or Kosovo are as likely as not to have focused on questions regarding what governments ought or ought not to have done – whether they should have intervened or not, employed sanctions or not, what their policy towards refugees ought to have been and so forth. Again there are many different moral standpoints, and even those holding to the contextual ethic will have had divergent views on the precise nature of that context and, hence, on what could best be done. For some the 'right' thing will have been to have become involved in the fray, even if it introduced a further element of turmoil in an already disordered situation and might be of dubious legal validity.

As indicated earlier in the text, non-intervention has long been the norm in international law, and intervention has been allowed only under exceptional circumstances: in particular where, paradoxically, it may be deemed necessary to preserve the society of sovereign states – in self-defence, at the invitation of an incumbent government, as counter-intervention and where there is a threat to peace, as defined by an international organisation such as the UN. But the law is itself expanding to include a raft of human rights conventions which till recently many would have regarded merely as statements of moral principle, but which governments may exploit to justify intervention, including armed intervention. Though at present the exact status of the body of humanitarian law is contested, the moralist has to consider the ethical pros and cons of intervention against regimes that are committing gross human-rights violations such as genocide, or in circumstances where people are struggling for national liberation against oppression or where governments are unable to protect people against mass starvation or ethnic violence. For just as there is a price to be paid for an intervention that goes badly wrong, as the Americans discovered in Vietnam and in Somalia, or that produces only superficial improvements and at considerable cost, as with the Nigerians in Sierra Leone, there might be an even higher price for inaction, as when Chamberlain bought 'peace in our time' by failing to stand up to Hitler in 1938. In practice, however, motives for intervention are rarely entirely pure, and an element of self-interest usually obtrudes. One has only to consider India's intervention in support of the Bangladeshis in 1971 or Vietnam's intervention in support of the oppressed Cambodians a few years later.

As regards the question about the morality or otherwise of, say, the NATO intervention in Yugoslavia, some argued that the Milosevic government was both genocidal and expansionist, that neither the Kosovars nor Yugoslavia's neighbours could be secure while its activities continued unchecked, and that the short-term suffering and disorder that would result from a military intervention would be a small price to pay for long-term stability. Others held that the Serbs who know their terrain better than any conceivable foe would not be easily intimidated into surrender by any combination of forces, and that the tally of casualties that would flow from an intervention would be too high. The only practicable course, therefore, was to further tighten sanctions and possibly arm the rebel KLA – Kosovo Liberation Army. Thus, we have two arguments with a moral dimension but with contradictory implications for policy and for international order.

Hence, it would be wrong to suppose, as did the Classical Realists, that decision-making automatically excludes any sense of international moral obligation. For decision-makers are not automata. They have the kinds of moral sensibilities of other people and in this sense the classical dichotomy between ethics and interests is probably nearer fiction than reality. Unfortunately, what is regarded as moral conduct by some may be seen as grossly immoral by others, even though there has been an attempt at an international consensus through the development of human rights legislation. On the other hand, the moral scruples of governments and peoples combined with a shrewd sense of political realities can and sometimes do serve to strengthen that modicum of order which has hitherto obtained in international society.

NOTES

1. A key text is, of course, Bull, H., *The Anarchical Society*, London, Macmillan, 1997.
2. Schwarzenberger, G., *Power Politics*, New York, Praeger, 1941 and Wight, M., *Power Politics*, Harmondsworth, Penguin, 1978.
3. For a comprehensive elucidation of 'power' see Minogue, K., 'Power in politics', *Political Studies*, October 1959, pp. 269–89.
4. See for example Miller, J.D.B., *The Nature of Politics*, London, Duckworth, 1965, pp. 13–23.
5. For an analysis of those rules and institutions, see, Bull, H., op. cit.
6. See for example Bourke, J., *An Intimate History of Killing: Face-to-face Killing in Twentieth-Century Warfare*, Cambridge, Granta, 1999.
7. Olusegun Obasanjo is, at the time of writing, no longer a former President as he was re-elected to the Nigerian Presidency in mid-1999.
8. See for example Roetter, C., *Psychological Warfare*, London, Batsford, 1974.
9. Britain's First World War propaganda is detailed and taken to task in Ponsonby, A., *Falsehood in Wartime*, London, Allen & Unwin, 1928.
10. See for example Doxey, M., *International Sanctions in Contemporary Perspective*, London, Macmillan, 1987; Lindsay, J., 'Trade Sanctions as Policy Instruments', in *International Studies Quarterly*, vol. 30, 1986; and Van Bergeijk, P., 'The impact of economic sanctions in the 1990s', *The World Economy*, vol. 18, no. 3, May 1995, pp. 443–55.

11. For a detailed analysis of the development of international human rights law and of the response of the international community to it, see Robertson, G., *Crimes Against Humanity, The Struggle for Global Justice*, London, Penguin, 1999.

12. Brierly, J.R. in Lauterpacht, H. and Waldock, C.H. (eds), *The Basis of Obligation in International Law*, Oxford, Clarendon Press, 1958, p. 69.

13. See for example Maddock, R., 'The Global Political Economy' in Bayliss, J. and Rengger, N. (eds), *Dilemmas of World Politics*, Oxford, Clarendon Press, 1992, especially pp. 126–8.

14. On 'rules of the game' and their implications, see Cohen, R., *International Politics: The Rules of the Game*, London, Longman, 1981.

15. Krasner, S. (ed.), *International Regimes*, New York, Cornell University Press, 1983.

16. See for example Midgley, E.B.F., *The Natural Law Tradition and the Theory of International Relations*, London, Elek, 1975; Donelan, M., *Elements of International Political Theory*, Oxford, Clarendon Press, 1990, pp. 7–21: Bull, H., 'Natural law and international relations', in *British Journal of International Studies*, vol. 5, July 1979, pp. 171–91; and Beitz, C., 'Bounded morality: justice and the state in world politics', in *International Organisation*, vol. 33, no. 3, 1979.

17. On the contextual ethic see for example Carr, E.H., *The Twenty Years' Crisis 1919–1939*, London, Macmillan, 1939; Bull, H., 'Justice in International relations', *The Hagey Lectures*, Waterloo, Ontario, The University of Waterloo, 1984; Butterfield, H., 'Morality and an International Order' in Porter, B. (ed.), *The Aberystwyth Papers*, London, Oxford University Press, 1966; and Stern, G., 'Morality and International Order' in James, A. (ed.), *The Bases of International Order*, London, Oxford University Press, 1973, 133–55.

18. The title of a lecture series delivered at the LSE in early 1999.

CHAPTER 10

POWER BALANCES AND ALIGNMENTS

It has been invoked by all the major international actors of the twentieth century: it was periodically operated by the ancient Greeks, Persians and Indians, though they had no name for it: it underpinned the operation of the Italian city states system, though it was not christened till the sixteenth century nor yet a theory or a set of principles: it was eulogised by seventeenth-century monarchs and enshrined as a principle of stability in a host of eighteenth-century treaties. Yet to one of the nineteenth-century apostles of free trade, John Bright, it was a foul idol to which hundreds of thousands of lives had been sacrificed[1] and to Woodrow Wilson it had been responsible for the First World War and was a symbol of all that was rotten in traditional politics and diplomacy.

Meaningless or too many meanings?

The subject, of course, is the balance of power, and, as a repository of much hyperbole, both positive and negative, by the eighteenth century it had become a subject of serious enquiry by a host of distinguished scholars, among them the French philosopher François Fénelon, the Scottish philosopher and diplomat David Hume, the English historian Henry St John, Viscount Bolingbroke and the German theorist Friedrich von Gentz. [2] Yet there was no agreed definition on what the balance of power was or what it was designed to do, which is perhaps why to John Bright's fellow nineteenth-century Liberal, Richard Cobden, the concept was entirely threadbare. It was 'an ... incomprehensible nothing; mere words, conveying to the mind not ideas but sounds'.[3] But if it had little or no meaning to Cobden, to many twentieth-century theorists balance of power had too many meanings, and as one of them put it, even IR teachers tend to 'slide blissfully from one usage of the term to another and back again, frequently without posting any warnings that plural meanings exist'. So what about those possible meanings?

Two scholars have done some particularly valuable linguistic spadework. Ernst Haas in an article 'Balance of power: prescription, concept or propaganda'[4] distinguishes between eight possible connotations, all mutually exclusive. And Inis Claude, quoted earlier admonishing colleagues who shift unknowingly from one connotation of the expression to another, in his book *Power and International Relations* produces another helpful inventory of possible definitions.[5]

The problem with 'power'

The first difficulty lies in arriving at a satisfactory interpretation of 'power'. As indicated earlier, it is one of the most nebulous terms in the vocabulary of politics. It has to do with capacity, quality, resource, relationship, status, structure, means, ends, and much more besides. But even if we beg a host of questions and define 'power' in this context as 'the capacity to produce intended effects', inducing targets thereby to act in ways contrary to their original intentions, balance of power can still be interpreted in at least three different ways.

10.1 BALANCE OF POWER AS A DESCRIPTION

Significant indicators

First, the balance of power serves as a descriptive term – to characterise any distribution of power, balanced or unbalanced. Here it denotes a kind of intellectual snapshot of the condition of international relations at a particular time. In the picture, so to speak, would be some perceived catalogue of assets capable of being mobilised in support of objectives. But even with it as a descriptive term, disagreements can arise about first the significant indicators in the balance and secondly the nature of the situation to which it refers. Regarding the significant indicators, traditionally statesmen and their advisors tended to assume that the answer depended largely on relative military capabilities, which is presumably why during the cold war the annual survey of the London-based International Institute for Strategic Studies, *The Military Balance*, was so eagerly sought after by politicians and diplomats as well as defence analysts from all over the world. And until the collapse of the Soviet Union, defence experts at the Pentagon took the conventional view that the disposition of the balance was to be found in totting up the military hardware and software available to Moscow and Washington and examining force levels and deployments, command and control systems, payloads, megatonnages and throw-weights (whatever they may be!).

However, even if one made the questionable assumption that the military factor was decisive, it was open to the objection that the military balance was not so easily measured, that there were many elements critical to the success or failure of a military enterprise that could not be readily quantified. The quality of weapons systems, for example, their mechanical reliability, the capacity to improve on them and obtain spare parts, the military advantage or otherwise of a state's location, size, terrain, etc., the degree of accord between political and military leaders, their resolve, their judgement, their ability to carry the country with them – in other words national cohesion and morale. In addition there is the all-important question of the cohesion of an alliance system. Although such factors vitally affect the success or otherwise of a military enterprise, none is easily measured.

Yet is the military factor necessarily the decisive test of power today, if 'power' is taken to mean the capacity to achieve objectives? After all, we have seen the collapse of one superpower, the Soviet Union, the humbling of the other by countries such as North Vietnam and Iran, the humiliation of France in Algeria and Indo-China, and of Britain in Egypt in 1956. And no matter how powerful Saddam Hussein's Iraq or Slobodan Milosevic's Yugoslavia, militarily they were no match for all those Western and other states they successfully defied for so long. Clearly any analysis of power balances has to take into account constraints as well as capabilities, intentions as well as deployments; and in assessing capabilities one has to consider more than just the military option. For an understanding of how small and weak powers can outwit, outmanoeuvre or defeat their more powerful rivals requires analysis of a range of diplomatic, economic, political and other mechanisms at their disposal, including the skill of leaders in being able to choose the appropriate pressures to the ends in view. One has only to consider, for example, the potential damage that could be inflicted on the advanced communications of a military giant like the US by the adroit use by a rival power or even a delinquent hacker of computers and the internet.

It was to shift attention away from purely military considerations that Soviet theorists came up with the idea of 'the correlation of forces',[6] in which political, economic and ideological factors featured heavily in the overall calculation of advantage, and though they may have got their sums wrong, in principle, looking for correlations rather than balances seems to be quite a sensible idea.

Definition of the situation

But there can be contention not only as regards the significant indicators in the balance but also over perceptions and definitions of the situation itself. Given the multiplicity and diversity of mobilisable assets involved, how is an equilibrium to be ascertained? And if the concept of equilibrium is abandoned in favour of something less precise such as an equivalence or rough parity, what one observer interprets as equivalence between two or more powers, another might construe as disequilibrium or imbalance. Those, for example, who saw Germany and France as finely balanced in 1940 would be forced to adjust their calculations later in the year following the French surrender – a failure of will rather than of weaponry. Disagreements can also arise as to the precise direction the balance is taking – whether, in other words, the balance is tilting towards or away from a particular power or group of powers.

During the cold war, for example, many talked of strategic parity between Moscow and Washington, though there were others equally convinced that the US enjoyed superiority in most fields, including the military, and were constantly overestimating the Soviet 'threat'. Ironically, many in the East shared the misperception that the world balance was tilting if not towards Moscow as such then in favour of socialism, and as evidence they pointed to the fact that by the early 1980s more countries than ever before were ruled by Communist or crypto-Communist parties. What they failed to notice, however, was that Communism's recent acquisitions were 'basket cases' – weak, impoverished and divided and a constant drain on the resources of Moscow or Beijing. To make matters worse, they were often in conflict with one another (consider, for example, the Sino–Vietnamese and the Vietnamese–Cambodian wars of the late 1970s) and often, too, at odds with themselves, with different Communist factions fighting it out in Ethiopia, Cambodia and Grenada. And in South Yemen, the hostilities between Communists became so intense at one time that Soviet officials had to take shelter in the British royal yacht *Britannia* to avoid getting caught in the crossfire. Not even Afghanistan was spared. While the Communists were being besieged by the Mujaheddin, rival wings of the party were also settling political scores with one another in the streets of Kabul. Thus, at the very time both Western alarmists and Communist propagandists were portraying the global balance as having tilted towards Moscow, the Communist movement was in fact debilitated, divided, nearly destitute and, as we now know, in serious decline. The greater the number of states in an organisation the greater the danger of dissension.

But even when there is a general acceptance that some kind of equilibrium or equivalence exists there is often disagreement on its exact nature. During the cold war some described the balance as loose, i.e. flexible, bi-polar, others as tight, i.e. inflexible, bi-polar; others, yet again, included in their description a significant third force, but could not agree on what it was. For some it was China, for others the non-aligned or even the EEC. Some even ventured beyond triangular conceptions to talk of a complex multipolar or polycentric world, at least in diplomatic and economic terms. Before joining the US administration in 1969 Henry Kissinger described the world as 'bipolar militarily but multipolar politically'[7] – a situation Richard Rosecrance characterised as one of 'bi-multipolarity'.[8] Subsequently Alistair Buchan spoke of a world which was strategically tripolar (strange, this notion of three poles!) – the US, the Soviet Union and China – and economically pentipolar, that is, balanced between five centres, which he detailed as the US, the Soviet Union, China, Western Europe and Japan.[9] But if there is deemed to be a central balance, there must be regional balances as well, in such areas as the Balkans, the Middle East, the Horn of Africa, the Indian subcontinent or South-east Asia. Here, again, however, the precise nature of such balances may give rise to controversy.

'Balance' and the prerequisites for peace

One further critical controversy relates to the implications of equilibrium or equivalence. Does peace lie in perceived equilibrium or perceived imbalance? For Churchill peace lay in the military superiority of the powers interested in defending the status quo. 'The old doctrine of a balance of power is unsound,' he declared in his famous 'Iron Curtain' speech in Fulton, Missouri in March 1946. 'We cannot afford, if we can help it, to work on narrow margins, offering temptations to a trial of strength'. Yet the theory of nuclear deterrence assumes the reverse. That the best guarantee of peace lies in mutual assured destruction, which implies a kind of equivalence, parity or sufficiency, even if not precise equilibrium.

As to whether bi- or multi-polarity is more likely to produce international stability, again the experts have been divided. As long ago as 1964 Kenneth Waltz, somewhat against the trend, was preaching the virtues of a bipolar system, arguing that in such a situation the rival powers deter each other while controlling conflicts between other states that might otherwise get out of hand.[10] It was a view strongly contested by Richard Rosecrance, Karl Deutsch, David Singer and others who claimed that bipolar systems merely accentuate antagonisms and generate multiple crises which can so easily degenerate into global conflict.[11] But such are the shifts in academic fashion that at a time of multiple civil and regional conflicts, Waltz's formulation seems less eccentric than it did all those years ago.

10.2 BALANCE OF POWER AS A POLICY

Balance of power is not just a descriptive term. It has a second set of meanings as a policy – a policy, central to Realism, for which order generally has to take precedence over justice. What kind of policy? Its critics assert that the term is so elastic as to be able to justify any state action. But in the classical writings on the subject – from Machiavelli to Morgenthau, from Hume to Holsti, from Burke to Bull and from Castlereagh to Churchill – the statesman is enjoined to aim for one of three objectives.

Equilibrium

First, to correct a dangerous imbalance by seeking to fashion an even distribution of power (i.e. of capacities to produce intended effects), as between his state and any potential rival or rivals. War was, traditionally, one of the means most commonly used. In his magisterial analysis of the Peloponnesian war, Thucydides concludes: 'What made war inevitable was the growth of Athenian power and the fear which this caused in Sparta'. In other words, it was only through hostilities that the Spartans felt they could redress the balance. But if Athens was so strong, how could Sparta deter or defeat her? Thucydides suggests, in addition, the existence of a diplomatic component. He attributes to one Spartan leader: 'Others may have a lot of money and ships and horses, but we have good allies', i.e. the notion that shrewd diplomacy can compensate for military, economic or technological weakness.[12] In fact, states will often use diplomacy as an alternative to war in attempting to achieve a perceived balance. An example would be the decision of Britain's Foreign Secretary Canning to call, as he put it, 'the New World into existence to redress the balance of the old',[13] after both France and Spain had come under Bourbon rule. It was a notion which found its American counterpart in the Monroe Doctrine of non-intervention in Europe in return for European non-intervention in the Americas.

A margin of strength

Since it may only take a minor change in capability to upset a perceived equilibrium, another recommended aim of the balance is the attainment of a margin of strength over any military or political rival. Here the word 'balance' is used in the sense of having a balance in the bank, i.e. a surplus not an equality of assets and debits. Pushed to extremes, possessing a margin of strength can come to mean predominance, and here balance comes to mean the opposite of its original sense – overbalance rather than balance. Certainly this was the understanding of Machiavelli who in *The Prince* warned: 'Whoever is the cause of another becoming powerful is ruined himself.'[14] Many of those Pentagon defence analysts referred to earlier seem to have had a similar conception when they spoke both of a 'balance' between the Superpowers and of 'negotiation from strength'.

The trouble with such an interpretation is that it can induce insecurity in rival states, thereby generating instabilities that might result in war.

The balancer

A third possible purpose might be to act as balancer, holding the ring between rival states and aligning first with one set of powers, then with another set of powers as the changing situation seems to demand. This, for example, had been Persia's role during the classic confrontations between the Greeks in the time of Thucydides, and for centuries this had been Britain's position in Europe, which is why it became known as 'perfidious Albion' – perfidious, because it could not be relied upon to maintain any alignment for long. It would change partners as its perception of the power balance on the European continent shifted. The nineteenth-century Prime Minister Palmerston summed up the position: Britain had no permanent friends. Only its 'interests' were 'eternal and perpetual'.[15]

Clearly, such balances can be pursued unilaterally or multilaterally, the latter either through alliances or alignments or even through institutions such as the nineteenth-century Concert of Europe, the Council of the League of Nations, the Security Council of the UN – all of them set up in part to manage the balance, as it were, give it a helping hand in the maintenance of order.

Purposes

But what was the point of this policy of balance? Basically it was regarded as an ordering principle in an unstable and threatening international environment which compelled states to combine and recombine for protection, and from the classical writings we can infer that its purposes embraced one or more of the following: (1) preventing the establishment of a universal empire; (2) preserving the existing international system and the independence of its political actors; (3) providing the conditions in which other institutions on which international order depends can operate – international law, diplomacy, international institutions, regimes, great power management, etc.; (4) deterring any potential hegemon by the threat of an effective collective response; (5) emerging victorious from any hostilities if deterrence fails, and reinstating the vanquished into international society.[16]

For many LDCs, the balance of power would appear to fulfil a further purpose. Here it becomes a calculated response to an internal threat, as for example when Egypt's President Sadat sought to silence his domestic critics by switching allegiance from Moscow to Washington and then using his growing ties with the US as a means of pressurising Israel to relinquish Sinai; or when Ethiopia's President Mengistu shifted to a pro-Soviet strategy in part to enlist the Kremlin's support against the Marxist–Leninist secessionists in Eritrea.[17]

Insofar as balance of power is designed to protect the independence of states as well as the stability of the society of states and hence interdependence, it can be seen as a form of enlightened self-interest, and in certain of its interventionist guises, as in the Gulf a few years ago and in Yugoslavia more recently, has appeal to pluralists as well as Realists. To maintain a balance of power or rectify one perceived to be shifting to its disadvantage, a state or group of states can employ a number of different techniques or mechanisms.

Techniques

Alliances

First, to form mutual security arrangements: alliances (bilateral or multilateral), counter-alliances or alignments to enable those involved to increase their overall bargaining and fighting power. On the other hand they tend to be short-lived. In the first place, alliances are not risk-free, for they can become hazardous if an ally becomes alarmingly provocative, prompting hitherto neutral states into hostility. In such circumstances member states may have to reconsider or even relinquish their tie, as did the Soviet Union when in the early 1960s Communist China's external and internal policies began to appear unnecessarily reckless.[18] Secondly, where alliances come into existence in response to a perceived threat, they tend to lose coherence when that perceived threat disappears or when some members come to regard fellow members as more inimical to their interests than the presumed enemy of them all. For years, NATO had been weakened by the growing rivalry between Greece and Turkey, and after the end of the cold war appeared to be floundering in the absence of a clear external enemy. If it had not found a new role for itself in the Balkans, NATO might conceivably have lost its Southern European members and then disintegrated. As it is, NATO has become one of the world's longest-standing alliances, but as it enlarges, maintaining internal cohesion could become even more problematic unless it faces or provokes some new external threat.

Intervention

A second technique for maintaining a perceived balance is intervention – a term with, again, many different definitions and involving different kinds of military, economic and political activity. However, one of the more useful comes from Oran Young in an article of 1968. 'Intervention refers to organised and systematic activity across recognised boundaries aimed at affecting . . . political authority structures . . . designed either to replace existing structures or to shore up structures thought to be in danger of collapse.'[19] Thus it can be offensive – aimed at changing a policy, an orientation, a government or a country's independent status – or defensive, with the aim of preserving the status quo or restoring the status quo ante in face of a rival bid to establish control. Among examples of defensive strategies could be cited the token forces sent to Russia in 1918 to try to restore the pre-Bolshevik regime, the Red Army shooting its way to Budapest or Kabul to try to prevent the overthrow of a Communist regime, the American landings in South Korea, South Vietnam, and in a host of Central and Latin American countries to try to preserve their administrations against Communist forces, or the French decision to back the Algerian military in its bloody mission to prevent the establishment of a freely elected Islamic regime. As it happens, such interventions tend to be counter-productive, especially when they prop up unpopular governments and alienate their populations. Moreover, unless requested by governments or authorised by a legally constituted world body such as the Security Council, such interventions are almost always illegal, though they can sometimes be morally justified on humanitarian grounds.[20]

On the other hand, some political, economic and diplomatic pressures and inducements which can effectively make and unmake governments are lawful and sometimes stand a better chance of success than direct military intervention. The collapse of Soviet power, for example, was not unrelated to the relentless political and economic pressure on Moscow by its Western opponents. By contrast, the continued existence of Israel in face of the hostility of its neighbours and many of its dispossessed Arab citizens may be said to have been due in part to the unfailing largesse of the United States.

Compensation

A third technique is what is called 'compensation', in which an increase in the components of power by one side is matched by its rival. In the eighteenth and nineteenth centuries, for example, this tended to involve agreed territorial adjustments. But the process was generally haphazard and without reference to the rulers or the inhabitants of those territories. Nobody asked the Poles at the end of the eighteenth century whether they wanted their country partitioned between Russia, Prussia and Austria for the sake of the European balance; nor was Peking's advice solicited as the European powers plus Japan carved out large slices of Chinese territory ostensibly to stabilise the world balance. Nor is the process of compensation necessarily by agreement between rivals. Mussolini reportedly seized Albania in April 1939 in compensation for Hitler's seizure of Czechoslovakia the previous month, and invaded Greece in October 1940 in response to Hitler's occupation of Romania. And when Poland returned to the political map after the Second World War it had no control over the process by which as a country it was moved westward, the Russians taking much of what had been eastern Poland and, without consulting the Germans now under occupation, handing over to Poland a large slice of German territory up to the Oder–Neisse line.

But compensation can be claimed for something more intangible than territorial deprivation, for example loss of prestige – as when certain diplomats are declared *personae non gratae* or when foreign businessmen are seized on charges of spying. And if there is a cold war between the countries concerned, as often as not such actions lead to tit-for-tat expulsions and a catalogue of arrests. We saw this amply demonstrated in relations between Britain and the Soviet Union and between Britain and Iran in the 1980s, and when in 1992 fanatical Hindus demolished a mosque at Ayodyha in Uttar Pradesh, fanatical Moslems wreaked compensatory vengeance against Hindu temples, in turn generating further retaliatory action by Hindus.

But compensation can also have a more positive side, as in recent arms-control negotiations. In the Strategic Arms Limitation Treaty of 1971, the United States permitted the Soviet Union to build more strategic weapons than itself in an attempt to preserve the balance. In more recent arms-control arrangements involving intermediate-range nuclear missiles, it was generally the Soviet Union which made the greater sacrifices, again in the interests, supposedly, of balance.

Spheres of influence

A fourth balance-of-power technique is that of spheres of influence, and in the hope of minimising friction each antagonist undertakes to respect what the other claims as its rights within its zone. From the mid-nineteenth century, for example, much of northern and western Africa was divided between the British and the French, and, generally speaking, each respected the spheres of the other. Much the same can be said for the Soviet and American spheres from the 1940s until the collapse of Eastern European Communism at the end of the 1980s – though the establishment of Communist and crypto-Communist regimes in Cuba, Nicaragua and Grenada, and President Reagan's crusade in the early 1980s against the 'evil empire' threatened to erode these spheres. On the whole, however, they were maintained, and we can each have our own idea as to whether this was a good or bad thing for the world.

Buffer zones

A fifth technique for managing the international balance is the establishment of buffer zones, generally small or weak powers situated between two or more greater powers. The underlying assumption is that each great power has an interest in preventing the others from controlling the zone and that the integrity of the small state in the middle is preferable to its falling prey to any of its great neighbours. At one stage or another Switzerland, Luxembourg, Belgium, Austria, Afghanistan, Nepal, Korea and Macedonia have all been called upon to play this role. Often for this purpose they are neutralised – that is, accorded neutral status in law by which they are prohibited from joining alliances – their neutrality being guaranteed by the powers. In time of war, however, there is in fact no guarantee that that guarantee will be respected, and in the case of Belgium and Luxembourg during both World Wars and in Korea from 1910 to recent times it was not.

Divide and rule

A sixth technique is one going back to ancient Rome and much used by the Italian city states – *divide et impera*, divide and rule. Here a power, often but not always a great power, exploits any disagreements between its opponents and competitors and attempts to sharpen their differences often by siding with an enemy's enemy in a dispute and then changing sides as the power situation seems to demand. While it flourished in the days of Empire, and was closely associated with British rule in particular, it shows no sign of going into disuse. Israel has been utilising this time-honoured device against its neighbours since the Arabs attempted to stifle the country at birth, while the decade of war between Iran and Iraq beginning in 1979 provided an opportunity for Western policy-makers to play off one protagonist against the other. More recently, Yugoslavia's President Milosevic was able to exploit disagreements between the various Western countries so as to obtain his objectives in Bosnia and Kosovo. That the strategy ultimately failed indicates that its utility may be short-lived.

Other techniques

Among other techniques in maintaining or restoring some kind of perceived equilibrium are diplomatic bargaining, generally in secret; the legal or judicial settlement of disputes; and partial and selective disarmament on the one hand and arms sales, arms races and, arguably, war on the other – arguably, because theorists disagree on whether resort to war can be considered a technique in the maintainance of the balance or its breakdown. What is clear, however, is that in the interests of balance, defeated powers tend to be, as it were, reinstated post-war to international society – as for example France after 1815, Germany after 1918, Germany and Japan after 1945, though the reinstatement of Iraq after the Gulf war has been but partial, owing to the continued contradictions between the ambitions of Saddam Hussein and the objectives of the victorious coalition.

10.3 BALANCE OF POWER AS A STATISTICAL TENDENCY

Having examined balance of power as a descriptive term and as a policy, it is time to consider a third connotation, which is of a supposed fundamental law of history or statistical tendency. This suggests that any power seemingly bent on establishing international ascendancy will sooner or later provoke a hostile and countervailing coalition. On one reading the process involves a rational and calculated response by national actors who react by making and breaking alliances in order to prevent any bid for hegemony. On another reading the balancing process arises without conscious effort and can be compared to a Newtonian conception of a universe in equilibrium, to a biological balance of nature between organism and environment, to economics, with its interest in a balance of forces such as supply and demand. In other words, when a Xerxes, Attila the Hun, Genghis Khan, Louis XIV, Napoleon, Hitler, Stalin or even a Saddam Hussein is perceived to be aiming at some kind of hegemony – local, regional or global – the balance automatically comes into play. On the other hand, the fact that some leaders often succeed in securing major territorial advantages at least in the short run suggests that if the balance is an automatic mechanism for limiting excessive power it tends to come into operation later rather than sooner. In the short run governments tend to try to avoid involvement, as was the case till recently with Serbian and Croatian expansionism and Hutu nad Tutsi extremism.

Such balance-of-power theories are structural or systemic, implying that (1) if the structure of the system as perceived alters, then, as Kenneth Waltz suggests in his *Theory of International Politics*,[21] the behaviour of governments tends to change, too, as new alignments are forged and old ones go into disuse; (2) the system as perceived with its emphasis on *raison d'état* imposes considerable uniformity of behaviour upon states regardless of their ideology, political culture, economic organisation or whatever – for this reason an official or state ideology, whether Marxism–Leninism, Islamic Fundamentalism or even Cobdenite liberal universalism tends to be seen by the theorists as largely a rationalisation of interests; (3) the system as perceived places limits on the policy choices available to governments; and (4) that as a consequence even radical or revolutionary governments are often obliged ultimately to act in part according to the foreign political agendas of their predecessors and of their neighbours. One need only think of post-revolutionary Russia or China, with the deradicalisation of their original agenda and their quest for recognition, credits and technological know-how.

10.4 CRITIQUES OF THE CONCEPT

Though at one time the balance of power had comparatively few critics, in the twentieth century it was under constant attack from pluralists and others, and on a combination of theoretical, empirical and moral grounds. Some claimed, with Cobden, that balance of power had no meaning at all: others, that if it meant anything it rested on generalisations both untested and untestable about the relentless pursuit by governments of power, in any of its guises.[22] For sometimes states clearly choose to play games other than those of power politics, and will even compromise their security in favour of ideological, religious, economic or other objectives. Indeed, some may even be prepared to concede survival itself, as when Korea submitted to the Japanese without a struggle in 1910 and Austria and Czechoslovakia to the Germans in the late 1930s.

Pluralists also claimed that balance-of-power thinking is complacent, impervious to the kaleidoscopic changes in the international landscape and simplistic, presenting a static, deterministic world in which state A's gain is state B's loss and all outcomes are determined by threat, display or use of force. To say that the policies of, say, Switzerland, Iceland or New Zealand rest on considerations of zero-sum power politics is patently absurd, even though every country in the world (apart from Costa Rica) has its own defence forces. And where is the power or group of powers to balance the US, arguably the sole Superpower, after the collapse of the Soviet Union?

But it is not only the theoretical, empirical and moral bases of the concept that has disturbed the critics, it is also the techniques employed to manage the balance. Woodrow Wilson held them directly responsible for the First World War[23] and his successors have accumulated a catalogue of complaints. They claim that the politics of the balance (1) prioritise order over justice; (2) elevate the interests of the greater over those of the smaller powers; (3) disregard international law; (4) are a source of war;

(5) are outmoded in a nuclear world, and (6) are irrelevant in an interdependent world. Some of those objections are more powerful than others, but they each merit an answer.

10.5 CRITIQUES OF THE CRITIQUES

As to balance-of-power thinking being intellectually threadbare, even meaningless, there is always a problem with a concept that is so ambiguous. On the other hand if students of IR were to be intolerant of ambiguity we would hardly have a subject at all. But with linguistic analysis we can sift out at least some of the applications of such terms, which have meaning to those who use them. As suggested above, throughout history balance terminology has been used, first, to characterise the state of international affairs – locally, regionally and globally; secondly, as a guide to policy – in particular in relation to the security dilemma and to the need to provide for future contingencies; and, thirdly, as a method of explaining recurrent patterns in international relations – the challenges and responses, the assertions and denials of sovereign status, the checks and balances on expansionism, etc.

As regards the claim that balance-of-power theories are untested and untestable, it is true that they cannot be validated in the way that one can verify say the boiling or freezing point of water. But then the nature of proof is always problematic in the social sciences. Because we are dealing as much with abstract conceptions as with the people entertaining them, we can never do the kinds of testing under laboratory conditions that the natural scientists can. However, while there is no proof, there is ample historical evidence to support many balance-of-power propositions. On the other hand such propositions need to be clearly understood, and, sadly, often they are not. First, most balance theorists do not hold that governments are motivated solely by the acquisition and exercise of power. They concede that governments generally have a broad agenda of aims and they do not necessarily exclude moral concerns from their analyses. E.H. Carr in *The Twenty Years Crisis* devotes a whole chapter to morality and, according to his biographer Jonathan Haslam, he tended, like many other Realists, to agonise over moral questions.[24] On the other hand balance-of-power theorists do suggest that administrations need to concern themselves with power capabilities and relations to have some chance of securing some of their ambitions, including their moral aspirations.

Secondly, such theorists do not posit an unchanging and unchangeable world. Though they portray a world of continued constraints and limitations, people like Richard Rosecrance point, among other things, to different patterns of power from the seventeenth century onwards, and to watershed periods,[25] such as the French revolutionary wars, the end of the First and Second World Wars, the collapse of East European Communism, the end of white minority rule in Southern Africa, etc. when one political configuration appears to have yielded to another.

Thirdly, balance theorists do not necessarily take a zero-sum approach. Men like George Kennan, Hans Morgenthau and Henry Kissinger were constantly searching for balances which might serve the interests simultaneously of a large number of states, including small states.

Fourthly, while such theorists did at one time tend to stress the military factor, those days have long since gone, and today they examine a wide spectrum of capabilities – economic, political, diplomatic, etc. – utilised by states in their quest for survival and prosperity.

The claim that balance-of-power theorists tend to stress order or at least stability over justice is probably true. On the other hand most would claim that unless there is a modicum of order, justice, in any meaningful sense, cannot in any case be secured. After all, where there is anarchy few benefit apart from the bandits, as has been only too clear in Afghanistan, Albania, Rwanda, Somalia, Bosnia, Georgia and Chechnya over the past few years. This is not to say, of course, that any order, say, a Hitlerite order, serves the purpose. It is, however, to say that the fight for a particular form of justice might be better served in an orderly than in a chaotic framework, and that this is not invalidated by the current global situation when there is only one preponderant power. After all, it is in Washington's interest to try to preserve a framework of order.

The claim that balance-of-power policies serve the interests of the great powers is, again, probably true, if the reference is to the central power balance and not to more localised regional balances. However, that those interests are always at odds with those of the smaller powers would seem unwarranted. Whether the smaller powers suffer or not depends on circumstances. True, during the cold war several East European and Latin American countries for a time appeared to lose the capacity to exercise effective sovereignty. On the other hand it could be argued that the interests of many a Third World country benefited from bipolarity as they were able to play off one set of hostile powers against another, often getting aid from both. In any case, it is open to smaller states to pursue balancing strategies of their own by attracting distant protectors, as has Israel in relation to the US, immersing themselves in the activities of regional and global international organisations and making adroit use of whatever economic, political, strategic or demographic resources they possess.

The notion that balance-of-power theory disregards international law is at best a half truth. Yes, 'balance' thinking has led to breaches of law. On the other hand it could be argued that without the kind of international order which balance of power is supposed to engender, the system of international law could not function properly at all.

What of the oft-heard claim after the outbreak of war in 1914 that balance-of-power thinking was largely responsible? One could, in fact, assert with equal justification that if only there had been some kind of balance in the form of an arms race before 1939, instead of a one-sided arms build-up by the Fascist powers, Hitler might have been deterred from some of his conquests and a Second World War might have been averted. Equally, if the 'Muslims' had had the weaponry of the Serbs and Croats the conflict in Bosnia might have been curtailed much earlier than it was. Significantly, the Bosnian Prime Minister, Haris Silaidjic, was of this opinion when he claimed that 'When power is balanced, you have peace'. The point is that though a particular war might result from a particular application of balance-of-power precepts, other applications might help to avert or curtail conflict.

The argument that the politics of balance are outmoded in a nuclear world seems to depend on a very narrow interpretation of world politics. Clearly the possession of such weapons in an increasingly complex and ever expanding international system introduces a novel dimension into balance mechanisms – as new weapons always do – but it does not necessarily render balance-of-power thinking obsolete. The balance of terror is, after all, but another variation of the balance of power, and in the meantime as between non-nuclear powers and as between nuclear and non-nuclear powers in, say, the Balkans, the Gulf, Southern Africa or Southern Asia, power considerations and the need for watchfulness, prudence and rational thinking are no less relevant today than before. The same argument applies in answer to those who claim that in an age of interdependence notions of balance are irrelevant. No matter how inter-dependent the world, sovereign status is still sought, attained, nurtured and prized, and it would appear, therefore, that notions of power balances are no more inapposite today than the notion of the state, the nation and international society – all of them mental constructs which continue to exert enormous influence on our thinking and behaviour.

NOTES

1. Wight, M., 'The balance of power and international order', in James, A. (ed.), *The Bases of International Order*, London, Oxford University Press, 1973, p. 86.
2. See for example Fénelon, *Oeuvres*, Paris, Lebel, 1835; Hume, 'Of the Balance of Power', in *Essays Moral, Political and Literary*, vol. I, London, Longmans, Green and Co., 1898; Bolingbroke, *Letters on the Study and Use of History*, London,

Millar, 1752, and von Gentz, *Fragments upon the Balance of Power in Europe*, London, Peltier, 1806.

3. Cobden, R., 'Russia' (1836) in *Political Writings*, vol. I, Ridgeway, London, 1868, p. 263.

4. *World Politics*, vol. 5, July 1953, pp. 442–77.

5. Claude, I., *Power and International Relations*, New York, Random House, 1962, p. 22.

6. Stern, G., *The Rise and Decline of International Communism*, Aldershot, Elgar, 1990, pp. 234–48.

7. 'Central issues of American Foreign Policy' in *Agenda for the Nation*, Washington DC, Brookings Institution, 1968.

8. Rosecrance, R., *Action and Reaction in World Politics*, Boston, Little, Brown, 1963.

9. *The End of the Postwar Era*, London, Weidenfeld & Nicolson, 1974.

10. 'The stability of a bipolar world', *Daedalus*, vol. 93, Summer 1964, pp. 881–909.

11. Rosecrance, R., 'Bipolarity, mutipolarity and the future', *Journal of Conflict resolution*, vol. 10, 1966, pp. 315–17; and also Deutsch, K. and Singer, J.D., 'Multipolar power systems and international stability', *World Politics*, vol. 16, 1964, pp. 390–406.

12. *The Peloponnesian War*, Harmondsworth, Penguin, 1976, p. 49.

13. Therry, R., *The Speeches of George Canning*, vol. VI, London, Ridgeway, 1828, p. 111.

14. Quoted in Padelford, N. and Lincoln, G., *International Politics: Foundations of International Relations*, New York, Macmillan, 1954, p. 198.

15. Speech in the House of Commons, 1 March 1848, *Parliamentary Debates*, Third Series, vol. 97, col. 122.

16. Bull, H., *The Anarchical Society*, London, Macmillan, 1977, pp. 101–26.

17. David, S., 'Explaining Third World Alignment', in *World Politics*, vol. 43, no. 2, January 1991, pp. 233–56.

18. See for example Stern, G., op. cit., pp. 173–95.

19. 'Intervention and the international system', *International Journal*, vol. 22, no. 2, 1968, pp. 177–87.

20. See for example Rosas, A., 'Towards some international law and order', *Journal of Peace Research*, vol. 31, no. 2, 1994, pp. 129–35.

21. *Theory of International Politics*, Reading, Mass., Addison-Wesley, 1979.

22. See for example Burton, J., *World Society*, Cambridge, Cambridge University Press, 1972; and also Rosenau, J., *The Study of Global Interdependence*, London, Pinter, 1980.

23. In a speech to Congress, 11 February 1918, Wilson spoke of the balance as 'the great game, now for ever discredited.'

24. *The Vices of Integrity: E.H.Carr, 1892–1982*, London, Verso, 1999.

25. Rosecrance, op. cit.

CHAPTER 11

DIPLOMACY – OLD AND NEW

In the previous two chapters we began to explore some of the elements comprising that modicum of international order that makes it possible to speak of an international society – the constraints and rules, written and unwritten, and the various ramifications of the notion of power balance. In this chapter we examine a further element – an institution which has, as it were, lubricated the intercourse between communities since the dawn of history – diplomacy. But first, what precisely is it?

11.1 CONNOTATIONS

Though the word 'diplomacy' would appear to be one of the least controversial in IR, like most of the terms of art in our study it has a variety of applications. There is one, however, which need not concern us here: where it becomes, especially in its American usage, a synonym for foreign policy, a subject considered in an earlier chapter. Of the many other connotations, five in particular will be considered here. First, and one of the oldest conceptions, the peaceful and orderly conduct of relations between political communities – tribes, city states, sovereign states or whatever. Secondly, the act of negotiation. Thirdly, the skills required for conducting negotiations – among them intelligence, tact, patience and empathy. Fourthly, and one of the most recent interpretations, the non-violent management of international relations by state agents and envoys through diplomatic institutions governed by rules of procedure and protocol. Fifthly, and more generally, what diplomats, professional or otherwise, do.

In fact we can identify most of these connotations by citing the different dimensions of the Gulf crisis between Iraq's original occupation of Kuwait in 1990 and the renewed bombardment of Baghdad and Basra by Anglo-American planes in 1999. Throughout the 1990s a host of diplomatic initiatives were in play, where diplomacy had to do with pressures, devices and stratagems designed as alternatives to the use of force. There were attempts at negotiations, and when these failed there followed the withdrawal of several Ambassadors, the collective severance coordinated through the UN of diplomatic ties; economic sanctions, military containment by the UNSCOM weapons inspectors and Secretary-General Kofi

Annan's attempts at UN mediation. When Washington and London decided that Saddam Hussein was still not sufficiently compliant they then resorted to a gamut of threats which may be in the arsenal of diplomacy but which appeared to lack the tact, subtlety and diplomatic finesse associated with traditional diplomatic language. These suggested that he was impervious to the normal diplomatic procedures, that he had made no concessions whatever in face of diplomatic pressure and that 'the only language Saddam understood' was 'force'. But for the champions of the kind of emollient language associated with the diplomacy of an earlier age, such 'megaphone diplomacy', with its tendency to demonise the Iraqi leader, was counter-productive and merely stiffened Saddam's resistance.

In this chapter particular attention will be paid to what diplomats do, but it also seeks to question the current wisdom that in an age of jumbo jets, fax machines, mobile phones, e-mail and satellite transmissions, diplomats are no more than glorified errand boys and girls.

11.2 EVOLUTION

Though diplomatic activity may be traced back to ancient times, as a profession diplomacy is comparatively modern. The Latin word 'diploma', derived from the Greek for 'to fold', originally referred to the stamped and folded metal plates the Roman authorities issued to those travelling on imperial roads or going abroad on official business. The 'diploma' was a kind of official pass and, when the term was extended to cover virtually any official document, a cluster of clerks was needed to index and preserve such documents in the imperial archives. A 'diplomatist', thus, was originally an archivist, but the archivist works on precedence and experience, as does the diplomat, and many medieval and Renaissance envoys were either archivists themselves or had been instructed by them. Hence the connection between the older and modern usage of the term 'diplomacy'.[1]

Pre-historic

In a classic work on the subject the former diplomat Harold Nicolson suggests a pre-historic origin in which warring tribes tire of slaughtering one another and seek a truce to bury their dead and possibly to try to reach some accord. Diplomacy represented, in other words, an alternative to force and involved sending messengers from one tribe to the enemy camp. These will have been people (often female) of impressive appearance and apparently unarmed, and to reassure their adversaries, their bodies will generally have been adorned with religious symbols or recognised emblems of peace. In addition they will have required courage, confidence, a good memory and, above all, a loud voice, since they were, after all, primarily heralds and messengers. For negotiations to follow, the envoys will have had to be accorded certain privileges, including the right to return unharmed to their people. In this respect, diplomatic immunity has to have been as old as diplomacy itself.[2]

Greek

Like many other aspects of international relations, diplomacy has not stood still, and when the ancient Greek city states began developing something akin to a regular system of inter-state communication and exchange, the need for diplomatic missions was greatly expanded. At the same time, however, the duties of an envoy became much more demanding, as henceforth they were required to be not only messengers but also negotiators, arbitrators and skilled orators equipped to argue their case before the popular assembly of the host state. But by now the diplomatic enterprise was also beginning to be associated with more sordid activities. Since a Greek mission often comprised several envoys, each representing a particular political faction, a diplomat would often spend as much time spying on fellow envoys as in pleading the cause of his city. And because an indiscreet remark or phrase could be taken out of context by a rival envoy and used back home as evidence of treachery, Greek diplomats soon developed the art of talking without saying anything. When politicians today use expressions such as 'let me make it absolutely clear', when the last thing they convey is clarity, 'in real terms', which means the kinds of terms favourable to their case, 'if I may say so', which means, 'try and stop me!' or 'if you will', 'with respect', 'at the end of the day', which generally mean 'don't interrupt me, I'm trying to think', they are following in a tradition of empty rhetoric which has a long history. Not for nothing did the ancient Greeks choose as patron of ambassadors and heralds the god Hermes, who was also the patron of vagabonds, thieves and liars.[3]

Roman

Under the Romans diplomacy had to fit into the imperial pattern. With their apparent disdain for what they regarded as 'barbarian' peoples, the Romans were reluctant to concede the principle of equality in diplomatic discussion and, in consequence, would often draft a treaty before meeting foreign envoys, and present a deadline to any raising too many objections. Should agreement fail to be concluded within the allotted time, the envoys might be stripped of their immunity, denounced as spies and transported back to their own country as virtual prisoners. And if agreement were reached, the Romans would sometimes take diplomatic hostages as a guarantee that there would be no backsliding – a practice which later, mercifully, fell into disuse. But Rome's impressive contribution to legal procedure was certainly not matched by any corresponding contribution to the art of diplomacy.[4]

Papal

If imperial Rome was rather cavalier about diplomacy, papal Rome was different. For as Italy's largest state and the fount of Christendom, the papacy needed soundly-based relations with the governments of Europe to ensure they kept doctrinally in line and to be in a position to settle local church/state disputes. And though the first ecclesiastical representatives were 'legates', people on temporary missions, by the late thirteenth century there were also 'nuncios', i.e. those whose missions were more prolonged and whose tasks were not very different from those later entrusted to ambassadors in a secular state – namely to represent and implement the policies of their sovereign. Soon they were to embrace the whole panoply of diplomatic practices utilised by the rest of the Italian peninsula: at best arbitration, negotiation, treaty-making and alliances; and of a more sinister nature, espionage, subversion, seduction (generally, but not invariably of the opposite sex), conspiracy and ingenuity in the use of poison and the stiletto.[5]

Byzantine

If papal Rome found its diplomats invaluable, the Byzantine Empire probably owed its very survival to them. Surrounded by 'barbarian' tribes, it needed to play off one potential enemy against another or else bribe, coax or convert them to Christianity, which called for another diplomatic dimension – reliable information about its neighbours. The Empire met the problem by appointing to foreign courts as more or less permanent envoys people with trained powers of observation and sound judgement who would regularly report back. In a department for external affairs based in Constantinople, the reports were carefully analysed, a policy hammered out and the envoys instructed on what line they should take – the first time diplomats had been 'on message' and diplomacy regarded as anything more than an improvised activity. On the other hand, because of their evident role as informers, Byzantine envoys were often so distrusted as to be virtually interned by the host country.

But the Byzantine emperors were themselves no more trusting and would generally keep their foreign envoys in virtual isolation. But to try to impress them, too, the Byzantines would mount endless military parades, often with the same troops entering by one gate, passing out by another, running round the back, changing uniforms and marching past again. Meanwhile, envoys coming within the Imperial Presence were often greeted with an elaborate, somewhat operatic ceremonial when, on rising from their obligatory kneelings before the emperor, they would have discovered that the imperial throne had mysteriously risen several feet in the air, while the carved gilt lions by the side of the chair of state were belching forth fire and giving terrifying roars. The secret, of course, lay in a complex system of pulleys worked by slaves, but contemporary accounts suggest that the more naive foreign envoys were indeed astounded.[6]

Renaissance Italian

Even though both medieval Rome and Byzantium were centres of what diplomatic interchange there was, diplomacy could hardly yet be called a profession, nor were there yet permanent embassies and rules of procedure. Diplomats in those days were generally expected to pay out of their own pocket for their travel and entertainment and the upkeep and staff of their foreign residence, which meant that they were generally wealthy aristocrats or else travelling salesmen who could pay for their keep by hawking wares round the local markets. Not surprisingly, diplomacy was an occupation not exactly overburdened with potential recruits, and until it became a regularly paid profession in the eighteenth century, governments often resorted to press-gang methods to recruit the wealthy. On the other hand, innovations by both papacy and Byzantium had pointed to the possibility that diplomacy might develop into a more organised system, and at about the time of the Renaissance, the Italian city states, with their interconnecting economic and security interests as well as their rivalries, began to turn their temporary missions into permanent legations and embassies.

It was in Genoa in 1455 that the Duke of Milan established the first recorded permanent mission, inaugurating in effect modern diplomacy. By the end of the fifteenth century most Italian capitals were hosting the permanent missions of their neighbours, and by the beginning of the sixteenth century the Italian states had established permanent embassies in London and Paris and at the court of the Holy Roman Emperor. Soon other governments followed suit. But many, if not most, countries continued to exercise close supervision of foreign envoys, not least because the diplomats of the sixteenth and seventeenth centuries often provided good grounds for suspicion. For they bribed courtiers, financed rebellions, encouraged opposition parties; they subverted, seduced, lied, spied and stole official documents, convinced that private and public morality were two different things. Hence, when Soviet and American intelligence would wiretap each other's embassies during the cold war, they were merely applying new technology to an old practice.[7]

Westphalian

In the Westphalian world, which was neither in a Hobbesian state of nature nor in process of moving towards a Kantian perpetual peace, diplomacy had to change if it was to uphold what international order there was. And change it did. By the late seventeenth century when the ambassador began to be viewed not as just an agent of his sovereign but as the physical embodiment of his master, entrusted with the power to interpret and, if necessary, decide policy, diplomacy began to be organised as a profession, if not necessarily a paying one. By now, the diplomatic resources of the state began to be arranged between separate ministries, diplomatic dispatches being regarded as state property rather than as the personal possession of the envoy, and soon the profession developed its own mores and social etiquette. By the beginning of the eighteenth century the diplomats appeared to possess a kind of corporate identity. Its members came from similar aristocratic backgrounds, spoke the same language, French (Latin, the language of the now declining Roman Church, having been discarded as the language of diplomacy), shared similar tastes and could argue, bargain and intrigue, swap gossip and mistresses generally without raising their voices. It was all very gentlemanly, polite, civilised, exclusive and secret.

Moreover, from 1716, when the French diplomat François de Callières published his treatise *De la Manière de négocier avec les Souverains* (*On the Manner of negotiating with Princes*), the profession now had a kind of bible, but one which could not have been further removed from the spirit of Machiavelli's *The Prince*. For example: 'The good negotiator will never base the success of his negotiations upon false promises or breaches of faith; it is an error to suppose ... that it is necessary for an efficient Ambassador to be a past master at the art of deception. Dishonesty is in fact little more than a proof of the smallness of mind of him who resorts to it and shows that he is too meagrely equipped to gain his purposes by just and reasonable methods.'[8] With such sentiments, de Callières probably did more than anyone to counteract the long-held view that diplomacy was a somewhat discreditable profession and the ambassador, in the words of the seventeenth-century British diplomat Sir Henry Wotton, 'an honest man who is sent to lie abroad for the good of his country'.[9]

On the other hand, diplomacy never entirely lost its reputation for sleaze. In fact the age of 'boudoir diplomacy', largely focused on Catherine the Great's much frequented bedroom in St Petersburg and involving some of the handsomest men in the diplomatic service, was yet to come. There were also to be far too many undignified wrangles over rank and precedence, with diplomats vying with one another, often violently, to be at or near the head of any ceremonial procession and demanding financial reparation or even a duel if their honour was impugned.[10] In an earlier era the Pope had tried to have the last word on the subject. In a memorandum of 1504 he had placed himself first among the monarchs of the earth, nominated the Holy Roman Emperor and his heir apparent as second and third and so forth, but the list fell into disuse as more and more rulers abandoned Roman Catholicism, and even Catholic monarchs increasingly questioned a proceeding that could adversely affect their own prestige.

Clearly, there was a need for some agreed formula for establishing rules of precedence and protocol to be set down and, in an agreement of 1815 drawn up at the Congress of Vienna following the French revolutionary wars, this was done. Even so, it is interesting that the conference hall had to be equipped with five doors of equal width and height so that the assembled monarchs could enter and depart simultaneously without anyone yielding precedence, and also that the conference table had to be circular, thereby eliminating the problem of who would sit at its head.[11]

At a subsequent conference, at Aix-la-Chapelle in 1818, it was agreed that precedence should be accorded not on the prestige or power of the diplomat's government but solely on the duration of his service in the country – the longest-serving Ambassador being referred to as the *doyen* or dean of the diplomatic corps and taking precedence over all the others. With the rules of precedence now standardised, henceforth the diplomat could concentrate on matters of substance instead of worrying about his place in the pecking order.

11.3 DIPLOMATIC FUNCTIONS

Until comparatively recently many an envoy would have to fulfil several different functions simultaneously. Nowadays diplomacy tends to be much more specialised. Even so, a single diplomat may be called upon to serve at different times in a variety of capacities. The Vienna Convention of 1961 codifying the laws and immunities protecting diplomats also sets out the range of diplomatic duties, and these may be summarised as follows.

1. Representation. This is a key function and can only occur in countries willing to accord some legitimacy to the diplomat's employers. Once the representative of a monarch, in an age of so-called popular sover-

eignty the diplomat has become the agent of a country or even of an institution, such as the UN, the EU or NATO. As such, the courtesies, privileges and immunities accorded the Ambassador, acting in his official capacity, are a legacy of the past, and resemble those normally extended to visiting heads of state. In this representative capacity the diplomat usually has an associated function – as old as diplomacy itself.

2. Communication. Though the means may have changed as governments can now communicate directly with one another, politicians have multiple agendas and often inadequate knowledge and thus still need the services of the diplomat to convey messages and reflect the government's views in accordance with instructions. If their views change overnight, as with absolutist kings or authoritarian rulers, the diplomat has to reflect and defend that change. For some this is not easy. For example, diplomats under Fascist and Communist governments (and sometimes under democracies as well) have often suffered crises of conscience in having to defend policies in which they do not really believe. The former US Ambassador to the UN, Adlai Stevenson, finally resigned after spending months defending a policy in Vietnam to which he was personally opposed. More recently, the former Minister Counsellor of the Yugoslav Embassy, a Bosnian Serb born in Sarajevo where his family still lived and where his brother ran one of the hospitals which had just been bombed, was in utter despair at the antics of some of his more militant fellow countrymen, and in a radio interview endorsed the policy of sanctions against the very government he was supposed to be representing. Needless to say, having failed to maintain the line he was supposed to be defending he was recalled to Belgrade and then banished to a minor post in a war-torn former Soviet republic.

3. Negotiation. Despite the frequency of 'summits' and other face-to-face meetings of politicians, the diplomats remain the key to successful negotiations, preparing the ground for their political masters or mistresses. Yet, though Harold Nicolson called diplomacy 'the art of negotiating between conflicting interests', this is perhaps an oversimplification since it presupposes that interests always conflict and that the diplomat has to reconcile them. In fact, of course, interests often overlap or coincide, and it is part of the diplomat's function to explore the degree to which common ground exists. Naturally when interests do conflict the diplomat is normally instructed to work at conciliation – a process that can continue even during a war. On the other hand in time of cold war the diplomat may be charged with making impossible demands so that the onus for rejection can be placed on the rival negotiator. This, for example, was the fate of many a disarmament or arms-control proposal in the 1950s and 1960s when

representatives of one superpower would issue a draft containing a unilateral advantage to itself which would naturally prove unaccept- able to its rival. Once the other side had, as expected, rejected the proposal it would be immediately branded 'a warmonger'. In effect, disarmament and arms-control negotiations and the 'peace propaganda' often accompanying them had become part of the fabric of the cold war.[12] Nonetheless, in general, diplomats are usually paid to secure positive rather than negative results, to achieve accord rather than rancour and bitterness.

4. Ingratiation – promoting good relations by winning friends and influencing people – and in an age of mass communications this will include academics, who like politicians, civil servants and journalists can help to shape minds and attitudes. Many an academic will have enjoyed the hospitality of envoys who thought we were worth cultivating. During the cold war, the writer, once a specialist on the Communist world, found the various Eastern European and the Chinese Embassies especially attentive. Significantly, the greater a country's unpopularity, the more lavish its hospitality, as in the case of the Czechoslovak Embassy before and after the reform movement known as the 'Prague Spring'. But ingratiation is not just about courting popularity. It also has to do with a fifth function of diplomacy.

5. The extraction of information. Gathering intelligence has long been a key diplomatic activity, and though journalists may often make important discoveries (it was for example a correspondent, Clare Hollingworth of the *Daily Telegraph*, who informed the British government on 1 September 1939 that the Germans were marching into Poland[13]), in an age of rapidly developing technology when access to and specialist understanding of classified government or commercial material are highly prized, the diplomats are often best placed to sift the relevant information. Once asked to explain the difference between a political attaché and a spy, a political attaché at the Yugoslav Embassy in London gave a revealing answer: 'There is an invisible line between normal intelligence gathering (i.e. from open sources) and espionage that you cross at your peril. If you go over that line and are a foreign national, you get arrested. If you are a diplomat and cross the line, you are declared *persona non grata* and thrown out'. It was a response all the more interesting for the fact that two or three weeks after that interchange the attaché in question was declared *persona non grata* and expelled.

Since academics in Communist countries were often government agents of a kind, many an eastern European diplomat wrongly assumed that the writer was too, and sometimes made the most ludicrous attempts to try to extract information which was never in my possession. For example, following a chance encounter with a Czecho-slovak diplomat in the 1970s, the writer found himself the envoy's guest at an expensive lunch in one of London's most exclusive res-taurants, only to be asked, after the aperitif: 'You have some papers for me?' Somewhat taken aback, I said, 'Yes, I have *The Times*, the *Guardian* and the *Herald Tribune*.' His reply: 'No, not such papers. Maybe you have something on British foreign policy.' 'Yes indeed', I remarked, 'there's a very good book on the subject by Fred Northedge, I don't know if you've read it.' 'No,' he countered, 'I am much more interested in something not published.' And there we left it. The writer discovered that there is such a thing as a free lunch, and the diplomat got virtually nothing but the bill. On the other hand, as is clear from both the so-called Iran- and Iraq-gate scandals, when Western governments were pursuing arms policies contrary to official policy, the quest for infor-mation can on occasion be a much more deadly and vicious game.

6. Protection. Promoting and securing what are perceived as the interests both of the state and of its citizens residing temporarily or permanently in the host country. This would include, among other things, securing consular access to any of its nationals in trouble or evacuating its citizens in the event of civil strife or hostility.

7. Recommendation, i.e. tendering advice to the home government on the basis of the diplomat's appreciation of the situation in the country to which he or she is accredited. As will be revealed later, such advice can still be critical in helping the government of one country to frame its policy towards another.

11.4 CRITIQUE OF THE 'OLD' DIPLOMACY

In sum, diplomacy is an important instrument of state policy, but since its aim is to minimise inter-state friction it is also a major instrument of international order. Why then did it come into such disrepute in the early twentieth century? Many held what they called the 'old diplomacy' to be responsible for the First World War. From liberals like Woodrow Wilson as well as Communists like Lenin, the 'old diplomacy' stood condemned for its secrecy, duplicity, unrepresentativeness, lack of political accounta-bility, outdated language and proceedings.[14] But perhaps the critics were confusing the formulation and substance of policy with its execution. Surely the diplomats were themselves no more responsible for the secret treaties prior to and during the First World War than they were for the spheres of influence arrangements after the Second. It was not the diplo-mats but the politicians who kept agreements secret. The diplomats were merely called upon to make the necessary arrangements. True, diplomatic discourse generally takes place in secret, but then it is hard to see how negotiations can be successfully concluded otherwise. After all, an accord generally requires flexibility, concession and compromise, something not easily achieved in public. In any case, if the expectations aroused by publicity are not met, there is always the danger of public recrimination, and that can hamper future diplomatic dialogue.

It would appear, for example, that Middle East peacemaking has been best served when conducted in secret, and that negotiations well publicised in advance often prove disappointing. In any case, it is doubtful whether the compromises necessary to pave the way, say, for Kissinger's visit to Peking in the early 1970s, President Sadat's to Israel in the late 1970s or for that matter Arafat's to Oslo to meet with Israeli officials in the 1990s could have been made without the strictest secrecy.

Interestingly enough, Woodrow Wilson, who had called for 'Open covenants, openly arrived at' became himself a convert to secret negotiations. When the peace treaty was being negotiated after the First World War he had two American marines with fixed bayonets standing guard outside the Palace at Versailles.[15] Clearly, when it came to the test, he opted for open covenants secretly arrived at, and nothing could have been more clandestine than the Rapallo treaty between Russia and Germany which was beginning to take shape even while the US President was pontificating about 'open covenants'. What this suggests is that the criticism of the 'old diplomacy', so-called, should have been levelled rather at the politicians who refused to publicise their treaty arrangements than at the diplomats who in this respect merely carried out their masters' instructions.

Moreover, though many hold that – with the growth of multilateral diplomacy through international, regional and transnational bodies – secret diplomacy is now a thing of the past, this is an illusion. True, the deliberations of the UN General Assembly and of the European parliament are open to public scrutiny. But what happens in the public forums is often far less significant than what goes on behind the scenes – in the delegates' lounges, the lobbies and even in the lavatories. It appears, for example, that the matter of the Berlin Blockade was more or less resolved in one of the urinals where the Russian and US Ambassadors happened to have a chance encounter.[16] But the stratagem they worked out together never hit the headlines at the time, and it is as well that it did not since any leak (i.e. of the stratagem) might have caused embarrassment and led to the shelving of the plan. The fact is that though international organisations may have changed the form, they do not necessarily alter the conduct of diplomacy. Diplomatic skills are needed as much in a multilateral as in a bilateral context.

As for duplicity, this may be part of the diplomat's brief, but this is again the diplomat acting on instructions. Normally, envoys are required to be truthful, but selectively and with significant omissions, since divulging the whole truth may create serious problems. For example, shortly after President Kennedy arrived in Berlin in 1963 to raise morale in that now divided city, a key State Department official, Chester Bowles, declared that 'we', meaning the US, 'would never fight for Berlin'. He was almost instantly dismissed, though the question many wanted answered was: did he fall because he had told the truth or because he had been lying? Whether true or false, the statement was clealy undiplomatic as it could only undermine the President's attempt to give heart to the increasingly isolated West Berliners. In diplomacy complete candour cannot necessarily be considered a virtue.

As to the criticism that the diplomatic service is both unrepresentative and unaccountable, here there may be valid grounds for complaint. Certainly till recently in Western Europe the profession tended to be drawn from the upper middle class, in the US it tended to be drawn from the wealthy, and in the Communist and Third World countries the recruits tended to be the trusties of the ruling party or establishment. However, in many countries it is changing. In Britain where diplomats were once almost exclusively 'Oxbridge' and disproportionately gay, the service now contains many heterosexuals from the Red Brick colleges and even more from LSE. Admittedly, it still underrepresents women and the ethnic minorities and has a rather traditional brand image of the kind of recruit it is looking for, but at least it draws them from a much broader spectrum than before.

If the profession lacks direct public accountability, just as the armed forces are ultimately responsible to the Ministry of Defence, so the diplomatic services are ultimately responsible to the Foreign Office, and at the head of each is an elected official subject to parliamentary scrutiny. In Britain a recent row over the decision to aid a counter-coup in Sierra Leone to restore democratic rule raised questions about where responsibility for policy lies and whether the diplomatic service was properly under control. The fact, however, that questions could be asked in parliament indicates that such matters are not beyond examination. Whether diplomatic activity should be shielded from the public gaze is a matter for debate. The 'traddies' argue that the public is neither knowledgeable nor interested enough and can be easily led astray by prejudices which the less scrupulous tabloids merely reinforce. The 'trendies' claim that such a view is elitist and outmoded. The debate continues.

Finally, regarding the point that diplomatic language and proceedings are archaic, it would be true to say that much of the more arcane phraseology has gone, but occasionally hallowed expressions surface from an earlier era that are unmistakable in their implications and possibly all the more effective for their undertone of politeness. Thus if 'Her Majesty's Government cannot remain indifferent to', or 'views with concern', or 'views with grave concern' some policy or other of a rival state, the implication is that Britain will take a strong line. If 'Her Majesty's Government declines to be responsible for the consequences' it is clear that diplomatic rupture or even war could be contemplated. The advantage of such conventional phraseology over clichés such as 'the only language Saddam (or Milosevic) really understands is force' is that they avoid personal abuse and maintain an atmosphere of calm while conveying warnings that are unlikely to be misunderstood – and clarity in diplomatic signalling is usually important, unless, of course, the government decides for whatever reason that its messages should be somewhat ambiguous.

11.5 A 'NEW' DIPLOMACY?

If these are the charges against what was called the 'old diplomacy', is there a 'new diplomacy', and if so what are its characteristics? Certainly, nowadays there is no shortage of 'summit' diplomacy between heads of state, 'shuttle' diplomacy as politicians venture to and fro between countries in contention and 'funereal' diplomacy as the ceremonials associated with the death of prominent personalities provide an opportunity for statesmen to meet and discuss matters of common concern. Nonetheless, there was in 1918 no abrupt transition, as some have maintained, from one form of diplomacy to another. As indicated earlier, elitism did not suddenly disappear from the diplomatic service, secret diplomacy did not suddenly yield to open, nor bi- to multilateral diplomacy. Apart from anything else, bilateral diplomacy continues even in a multilateral setting. In any case, multilateral diplomacy was by no means a twentieth-century innovation. After all, long before people talked of a 'new' diplomacy there were multilateral conferences in Westphalia in 1648, in Vienna in 1815; there was the Congress of Paris that ended the Crimean War in 1856 and the Congress of Berlin which attempted to settle the tangled affairs of the Balkans in 1878 . . . and so on.

On the other hand, the vast increase in the number of states and of international institutions, combined with technological innovations in modern communications, could not but have had a powerful effect on diplomacy. In the first place, it has led to the globalisation of what had hitherto been a largely European institution, resulting in a proliferation of embassy and consular posts and of specialised attachés with a particular interest in the military, the economy, the press, legal procedure or whatever. Indeed, in today's complex world the generalist as distinct from the specialist diplomat may be at a disadvantage. Secondly, it has widened the diplomatic agenda from discussions largely of security issues to include matters of trade and economics, migration, environmental and health problems. Thirdly, negotiations have to take place against a background of burgeoning information networks, of international press, radio and television and of direct discussions either face-to-face or fax-to-fax or phone-to-phone between heads of government, often bypassing traditional diplomacy. Fourthly, there is perhaps not the same reverance for diplomatic institutions as hitherto. Diplomatic immunity is abused more often than before; diplomats all too frequently engage in spying, infiltration and 'megaphone diplomacy', i.e. propaganda and invective; and too many diplomats have become targets for hostage-takers, a particularly notorious example of which occurred in Lima, Peru, in 1998 when nearly 100 diplomats were detained in the Japanese embassy for several weeks.

Fifthly, non-diplomatic personnel are increasingly either having diplomatic influence or being involved in activity affecting diplomatic ties. Among those who have helped shift the diplomatic agenda are the American oil magnate Armand Hammer, a friend of Lenin who for years acted as a go-between for the United States and the Soviet Union; the academic Hedley Bull, whose book on *The Control of the Arms Race* helped create a climate of thought leading to the Strategic Arms Limitation Treaty of 1971; the academic economist Jeffrey Sachs, whose ministrations to Moscow accelerated Russia's break with the command economy; the pop star Bob Geldof, whose 'Band Aid' concerts gave fresh impetus to the concept of economic assistance; and the financier George Soros who used the vast fortune he accumulated in speculating against sterling in the early 1990s to support democratisation in post-Communist Eastern Europe. By extension, the activities of some private individuals can have diplomatic effect, as for example when Salman Rushdie's novel *The Satanic Verses* prompted Iran's former leader, the Ayatollah Khomeini, to issue a *fatwah* ordering Rushdie's death for blasphemy, thereby provoking a diplomatic row between Britain, Rushdie's domicile, and Iran. Meanwhile, the activities of a Saudi dissident who sent daily faxes from his London flat to his country, with embarrassing revelations about the Saudi monarchy and the extent to which MNCs had penetrated the diplomatic profession and could exert diplomatic pressure in the Middle East, illustrates how multifaceted diplomacy has become.

11.6 THE DIPLOMAT TODAY

To return to the question posed at the beginning: has the diplomat become a mere errand boy or girl? If the profession had declined into almost insignificance it is doubtful whether there would have been such a burgeoning of diplomatic posts. In international politics as in international business, where captains of industry could conceivably settle all their affairs directly, the operative work is more adroitly and economically handled through intermediaries. In any case none of the diplomatic functions itemised earlier has lost its salience. For a new state, the symbolic ceremonial functions of diplomacy are regarded as of especial importance, while the numbers of diplomats still being expelled for 'conduct unbecoming' suggests that intelligence remains a key consideration. Indeed, given the fearful consequences of political miscalculation in a nuclear age it could be argued that the communication and mediation skills, information-gathering and advice that the diplomat can tender are more important than ever. After all, even if politicians insist on getting in on the diplomatic act, they are often ignorant of the finer details and can so easily hamper successful negotiation unless fully briefed by the diplomats who generally prepare the ground beforehand. In any case reliance on media rather than diplomatic reports from a region is risky, as the work of journalists is often highly selective, written in haste to a deadline or tailored for a particular partisan audience.

But do politicians appreciate the value of the diplomatic enterprise? Perhaps not always enough. Nonetheless, Presidents Kennedy and Johnson would repeatedly recall their ambassadors from Moscow for consultations, and during the Cuban Missile Crisis of 1962 the American ambassador in Moscow was one of the main communications links between the White House and the Kremlin.[17] And as the writer discovered from a former student who had been among the first Canadian diplomats in Communist China, when two countries have little understanding of one another or have lost contact over the years, what the diplomat says can be very influential. And she confided that in the early 1970s diplomats like her more or less made Ottawa's policy towards China.

By contrast, lack of diplomatic expertise in an area of extreme sensitivity can be a serious handicap, as when in the 1960s during the Vietnam War Washington was obliged to rely heavily on the reports of American politicians and Generals in Saigon, Phnom Penh and Vientiane, virtually none of whom spoke the relevant languages or was an authority in the region. This was because the real experts had been sacked during the anti-Left purges of Senator Joseph McCarthy, and in their absence the US decision-makers had to rely on accounts that were often shallow, ignorant and misleading.[18] Perhaps, if America's placemen in South-east Asia had studied *Structure of International Society* it might have ended differently. At least they might have asked some more searching questions before giving their woefully inadequate answers.

NOTES

1. Nicolson, H., *Diplomacy*, 3rd edn, London, Oxford University Press, 1963, pp. 9–12.
2. See Numelin, R., *The Beginnings of Diplomacy*, Oxford, Oxford University Press, 1950, p. 124.
3. Roetter, C., *The Diplomatic Art*, London, Sidgwick & Jackson, 1965, pp. 9–11.
4. Ibid., pp. 11–12.
5. Ullman, W., *The Growth of Papal Government in the Middle Ages*, London, Methuen, 1955, p. 292.
6. Roetter, C., op. cit., p. 14.
7. Nicolson, H., op. cit., pp. 20–2.
8. Quoted in ibid., p. 57.
9. Quoted in ibid., p. 21.
10. Ibid., pp. 98–100.
11. Hartmann, W.H., *The Relations of Nations*, 2nd edn, New York, Macmillan, 1964, p. 93.
12. See, Spanier, J. and Nogee, J., *The Politics of Disarmament*, New York, Praeger, 1962.
13. Hollingworth, C., *The Three Week's War in Poland*, London, Duckworth, 1940.
14. For an informed discussion of the 'old' diplomacy and the 'new', see Watson, A., *Diplomacy: The Dialogue between States*, London, Eyre Methuen, 1982, pp. 132–57 and 212–26.
15. See for example Walworth, A.C., *Woodrow Wilson*, Baltimore, Penguin, 1969, p. 148.
16. This is implicit in the account in Truman, H.S., *Memoirs*, vol. 2, New York, Doubleday, 1956, pp. 30–1.
17. Beschloss, M.R., *Kennedy versus Khrushchev: The Crisis Years 1960–3*, London, Faber, 1991.
18. See for example Halberstam, D., *The Best and the Brightest*, New York, Random House, 1972.

CHAPTER 12

IMPERIALISM

Given that imperialism, in one or other guise, has existed more or less since the dawn of history it is surprising that few recent textbooks on IR have much to say on the subject. Indeed, some do not mention it at all. Perhaps their authors can find no place for it in an era which is supposed to celebrate self-determination and the right to safeguard national identity. Yet the kind of expansionism involving an essentially unequal relationship between political entities – which is at the heart of the imperial idea – is surely as relevant today as ever. After all, for many living in the vicinity of countries such as Russia, the United States, Iraq, Syria, Israel, Libya, Liberia, Rwanda, South Africa, China, Vietnam, India, Serbia and Croatia, imperialism still represents something very real. And in some of the world's poorest countries what is called 'imperialism', both past and present, is still eagerly seized upon, rightly or wrongly, as the source of their present plight.

12.1 CONNOTATIONS

A philosophy

To place imperialism in perspective, it is necessary, as usual, to tease out the different strands of meaning to the concept. First, imperialism has long been a philosophy – the idea that certain kinds of governments should undertake the burden, the responsibilities or perhaps the satisfaction of extending their rule to other lands. Often, as in nineteenth-century mid-Victorian Britain, it was presented in mythical, even semi-mystical terms. Supposedly, it had to do with a nation's destiny and duty. Imperialism, in other words, represented the fulfilment of some kind of service in which there were no trophies to be won, save the pleasure of knowing that an obligation had been met – a *'mission civilisatrice'* accomplished, 'the white man's burden' shouldered. As one of Britain's great viceroys, Lord Curzon, put it in his book *The True Imperialism*, written in 1908: 'In Empire ... we have found not merely the key to glory and wealth, but the call to duty and the means of service to mankind'.[1]

Nor has such a notion been out of fashion for all that long. As late as 1947, for example, at the British Conservative Party's annual Conference, the philosopher/statesman L.S. Amery was introduced, to huge cheers, as 'the greatest imperialist in our midst'.[2] And in the light of the dismal post-imperial experience of some of the peoples of the former British Empire, the Soviet Union and Yugoslavia, the philosophers of imperialism may again be raising their heads above the parapet.

Imperialism has also been championed at various times by the devout, especially by Christians and Muslims who have sought to attract what they regard as 'lost souls' to their own supposedly superior values and norms. This often meant, of course, depriving the indigenous peoples of the very essence of their traditional culture and religious practices. In an earlier chapter we traced the rapidity and reach of the spread of Islam from the seventh to the fifteenth century. Later, when the Americas first came within the ambit of Europeans, they presented a field for spiritual conquest as well as trade, and a host of Catholic and Protestant mission-aries followed in the wake of the European explorers. Indeed, the mission-aries often served as imperialism's advance guard.[3] For example, once the London Missionary Society had succeeded in converting the natives of Tahiti to Christianity and prohibiting in the process the wearing of flowers, tattooing, dancing and the singing of songs other than hymns, it had effectively prepared the ground for European dominion, and the French established it. And in the nineteenth century the prospects of spreading the Gospel among 'heathen' tribes encouraged both European and American missionaries to promote the colonisation of Africa and the acquisition of extra-territorial rights in China and India.

But imperialist philosophies were not the preserve merely of the Right and the self-righteous. They also found favour with certain liberals (the so-called Limps or liberal imperialists),[4] like Bertrand Russell and Herbert Asquith. It was their belief that Western rule and the spread of education could liberate non-Western societies from despotism, oppression and poverty and, paradoxically, create the conditions for the end of imperial-ism, hastening the dawn of a new and harmonious world order. To them, someone like Gandhi, a Western-educated lawyer influenced by a West-ern-derived ideology, symbolised the virtues of the imperial system. It was a view not unlike that of the proponents of Athenian expansionism during the time of Thucydides. And to the poet Tennyson, the age of empire was an augury of a world in which 'the war drum throbb'd no longer and the battle flags were furled in the Parliament of Man, the Federation of the World'.[5] And though the agents of empire were white *men*, many women of liberal views believed that the colonial reordering of society could emancipate women from traditional customs which had turned them into virtual slaves or prostitutes.[6]

A similar sentiment seized some on the left, notably Bernard Shaw, H.G. Wells and the founders of LSE – Sidney and Beatrice Webb. Like

Karl Marx, who had once praised British imperialism as 'the subconscious instrument of history in bringing about [social] revolution in Asia',[7] they also saw imperialism as progressive. It brought Western civilisation, efficient government, industrialisation and democratic structures to backward peoples while creating a potentially revolutionary class of workers and raising their political consciousness. In addition, the founders of LSE, with their faith in science in general and the social sciences in particular, relished the creation of large, well-governed multinational units in which technology could serve the cause of social advancement. This is presumably one reason why in one of their more 'dotty' discourses they welcomed what they called the Soviet 'civilisation' of Stalin,[8] whom they appeared to regard as an experimental social scientist worthy of an M.Sc in Social Policy (with Distinction). And it is, probably, no accident that the first Director of LSE, W.A.S. Hewins, chosen by the Webbs for his compatibility with their views, left the School to become Secretary to the arch-apostle of British imperialism, Joseph Chamberlain, who was to become Colonial Secretary in the Liberal government of 1905.

Others, however, made no secret of their ethnocentric and frankly racist justification for imperialism. The more extreme were Social Darwinists who, long before Hitler, held that there was a hierarchy of races and that it was the destiny of certain ethnic groups or civilisations to rule over those they deemed inferior or weak. Some, such as the German composer Wagner, had nothing but contempt for those they judged 'inferior'; others such as the British adventurer, Cecil Rhodes, persuaded themselves that there was a kind of harmony of interests when the superior governed the inferior. Rhodes summed it up by declaring in that high voice of his: 'I contend that we British are the first people in the world and the more of the world we inhabit the better it is for the human race'.[9] Such a sentiment fitted in with the idea of Britain presiding over 'an Empire on which the sun never sets' which was championed by the popular press largely because of its appeal to the newly enfranchised factory workers. Significantly, however, those advocating the expansion of their country's particular form of rule tended to use double standards, seeking to deny to others any claim to an enlargement of dominion.

A policy

But imperialism has a second connotation, where it becomes a policy, as distinct from a philosophy of expansion – because it is possible to have one without the other. A government, that is, may fail to realise the expansionist aspirations of some of the theorists. Alternatively it can acquire territory and dominion, as China did so often in the past and Israel much more recently, in consequence not of any theory of expansion but of an attack against it which misfires and leads to the invader being absorbed by its potential victim.

As a policy, 'imperialism' may be passive – that is, conserving an empire already in existence – or active – involving the extension of dominion or rule; pragmatic – that is, a reaction to circumstances – or planned. As a plan it may be aimed at territorial expansion in general or else may target a specific territory, strategic waterway or resource. Further, 'imperialism' may or may not involve 'colonisation', that is, the creation of sizeable settlements of nationals from the imperial power. In addition, the area targeted for expansion may be overseas or over contiguous territory, though because it is more apparent when it involves overseas expansion, many Americans during the height of the cold war persuaded themselves that their country in contrast to the Soviet Union had never been imperialistic. Ironically, many of them, with an evident disdain for or ignorance of history, hailed from California, Texas or New Mexico – once, of course, part of Mexico proper. Further, imperialist expansion may involve the acquisition of land and/or the extension of control, and its exercise may be direct, involving a transfer of sovereignty through conquest or political absorption, or indirect, entailing the exploitation of political, economic, diplomatic or strategic advantage, while the form of sovereign independence is maintained.

Protectorates, mandates and trusteeships

Legal arrangements providing for a measure of self-government may sometimes be devised to mitigate the exercise of imperial power. For example, in a protectorate such as Basutoland (Lesotho), Bechuanaland (Botswana) and Swaziland, controlled by the British from the 1880s to the 1960s; Manchukuo (Manchuria), governed by Tokyo from 1932 until the end of the Second World War; Albania, under Italian protection in the 1920s and 1930s; and Slovakia and Croatia, both German-sponsored protectorates in the 1940s, whatever vestigial elements of self-government remained were largely in the gift of the protecting power.

Among other forms of modified imperial control were the League of Nations Mandates and the UN Trusteeships in which territories, most of which had never previously enjoyed independence, were placed under the control of a power entrusted to prepare them for self-government and eventual sovereignty. One of the last such states to gain independence was the former German colony of South West Africa and which, freed from South African trusteeship, took the name of Namibia. However, the trusteeship idea is by no means defunct. For in effect, since the Dayton Agreement of 1995, much of Bosnia has been a virtual trusteeship territory, administered by a combination of NATO powers together with

Russia, and the same fate would appear to have befallen Kosovo and to lie in store for some of its neighbours.

Indirect control

Spheres of influence

The more indirect method of imperial domination may or may not involve the acquisition of territory or disturbance to the political structure of a country. The most visible indicator of indirect control is the sphere of influence, by which competing great powers delineate their areas of dominance. Perhaps the most preposterous example was the 1494 treaty between Spain and Portugal demarcating their spheres of discovery and more or less dividing the world between them. More recently there was the Monroe Doctrine of 1823, by which the Americas were to be free from European colonisation and by implication free for American intervention, and later the various arrangements between the nineteenth-century European powers for the partitions of Africa and of the Near East and between the European powers and Japan for the semi-partition of China.

Contemporary historians can cite as examples the accord between Churchill and Stalin in 1944 mapping out the post-war political contours of Eastern and South-eastern Europe, and the so-called 'Brezhnev Doctrine' of 1968 whereby Moscow and its Warsaw Pact allies claimed the right to intervene in any Eastern European country where they deemed Socialism to be at risk. Though such agreements do not necessarily infringe sovereign rights, in practice they may seriously undermine a country's ability to exercise its sovereign power. It becomes in effect a client state, though, as indicated by the changing political fortunes of the Americas, Eastern Europe, North Africa and East Asia, eventually states once regarded as within the sphere of another may resume the independence to which they are theoretically entitled.

'Neo-colonialism'

Less visible, perhaps, but often equally subversive of the ability to exercise sovereign power is what the late Ghanaian President, Kwame Nkrumah, called 'neo-colonialism',[10] and which creates what many Latin American theorists call a situation of *dependencia* – dependency – in which the possibilities for independent action are limited. What, then, characterises the neo-colonialist relationship? The declaration of the 3rd Afro-Asian Peoples' Conference in Cairo in 1961 spelled it out in rather colourful, if somewhat tendentious language. The gist is as follows: the maintenance by the former imperial powers of effective control over the newly sovereign countries through a) puppet governments; b) federations linked to the former imperial power; c) the sponsorship of artificial political entities, such as for example Katanga in the Congo or Baganda in Uganda; d) the exploitation of economic dependence; e) integration into economic blocks controlled by the former colonial power; f) economic infiltration through capital investments, loans, and monetary or technical aid; g) continued control of monetary policy and finance, and h) the establishment of military bases under the guise of scientific research stations or training schools.[11]

If, indeed, many LDCs are prey to many of these, their chances of enjoying the substance as well as the form of independence will be strictly limited.

Cultural imperialism

A further and even less visible type of informal imperialist penetration relates to the technology of communications. If, as is often suggested, the continued use of European languages remains one of the most significant links between the LDCs and their former imperial masters, developments in communications merely reinforce that tie. Though the LDCs are beginning to create news agencies of their own, such as IRNA, the Iranian news agency, and the various media networks of the Middle East, these are comparatively few and far between, which means that Western agencies, many owned, controlled and/or staffed by Americans, have tended to dominate the news outlets. And while there are Third World TV networks which broadcast to several countries simultaneously – for example MBC, owned and largely controlled by the Saudis – there is no Third World equivalent of CNN, SKY, the European Broadcasting Network or BBC World Service TV which take an increasing share of viewing time in the LDCs and whose broadcast content will frequently undermine that of the local media. Meanwhile, the news coverage of the LDCs, like their trade, has tended to be geared towards the developed countries, as the journalists of the developing countries reflect the news values and concerns of the elites who manage the networks often on behalf of outside interests. Moreover, those indigenous journalists who broadcast or write about the affairs of the LDCs are themselves often Western-trained and apt to perceive LDC events through, as it were, Western eyes.[12]

It is partly for this reason that sub-Saharan Africa rarely gets a good press and that comparatively few features on South Asia or Latin America explore subjects other than corruption, ineptitude or ethnic and religious division. And it seems standard practice to dwell on 'terrorism', 'fundamentalism' 'intransigence', 'fanaticism' or 'ostentatious wealth' in articles on the Middle East. With the development of digital transmissions,

Western domination of the news networks could well be further accentuated until the poorer LDCs can afford their own satellites. No wonder many speak of the need for a new, non-Western-dominated information order!

Combined with this wily form of Western informal penetration, there is another. Some call it Coca Colonialism or Pepsicology, in which the transmission of ideas through education, secular and religious, technological transfer and trade serve to inculcate a range of Western ideas into non-Western minds. If in practice the influence of prolonged encounters with other cultures has always been a two-way process, with Western tastes in food, drink, medicine and fashions being changed by oriental silks, tea, coffee and now acapuncture, herbal medicine, meditation, judo, the kebab, the curry, the chow mein, etc., and Islam, Zen Buddhism and Krishna consciousness attracting more and more Western converts, the transfer from East to West seems somehow less destructive of traditional values than the transfer from West to East – perhaps because the West has usually had the military or economic advantage.

A structural relationship

But imperialism is not just a philosophy and a policy. For structuralists, and especially Marxists, such as Lenin and Wallerstein, it is essentially a relationship – one of inequality as between dominant and dependent. It may be that objectively the dominant do not seek hegemony and that an unequal relationship eventually becomes more of a liability than an asset to the dominant. S. Gopal in a book on *British policy in India* suggests that by the beginning of this century the costs of maintaining Imperial India may have outweighed the benefits in terms of the massive budgets required to defend it from its many foes – external and internal – the hostility of Britain's European neighbours to its very existence, the massive death toll and the untold personal hardship and frustration involved in governing it.[13] Nonetheless, for the structuralist, that unequal relationship persists, since it is independent of conscious planning or desire. Indeed, it is a manifestation of a pattern of structural inequality inherent in all social situations – in, say, the family as between parents and children or between men and women, in society as between teachers and pupils, governments and the governed.

On the other hand, given the nature of world capitalism there are, according to Marxist theorists, particular economic patterns which reinforce the relationship of dominance and dependency even after the end of formal empire. So what are these patterns? They comprise relations of unequal exchange as between a dominant centre, that of developed capitalism, and a dependent periphery, comprising the economies of

LDCs, in which there are common interests between 'the centre of the centre' and 'the centre of the periphery', i.e. the elites of the LDCs. Rather like the theorists of 'neo-colonialism' the Marxists hold that the subordinate status of the LDC is perpetuated by hierarchical structures which

1. weight terms of trade heavily in favour of the industrialised;
2. facilitate foreign penetration of development projects in the peripheral states through credit and technical expertise, which generally serve the long-term interests of the industrialised;
3. deepen and entrench internal inequalities within the LDCs as their elites are bribed or else co-opted to serve foreign interests;
4. sap indigenous cultures of their vitality by subjecting them to a creeping tide of western cultural penetration, and
5. help reinforce ties of dependency through the discouragement of regional cooperation among the LDCs themselves.[14]

The effect of this unequal relationship on the economies of the LDCs is either their systematic exploitation, their marginalisation through 'imperial neglect' or their dependent development, according to which any industrialisation benefits only a minority, while the country's legal 'independence' becomes empty of all practical content.

Since, as indicated earlier, the structural relationship of dominance and dependency can be understood as occurring in a variety of social situations, increasingly it is being applied by ethnic, religious or national minority groups to refer to the political arrangements of states in which they feel their capacity for self-realisation, self-expression or self-determination is being denied. It is this sense of being dominated by an alien presence – in Moscow, Belgrade or Prague – that led to the break-up of respectively the Soviet Union, Czechoslovakia and Yugoslavia. It is the same sense that leads to secessionist movements in Chechnya, in the Crimea, now part of the Ukraine, in many of the other successor states of the Soviet Union and of Yugoslavia as well as in multi-ethnic states such as Congo, Angola, Iraq, India, Indonesia, China, Spain and even Britain. Here imperialism does not presuppose the primacy of economics. It is simply equated with a relationship perceived as denying the realisation of national, ethnic or religious aspirations.

12.2 EXPLANATIONS

If 'imperialism' is a philosophy, a policy and a structural relationship of inequality, are not expansionism and resistance to it part and parcel of the fabric of international relations? Realists, of course, would claim that they are, as would Marxists, though they can envisage an end to 'imperialism', but only after the transformation of world society through a revolutionary process. For some pluralists, however, a post-imperialist world is possible without the revolutionary overthrow of capitalism. But to account for the persistence of imperialism, there would appear to be two different modes of explanation – one based on psychology and stressing conscious motivation; the other based on structural analysis.

Psychological

Drawing on both Thucydides and Hobbes, Martin Wight in his book *Power Politics* attributes the frequent incidence of both imperialism and war to three chief motivations – gain, fear and doctrine.[15] Though it is not entirely clear in Wight's text whether the relevant psychological drives are those of individual statesmen or of the ruling body or can be imputed somehow to the state itself, can Martin Wight's classification help us understand the forces that impel countries to expansion?

Gain

When the talk is of the need for 'a place in the sun', 'living space', 'warm water outlets', 'natural frontiers', 'frontier rectifications', etc. it is the language of acquisition, of seeking to extend control or dominion for the benefits it supposedly brings. And what are these benefits? They can take the form of guaranteed markets and of sources of raw materials, precious metals, precious minerals, geo-strategic areas – waterways, sheltered harbours, hilly vantage points, railway junctions, and spacious underground facilities for nuclear testing – good agricultural land and of course populations which can be seen as a reservoir of man- and woman-power. Finally they can involve the acquisition of terrain for the settlement – the word is 'colon', from which we get the word colonisation – of the young and restless looking for adventure or a sense of purpose, which is in part why many young Frenchmen joined the Foreign Legion and ended up in Algeria or West Africa. John Stuart Mill called the colonies 'a vast system of outdoor relief for the younger sons of the upper class',[16] and certainly they have served as dumping grounds for surplus populations, as in the case of Japanese expansionism in the 1930s and 1940s.

Nor is such expansion necessarily confined to the greater powers. After all, many of today's minor powers once went through an imperialist phase: Spain and Portugal from the fifteenth to the eighteenth century, Switzerland at the end of the fifteenth and beginning of the sixteenth centuries, Sweden and Holland in the seventeenth century, Belgium in the nineteenth century. And more recently Poland, India, Indonesia, Egypt,

Ghana, Libya and Iraq, among others, have put in bids for territory not originally theirs.

Fear

Martin Wight's second motivation for imperialism is fear. If at first sight this seems a curious stimulus, one has only to recall such adages as 'attack is the best form of defence', 'kill or be killed' and to consider the notion of the pre-emptive strike, of 'getting them before they get you'. Here it is an essentially defensive reaction to a perception of threat. The 'scramble for Africa' at the end of the nineteenth century was motivated in part by the fear of certain powers that they would be left behind and find the world balance tilting against them. This would seem to have been the case, for example, with Germany, which came into the 'game' late, after Bismarck had declared that his country was 'satiated' and which did very little to develop, exploit or even populate its African colonies. Alternatively, a country might acquire terrain where it can, as its rival acquires territory elsewhere. It is sometimes said, for example, that Italy seized Albania in April 1939 as a direct result of the perceived power imbalance occasioned by Germany's thrust into Czechoslovakia the month before.

Sometimes, the impetus can be strategic or defensive – in order to safeguard existing possessions. The British, for example, were constantly involved in overseas intrigues to safeguard trade-routes to India. More recently the strategic urge has been largely to defend the home territory, as when the Soviet Union invaded Finland and took over the Baltic States – Latvia, Lithuania and Estonia – partly to safeguard the area around Leningrad, at a time when Germany was advancing into southern and eastern Europe; or when South Africa made its repeated incursions into Mozambique, Angola and the other black states of southern Africa where the ANC had their guerrilla bases; or when Israel moved to carve out a slice of southern Lebanon and to occupy the West Bank and the Gaza strip in time of hostilities, and decided to hang on to them. Incidently, it is fear of a repetition of the genocidal activities of the Croats in World War II that the Bosnian Serbs often gave as their reason for what others called 'ethnic cleansing' and the attempted acquisition of terrain from Croats and Muslims. It was, however, a policy which would backfire since the Serbs were themselves to be 'ethnically cleansed' from Krajina. As in the other cases cited, we can make our own judgement as to whether or not fear has been the real impulse behind these activities.

Doctrine

Doctrine is Martin Wight's third category. Earlier, reference was made to expansionist philosophies, and ever since biblical times, if not before, people have sought to spread their cherished beliefs by the sword if peaceful means do not work. The salvation of souls, that is, has long provided the pretext for the crusade or the *jihad* – the holy struggle – and of course other creeds, both left- and right-wing, internationalist as well as nationalist, have provided the stimulus for the extension of domain. But faith in science can also be the spur. For the scientifically inclined are often obsessed with the conquest of nature, and this can involve the impulse to control the very terrain that will enable them to conduct their experiments, just as it provides the incentive for the exploration of space and of the ocean bed. Sadly, all too many doctors of medicine and scientists willingly chose to serve Hitler's various experiments at home and abroad, or for that matter those of Stalin, Apartheid South Africa or Saddam Hussein. And if the political records of former doctors such as Hastings Banda of Malawi, Sali Berisha of Albania, Radovan Karadzic of the Bosnian Serbs and Mahathir Mahomad of Malaysia are not above reproach, perhaps it has something to do with their former role in having the power of life and death over people.

Prestige

Two more motivations should perhaps be added to those of Martin Wight. The first is prestige or reputation. The quest for either personal fame or national glory, *la gloire*, is often sought by those who assume that the more extensive the area under control, the higher the standing and status internationally. Alternatively, expansion may be a belated riposte to a past humiliation. Mussolini's seizure of Abyssinia in 1935 appears to have been to avenge the Italian defeat by Abyssinian forces in Adowa in the 1890s, while many of Milosevic's policies seem to be informed by memories of past injuries inflicted on the Serbs by Croats, Bosnian Muslims and Albanians.

Distraction

The second addition to Martin Wight's categorisation is that of distraction, as when a leader or a ruling body embarks on a foreign adventure in order to direct attention away from domestic discontents – as it can be argued that Cambodia's Pol Pot did in the country's frequent incursions into Vietnam in the 1970s, Argentina's General Galtieri in trying to seize the Falklands/Malvinas in the 1980s, and Slobodan Milosevic in a series of adventures starting with the suppression of Albanian autonomy in Kosovo in 1989, continuing with the attempt to carve out a Greater Serbia in Croatia and Bosnia and ending with a policy of attempted suppression of the Albanian Kosovars. And many see in some of President Clinton's more controversial foreign undertakings – both military and diplomatic – a desperate attempt to deflect the domestic agenda.

The value of psychological explanations

The kind of classification suggested by Martin Wight has value so long as his suggested motivations are not taken as mutually exclusive. After all, to understand, say, Baghdad's occupation of Kuwait one has to draw on virtually all five. Gain – given Kuwait's oil reserves and outlet to the sea; fear – given Kuwait's reported over-production of oil which drove down the price and its habit of syphoning off oil from Iraqi territory; doctrine – in this case nationalism combined with anti-imperialism, in that Kuwait was regarded as an appendage of the West. Saddam Hussein also drew, but far less convincingly, on Islamic as well as Arab nationalism; reputation – if ever a man sought *la gloire* it was Saddam Hussein, especially after a prolonged, expensive and unsuccessful war against Iran; and, finally, distraction – a clear motivation given that within the space of a decade Iraq had gone from riches to rags, Saddam Hussein's grandiose military schemes having indebted and impoverished one of the world's wealthiest countries.

But as the Iraqi example shows, the long-term effects of expansionism can often be counter-productive, as other countries or combinations of countries, in the best balance-of-power tradition, launch a counter-offensive against a state which challenges the existing distribution of power. In the case of the struggle against Iraq, it might be interesting to consider how far each country in the original Gulf War coalition was motivated by gain, fear, doctrine, reputation or distraction.

But theories in accounting for imperialism are to be found not merely in psychological but also in structural terms, that is, without reference to conscious choice or motivation.

Structural theories

Political

One of the most pervasive theories is political and based on the simple proposition, to quote the historian Lord Acton, that 'Power tends to expand indefinitely, and will transcend all barriers, abroad and at home, until met by superior forces.'[17] And in *The International Political System*,

F.S. Northedge suggests that the propensity of states to expand their territory, interests or influence abroad is but one example of a cycle that in his view characterises all social organisms, in which birth is followed by growth, and then eventually decay and demise. For him 'the state . . . is an imperialistic animal, just as the beaver is a dam-building animal'.[18]

Sociological

A second structuralist theory is sociological, and based on the analysis of particular kinds of social systems. From Kant to Woodrow Wilson and probably down to Ronald Reagan, people have viewed imperialism as an outcome of elitist, authoritarian and despotic governments. For Plato, through Burke, down to the Webbs, the most potent source of imperialism would be the demagogue and the populist. And whereas the late Elie Kedourie would have seen imperialism as an outcome of nationalism, Mazzini in the nineteenth century would have seen it as stemming from the denial of nationalist sentiment. Only when states and nations coincided would there be an end to imperialism and war. For Kedourie, in contrast, nationalism begins as a demand for separation and secession from a multinational state, but as soon as the new state is formed, the same spiritual vitality which inspired the independence struggle is diverted into expansion, since the force released by the quest for national liberation cannot be contained within the national state. But, of course, when nationalism becomes imperialism it in turn engenders resistance among those whose own national identity is threatened by it, and so there is an endless cycle of thrust and counterthrust.[19] Those subscribing to this theory might select a host of examples from the Roman Empire to the Empire of Napoleonic France and down to the more recent actions of Russia, Germany, Italy, Japan and currently what is left of Yugoslavia. However, doubtless those with an alternative view would select examples in which the nationalist dimension was missing.

Economic

Thirdly, there are a host of structural economic theories, many designed to explain what they call 'modern' imperialism. The reason the term 'modern' is appended is that its proponents see in capitalism the cause of imperialism in the last 100 years or so but are well aware that the phenomenon is far older than the capitalist system. Among the better known theories are, first, that of the English economist J.A. Hobson whose study of *Imperialism* of 1902 attributes the phenomenon to the existence of maladjustments in European capitalism and suggests that imperialism might be avoided if improvements were made to the capitalist system itself.[20] Another treatise is that of Lenin who in *Imperialism, the Highest Stage of Capitalism* of 1916 transformed Hobson's thesis into a determinist theory, suggesting that imperialism was an inevitable outcome of capitalism in what he called its 'monopoly stage', i.e. when the system is dominated by business cartels and finance houses have an overwhelming need to export surplus capital. At this stage, he says, 'the division of the world by the international trusts has begun and in which the partition of all the territory of the earth by the greatest capitalist countries has been completed'.[21] For contemporary Marxists like Wallerstein in his *The Capitalist World-Economy*, the outcome is one of exploitation by the developed 'centre' economies and the underdevelopment and economic stagnation of the 'periphery', with a number of Fascist, state Socialist or Third World countries forming a 'semi-periphery' whose ultimate direction depends on circumstance.[22]

Though these have been influential theories, they are, like most theories, flawed. First, they fail to explain imperialism before the age of capitalism. Secondly, history does not invariably show a coincidence of surplus capital and imperialist venture. Thirdly, the suggestion that the imposition of imperialism is always to the disadvantage of the colonised is questionable. While its political and psychological effects may be difficult to determine, economically at any rate imperialism has often proved to be an engine of development, introducing more efficient methods of production and spawning industries serving the local market. Fourthly, the contention that a power has to possess foreign territory in order to export capital is bogus. Indeed, it could be argued that the imperialist countries of Western Europe and Japan were never so prosperous as when they had divested themselves of their colonies. But then a neo-Marxist of the *dependencia* school would suggest that imperialism does not require formal empire. All that is needed is a structural relationship of dominance and dependency – which, they would argue, still exists.

International systemic

There is one final structural theory which was alluded to earlier in the text and which merits a mention here. In his *Theory of International Politics* Kenneth Waltz espouses what is called 'structural Realism', in which he suggests that states tend to expand not because of any psychological impetus but because of the fact of their existence in a world without government, in which power is dispersed, life is precarious and there is no sense of international solidarity. In such an insecure, system-dominant world in which each state faces a security dilemma, expansionism is a way, he claims, of coping with the logic of the situation.[23]

12.3 CAVEATS

Earlier, reference was made to the Northedge contention that states are inherently imperialistic. There is a sense, as indicated in the first chapter, in which states are inherently nothing but social constructs and personified abstractions. On the other hand, they have an existence in our minds and as such shape our behaviour, and when we think of the state we often imagine it as capable of and often involved in expansion. On the other hand, we may also conceive of particular states as having contracted over the years. In the past decade alone Russia, Yugoslavia and Ethiopia have shrunk and Czechoslovakia has split into two separate states, its so-called 'velvet divorce' occurring more or less amicably, not unlike an earlier divorce in this century – that of Norway from Sweden. Nor is the voluntary cession of territory necessarily a twentieth-century phenomenon; in the eighteenth century at the end of the Seven Years War, Britain handed France several West Indian islands it had captured and in the nineteenth century Britain transferred the Ionian isles to Greece. And there have been other examples.

Do such concessions occur only in response to external pressure? They generally happen in response to pressure, but the operative pressures may be internal rather than external and the result may be a leaner and possibly fitter country, better prepared than before for the cut-and-thrust of power politics, like France after being forced to cede Algeria. Conceivably Britain, which fought to prevent Irish independence, would be better off without Northern Ireland, but of course it requires a majority of the people of Ulster to bring it about. Nor is it always the case that powers attempt to stem their decline in territory and status. Venice, Portugal, Denmark, Sweden and Holland seem to have gradually resigned themselves to a lesser role than in the historic past. So did Turkey, though there are signs now in Cyprus, Northern Iraq and beyond of a desire to exert greater influence than in the past half-century or so. But such are the vicissitudes of international politics that it would serve little purpose 1) to define imperialism in a narrowly restrictive way; 2) to seek a single factor or monocausal explanation for it; and 3) to suggest that all states are imperialistic all the time, even if it may sometimes look like it. True, all states, large and small, weak as well as strong, seek to expand their influence, but that they seek to expand their terrain and all the time is a dubious proposition, and to call the desire for greater influence 'imperialistic' is, surely, stretching the meaning of the term rather too far.

NOTES

1. Quoted in Thornton, A.P., *The Imperial Idea and its Enemies*, London, Macmillan, 1958, p. 72.
2. Quoted in Northedge, F.S., *The International Political System*, London, Faber, 1976, p. 224.
3. See for example Tuck, P.J., *French Catholic Missionaries and the Politics of Imperialism in Vietnam 1857–1914*, Liverpool, Liverpool University Press, 1987; Varg, P., *Missionaries, Chinese and Diplomats: The American Protestant Missionary Movement in China 1890–1952*, Princeton, Princeton University Press, 1958; Langer, W.L., *The Diplomacy of Imperialism*, New York, 1951; and Moon, P.J. *Imperialism and World Politics*, New York, 1936.
4. Thornton, A.P., *Imperialism in the Twentieth Century*, London, Macmillan, 1980, p. 154.
5. From 'Locksley Hall', 1842.
6. See for example Oliver, C., *Western Women in Colonial Africa*, Westport, Conn., Greenwood Press, 1982.
7. Marx, K., *The First Indian War of Independence 1857–1859*, Moscow, Progress Publishers, 1959, p. 33.
8. Webb, S. and B., *Soviet Communism: A New Civilisation*, 3rd edn, London, 1944.
9. Quoted in Carr, E.H., *The Twenty Years Crisis*, London, Macmillan, 1962, p. 76.
10. His views were spelled out in *Neo-colonialism*, London, Nelson, 1965.
11. 'Neo-colonialism' in *Voice of Africa*, vol. I, no. 4, April 1961, p. 4.
12. See for example Mowlana, H., Gerbner, G., and Schiller, H. (eds), *Triumph of the Image: The Media's War in the Persian Gulf – A Global Perspective*, Oxford, Westview, 1992.
13. Gopal, S., *British Policy in India 1858–1905*, Cambridge, Cambridge University Press, 1965, pp. 120–1.
14. Immanuel Wallerstein, Paul Baran, Raul Prebisch and André Gunder Frank are leading exponents of this theory, while a non-Marxist, Galtung, J., in 'A Structural theory of imperialism', *Journal of Peace Research*, vol. 13, no. 2, 1971, pp. 81–94 puts the argument particularly clearly.
15. Op. cit., p. 138.
16. Quoted in Zilliacus, K., *The Mirror of the Past*, London, Gollancz, 1944, p. 32.
17. Lord Acton, *Lectures on Modern History*, London, Macmillan, 1952, p. 156.
18. Op. cit., p. 203.
19. Kedourie, E., *Nationalism*, London, Hutchinson, 1960.
20. Hobson, J.A., *Imperialism*, London, Nisbet, 1902.
21. English translation, New York, 1933, pp. 80–1.
22. Cambridge, Cambridge University Press, 1979.
23. Reading, Mass., Addison-Wesley, 1979.

CHAPTER 13

WAR

13.1 ATTITUDES TO WAR

It is one of the paradoxes of our time that though analyses of the causes of war proliferate and the peace researchers come up with ever more sophisticated techniques and strategies for conflict avoidance or resolution, war continues to take a heavy tally of lives. And if its epicentre has appeared to shift from Europe to the so-called Third World, and its character from inter-state to intra-state conflict, the hostilities in 1999 between NATO and Yugoslavia over the future of Kosovo served as a reminder that war can still break out in any continent at any time. Those who argued that nuclear weapons, with their potential threat to humankind, would bring an end to warfare will have been sadly disillusioned. For even if conflicts between the nuclear powers have been kept within bounds, clearly they do not prevent wars between non-nuclear powers. Nor, indeed, does the existence of such weapons inhibit war between powers one of which has a nuclear capability, even though, as the Americans learned in Vietnam and the Soviets in Afghanistan, awesome military strength is no longer decisive. Sadly, there has not been a single war-free year since the devastation of Hiroshima and Nagasaki in 1945.

And yet the First World War was to have been the 'war to end all wars'. The senseless slaughter, the massive toll of mangled bodies, the enormous devastation would, it was argued, serve as a warning to any future leader bent on hostilities, while new institutions such as the League of Nations with its provision for collective security would ensure that aggressors were either deterred or severely punished. So what went wrong? Why, even after the countless lives lost in the fields of Flanders, were there to be so many additional mutilated corpses – in the plains of Central Europe, the waters of the Atlantic and the Pacific, in the once-bustling cities of Hiroshima and Nagasaki, the frozen wastes of Korea, the jungles of Vietnam, the deserts of Ethiopia, Sudan, Somalia and Zaire, the mountains of Bosnia and Kosovo and in so many other theatres of war throughout the five continents? And why even today do the hapless victims of war – often innocent women and children – lie strewn throughout Rwanda, Congo, Sudan, Algeria, Afghanistan, Chechnya, Croatia, Bosnia and Kosovo?

From talking to male veterans and survivors in particular, one might perhaps get a clue as to why war, in the sense of organised and protracted military conflict, persists. For though they will lament the loss of comrades, they are often nostalgic about life in the trenches or bomb shelters and about past battles when adversity and hardship were shared and there was a heightened sense of solidarity and comradeship.[1] And most of us will know people who eagerly wrap themselves in the national flag or take up the cudgels on behalf of some religious, ethnic, class or even gender-based cause to be able to fight the enemy, metaphorically or literally, and with a clear conscience.

Nor is this anything new. After all, the ancients worshipped, among other deities, the gods of violence, if only to get on the right side of them. The Hindus of India had Shiva, the often vindictive King of the Beasts, and his even more destructive spouse Kali. The Scandinavians had Odin, Wotan of the Wagnerian Ring cycle, and Thor who hurled thunderbolts at his enemies. In Greece Ares and in Rome Mars were celebrated as the gods of war. The sacred texts of the world's three monotheistic religions are full of war imagery and of divinely legitimised violence. The Jewish Lord of Hosts 'smites' his enemies, a notion much in the mind of those Jewish fanatics who rejoiced when Israel's former Prime Minister Yitzhak Rabin was murdered. The Christian is directed to put on 'the breastplate of righteousness', 'the helmet of salvation' and 'the sword of the Spirit', which is presumably why some, with a clear conscience, can kill abortionists,[2] while the Moslem is promised a reward in heaven if he dies in the defence of Allah and his cause. Perhaps this is why neither the Iranians nor the Iraqis during their decade of war from 1979 flinched from sending children into battle. Indeed an assassin (an Arabic word) who eliminates one of the enemies of Allah has a particularly honoured place (not unlike the Kamikaze warriors so greatly revered in the Japanese Shinto tradition).

The willingness of people to resort to collective violence in defence of a principle led the American scholar, Samuel Huntingdon, to envisage a millennium of globalised tribal conflict in what he calls the 'clash of civilisations'. He argues that while war was between princes until the Peace of Westphalia, between states until the First World War and between ideologies until the end of the cold war, the battle lines of the future will be drawn up between various combinations of civilisations, which he defines as Chinese, Japanese, Islamic, Hindu, Orthodox, Western, Latin American and African.[3] He has, however, little to say about cooperation between civilisations (if only on the basis of 'my enemy's enemy is my friend') or about serious strife within civilisations, of which there have been not a few within recent years.

Between the two contrasting attitudes to war – one seeing it as destructive of value, the other regarding it as a mechanism for upholding values

– the historical record reveals a variety of conflicting views. For some, warfare is an adventure, even a kind of recreation, and indeed both the Crimean and the American civil wars became spectator sports as families and friends of the combatants gathered at the front to watch the contest in what was literally a 'theatre' of war. And since time immemorial warfare had been viewed as a kind of virility test, with the warrior cutting a rather glamorous if not always a very imaginative figure, and even now military displays tend to be spectacular demonstrations of glory, magnificence and testosterone.

A 'disinfectant'

Ironically, it was often weaklings who were most attracted to the Social Darwinist idea of the survival of the fittest. For example, at the end of the nineteenth century, Friedrich Nietzsche (who had been ill for most of his life and finally succumbed to syphilis and insanity) suggested that 'For nations that are growing weak and contemptible, war may be prescribed as a remedy'.[4] Similar views were held by people such as the British writer Robert Louis Stevenson (another chronic invalid) who had created Mr Hyde as well as Dr Jekyll; by Gabriele d'Annunzio, the Italian poet who had inspired Mussolini; and by the British economist and philosopher John Maynard Keynes, who at one stage held that war was an economic necessity in that it 'cut unproductive primitive peoples down to size'.[5] It was, however, the German General von Bernhardi who gave what might be termed 'the disinfectant theory of war' its most articulate expression. In his *Germany and the Next War* of 1912 he claimed: 'War is a biological necessity ... Without war, inferior or decaying races would easily choke the growth of healthy budding elements and a universal decadence would follow.'[6] War, in other words, purified society, purging the body politic of its ailments.

A political expedient

Fortunately, most modern politicians do not think in these terms. For them war is not so much a biological or economic necessity as a political expedient designed to secure vital objectives, and is more often than not a last resort. Their guru, insofar as they have one, tends not to be Nietzsche but von Clausewitz, who in his classic study *Vom Kriege* (On War), written in 1823, described war as 'a continuation of policy by other means', and as being intended 'to compel our opponent to fulfil our will'.[7] It must, therefore, have clear objectives and be a means of influence, never an end in itself, with the means tailored to the objective.

A religious duty

For yet others the justification is not pragmatic but ideological or even theological. In both Bible and Koran war is represented as in some sense a demonstration of the Divine purpose, either as punishment for sin or as an appropriate means for spreading the Word. In deciding to expel the Muslims from Spain in the ninth century and setting the precedent for the Crusades, the Emperor Charlemagne was acting in part on his understanding of the New Testament, and already the priests were beginning to bless the weapons belonging to the defenders of Christianity. By the end of the eleventh century Pope Urban II was invoking the crusading spirit in the cause of liberating Jerusalem from Islam. Not surprisingly the Muslims, who had been fighting for much of their existence, had their answer in the form of a counter-crusade or *Jihad*.

A political duty

But if some saw war or a particular war as a religious obligation, others were to regard it as a political duty. For Marx and the Marxists the 'inevitable' overthrow of capitalism could be hastened by the exercise of collective will-power. For Lenin and the Communists, the Marxist had the responsibility, as it were, to 'give history a push' by waging unceasing struggle and by all means, including violence, to destroy the citadels of capitalism.

A moral duty

If the Marxists saw war as a political obligation in the creation of a better world order, others saw it as a moral duty in the preservation of what already exists. For example, that ardent nineteenth-century champion of national self-determination, J.S. Mill, believed that where a country's very existence was imperilled by foreign intervention, other states had an obligation to counter-intervene, if necessary by force, to restore the independence of the subjugated state. As he put it: 'Intervention to enforce non-intervention is always rightful, always moral, if not always prudent.'[8] It was the kind of sentiment, moreover, which impelled the UN to become involved in Kuwait, and belatedly in Bosnia, though it raises the question as to why the UN intervened in these particular conflicts and refrained from intervention in others which were, arguably, no less morally compelling.

But the moral case for military intervention is not just a matter of assisting the victims of foreign invasion. Where there are accounts of unspeakable actions by tyrannical rulers or indisciplined soldiers, whether in Iraq, Bosnia, Serbia, Rwanda or Congo (Zaire), calls for what is called 'humanitarian intervention' intensify, and tend to gather momentum after an especially shocking atrocity hits the headlines.[9] For example, NATO's controversial decision to take up arms on behalf of the Kosovars has to be seen in the context of the earlier and widely reported massacres at Vukovar (Croatia), Srebrenica (Bosnia) and Racak (Kosovo) – some of the worst atrocities Europe has witnessed since the Second World War. Though people can be very selective in their moral indignation (the Kosovars, for example, have received far more sympathy than the Serbs brutally expelled from Krajina in Croatia), the argument for intervention in particular cases can sometimes unite people across the political spectrum as well as revive religious notions of 'the just war', with its attendant notions of 'just cause' and 'proportionality' as regards means. In Britain, for example, the campaign to assist the Kurds and the Marsh Arabs of Iraq and to expel the Iraqi forces from Kuwait in 1990 found the Archbishop of Canterbury, left-wingers such as Professor Fred Halliday, liberal intellectuals such as Michael Ignatieff and right-wing Conservatives such as Margaret Thatcher on the same side. It is also worth noting, however, many of those opposing intervention had equally strong moral convictions, not least the fear of doing more harm than good.

Conscientious objections

While resort to threat, display or use of force has always found defenders, there have also always been pacifists, who object to all war, as well as conscientious objectors who object to particular wars – and in recent times, especially in the West, anti-war sentiment has grown. This is partly because of television which, in bringing home the horror as well as the pity of war, encourages a 'keep out!' as well as a 'let's get involved!' mentality.[10] Partly, too, it has to do with fear of nuclear escalation with its potential threat to the planet. It may also have something to do with the spread of education, though since some of the most highly educated people have also been among the most brutal, it is difficult to be sure.

It was, however, among the politically aware in nineteenth-century Europe that the animus against war first began to spread. For liberal apostles of free trade, such as Cobden and Bright, war was not so much wicked as irrational. It undermined the good order on which commerce depended. And in the twentieth century the idea that war was irrational received its most eloquent expression in the essay *The Great Illusion*, by the influential sage, Norman Angell – the illusion being that war could be to anyone's long-term benefit.[11] Though it might bring short-term commercial and political gain, it could only contain the seeds of further conflict – and the outbreak of the Second World War seemed merely to vindicate Angell's analysis of thirty years before.

A similar idea found expression in the First and Second Socialist Internationals of the nineteenth century, among people such as Eduard Bernstein representing the Social Democratic wing of the Labour movement. But whereas the liberal internationalists held that almost nobody benefited from war, the Social Democrats suggested that some did – what has become known as 'the military–industrial complex' – but for the working class to take part in an activity from which only 'the bosses' could benefit was irrational.

Finally, there were the thoroughgoing pacifists who held that all war was wrong. Some were of a religious inclination, such as the Quakers. But there were secular pacifists, too – some, life-long, such as the writer Aldous Huxley and the composers Benjamin Britten and Michael Tippett; others pacifists for a time, such as the philosopher Bertrand Russell who abandoned his pacifism during the Second World War. Though they had different starting points, they all believed that no cause was worth killing for.

On the other hand, a principled refusal to countenance violence can encourage the violent, and many still believe that some causes are worth fighting for, even if they would refuse, as does CND, to sanction the deployment of particular weapons. But that some can contemplate nonnuclear but not nuclear combat is a reminder that there are different kinds of hostilities.

13.2 TYPES OF WARFARE

Civil

There are first, civil wars, and increasingly these are the most characteristic violent conflicts of our time. Though they are sometimes limited to skirmishes between rival factions within a ruling clique, as for example in Central and Latin America, more often they polarise whole populations. Typically they begin with street violence, graduate to acts of terrorism – random or selective – then to insurgency and finally to protracted civil conflict. When this happens, as in Russia in 1918, Spain in the 1930s, Vietnam in the 1960s and 1970s or more recently in Algeria, Afghanistan, Bosnia, Croatia and Kosovo, such conflicts tend to be especially brutal. For women, children and hospitals do not merely get caught in the crossfire. They are often prime targets in a struggle which pits whole communities – ethnic, religious, political or whatever – against one another, making combatants out of anyone capable of holding a gun.[12]

And where the outcome could possibly affect the overall international situation, outside powers tend to get involved either as participants as in Russia, Spain and Vietnam, or as peace-keeping mediators as in Bosnia, Somalia and the Middle East, though, as such examples indicate, far from curbing hostilities, the external presence may merely prolong them.

Liberation

When the conflict is between the existing authorities and those attempting to secure some kind of national liberation, it can again involve much brutality. And when it takes the form of attempted secession from a larger contiguous entity, as in Eritrea, South Sudan, East Timor, Tibet, Kashmir, Chechnya, the Serb-dominated parts of Bosnia and, of course, Kosovo, the geographical proximity of the warring factions probably makes it even more bloody than a struggle for liberation from an overseas colonist. Moreover when, as often happens, national liberation fails to bring greater individual fulfilment, as has been the experience of the Iraqis, Afghans, Malawis, Georgians, to say nothing of the Bosnians, future conflicts are not only possible, they are likely. The Indian sub-continent serves as an ominous precedent. First India, then Pakistan, then Bangladesh, and what next? An independent Kashmir, Sindh or Punjab, perhaps? And what future for Yugoslavia – once regarded as the most 'civilised' of the Communist states and more recently prey to the most barbaric communal hatreds as the country shatters into more and more fragments?

Limited

One of the more ambiguous terms in the inventory of conflict is that of 'limited war'. Though it implies constraints on the scope, scale and intensity of hostilities, there appears to be no consensus on when a war ceases to be limited. After all, though the Thirty Years War of 1618–48 was confined largely to Central Europe, the devastation and destruction during this lengthy vicious conflict was colossal. An estimated six million people are believed to have perished, that is, about 40 per cent of the central European population of the time, and as much as 75 per cent of the population of Bohemia, now part of the Czech republic.[13]

If one considers the Vietnam War of 1961–75 again, though limited in geographical area, in the number of states participating and in the scale of violence in the sense that the US resisted the temptation to take it to the nuclear threshold, American planes nonetheless dropped some twenty million high-explosive fragmentation bombs – far more than in the Second World War, which no one regards as a limited war. Moreover, US strategy involved chemical agents and defoliants such as the notorious 'Agent

Orange' – never in use during the Second World War – which devastated much of the country's agricultural land and forestry and took Washington within a whisker of breaking the 1925 Geneva Conventions on chemical warfare. By the end of hostilities, some two million had been killed, a further four million seriously injured and seventeen million or so (one-third of the entire Indo-Chinese people) displaced.[14]

In view of the fact that the two World Wars of this century began as local or regional conflicts – the first in the Balkans, the second in the Far East – the term 'limited', as in the phrase 'limited war', would appear to need some qualification. 'Limited' in what sense?

Proxy

The notion of 'war by proxy' is more easily defined than exemplified. It occurs when state A encourages the people of state C to take up arms against state B, which happens to be its own adversary. It is claimed, for example, that both Korean and Vietnam Wars come into this category, that the real instigators were the Soviet Union – the patrons of North Korea and North Vietnam – and the US – the patrons of South Korea and South Vietnam – and that the so-called Third Indo-China War between Cambodia and Vietnam in 1978 was really a Sino-Soviet war by proxy. The trouble with this kind of ascription is that even if true at one level, there is generally another level at which the war is a local affair dealing with local concerns. In the case of Korea, given that in the summer of 1950 the then South Korean leader Syngman Rhee was clinging to power despite having been massively defeated in a recent election, the North Koreans would have been tempted to attack either because they believed the South to be divided and therefore vulnerable or alternatively because they feared the South might strike northwards to give Syngman Rhee a pretext to retain power.[15]

Total

If there are problems about the notion of 'limited war', there are far fewer difficulties with the contrasting concept of 'total war'. Given currency during the First World War, it indicated a conflict in which the total resources of the countries involved were mobilised for victory, while millions were conscripted into the forces or war industries, and even in the most laissez-faire economies, governments took virtual control of industry, farming and labour. As the scale and intensity of the war mounted, the conflict was increasingly portrayed as a Manichean struggle between good and evil, light and darkness, civilisation and barbarism, in which a whole way of life was deemed to be at stake. In this sense victory,

too, had to be total, involving unconditional surrender and the disarmament and demobilisation of the vanquished – all very different from, say,
the Bismarckian wars of the nineteenth century or the Russo-Japanese
conflict of 1904–5 fought by limited means for limited objectives. Though
both World Wars were 'total' in the sense described, the seeds of 'total'
war had been sown at the end of the eighteenth century during the French
revolutionary wars when the authorities in Paris introduced the *levée en
masse* (conscription), conducted an intense propaganda campaign and
yoked the country's productive capacity and its civil service to the war
effort.

Nuclear

One final category – nuclear war – remains, mercifully, hypothetical
though the atom bomb was used to end the Second World War and an
increasing number of states have nuclear weapons or else access to nuclear
know-how. On the other hand, a nuclear capacity does appear to have a
sobering effect on those in possession. The US and the Soviet Union,
which were in conflict on so many different levels simultaneously, took
care not to be pushed over the brink in any altercation; China stopped
preaching the virtues of nuclear war after exploding a nuclear device in
1964, while India and Pakistan have also kept their multi-layered conflict
within bounds since both acquired a nuclear capacity. True, neither
country, so far as we know, yet has a retaliatory capacity and hence the
deterrence of mutual assured destruction (MAD) does not at present
operate between them. On the other hand, given that neither power lacks
allies, a nuclear first strike may reasonably be said to be virtually ruled
out, even though hostilities between them by conventional means are not
precluded.

On the other hand, such a proposition presupposes rational decision-
making. But what, say the pessimists, if there is a lack of rationality on
one side or the other? Might not a nuclear war come about by miscalculation or misunderstanding? It is, of course, true that mechanical failures
have occurred in nuclear-related technology. At one time, for example, a
flock of starlings appeared on a computer screen as a cluster of airborne
missiles. And the lessons of what happened in 1983 when Soviet intelligence detected an alien intruder over the USSR's vital Far East nuclear
installations, only to discover after shooting it down that the intruder was
in fact a Korean passenger plane that had strayed off course, may still
have to be learned. On the other hand as political and military establishments acquire greater understanding of the possible errors that nuclear-
related computers can make, they build greater 'fail safe' mechanisms into
them, while the numbers of fingers on the nuclear safety-catch ensure that

the nuclear trigger is rarely at the disposal of a single fallible and perhaps irrational leader.

13.3 WAR: A CALCULATED ACT?

This is not to say that strategic nuclear war could never come about by accident. After all, military manoeuvres designed to put pressure on an opponent could conceivably be understood wrongly as indicating an intention to attack. Certainly in both the First World War and the more recent conflicts over the Falklands, the Gulf and Kosovo there were miscalculations regarding intentions and resolve, while the Six Day War in the Middle East was arguably sparked off by false reports regarding Israeli intentions which Moscow fed to Syria and Egypt.[16] A further danger could stem from the issuing of an ultimatum which begins as an elaborate bluff but which has to be followed by military action if credibility is to be maintained. And some fear that leaders like Saddam Hussein or Kim Jong Il or a group of terrorists might not be constrained by the kinds of factors which have hitherto deterred states from a nuclear attack on one another.

On the other hand, wars normally are the result of the calculation of one or both parties to it and rarely a matter of chance.[17] Since, moreover, a nuclear strategy calls for the kind of extensive command, control and delivery systems which can be detected by 'spy-in-the-sky' satellites and which a terrorist group is unlikely to possess, the danger of any such strike is minimal. Not since the Cuban missile crisis has the world faced any serious possibility of nuclear war by miscalculation.

13.4 SOURCES

Human nature

As organised and protracted conflict between rival groups has been endemic in human affairs since the dawn of history, thinking people have long speculated on its cause. In his *Man, the State and War*,[18] Kenneth Waltz examines the literature on the subject and identifies three main bodies of theory. The oldest of them attributes war to some defect in human nature. In any school playground, sports field, boardroom or even senior common room, competition, contention and conflict are the norm. If such emotions are transferred to political groups and get out of control, say the Hobbesian Realists, violence results. Psychologists such as Freud and William James, being in the business of exploring the dark recesses of the subconscious, would agree and point out that even normally well-balanced individuals, if frustrated, provoked and enraged will commit acts which under less extreme circumstances they would themselves deplore, as when after losing so many comrades in battle, ordinary American GIs gunned down innocent women, children and even babies at My Lai in Vietnam.

Some theorists of a more religious disposition, from St Augustine to the psychoanalyst Jung, trace the source of what they see as man's violent disposition to the biblical story of the fall of man, and view war as a manifestation of sinfulness – of turning away from God. The more apocalyptic, such as the Jehovah's Witnesses, envision sinful man as moving towards a final global holocaust – Armageddon – before God establishes his Kingdom (apparently reserved for Jehovah's Witnesses) on earth. Other theorists, such as Robert Ardrey and Konrad Lorenz, in the mould of Darwin, Huxley and Bernard Shaw, take an anthropological view and regard war as a disreputable relic of an earlier age when we were savages and used the spear not just for hunting.[19] Yet others, such as the ethologist Niko Tinbergen, trace it even further back – to man's supposed animal ancestry,[20] though some animal 'liberationists', ironically not averse to using violence themselves in defence of their cause, contend that calculated and purposeful violence is a human institution and not to be found in the animal kingdom at all.

Yet if war is inherent in human nature, why are there not organised hostilities all the time? Why do wars occur at certain times and not at other times? The idea that human nature is the cause leaves crucial questions unanswered.

Socio-political systems

An alternative theory, at least as old as Aristotle, holds that the cause is not so much in man himself as in the way society is organised. In the eighteenth century, dynastic rivalries had been responsible for a series of conflicts – hence the wars of Spanish, Polish, Austrian and Bavarian succession. And in the twentieth century, after the First World War, for which many held the Kaiser and his fellow autocrats responsible, there was a spate of theories about the war-making propensity of autocracies. In the view of Woodrow Wilson, for example, the voice of the people was the voice of reason and governments responsive to what he called 'the organised opinion of mankind' would desist from war-making. If such an idea seemed to fly in the face of the kind of war nostalgia described at the start of this chapter, it reflected the widespread 'never again!' mentality in the victorious powers, and gained fresh impetus with the rise of Soviet

Socialism and of Fascism in the 1920s and 1930s, both of which were regarded by many as modern despotisms and, hence, harbingers of war.

But if liberals traced the origin of war to a lack of democracy, less liberal thinkers such as Plato through Burke down to the Webbs tended to see the cause in an excess of it. Or rather to demagogues who court the popular will and then lead a gullible public to disaster. For evidence they could cite any number of leaders who, faced with a loss of popularity, resort to overseas adventures. Was it mere coincidence, for example, that in 1914 Vienna was suffering from the restlessness of its polyglot peoples, Berlin from the agitation of the Social Democrats, St Petersburg from strikes and hunger marches, and London from the terror tactics of the IRA? And was there no possible connection between Clinton's domestic difficulties and a US raid on a chemical factory in Sudan on the eve of impeachment proceedings? And did not the Soviet international affairs specialist Georgi Arbatov have a point when in 1988 he warned Western reporters: 'We are going to do something terrible to you. We're going to deprive you of an enemy'?[21]

The founder of modern communism, Karl Marx, would have agreed that there was a close connection between domestic problems and overseas adventures, save that he saw them as a result of coping with specifically economic difficulties, inevitable under capitalism. Lenin was even more categorical, and considered that monopoly capitalism, which occurs when the system is in the hands of cartels and combines, must foster imperialism and ultimately war.

One nineteenth-century contemporary of Marx, Mazzini, put the cause of war down to not despotism, demagoguery or capitalism but to the denial of national self-determination. Nations whose group identity had been denied political expression would go on struggling until having achieved international legitimacy in the form of sovereign statehood. Only when states and nations coincided would war be abolished. In this view, nationalists are rather like the supporters of a football team who following a defeat launch all-out war on the fabric of an excursion train on their way home. Their victory alone will solve the problem.[22] A century later, the political scientist Elie Kedourie advocated exactly the reverse. However noble and enlightened its origins, nationalism had become hostage to collective hatred, and only when its aspirations were checked by rational thought and action could we envisage an end to inter- and intra-state conflict.[23]

But if Professor Kedourie is right, what of the wars long before nationalism ever existed? If Lenin is on the right track, what of the many conflicts between Communists? As for the idea that despotism, Communism or Fascism represent the main danger, is the record of liberal democracy so much more impressive? After all, despite what thinkers from Kant to Michael Doyle have suggested about the peace-inducing properties of representative government,[24] the Amritsar and My Lai massacres, the brutalities during the Algerian struggle for independence from France and the maltreatment of the indigenous peoples of the Americas and Australia were all committed by the agents of liberal democracy. Sadly, no political or economic system to date appears to have avoided bloodshed on the grand scale, and for this reason some theorists have offered yet a further mode of explanation as to the causes of war. They look not to any particular political or economic arrangement within the state but to the system of states itself, seeing war as a product of collective insecurity in a divided world lacking government or moral consensus.

The international system

It was probably Thucydides who first saw war not so much in terms of human or societal failings but rather as a product of the security dilemma facing all states in conditions of international anarchy. Since then, many others have made their contribution – from Hobbes to Rousseau, through Hans Morgenthau to Kenneth Waltz. But perhaps the predicament was best summed up by a man who basically deplored the international system he was writing about – the Christian pacifist Martin Wight. For him war represented the most violent expression of the anarchical nature of the international system and the most extreme way in which states choose to control their destiny. And in his book *Power Politics* he suggests: 'The fundamental cause of war is not historical rivalries, nor unjust peace settlements, nor nationalist grievances, nor competitions in armaments, nor poverty, nor the economic struggle for markets and raw materials, nor the contradictions of capitalism, nor the aggressiveness of Fascism or Communism; though some of these may have occasioned particular wars. The fundamental cause is the absence of international government; in other words the anarchy of sovereign states.'[25]

It was left to Martin Wight's student, Hedley Bull, to add that war might also be undertaken either to transform the international system, as in some revolutionary agenda, or else to preserve it in face of challenge.[26]

13.5 TERMINATION OF HOSTILITIES

It is always much easier to start than to end a war, and one of the problems for both combatants and observers is to determine whether hostilities have indeed ended. After all, from the painful experience of both Bosnia and Angola, we have become painfully aware that ceasefires, peace negotiations and even peace treaties do not necessarily resolve a conflict. For whether war ends in the victory of one side, mutual exhaustion and stalemate, compromise or in third-party intervention, the dissatisfaction or resentment of one side or the other can always lead to further hostilities later on. Can we be quite certain that the conflict, say, between Iraq and Kuwait or between the various factions in Bosnia is finally over?

13.6 CONSEQUENCES

Clearly, wars can be major catalysts for political and economic change, often unintended. Those instigating them, for example, frequently end up on the losing side, while none of those responsible for the First World War would have envisaged either the Bolshevik Revolution, a direct result of the conflict, or the birth of Israel, an indirect long-term consequence, Britain's General Wingate having offered the Jews a Middle Eastern homeland in return for their labours during the war. And Hitler no doubt turns in his grave at the thought that his invasion of the Soviet Union ultimately produced Communist rule in East Germany and the rest of Eastern Europe.

Economic

Equally unpredictable are the economics of warfare. War has, of course, always been expensive, but the costs of modern hostilities can be astronomical, not only in direct military expenditures but also in terms of devastated real estate and capital equipment, lost production and trade, depleted resources, welfare payments for victims, the resettling of refugees and so on.[27] Such massive costs can impoverish even victorious countries, creating the conditions for economic depression, political instability, civil strife and even revolution, as in the 1920s and 1930s.

Political

Politically, the after-effects of an exhausting war are also problematic. Resistance to national secessionism may be weakened, and new, possibly unviable states created whose very instability can become the harbinger of further international strife, as in 1939. On the other hand the very precariousness of the post-war order may lead, as in 1919, 1945, 1947 (when Marshall Aid was proffered) and 1957 (when the Treaty of Rome was signed) to the creation of new international institutions to stabilise the system and encourage mutual aid and cooperation. However, since the victorious allies tend to fall out with one another, such order as there is may depend on the forging of new alliance partnerships, as in the case of France and Germany in the 1950s.

Psychological

Psychologically, the end of a prolonged and costly war tends to produce paradoxical effects. On the one hand bitter memories and apprehensions for the future may simply prolong traditional rivalries and heighten war preparedness. On the other hand they can also have a moderating influence, dampening enthusiasm for a future resumption of hostilities. In terms of ideology and religious principle, the effect of victory is often to strengthen conviction: the effect of defeat to weaken it; and it is after a lost war, particularly one perceived to have been mismanaged, that revolutions and counter-revolutions tend to occur – witness the spate of Communist, nationalist and Fascist revolutions in Central and Eastern Europe following both World Wars.

The ultimate resolution?

Do wars ever settle anything? The term 'settle' suggests the end of a process, and in fact we can never be certain that a war has reached its final termination. As Christopher Coker puts it: 'The cessation of hostilities and the end of war are not always the same'.[28] Nor we can ever assume that a contentious problem which has been the occasion for violence is resolved for all time. On the other hand some wars do result in the creation of new states, changed borders and transfers of population which seem to stand the test of time, even if still resented by those connected with the losing side. Other wars, however, settle nothing and merely fuel the grievances that result in further hostilities.

13.7 IS WAR INEVITABLE?

For neo-Liberals such as Francis Fukayama war is not only not inevitable, it is destined to disappear with the global spread of capitalism. Like Cobden and Bright a century and a half before 'the End of History' he believed that free trade and warfare are ultimately incompatible. On the other hand, Realists like Martin Wight have tended to think that war is inevitable, even though he held that 'particular wars could be avoided',[29] presumably by deterrence, diplomacy, third-party mediation or a reappraisal of the situation by one or other side. But, of course, it all depends on what is meant by 'inevitable'. If it implies a permanent process, clearly wars are not inevitable. They occur at some times in some places and not at other times in other places. If, on the other hand, by 'inevitable' is meant a phenomenon likely to recur at some time in the future, then this seems more plausible, especially if one includes low-intensity and protracted civil conflicts. But is the past always a guide to the future? Since habits and institutions can change, it is often dangerous to project the past into the future. Surely we can have no warrant for believing that anything is inevitable except, possibly, as Benjamin Franklin once put it, 'death and taxes'. What we *can* say is that war occurs with sickening statistical frequency, and that though there have been useful suggestions for reducing its incidence, scope and scale, sadly, no one has yet come up with a foolproof formula for eradicating it.

NOTES

1. The complex motives serving to explain war nostalgia are explored in Bourke, J., *An Intimate History of Killing: Face-to-face Killing in Twentieth-Century Warfare*, Cambridge, Granta, 1999.
2. On the ambiguities of 'the religion of love' in practice, see for example Martin, D., *Does Christianity Cause War?*, Oxford, Clarendon Press, 1997.
3. *The Clash of Civilisations and the Remaking of World Order*, London, Simon and Schuster, 1997.
4. Quoted in Joad, C.E.M., *The Bookmark*, London, Westhouse, May 1945, p. 99.
5. Report in *The Times*, 30 January 1998.
6. Quoted in Brend, W., *Foundations of Human Conflicts*, London, Chapman & Hall, 1944, p. 89.
7. Harmondsworth, Penguin, 1982, p. 101.
8. 'A few words on non-intervention' in *Dissertations and Discourses*, New York, 1873, pp. 261–2.
9. See for example Pugh, M., 'Peacekeeping and Humanitarian Intervention' in White, B., Little, R. and Smith, M. (eds), *Issues in World Politics*, Basingstoke, Macmillan, 1997.
10. On the effects of television on popular attitudes to intervention see Shaw, M., *Civil Society and Media in Global Crises*, London, Pinter, 1996.
11. [1910], New York, Arno, 1972.
12. Kaldor, M., *New Wars and Old Wars*, Cambridge, Polity, 1998.
13. See for example Wedgwood, C.V., *The Thirty Years War*, New Haven, Yale, 1939, p. 516.
14. Barnaby, F., *Future War*, London, Michael Joseph, 1984, pp. 116–17.
15. Nathan, J. and Oliver, J., *United States Foreign Policy and World Order*, Boston, Little, Brown, 1976, pp. 143–4.
16. Yapp, M.E., *The Near East since the First World War*, London, Longman, 1991, p. 417.
17. See Blainey, G., *The Causes of War*, London, Macmillan, 1973.
18. New York, Columbia University Press, 1959.

19. Ardrey, R., *The Territorial Imperative*, New York, Atheneum, 1966, and Lorenz, K., *On Aggression*, New York, Harcourt Brace, 1966.
20. His views were elaborated on a BBC programme *War and Peace in our Time*, 10 February 1984.
21. Quoted in Kegley, C. and Wittkopf, E., *World Politics: Trend and Transformation*, 7th edn, London, Macmillan, 1999, p. 95.
22. Mazzini, *Selected Writings*, Gangulee, N. (ed.), London, Lindsay Drummond, 1945.
23. *Nationalism*, London, Hutchinson, 1960.
24. See for example Doyle, M., 'Kant, Liberal legacies and foreign policy', Parts I and II, *Philosophy and Public Affairs*, vol. 12, nos. 3/4, 1983, pp. 205–35 and 323–53.
25. Wight, M., op. cit., Harmondsworth, Penguin, 1978, p. 101.
26. *The Anarchical Society*, London, Macmillan, 1977, pp. 184–99.
27. The costs of modern warfare are essayed in Kaldor, M., op. cit.
28. 'How wars end', *Millennium*, vol. 26, no. 3, 1997, p. 615.
29. Op. cit., p. 137.

PART V

NON-STATE ACTORS

CHAPTER 14

INTERNATIONAL ORGANISATIONS: GLOBAL AND REGIONAL

If the last chapter examined the factors behind the sad recurrence of war, this one focuses on the hopes of those priests, philosophers and potentates who had sought to eradicate it altogether and had devised plans for a more just and orderly world. What generally lends urgency to the search for the ultimate panacea is the experience of a particularly bloody and brutal conflict. Certainly the senseless slaughter of the First World War occasioned a profusion of proposals and projects, some more 'dotty' than others, but in the end people like Alfred Zimmern, Philip Noel-Baker, Norman Angell and Woodrow Wilson came to believe that in the idea of a League of Nations dedicated to international cooperation, peace and security, they had found that long-sought-after formula.

14.1 BEFORE THE LEAGUE

Influences on the architects

The League had not been conjured out of thin air. It represented a refinement of ideas and institutions around for centuries. Among the better-known visionaries with blueprints for a better world were Cruce, the Duc de Sully, Penn and the Abbé de St Pierre. But perhaps the most celebrated was Immanuel Kant's *Perpetual Peace* of 1795.[1] Couched in the form of a draft treaty, it anticipates in substance and in style the ideas of both Marx and Woodrow Wilson. Like Wilson, Kant believed war was an inevitable product of authoritarian rule and the insatiable drive of such systems for material gain. Writing at the time of the French Revolution, he argued – fifty years before Marx – for a transnational struggle to overthrow absolutism worldwide. As part of the process he envisaged the creation in one country after another of assemblies in which the common people would have a real say in their political destiny. In his view, such assemblies would refuse to sanction or finance war unless the Republics they served (and by Republic he meant a constitutional or democratic state) were threatened by some foreign autocrat. And he anticipated Marx in holding that there was a law of history that made the attainment of perpetual peace as inevitable as it was desirable. For, as a former teacher of geography, Kant had observed that the drive for security and material welfare that propelled men into war could also draw them together in cooperative endeavour. And though he did not think that the abolition of separate sovereignties was possible in the foreseeable future, he suggested that once states shared republican constitutions, a federal or confederal union of states would emerge, eventually to lead, as communism is supposed to lead, to the withering away of the state and the creation of a community of humankind.

What made this and other such schemes relevant was that the League's chief architect, Woodrow Wilson, had been a Professor of Politics: many of his advisors were likewise intellectuals with an interest in politics, philosophy, history and the classics and since they were well aware of such blueprints, it would be surprising if they had not been influenced by them.

But there were additional influences.[2] First, the historical legacy of confederal schemes, from the Swiss Confederation of the late thirteenth century, through the American Confederation of the late eighteenth century and beyond. Secondly, the post-Westphalian mechanisms for establishing and maintaining international order, such as international law, diplomacy and balance of power. Thirdly, the legacy of the Congress or Concert system established at Vienna in 1815 in which the five Great Powers of Europe met periodically to discuss and if possible resolve some of the world's major political and military problems. Fourthly, the examples of specialised international agencies such as the European Commission for the Danube, the Universal Postal Union and the International Red Cross – products of the massive growth of international trade and communications in the nineteenth century. And among additional international mechanisms for peaceful settlement on which the Covenant's architects could build was arbitration which, though by no means new (references are to be found in Grotius and even in Thucydides), had become fashionable after the Hague Conferences of 1899 and 1907 had established a Permanent Court of Arbitration.

14.2 THE LEAGUE

Organs

Emerging from the peace conference after the First World War, the League, therefore, was built on a legacy of ideas and experience. On the other hand it was a pity that President Wilson, imbued with the notion of making future wars impossible, insisted that the League be an integral part of the post-war peace settlement, since those governments that resented what they saw as an unjust accord were almost bound to transfer their animosity to the League itself. Since, too, many of those involved in fashioning the UN 25 years later saw in the League a model of how *not* to construct an international institution, it is important to examine its structure.

The League had four principle organs: an Assembly in which all participating states were represented; a Council containing the five major victors of the First World War plus ten others elected by the Assembly; a Secretariat, and a Court with nine judges at its disposal. Throughout, however, the major problem was lack of effective power. Assembly and Council could make only recommendations, not binding resolutions, and member states could interpret the recommendations as they chose. In any case recommendations had to be unanimous, which greatly hampered the ability of either organ to achieve agreements. As for the Secretariat, it lacked any executive function, while the Permanent Court of International Justice could adjudicate only if members submitted their disputes to it or asked for an advisory opinion.

Agenda

True, the League was concerned with more than just threats to the peace. Specialised agencies under its auspices sought to promote inter-state cooperation in fields such as labour, transport, communications, finance, public health and welfare. And under the Mandates system it promoted the well-being and development of the inhabitants of the former colonial territories of the Ottoman Empire and of Germany, effectively preventing their annexation by the Allied powers. Yet despite such activities, grudgingly financed by the member states, the organisation's primary aim was to establish what Woodrow Wilson called 'a new world order'. It was to replace the old, de-centralised balance-of-power mechanism with something more centralised and regulated, i.e. collective security through collective deterrence. It was also to promote the peaceful settlement of disputes as well as disarmament. How did it fare?

Record

Since in the 1920s the League faced no direct challenge from a major power, it was able to chalk up some successes. It helped defuse tensions on the Albanian/Yugoslav frontier in 1921, prevent hostilities between Sweden and Finland over the Aland Islands, deter a war between Greece and Bulgaria in 1925, settle a frontier dispute between Turkey and Iraq in 1926 and end the 'state of war' between Poland and Lithuania in 1927.

But in the 1930s, a decade of economic depression and national self-absorption, the successes were few and far between, and the League faced a series of challenges from the greatest military powers of the day for whom rearmament, not disarmament, was the priority.[3]

First to challenge the new world order was Japan, aggrieved that the peacemakers of 1919 had not granted it a bigger share of the spoils of war. Already militarised by the time Hirohito ascended the throne in the mid-1920s, Tokyo in 1931 embarked on the Tanaka plan of territorial expansion in Asia and beyond. An incident against a Japanese patrol guarding the South Manchurian railway provided the pretext for Japanese troops to sack the local Chinese barracks and thence to occupy the whole of Manchuria, China's vast and most prosperous province. Clearly the League's deterrent posture had failed, and under the collective security arrangement economic or military sanctions should have been applied against Tokyo. Yet in offering nothing beyond a mere rebuke, the League failed to provide an effective deterrent against further Japanese attacks, and over the next fourteen years Tokyo launched one assault after another on China, not hesitating to use poison gas in the process. When the League took the modest step of issuing a report branding Japan as an aggressor, the Japanese envoy stormed out of the League Assembly, and Tokyo's onslaught against China went on. Already the League's policy of collective security stood exposed as a sham.

Soon another delegate was to pack his bags – the representative of Germany, now under Nazi rule. Adolf Hitler, who had come to power in 1933, had never hidden his intention of restoring his country to greatness and avenging those he claimed had humiliated Germany in the peace of 1919. And as German rearmament and expansionism were incompatible with League membership, Hitler pulled his country out, even though Berlin's departure came a full two years before Hitler was ready to go on the attack. While he finalised his plans another dictator took action.

In Italy Mussolini, the architect of Fascism, saw himself also as the architect of a new Roman empire, centred around the Mediterranean. But first he sought revenge against Abyssinia, a country which had humiliated an Italian force in the 1890s, and in October 1935, following an incident he was able to turn to advantage as the Japanese had done in Manchuria, Mussolini sent in the troops. Against defenceless civilians and soldiers whose only weapons were spears, bows and arrows and bare knuckles Mussolini used the air force, tanks, machine guns and poison gas. It was an unequal contest, and flying to Geneva in the country's only plane, the Emperor of Abyssinia pleaded with the League to take effective action. But in vain. As in Manchuria, there was to be no military rescue. Though the League imposed a modest range of economic sanctions, their implementation was so half-hearted as to make little difference to Mussolini's war effort. And the Abyssinians capitulated.

The League's failure to take decisive action yet again was noted with satisfaction in Berlin as well as in Rome. And in 1936 Hitler was ready. In defiance of the Versailles accords, Germany reoccupied the Rhineland. Two years later, it forcibly absorbed Austria and then demanded that Czechoslovakia cede the German-speaking area known as the Sudetenland. In the ensuing crisis, the leaders of Britain, France and Italy met Hitler at Munich, and in return for a German pledge not to annexe the rest of Czechoslovakia, successfully pressured Prague to concede to Hitler's demand. Since war had been averted, Britain's Prime Minister Chamberlain claimed, on his return from Munich, that he had brought 'peace in our time'. Others, however, called it 'appeasement' – giving in to blackmail. And in March 1939, the bankruptcy of this policy stood revealed, as Hitler reneged on his pledge and seized the rest of Czechoslovakia – one of Europe's most prosperous and militarily advanced states, whose annexation was of inestimable benefit to the German war machine.

While Germany digested its fresh acquisitions, Mussolini's ambitions turned to one of Europe's smallest and most backward states – Albania – in April 1939 annexing what was already a virtual Italian protectorate. Meanwhile in Spain, Italian and German military assistance helped to tip the balance in favour of the country's Fascist dictator, General Franco, after three years of civil war. Belatedly, the members of the League began to take their responsibilities seriously. In August 1939, with Poland under threat of a German attack, Britain and France offered Warsaw their joint protection. Given the dismal record of the League, Hitler was unimpressed. But the die was cast. Two days after 1 September, when Germany invaded Western Poland, Chamberlain, who had tried so hard to avert war, found himself declaring it. Other declarations followed, and the Second World War, which some saw as a direct consequence of Japan's unhindered conquest of Manchuria, had now begun in earnest. (Sixty years later the League's successor, the UN, was to recall that unhappy precedent in deciding that Kuwait must not be allowed to suffer the same fate as Manchuria, Abyssinia, Czechoslovakia, Albania and Poland in the 1930s.) But while Britain and France struggled to contain the Nazi threat, they soon had to contend with a further and unexpected series of aggressions.

Less than a month after a non-aggression Pact with Nazi Germany, its ideological foe, Stalin's Russia occupied eastern Poland. Whether or not a defensive measure, the Soviet action, so soon after the Nazi onslaught, served to wipe Poland off the political map yet again. Three months later, Moscow seemed to have the same fate in store for Finland, once integral to the Russian empire. This time, however, its unprovoked attack led to the Soviet Union's expulsion from the League. But the gesture was meaningless, since after a decade of creeping paralysis the League was already effectively dead. Whether the League had failed the nations or the nations the League is debatable.[4] Clearly, however, in both theory and practice it had been deeply flawed.

Flaws

1. It had been part and parcel of a peace settlement that several countries thought unfair, and were determined, when strong enough, to overturn.
2. It had been crippled from the start by America's refusal to join – an irony, since the League was largely the brainchild of that country's own president.
3. The powers of its various bodies had been far too limited for effective action. Council and Assembly could not make binding decisions, and any government was free to reject or resist any recommendation.
4. Since aggression, which would necessitate a League response, lacked clear definition, it was often difficult to secure a consensus for action. For what appeared to some as aggression was defined by others as a legal retortion to an aggression against it. And in determining whether or not an aggression had occurred, states tended to be partisan – reluctant to admit that, say, an ally might be an aggressor or a foe the victim of their ally's aggression.
5. Even when the League agreed that an aggression had occurred, it was one thing to respond collectively when the perpetrator was a small power, another when the aggression was committed by one or more great powers, which was the situation the organisation faced many times in the 1930s. In such circumstances apprehensions tended to rise, and with them increasing resistance to effective action.
6. The League had in any case been largely Eurocentric, and its members had shown a lack of concern when the arena of aggression was in Asia (as in Manchuria), Africa (as in Abyssinia), or Latin America (as when Bolivia and Paraguay fought a three-year war in the 1930s over the uninhabited river basin known as the Chaco. Significantly, it was the American states and not the League that worked out a peace to conclude the Gran Chaco War).
7. Several governments, having joined the League not out of conviction but for fear of popular disapproval if they did not, were in fact opposed to the very principle of combining for collective security. Quintin Hogg, later Lord Hailsham, spoke for many when he declared: 'I believe it is right to fight for . . . King and country. But it's against nature . . . to be called to die for someone else's King and country.'[5] The aggressors

were able to get away with it in part because too few were prepared to die for another's 'King and country'.

8. The League had tended to concentrate too narrowly on the problem of inter-state war and was insufficiently focused on the kinds of political resentments and economic and social conditions that might be a contributary cause.

14.3 THE UNITED NATIONS

Learning the lessons

After analysing the essential flaws in the constitution, composition and performance of the League, the framers of the UN Charter 25 years later were determined to learn the lessons.[6]

1. Though the UN arose out of the wartime anti-Fascist coalition, it was not tied to any particular peace settlement after it, and, unlike its predecessor, did not regard the post-war arrangements as sacrosanct or beyond discussion.
2. Switzerland excepted, the UN's membership is virtually universal, the US as well as the Soviet Union having been among its original signatories. Indeed, with 185 states, compared to the original 51, it has become far larger than anyone envisaged, and its membership seems destined to increase still further as aspiring nations seek to make good their claims to independence.
3. The Charter gave the UN powers conspicuously lacking in the League. It was to have its own armed forces, to deny the veto to all but the five permanent members of the Security Council and to empower the Council to call for collective action against any power it deemed an aggressor, ranging from a reprimand or rebuke, through economic sanctions to military force.
4. The UN was to have a broad agenda, in keeping with its wide-ranging membership, many of whom were more interested in 'justice' than in 'order' and in the problems of development than in the security dilemma. Though peace and security took priority, the UN was also to try to solve international economic, social, cultural and humanitarian problems. It was to have as its province, therefore, any question affecting inter-state relations; though not unless international peace was thought to be at risk was it to intervene militarily in matters of domestic jurisdiction.

Organs

As is generally known, the UN has a General Assembly, comprising all 185 member states, but with the power only to make recommendations, and a Security Council of fifteen members which can make binding decisions, provided the five powers with the veto can agree.

There are, in addition, four further major organs. One of these is the Economic and Social Council (ECOSOC), elected by the General Assembly every three years to initiate studies, establish commissions, call international conferences and make recommendations on issues concerning economic, social and humanitarian issues. One of its subsidiaries, the United Nations Conference on Trade and Development (UNCTAD), works closely with the UN's specialised agencies such as the Food and Agricultural Organisation (FAO), the World Health Organisation (WHO), the International Labour Organisation (ILO), United Nations Educational, Scientific and Cultural Organisation (UNESCO), United Nations Children's Emergency Fund (UNICEF) and the World Bank through which it helps to channel loans and technical assistance to some of the world's poorer countries.

Another UN body, the Trusteeship Council, was to take over the work of the League committee dealing with the Mandated territories, though it acquired additional responsibilities – territories once under German and Japanese control and mainly in the Pacific. With all its charges independent, the Council has successfully completed its mission.

Another UN organ, the International Court of Justice (ICJ), the successor of the PCIJ, also plays an important role, together with a further UN body, the International Law Commission, in developing international law, not least in new areas such as the environment, outer space, the polar regions and the seabed, and in highly contentious areas involving the delineation of individual, group and human rights.

Finally there is the UN Secretariat, a much more substantial body than under the League: indeed, it is often accused of being too substantial in that many of its several thousand highly paid international civil servants in New York and Geneva appear to have little to do. Nonetheless the gainfully employed are there to gather, publish and distribute data, prepare special studies on international problems and service the multitude of meetings under the UN's auspices. More importantly, perhaps, its Secretary-General has become an important figure in his own right. He may take independent initiatives which in his view advance the principles of the Charter, as when in 1998 Kofi Annan mediated in the dispute between Iraq and the coalition against it; he may also frustrate action he deems unwise, as Washington claims his predecessor Dr Boutros Boutros Ghali did in respect of its projected air operations in Bosnia.[7]

Difficulties

No matter how the UN has in fact developed, the original expectations of the organisation were probably too high and, not surprisingly, experience has failed to match up to them.[8]

1. Though the veto and the UN's New York headquarters ensured US membership, the organisation's performance has been shaped by the world political context, and any assessment of the UN's record has to take into account the environment within which it operates. The cold war greatly hampered the functioning of the Security Council and made it virtually impossible to create a permanent UN standing army. For the veto would be used whenever the major interests of either Superpower was involved, and neither Moscow nor Washington would sanction an international force it could not control. The one exception during this period – the creation in 1950 of a UN force to fight in Korea – only transpired because of the Soviet Union's absence from the crucial meeting which took the decision. Had it been present it would undoubtedly have rejected the claim that North Korea had been the aggressor. Later, the commitment to global collective security would be further undermined by the appearance of rival regional defence associations, such as NATO and the Warsaw Pact, and the refusal of the Superpowers to pay for peacekeeping operations of which they disapproved.

2. When the Superpowers did have matters of common concern to discuss, they would often deal with them outside the aegis of the UN. The UN was not involved, for example, in the treaty neutralising Austria, the 'hot line' between Moscow and Washington, the SALT treaties or the creation of the Conference on Security and Cooperation in Europe, which was to play a crucial role in the unravelling of Communist power in Eastern Europe.

3. Many of the more divisive issues preoccupying the Powers have not easily lent themselves to UN action because of their implications for domestic jurisdiction and the precept of non-intervention. Thus, though civil conflicts have mushroomed in recent years, along with human rights violations, the case for UN intervention has had to be balanced against the commitment to national sovereignty and self-defence.[9] And until a beleaguered government calls for its help or the Security Council deems there to be a general threat to peace or a danger of genocide, the organisation tends to avoid direct involvement.

For this reason, some states do not even bother to seek UN help. According to Ernst Haas, of 300 or so military conflicts between 1945 and 1984, fewer than half were referred to the UN.[10] It was never asked to conciliate such contentions as the French–Algerian war or the troubles in the Basque region, Northern Ireland or Chechnya. And even where its help is sought, by minorities such as the Palestinians, Kashmiris, Kurds, the Christians of South Sudan, the East Timorese in Indonesia, the Muslims in Bosnia or the Kosovars in Serbia, partisan politics will often delay or inhibit UN action. And when the UN does act, it cannot guarantee a successful resolution – as the expensive fiascos in Somalia and Angola demonstrate only too clearly.

4. On welfare, and its commitment to reducing the disparity between rich and poor, the UN's performance has been mixed. On the one hand the General Assembly and the various bodies under ECOSOC set standards and have served to dramatise the plight of the poor, the malnourished, the persecuted and the dispossessed. In addition, the UN's various agencies have been generous in allocating funds to the needy. Smallpox has been eradicated and epidemics of cholera, typhoid and malaria controlled thanks to the work of the WHO, which has also been in the forefront of the drive to inform people about birth control and the danger of AIDS. In many parts of the world, too, agricultural yields have been improved, together with local diets, thanks to the work of the FAO. And, of course, the Trusteeship Council has successfully completed its mission of promoting self-government and independence.

On the other hand, for all the UN's good work, the gap between the extremes of wealth and poverty both within or between states, has, if anything, widened. In part this reflects the fact that in many of the LDCs, population growth far outstrips economic growth. But narrowing the gap is made more difficult by corruption, inefficiency, indebtedness and civil strife in many of the LDCs, compounded by often adverse international trading conditions.

Moreover, Third World appeals for more development and technical assistance, duty-free access to Western markets, long-term commodity agreements at stable prices, the cancellation or reduction of debt – summed up in the notion of a New International Economic Order – have tended to get an unsympathetic response. Nor can the wealthy and powerful be compelled to concede on the matter since the UN, like any other political institution, reflects the competing objectives of its members and can only do what in the end the more prosperous are prepared to pay for.[11] As an organisation, it is as good or as bad as the states comprising it.

5. A host of new issues have appeared on the international agenda never in contemplation when the UN was founded. Climate change, environmental pollution, resource depletion, the population explosion, transnational crime and terrorism, the spread of AIDS, nuclear proliferation,

chronic debt and so on are matters for the treatment of which the organisation has yet to develop appropriate mechanisms. Meanwhile, the meagre results of the UN-sponsored summits on environmental degradation from Rio in 1992 to Kyoto in 1997 have hardly matched up to the seriousness of the problem.

6. In terms of its administration, where promotion is based on government quotas rather than merit, the UN has been plagued with staff of poor calibre, and the bureaucratic structure is widely thought to be in drastic need of reform. The reluctance of some of its largest donors, including the US, to pay their arrears merely compounds the problems of corruption, nepotism and mismanagement infecting its bloated bureaucracy. Too much capital goes into providing plush accommodation and perks for its administrators, too many of its agencies duplicate the work of other agencies, too many committees continue in being long after their work is done, while much of the UN's balloting and budgetary work is outdated and unfair. The Security Council, for example, reflects the pattern of power of 50 or more years ago, while the General Assembly's voting system leaves much to be desired when the 8 countries who pay 70 per cent of the UN's budget command only 8 votes and tiny Nauru and gigantic China have an equal say. Surely, too, it is unfair when bankrupt countries such as Russia and the Ukraine are levied far higher charges for peacekeeping operations than Saudi Arabia and Singapore, which are classified as less developed countries.[12]

Facilities

On the other hand Kofi Annan, whom Washington clearly hoped would reform the institution, has already begun the process by trying to pare the central budget, cut out wasteful duplication and pension off the more corrupt time-servers. In any case, for all its failings, the UN's very existence serves to focus attention on issues of global concern and provides a valuable framework for the handling of international crises, economic and environmental as well as political and military. It is not, however, a world government, and if it did not exist much of its work could be undertaken by regional and non-government organisations, by bilateral discussion, by conventional diplomacy or by the exercise of hegemonic power. As noted above, such expedients tend to be called into play when the UN is unable, for one reason or another, to act. On the other hand, in providing a framework for international cooperation and an instrument of international order, the organisation has far more to offer than meets the electronic eye. Moreover, the fact that representatives from countries hostile or indifferent to one another can be in continuous contact in the lobbies and lounges behind the scenes may serve to defuse tensions and encourage compromise.[13] What happens away from the public gaze may be more important than what society discerns.

And when conflicts are not being resolved by rational discussion, they can sometimes be deflected in debate, when the UN becomes a kind of safety valve for those who can discharge verbally much accumulated resentment and anger. In this sense the organisation has a quasi-psychiatric function in which the protagonists act out their quarrels in place, as it were, of physical combat. But the UN has an additional quasi-psychiatric function. It can serve as a face-saving mechanism for states which have to make a policy climbdown. For example, Britain and France probably called off their 1956 Suez adventure because the US secretly issued a number of economic and other threats. However, it made a pull-out much easier when they could say it was in response to UN pressure. And though the real reason for Premier Khrushchev's decision to remove Soviet missiles from Cuba in 1962 was Kennedy's threat to go to the brink of nuclear war if they were not withdrawn, the UN's request for their removal made it easier for the Soviet leader to back down.[14] Later, the UN provided the escape route by which the Soviet Union could withdraw from the 'bleeding wound' of Afghanistan, and the fig leaf whereby NATO could legitimise its protection force in Kosovo.

Peacekeeping

Interestingly enough, the UN has in some respects exceeded the hopes of its founders. It has, for instance, developed techniques for what former Secretary-General Dag Hammarskjold called 'preventive diplomacy', in which it attempts with the assistance of forces from small and medium powers to resolve local conflicts before they escalate to crisis point. And in recent years UN peace-enforcement, to compel compliance with UN resolutions, peace making, which is about the process of securing a truce between warring factions, and peace building, which aims to create conditions making a relapse into war unlikely, have been supplemented by numerous peace-keeping operations designed to monitor and support any accord between antagonists. Further, the duties of such peacekeeping forces have been greatly expanded over the years, as have their operations,[15] and in 1988 the organisation was awarded a Nobel Peace prize for its endeavours.

At first it involved simply interposing troops between combatants in an inter-state war, as when in 1956, on the retreat of Anglo-French forces from Egypt, a UN Emergency Force (UNEF) was placed in the Sinai peninsula to keep Egyptian and Israeli troops apart. However, the presence of such a force has to be approved by the state on whose territory it is situated, and if, as happened in 1967, that consent is later withdrawn, the force must go. In this case, UNEF's departure ushered in a new round of Middle Eastern hostilities – the Six Day War.

The next peacekeeping force found itself in a situation with which, strictly speaking, the UN was not supposed to deal – a civil war in a newly independent country. The country was the Congo, and the government, which had taken over after the hasty retreat of the Belgian colonists, was unable to keep control. When, however, it looked as if the Belgians and the Russians who supported different factions in the conflict might become deeply embroiled, the UN declared the situation 'a threat to peace' and with the consent of members of the Congolese administration, which had in effect been toppled, voted to send in UN troops. The troops played a controversial role, sometimes firing before being fired on, but by 1964 they had re-established order.[16] They had not, however, restored the original left-wing government, but a right-wing administration of which the late dictator, President Mobutu (one of those immensely rich rulers of a potentially wealthy country he had impoverished), was the direct successor.

A third UN peacekeeping force was again involved in a domestic dispute, but this time with the explicit backing of all the protagonists. The venue was Cyprus, the date 1964, and the UN force there was to police the lines between the hostile Greek and Turkish communities. Despite the presence on the island since 1974 of a quite separate Turkish force, after a coup designed to unite Cyprus with Greece in the teeth of Turkish Cypriot hostility, the UN force remains. Until recently it appeared to play a constructive role in separating the protagonists, but tensions on the divided island have been mounting alarmingly, and the UN can hardly of itself defuse the crisis for which both Cypriot and Turkish governments must share considerable responsibility.

In the past two to three decades peacekeepers have again been sent to Sinai, to the Golan Heights between Israel and Syria (one of the more successful UN enterprises!), to Southern Lebanon (one of the least successful!), and more recently, when the 'blue helmets' were increased from 4,000 to over 70,000, to Somalia (a disaster!) and Bosnia (no disaster, but no triumph either!). They have also become involved in monitoring ceasefire lines in places such as Afghanistan and on the Iran/Iraq border; in disarming insurgents, as in Nicaragua and El Salvador; in mine clearance, as in Cambodia and Angola; in preparing for and supervising elections, as in Cambodia, Nicaragua, Namibia and Haiti; in securing humanitarian assistance, as in Bosnia; in attempting to protect enclaves of minorities, as in Iraq, Croatia, Bosnia and Serbia; in pre-empting the possibility of hostilities, as in Macedonia; in documenting war crimes, as in Rwanda, Bosnia and Kosovo; and in a variety of capacities following the Gulf War when the UN, having first sanctioned a military force to chase the Iraqis out of Kuwait, then created a United Nations Special Committee (UNSCOM) to monitor the ceasefire and dismantle Baghdad's weapons of mass destruction.

But the effectiveness of such operations tends to be proportionate to the support – financial, military and political – they receive from the Security Council. Moreover, as indicated earlier, peace-keeping is one thing: peace-making another,[17] and if the former is often risky and not always success-ful, the latter – so often involving missions impossible – can be even more hazardous. It is precisely because there was so little peace for it to keep that the UN, following its débâcle in Somalia in the early 1990s, was wary of getting too enmeshed in either Bosnia or Kosovo, which were primarily civil conflicts in which those who know their mountains have a substantial military advantage over those who do not. In any case there was always the fear that, as in Cyprus, the UN would be involved in an open-ended commitment or in establishing a virtual protectorate or trusteeship with all the political and resource implications this could involve. In the event, the UN was drawn into Bosnia and Kosovo and with no clear exit strategy.

Though often bitterly criticised, the UN's peacekeeping services are still much in demand, even if, largely at Washington's behest, NATO is in effect shouldering some of their functions. As Kofi Annan has discovered, far too many people want the UN to do far too many things, but are not prepared to give it the financial backing it needs with which to do them properly. In short, UN peacekeeping is overstretched, under funded and often unable to cope unaided.

A new world order?

The record, thus, is somewhat patchy, and a disappointment for the idealists who expected too much. But in fact the UN's performance, particularly in matters of 'low' politics, has been not unimpressive given the competitive nature of international society. On the other hand hopes that the end of the cold war would place the UN at the hub of a new world order have not been realised. Certainly, as regards Kuwait the Security Council temporarily found a degree of cohesion hitherto lacking. But the five Permanent members of the Security Council evidently have no intention of curbing their role in supplying arms to the world's trouble spots. In any case, the vision of a new world order was largely based on the Western tendency to exaggerate the extent to which the Soviet Union was responsible for most of the world's troubles, and to underplay the threats to international stability of unresolved nationalist, ethnic, religious, economic, territorial and other rivalries that had little to do with the cold war.[18] In fact now that the cold war is over, such rivalries are being given free rein, posing threats to the interests of those not immediately involved.

14.3 REGIONAL ORGANISATIONS

Where, does this leave the regional organisations? Though there is in theory no necessary contradiction between regional and global integration, in practice the more united the regions the more fragmented international society could become.[19] For such organisations as the European Union, the North American Free Trade Area (NAFTA) and the Association of South East Asian Nations (ASEAN) have distinctly protectionist overtones, and threats of trade wars between them surface periodically. On the other hand it is not yet clear how solid these economic blocs are or for how long they can retain their residual trade barriers in face of the operations of the World Trade Organisation.

The European Union

In the case of the European Union which, as distinct from NAFTA or ASEAN, is supposed to be committed to the collective management of the region's domestic and foreign affairs, enthusiasts and critics alike are apt to exaggerate its progress to date. Conceived in 1957 as a common market among its six founding nations – Belgium, France, Italy, Luxembourg, the Netherlands and West Germany – the European Economic Community soon removed internal customs barriers and imposed a common external tariff. In 1973 the EEC was joined by Denmark, Ireland and Britain, in 1981 Greece, in 1992 Spain and Portugal and in 1995 Austria, Finland and Sweden, by which time the organisation's name had been changed to European Union.[20] By the end of the century the EU was preparing to incorporate former members of COMECON, the Communist economic pact. In theory it was by now a single market, committed to a single currency, a regional central bank and a common foreign and defence policy. In practice, however, the organisation was a Union in idea rather than in reality.

In the first place, in 'opting out' of some of these proposed arrangements at Maastricht in 1992, Britain created a precedent for others to follow. Monetary union, from which it stands aloof, is also spurned, at least for the time being, by two other members, and in many other areas of significance, the Union appears disunited. On immigration controls, taxation, the management of the European bank, beef imports, fishing rights, Iraq, Bosnia and even Kosovo, it has been something of a free-for-all. And as regards its unelected but powerful Commission which can initiate and execute policy, many complain of a 'democratic deficit'. Could it be that national sentiment tends to reassert itself the more the exercise of sovereignty seems to be diminished?

Certainly, many of the Union's original objectives have been outdated by events. With many of its members hovering around recession, and the Euro declining in value, some perceive the EU to be a failing economic organisation. The idea that it might become a kind of third force between the Superpowers has been outmoded with the end of the cold war, and those hoping to use it to keep Germany divided have already lost the struggle. On the other hand, the evident tensions between the European and North Atlantic wings of NATO during the conflict over Kosovo reinforced the notion that the EU has to assume greater responsibility for regional defence, while the strengthening of the institutional arrangements for a Common Foreign and Security Policy suggests that the EU is giving priority to the adoption of a common position. There is, thus, a kind of dialectic between integration and fragmentation which complicates its operations and in turn affects the functioning of other political and economic institutions, regional and global, intergovernmental and non-governmental.

Security – regional and global

On the other hand, though some see regional organisations as undermining the collective security aspirations of the UN, they can promote regional order.[21] After all, Commonwealth forces helped to monitor a peaceful transfer of power in Zimbabwe in 1980, Nigerian-led ECOMOG forces have sought to restore democratic rule to Sierra Leone, Russian-led troops of the Commonwealth of Independent States (CIS) have tried to moderate conflicts in the former states of Soviet central Asia, while NATO forces have been used, with varying degrees of success, in peacekeeping operations in former Yugoslavia. But the relations between regional and global institutions are no less complex than those between inter-governmental organisations (IGOs) and international non-governmental organisations (INGOs). The next chapter attempts to untangle some of the complexities.

NOTES

1. [1795], New York, Bobbs-Merrill, 1957.
2. See, Hemleben, S.J., *Plans for World Peace through Six Centuries*, Chicago, Chicago University Press, 1943; York, E., *League of Nations, Ancient, Medieval*

and *Modern*, Swarthmore Press, London, 1928; and Woolf, L., *International Government*, New York, Brentane's, 1916.

3. Northedge, F.S., in *The International Political System*, London, Faber, 1976, provides an interesting account of the pressures leading to the collapse of the League, pp. 91–101.

4. See Manning, C.A.W., 'The "failure" of the League' in Cosgrove, C. and Twitchett, K. (eds), *The New International Actors*, London, Macmillan, 1970, pp. 105–23.

5. From a BBC broadcast of June 1934.

6. Goodrich, L.M. and Simons, A.P., *The Charter of the United Nations – Commentary and Documents*, 3rd edn, New York, Columbia University Press, 1970; also Nicolas, H., 'From League to UN', *International Affairs*, November 1970, Special Issue.

7. For a more detailed analysis of the UN system see for example Luard, E., *The United Nations: How it Works and What It Does*, 2nd edn, New York, St Martin's Press, 1994.

8. See for example Roberts, A. and Kingsbury, B. (eds), *United Nations, Divided World*, 2nd edn, Oxford, Clarendon Press, 1993; and also Righter, R., *Utopia Lost: The United Nations and World Order*, New York, The Twentieth Century Fund Press, 1995.

9. See, for example, Pugh, M., 'Peacekeeping and Humanitarian Intervention' in White, B., Little, R., and Smith, M., *Issues in World Politics*, London, Macmillan, 1997.

10. *Why We Still Need the United Nations*, Berkeley, University of California, 1986.

11. See Thomas, C. and Reader, M., 'Development and Inequality', in White, B. *et al.*, op. cit., pp. 90–110.

12. For a more detailed analysis of the possibilities of and prospects for UN reform see for example Mingst, K. and Karns, M., *The United Nations in the Post Cold War Era*, Boulder, Westview, 1995.

13. Alger, C.F., 'Personal contact in international exchanges' in Kelman, H.C. (ed.), *International Behaviour*, New York, Holt, Rinehart and Winston, 1965, p. 527.

14. See for example O'Brien, C.C., and Topolski, F., *The United Nations: Sacred Drama*, London, Hutchinson, 1968.

15. See Peck, C., *Sustainable Peace: The Role of the UN and Regional Organisations*, Lanham, MD, Rowman and Littlefield, 1997.

16. O'Brien, C.C., *To Katanga and Back*, London, Hutchinson, 1962.

17. Rikhye, I.J., 'Peace keeping and peace making' in *Peace-keeping: Appraisals and Proposals*, Oxford, Oxford University Press, 1983, pp. 5–18.

18. Eban, E., 'The UN idea revisited', *Foreign Affairs*, vol. 75, no. 5, September/ October 1995.

19. See Jones, W.S., *The Logic of International Relations*, 6th edn, Glenview, Ill., Scott and Co., 1988, pp. 226–8.

20. For a detailed examination of the problems and prospects of the EU see for example Redmond, J., and Rosenthal, G. (eds), *The Expanding European Union*, Boulder, Colo., Lynne Riener, 1997; and also Wallace, H. and W. (eds), *Policymaking in the European Union*, 3rd edn, Oxford, Oxford University Press, 1996.

21. See Smith, M., 'Regions and regionalism', in White, B. *et al.*, op. cit., pp. 69–89.

CHAPTER 15

TRANSNATIONAL MOVEMENTS AND ORGANISATIONS

15.1 TRANSNATIONALISM PRIOR TO WESTPHALIA

So far the argument above may seem to have been somewhat old-fashioned in that the main emphasis has been on sovereign states. But, of course, the state was never the sole actor in world politics, if by actor one means an entity which enjoys a degree of autonomy, has a constituency which it represents and an arena in which it can exert influence. After all, prior to the sovereign state, the significant political, economic, social and cultural actors had to be subnational, transnational or supranational – city states, feudal fiefdoms, principalities, duchies, kingdoms and empires; clans and tribes; corporate economic bodies such as the Hanseatic League and the Merchant Adventurers; great banking and finance houses; and the religious establishments.

Ideas, moreover, had always been transnational. When social or political bodies interacted, assumptions, concepts, creeds, doctrines and dogmas could always be transmitted from one to another. At the same time, of course, the impact of inventions and new technologies could never be confined just to their countries of origin. Meanwhile the discoveries of voyagers such as Columbus and da Gama helped to reshape the intellectual, geographical and political horizons of the medieval world, though often to the detriment of the natives of the New World who were unwittingly introduced to the diseases, viruses, bacteria and parasites of the old.

Before the age of the sovereign state, loyalties, too, tended to be largely transnational. Most Europeans of the fifteenth and sixteenth centuries would probably have identified themselves first and foremost as Christians, that is, as a community of persons sharing the same faith. A few might also have considered themselves 'European', a novel concept indicating a culture forged by a Church claiming to be the inheritor of Graeco-Roman as well as Christian civilisation. In a sense, Europe would have been defined in terms of what was regarded as non-European, and increasingly the boundary was held to lie at the point where Christianity encounters Islam.[1] This is, perhaps, why historians of European origin tended to ignore the Egyptian contribution to Graeco-Roman and hence

European civilisation, and why even today many express surprise at the existence of European Muslims in the Balkans.

Where loyalties were not transnational they were often subnational – to individuals and groups within existing frontiers, to feudal lords, barons or local squires, to abbots of a particular monastery, to guilds – friendly societies that took care of the elderly, the sick and the unemployed members of a craft. Yet others found their sense of identity in a kind of local patriotism, in attachment to their region, province or town. Popular allegiance to king and country did not come until later.

15.2 TRANSNATIONALISM SINCE WESTPHALIA

Religious and political affiliations

Even after the appearance of the sovereign state in the sixteenth and seventeenth centuries, non-state actors continued to play a significant role. In fact the state system was always part of a wider system of political, economic and social interaction.[2] The Papacy and the Holy Roman Empire still counted millions of devotees long after Westphalia, while semi-autonomous principalities, duchies and archbishoprics continued to command allegiance even within the new kingdoms.

Class and cultural affiliations

There were, in addition, transnational class, ideological and other kinds of ties. For all their insistence on sovereign independence, the rulers of Westphalian Europe tended to be linked by cultural and religious bonds and often, because of dynastic marriages, by ties of blood. Indeed, so cosmopolitan was the royal profession that many rulers were not even nationals or native speakers of the countries they governed. In 1688 for example a Dutchman, William, became King of England, and in 1714 a Hanoverian, George, who hardly spoke English at all and despised the country and most of its people. Moreover, those serving the royal households often had no national stake in the system. The entourage of Peter the Great and of his successors in Russia were largely German, while for years Italians helped run the French royal household.

Ideological ties and movements

By the eighteenth century, the world of ideas was being revolutionised by theorists and political activists whose sympathies could not be confined to any particular state. For example the philosophers of the Enlightenment, who had a marked impact on our conception of modernity, inspired both American and French revolutions, and in turn promoted the paradox of trans-national nationalism, as militants in 1830 and 1848 used the newly invented trans-continental railways to foment revolutionary nationalist uprisings in one capital after another. And, of course, the contagious ideas of the French socialists and communists which inspired Marx and Engels indirectly contributed to the development of trade unions, cooperatives and welfare legislation and spawned the Socialist Internationals of the nineteenth century and the Communist (Third) International of the twentieth century.

ECONOMIC NON-STATE ACTORS

Trading companies

Generating not so much devotion as power were a host of economic non-state actors, of which the transnational trading organisation was perhaps the most important. Though Susan Strange in *States and Markets*[3] suggests that the relations today between transnational companies and the state constitute a 'new dimension of diplomacy', this is rather an oversimplification. For the political and economic influence of many of the trading organisations of the seventeenth to nineteenth centuries, such as the British East India Company, the various companies specialising in trade with the Americas and, in particular, the Hudson's Bay Company, was enormous. The East India Company, for example, in effect ruled much of India and South-east Asia for more than a century, employing its own armed forces to acquire territory and secure exclusive trading rights, and training native armies to keep out missionaries as well as rival traders.[4] In addition, it claimed the right to restrict tea imports from countries not under its control, and it was when this was applied to America that a Company tea cargo was sabotaged in Boston harbour, in turn precipitating the revolt of the American colonies. The Company also introduced opium to China, leading ultimately, of course, to the opium wars. How many modern MNCs can boast a comparable record of the use and abuse of power?

Finance houses

A second important set of significant non-state economic actors were the finance houses. For example, the German Fugger banking firm played a key role in determining who in 1530 would wear the crown of the Holy Roman Empire. That it went to Charles V of Spain was largely because the bank lent him enough florins to enable him to buy it. And in fact the Fugger balance sheet of 1546 shows debts from a German emperor, the city of Antwerp, the kings of England and Portugal and the Queen of the Netherlands. At one time the Pope was also in debt to this particular firm.[5] Though such actions predate the sovereign state as such, the Fuggers and the other great banking houses were to provide the backing for the expansion of international enterprise and commerce even after Westphalia.

Craftsmen

A third and increasingly important group of economic actors were what might be termed the transnational craftsmen – skilled workers and inventors who could be lured from one country to ply their trade in another. In a period innocent of the passport, immigration quota and work permit, and under the protectionist system that developed in the seventeeth and eighteenth centuries, to be known as 'mercantilism', such craftsmen were much sought-after by governments which would provide free dwellings, tax exemptions and a production monopoly to entice them into taking up residence – as many thousands did.[6]

The international economy

A fourth non-state actor was the international economy itself, whose power to influence policies and events seemed to grow as some of the restraints, regulations and restrictions of mercantilism gradually withered before the onslaught on them by Adam Smith and other free-trade economists.[7] Then, as now, free trade proved a seductive doctrine, especially among merchants and manufacturers in the 'have' as against the 'have not' countries. But as more and more governments began to act upon it, domestic markets became increasingly sensitive to what was happening in the international market. And just as the revolutions in British commerce, industry, agriculture and transportion reverberated on the international economy, so (as today) the international economy began to constrain the actions of governments.

For example, the unemployment, poverty and destitution noted by Marx and Engels during the 1840s was clearly not confined to any one state. For that era's slump affected all the countries in which the authors of *The Communist Manifesto* were exiled – Prussia, France, Belgium and Britain – and many others besides. By the same token the massive boom from the 1850s till the late 1870s, which had so surprised Marx and Engels, also impacted on most trading countries simultaneously. And during the twentieth century the pattern was repeated: a worldwide boom in the first decade; a global depression in the 1930s; a global boom in the 1960s; world recession creating a serious debt crisis in the 1980s and 1990s; global recovery in the mid-1990s, somewhat undermined by economic crisis in the Far East, in Russia and in Brazil that threatened to spread.

Benevolent organisation

Among other influential non-state actors, some had a markedly anti-commercial bias, as for instance the anti-slavery movements in Britain of the late eighteenth and early nineteenth centuries. For, having captured the public imagination, they helped to create a climate leading to the abolition of the slave trade in Britain in 1807 and throughout the Empire in 1833. Though Britain's example invited emulation, it took some time and not a little violence for, say, the plantation owners of the Southern American states or the Arab traders in East Africa to get the message. And even today slavery survives in parts of Africa, Mauritania especially, as does indentured labour in Asia and the Middle East.

Other non-national allegiances

In Africa, Asia and the Middle East, until the imposition of imperial rule, the conception of the sovereign state was largely unknown and loyalties were of necessity non-national. And since for their own reasons the imperialist powers would often encourage or exploit those local allegiances, indigenous loyalties based on tribe, traditional political and cultural entities or tributary relationships have tended to persist.[8] In this sense, the Hausa, the Hutu, the Zulu, the Kikuyu, the Baganda or the Ashanti have continued to play politically significant roles long after the independence respectively of Nigeria, Rwanda, South Africa, Kenya, Uganda or Ghana. In similar vein, the Overseas Chinese have tended to retain a strong attachment to the Zhung Guo, the Central Land, while successive Chinese governments have operated the 'ius sanguinis', the 'law of the blood', making themselves responsible for the welfare of Chinese communities in any part of the world. Sadly, such sub- and trans-national loyalties often antagonise fellow citizens with different affiliations, leading to tragedies such as the massacre of the Chinese in Indonesia, the Ibo in Nigeria or the Tutsi in Rwanda.

Individuals

Finally, no account of traditional non-state actors would be complete without reference to people whose actions, singly or collectively, contribute to the making of history. For one does not have to be of liberal inclination to know that individuals are not merely passive agents of impersonal forces. Ultimately it is individual statesmen and women, politicians, civil servants, businessmen and women, bankers, workers, soldiers, tribal chiefs, religious leaders, philosophers and the like who mould the destinies of nations, and individuals who are asked to realise their designs, and the dynamic interplay between those who conceive, direct and implement policy determines the changing course of world politics and economics.

15.3 CHALLENGE TO STATE PRIMACY?

If states were never the sole participants in world politics, and the non-state actor never wholly subordinate to the state system, why do so many teachers of the subject, including the present writer, continue to talk about the primacy of the sovereign state?[9] The answer depends on how one interprets the expressions 'primacy' and 'sovereign state', and on the realms of discourse to which they are applied. The term 'primacy' suggests the existence of a range of entities of which one in particular takes precedence. The term 'sovereign state' here refers to a political entity which has obtained recognition as a legal person, and is thereby the bearer of legal rights and duties. Here the question of state primacy will be in four separate contexts – the legal, the political, the functional (that is, as an instrument for promoting world order), and the economic.

Moral

First, however, it is necessary to dispose briefly of the question in one further realm of discourse – the moral. Though morality may or may not have an objective existence, what we as individuals understand by morality rests on a subjective judgement. For the Classical Realists, the state was the ultimate source of moral authority and was to be regarded as having claims morally prior to those of other bodies or individuals. But few people today would subscribe to such a notion, for it would imply that the dictates of, say, a Hitler, 'Papa Doc', Mobutu or Saddam Hussein had to be obeyed not because it might be politic or expedient to do so but because the edicts of these dictators had moral force. Once again it must be stressed that the state is no more than a personified abstraction, and it is an axiom of democratic politics that those exercising power in its name must be accountable. An authoritarian state, therefore, can have no moral claim on its citizens, and if one is to obey it, it is because one is compelled, not because one is morally obligated to do so.

Legal

As to whether the state can be considered to have primacy in a legal sense, there is not much doubt as to what was till recently the answer. For the system of international law bequeathed to us by Grotius made the state the sole bearer of international legal rights and duties. Individuals, groups, corporations and collective entities other than states might have moral, but not legal entitlements and obligations. They might be objects but could not be subjects of international law. They had no right to full diplomatic representation, to make treaties, new law, war, and so forth.

IGOs and INGOs

However, in the twentieth century, the notion of the state as sole international legal actor began to be chipped away. In the first place, global, regional or functional inter-governmental organisations (IGOs) – the League, the UN, NATO, the EU – were starting to acquire corporate international legal personality, with substantial title to rights and duties, even if not on a par with those available to the sovereign state. The same goes for the international non-governmental organisations (INGOs) such as Greenpeace, the Save the Children Fund or Amnesty International, etc., whose number and impact have grown so markedly since the 1960s that some 15,000 NGO representatives attended the Rio Earth Summit of 1992 as governments sought to tap their expertise concerning the ecological challenges we face. Meanwhile commercial and trading multinationals such as Microsoft, EXXON or ITT, whose priorities and practices can substantially affect social and political as well as economic agendas, have also been acquiring a status in international law, but again not quite on a par with that of the sovereign state.

What of the 'supranational' institutions which by definition have power over the state? In the first place, such bodies of international civil servants or technical experts are empowered and can be dissolved by the states over which they exercise jurisdiction. Secondly, their activities as yet scarcely dent state sovereignty. For example, no sensible government is going to object to the actions of the World Health Organisation in eradicating smallpox or curbing AIDS; and although the European Commission is often involved in controversy, it is little more than an expensive talking shop, while the EU's operative decisions are still made by the Council of Ministers in which every member state has a voice.

Nations

What of the 'nation' as distinct from the state? When Woodrow Wilson promulgated the right to national self-determination, he was implying that the nation as distinct from the state was entitled to legal status. Most lawyers at the time would have disagreed. Self-determination was a moral not a legal principle. However, more recently, as secessionist, 'ethnonational' and 'liberation' groups have proliferated, some legal theorists have questioned this. In the 1970s and 1980s, certain Soviet writers held that National Liberation Movements such as the PLO, the Kurdish Liberation Front or the Tamil Tigers had international legal personality, but this view was bitterly contested by more traditional thinkers, not least since Moscow was highly selective about the movements to which it was prepared to attribute legal personality. While, for example, it recognised the PLO and the African National Congress (ANC) as legal persons, it denied recognition to Latvia, Lithuania and Estonia, sovereign states incorporated into the Soviet Union without their consent, and switched from supporting to opposing the Eritrean Liberation Movement after the Marxist–Leninist Mengistu became President of Ethiopia. Thus, although such movements present an increasingly formidable challenge to many states in that their secessionist or irredentist claims command considerable support, their legal status remains contentious.

Non-sovereign states

What of realms, provinces or states that are sizeable but not sovereign – Scotland, say, or Quebec or California? Are they beginning to develop a legal personality hitherto lacking? For years Scotland and Wales have had their own rugby and ice hockey teams, and if they play England the game is regarded as an international. But that, strictly speaking, gives neither Scotland nor Wales significant legal character. On the other hand, now that they have their own parliamentary assemblies and that Quebec has what it regards as 'national' offices in London, Paris and the Francophone countries of Africa, some international lawyers argue that some legal threshold may have been crossed. It is, again, a contentious issue.

Individuals

Finally, what of the legal status of the individual? Since the Second World War individuals have been increasingly regarded as subjects as well as objects of international law. For example, when the Universal Declaration of Human Rights was first agreed in 1948, most lawyers assumed it was no more than a statement of moral principle, not a set of legally binding ordinances. And even now, a few post-modernists still hold that the notion of universal human rights can have no legal validity: that rights are culturally specific and that to pretend otherwise is a form of cultural imperialism. However, after the European Convention of Human Rights was signed in 1950, opinion among lawyers began to shift, and by 1966 when two human-rights covenants were agreed, the one concerning civil and political rights, the other with economic, social and cultural rights, most lawyers took them to be legally valid. Today it is also accepted that like slaves of old, refugees enjoy certain rights under international law; though what the law says is one thing and implementing it another, and in the meantime distinguishing between refugees and economic migrants is often made difficult by the problem of checking the claim to asylum of the would-be refugee. It is also now a commonplace that individuals with a grievance against some European institution or national legal body may ask for an adjudication from the European Court of Human Rights and these are usually accepted, witness the number of legal rulings which Britain, so often in the European dock, has had to set aside to comply.

On the other hand, even though many German and Japanese officials were sentenced, respectively, at the 1940s Nuremberg and Tokyo war crimes courts for failing to disobey authorities issuing monstrous and inhuman commands, such as the killing of innocents, mass murder, genocide, etc., human rights legislation has not achieved the salience its promoters had hoped for. When, for example, a community becomes brutalised through fear, misplaced political or religious zeal or ethnic hatred, laws on human rights, genocide or torture are generally no deterrent, especially when a breach brings little effective redress. And even where they are regarded as relevant, they seem to invite verdicts that are essentially partisan. After all, Nuremberg and Tokyo were the products of an allied victory, the Court's judgments the rulings of the winning side; while more recent controversies regarding human rights were often rooted in cold war politics, with each side using the notion as a stick to beat its cold war opponents.[10] The Western powers would chide the Communists for their lack of civil liberties; the Socialist countries would denigrate the Western record on economic and social rights – the right to a job, to welfare provisions, to a roof over one's head, and so forth – while the newly independent countries would admonish their former colonial masters for the denial of full collective rights, i.e. for failing to deliver the substance as well as the form of independence.

In the post-cold war period, there were to be fresh controversies over alleged war crimes. As in the cold war era, sadly, most go unpunished, but where there is an attempt to bring perpetrators to justice, as in the Court in Arusha, Tanzania, dealing with the Rwandan genocide or the proceedings of the International Tribunal on Bosnian War Crimes in The

Hague, there is always the question of the fairness of the proceedings and of the impartiality of the adjudicators. In particular, how, since there is no victorious army as such in either Rwanda or Bosnia, are suspects to be identified and rounded up, and, with people like the indicted war criminals Karadzic, Mladic and 'Arkan' apparently free to go about their business, is there not a danger that only a few 'squaddies' face trial and not their commanders? In any case, how are the Bosnian Serbs, who comprise by far the largest number of suspects in the Hague trials, to be persuaded to yield those indicted by the tribunal if the Croats and Muslims are reluctant to hand over theirs? And, of course, the question of indictments over the massacres of Kosovars raise fresh problems regarding culpability and the mechanics of capture and arrest.[11]

Moreover, since the projected International Court of Human Rights has yet to materialise, the legal profession is in two minds as to the competence of national courts in trying foreign nationals for alleged human-rights violations. And, of course, when the perpetrator is a former Head of State whose alleged violations occurred when acting in his public capacity, there is a further question as to whether he can be held accountable at all. The variety of legal views on the matter were well illustrated in the controversy surrounding the various judgments on the extradition to Spain of Chile's former President, Augusto Pinochet.

Thus, since controversy seems to surround virtually every ascription of legal personality to non-state actors, it would be premature to argue that the state had lost its legal primacy. The most one can argue is that it is no longer regarded as the sole bearer of rights and duties under international law.[12]

Political

What of the political as distinct from the legal realm? Can it be demonstrated that the state had a primacy it has now lost? Pluralist writers, such as James Rosenau, John Burton and Richard Mansbach believe that it can – that the state, once a kind of impermeable billiard ball with a hard impenetrable outer shell, has become so penetrated transnationally, supranationally, subnationally and internationally that it can no longer be regarded as politically supreme. Leaving aside the debatable question as to whether the state ever was impermeable and impregnable, certainly it cannot be denied that the number of NGOs has greatly multiplied in the twentieth century, that the impact of the MNC on the world economy has been dramatic, and that vast networks of exchanges, contacts and connections, including those of the Mafia and other criminal fraternities, have developed apace. Moreover, that the revolution in global communications, with its instant relay of messages and pictures and the opportunities for foreign travel, has created unprecedented mutual awareness throughout humankind. As a consequence, political organisations of all kinds, states included, are probably more interdependent, that is, more sensitive and vulnerable to one another, than before. One has only to consider the speed with which, after intense media coverage, one apparently impregnable Communist government after another collapsed a decade ago, helping in the process to dislodge in their wake the seemingly secure Apartheid regime in South Africa.

Geographical spread

Yet while the role of non-state actors may have significantly increased, that of the state may also be said to have been on the rise. In the first place, whereas a century or so ago as a form of political organisation the sovereign state was largely confined to Europe, its geographical spread in the twentieth century has been remarkable. Today there are 186 of them, i.e. three and a half times as many as only 55 years ago, and the demands of the Chechens, Palestinians, Kashmiris, Pathans, Timorese, Tibetans, Kurds, Kosovars, Quebecois, Basques, Scots, among others, suggest that the number is likely to rise still further. Admittedly, there are mini- and micro-states such as Nauru and Vanuatu which can barely function on their own, as well as states in apparent decomposition such as the Congo, Somalia and Yugoslavia. And as some states show signs of disintegration, others show an interest in confederation or even federation. Even so, neither fragmentation nor integration suggests the obsolescence of the state as such – merely an alteration in their total number and size. Sovereignty remains a status still eagerly sought-after throughout the world, and no government could afford to claim that transnational forces have destroyed its capacity to govern.

State control

Secondly, while prior to the twentieth century such matters as international trade and commerce, migration, social, ideological and religious affairs were left largely to the private sector, these have now tended to come under the scrutiny if not the control of government. In a sense the state may be progressively eroding the independence of initiative once enjoyed by the international businessman and banker, the labour organisation, the sporting body, the Churches and political parties. For example, the East German government approved a regime giving such heavy doses of steroids to their athletes as to turn their female competitors into virtual men while, till recently, well-meaning Social Democratic governments in Norway, Sweden and Denmark were ordering the incarceration, sterilisation or lobotemisation of social misfits, the illegitimate, the backward and the poor. In other words, while the pluralists see transnationalism as moving into the preserve of the state, the Realist can argue that the reverse is also true, and that the enlargement of the functions of the twentieth-century state erodes much of the previous autonomy of the non-state actor. Perhaps the truth is of an overall expansion of the international dimension of policy in which both the state and non-state organisations have an increasing share.[13] Certainly there is no zero-sum relationship between state and non-state actor. The expansion of the one does not have to mean a contraction of the other.

Perhaps this interpenetration of the national and the transnational can best be illustrated by a consideration of the recent fate of the Communist movement. By the mid-1970s when Communism had become the ruling ideology of more countries than ever before or since, governments on both sides of the cold war divide perceived that the world balance of forces was moving towards Socialism. But this was an illusion, since at the time the Communist movement was probably more divided than before or since. There were serious tensions between the Soviets and the Chinese; the Chinese and the Vietnamese had come to blows; there were to be hostilities between the Vietnamese and the Cambodians and a civil war between Communist factions in Cambodia, Afghanistan, the Yemen, Ethiopia and Grenada. Thus the greater the number of Communist states, the greater the divisions. A similar dialectic is to be found in Islam. As with Christianity, Islam has a global mission. It is universal in aspiration and when it feels under threat, either from Jewish extremists in Israel, Hindu militants in India or Christian fanatics in the Balkans, the rhetoric is one of unity and community. Yet, as with Christianity or for that matter Communism, theory and practice are often at odds, and a commitment to Islam has failed to bring unity in, say, Afghanistan, Pakistan, Yemen or Somalia.

Functional

As to whether the state has primacy in the quest for world order, it is clear that many attribute the disorder, economic injustice and ecological mismanagement in the world by and large to the state. On the other hand since violence, economic injustice and man-made environmental degradation long predate the modern state system, the state can hardly be held entirely responsible for them. Were conflicts more acceptable when they involved people like Xerxes, Attila the Hun and Ghenghis Khan? Was there a fairer distribution of global wealth and greater respect for the global commons and the environment when transnational relations and tribal loyalties were supreme?

Such an analysis, moreover, neglects what Hedley Bull calls 'the positive functions of the state',[14] first, in imposing order domestically, the manifest importance of which can be demonstrated by its absence in countries such as Somalia, Sierra Leone or what was Yugoslavia; secondly, in preserving a framework of international co-existence, no matter how imperfect, through legal and other constraints; thirdly, in providing the kinds of institutional and other structures within which international cooperation can grow; and fourthly, in raising issues which would never have reached the international agenda before – the management of the world economy and environment, the promotion of racial equality and womens' rights, population limitation, literacy, government accountability, etc. And Bull concludes that the state system can sustain not only coexistence but also cooperation in an array of shared goals, and that therefore even in the promotion of world order the state may have a claim to primacy.

Economic

The role of the multinationals

If the above is at odds with much current thinking, which is of the decline or the obsolescence of the sovereign state, the following observations regarding the non-state actor in economic affairs will doubtless raise further objections among those believing that the state has lost its primacy. Clearly, many advanced industrial states are undergoing a kind of post-industrial revolution, international in scope and technological in basis. Thanks to advances in communications, transportation and management, investment, production and marketing have become increasingly internationalised. The successful multinational enterprise can integrate whole sections of economies across state frontiers, draw on a common pool of financial and human resources, employ a multinational team, pursue a common strategy, and encourage managers to give their primary loyalty to the corporation as a whole rather than the states in which they are based. Though many such enterprises are relatively modest in size, the top 100 or so are massive. Because of the economies of scale and the advantage of locating where skilled labour is cheap, where foreign exchange is in short supply and imported goods subject to high tariffs, the more powerful enterprises will tend to ever enlarge their spheres of operation. The net effect is that the annual sales turnover of a corporate giant such as General Motors, Ford or Mitsui exceeds the GNPs of all but a score of states. Such massive operations are bound to affect the workings of the international economy and to challenge the very attributes of sovereign statehood, in which a government controls both national territory and the economy and serves as the focus of national loyalty. But do the MNCs in fact threaten the state?[15]

Certainly they often stand accused of political interference. Evidence suggests that the Anglo-Iranian oil company (later BP) played a key role in restoring the Shah of Iran to power after a popular rising led to his expulsion in the early 1950s, and that the United Food Company was instrumental in helping to remove a newly elected left-wing regime in Guatamala in 1954. And there is little doubt of ITT's role in helping to destabilise Allende's Chile in the 1970s, precipitating the coup of General Pinochet. Not for nothing did the author of a book on ITT call the multinational organisation *The Sovereign State*.[16]

Moreover, some MNCs are under attack for embarrassing the governments of the countries in which they have their headquarters by apparently pursuing policies counter to national policy, as when British- and German-based companies supply military equipment to pariah states such as Iraq and Libya or assist a counter-coup in Sierra Leone.

At the same time the MNC has been assailed for sabotaging the economies of some states by taking decisions in one country adversely affecting workers in another – as when in 1993 Hoover suddenly switched production facilities from France to Scotland or more recently when some hard-pressed Japanese and South Korean firms decided at short notice to curtail their economic interests in Europe. That MNCs cause environmental damage is another frequent cause of complaint, especially in oil-bearing countries such as Nigeria or Colombia. But it is not only their activities in overseas countries that fuel criticism, it is also what they do to the countries in which they have their head offices. They stand accused, for example, of forfeiting jobs and markets in the home state as their overseas investments and technological transfers create overseas competitors. So how justified are these criticisms?

Whether the net effect of MNC activities is beneficial or malign depends not just on the MNC but also on the states in which it operates. On the positive side MNCs can provide the investment and know-how that help fund development, disseminate skills and generate employment. In addition the networks of international as well as transnational relationships that they maintain can provide governments with potentially valuable levers of influence. More negatively, they can create situations of dependence, inhibit the growth of local industries and technologies, despoil the environment and sow confusion by suddenly switching investment and market priorities.

Clearly, the stronger, mainly Western developed countries can exert greater leverage over MNC activities than the less secure, less stable states of Africa, Latin America and Eastern Europe, and limit whatever damage MNCs may cause, wittingly or unwittingly. And yet even the less developed countries can learn in time how to put pressure on the MNC, particularly if they collaborate with countries in positions similar to their own. In any case governments can profit from the realisation that the MNC probably needs them as much as they may need it. After all, without their consent the MNC cannot act. Sadly, however, many politicians can be bribed into granting the MNC more intrusive powers than it really needs for its economic activities.

Nonetheless, the days when the MNC could ride roughshod over national interests have largely gone. For much of the high-handed political behaviour associated with them in the 1950s, 1960s and 1970s probably had less to do with the enterprises themselves than with the cold war concerns of the US, from which many MNCs originate, for often they acted as a vehicle for American foreign policy. For example, the Board of Directors of ITT which helped to bring down the Allende regime in Chile had so many ex-CIA, ex-Pentagon, ex-State Department officials that many saw it as a hidden arm of US diplomacy.

The reaction

But such intrusion combined with the other negative features of MNC activity produced an inevitable reaction, and the competition among MNCs to find suitable host countries provides even the poorest with a bargaining chip. By the late 1970s, therefore, many potential host countries were imposing conditions before granting extensive powers to the MNC. And, of course, where the 'trickle-down' benefits of MNC operations fail to materialise, governments can employ an arsenal of penalties, from additional controls to the ultimate sanctions of nationalisation, expropriation or expulsion. True, the more extreme the measures the greater the danger of economic dislocation. But then Egypt survived its nationalisation of the Suez Canal Co. and Guyana the take-over of Booker's Bros.

15.4 THE ROLE OF THE STATE

Today a balance seems to have been struck in which the state has as much leverage against the MNC as the MNC has against it. Thus, there is no reason for their relationship not to be mutually beneficial. So what are we to conclude? (1) That non-state actors and transnational forces are and always were a fact of life in world politics; (2) that while many see them as a challenge to the state, others see the state as posing an equally powerful challenge to them; (3) that though their role is evolving, it cannot yet be demonstrated that the state has had to yield primacy to any other body; and (4) that no matter how penetrated the state, its continued existence appears to fulfil a psychological need, and as such seems destined to continue as a focus for Palestinians, Kashmiris, Chechens, Kosovars, *et al.* whose aspirations for national self-determination are denied.

NOTES

1. Roberts, J., *The Triumph of the West*, London, BBC, 1985, pp. 96–7.
2. See Keohane, R. and Nye, J. (eds), *Transnational Relations and World Politics*, Cambridge, Mass., Harvard University Press, 1971.
3. London, Pinter, 1988.
4. Trevelyan, G.M., *English Social History*, London, The Reprint Society, 1948, pp. 216–22.
5. Huberman, L., *Man's Worldly Goods*, London, Gollancz, 1937, pp. 95–6.
6. Ibid., pp. 127–9.
7. Smith, A., *Wealth of Nations* [1776], ed. and introduced by Cannan, E., London, Methuen, 1930.
8. See for example Connor, W., 'Nation building or nation destroying?', *World Politics*, vol. 24, no. 3, 1972; also Shehadi, K., *Ethnic Self-Determination and the Break-up of States*, Adelphi Paper No. 283, 1993.
9. See Bull, H., 'The state's positive role in world affairs', *Daedalus*, vol. 108, no. 4, pp. 111–23 for a thought-provoking analysis of the continuing significance of the state.
10. On the essentially partisan approach to human rights during the cold war see for example Pettman, R., *State and Class: A Sociology of International Affairs*, London, Croom Helm, 1979.
11. Some of the legal, moral and practical problems regarding war crimes tribunals are discussed in Ignatieff, M., *The Warrior's Honor*, London, Chatto & Windus, 1998, pp. 178–84.
12. The question of legal personality receives cogent exposition in Higgins, R., *Problems and Process: International Law and How we use it*, Oxford, The Clarendon Press, 1994, pp. 39–55.
13. Bull, H., *The Anarchical Society*, London, Macmillan, 1997, pp. 270–73 and 276–81.
14. See n. 9. Bull's view on the continued viability of the state is reaffirmed in Buzan, B., 'Focus on: The Present as Historic Turning Point', *Journal of Peace Research*, vol. 30., no. 4, 1995, pp. 385–98, and challenged in Horsman, M. and Marshall, A., *After the Nation-State: Citizens, Tribalism and the New World Disorder*, London, HarperCollins, 1995.
15. The relations between states and MNCs are essayed in Strange, S., 'States, firms and diplomacy', *International Affairs*, vol. 68., no. 1, 1992, pp. 1–15, and Hocking, B. and Smith, M., *World Politics*, 2nd edn, Hemel Hempstead, Harvester Wheatsheaf, 1995, pp. 95–120.
16. London, Hodder & Stoughton, 1973.

PART VI

THE INTERNATIONAL
POLITICAL ECONOMY

CHAPTER 16

INTERNATIONAL ECONOMIC ORDER AND DISORDER

In the standard International Relations textbooks of a generation ago, when the emphasis tended to be on the state and on the recurrence of inter-state confict, the international political economy received scarcely a mention. Though there were a few somewhat tedious works on the subject, they usually catered for specialists in Economics rather than for generalists in International Relations. The most the student of IR could expect were periodic references to economic pressure, aid, sanctions, and to such organisations as the IMF and the European Economic Community; but little attempt was made to explore systematically the dynamics of the international economy or its impact on international political structures. Nor was there much attention to how the changing fabric of international politics shaped the international economy. Today, however, as 'low' politics, i.e. socio-economic activity, has in effect become 'high' politics, as politicians, businessmen and bankers attempt to regulate the world economy and governments often stand or fall by their success at economic management, it is different. Economic matters now have a high visibility and no self-respecting IR course could be complete without consideration of the politics of international economic relations.

Whereas in diplomatic and international legal matters the focus is generally on states, in international economic questions equal weight must be given to the actions of individuals, of groups and of corporations as well as states, and at issue is the 'behaviour' of an entity no less abstract and yet no less compelling than that of the state, namely the market. As the volume and value of international economic transactions have grown, a sudden slump in, say, Thailand, South Korea or Japan or the collapse of the rouble can have knock-on effects throughout what is becoming a global market place. In this chapter and the next we trace the pattern of international economic relations from the earliest days, even before the development of the state system, down to the present, and examine the theoretical debates which have helped to shape the international political economy.

16.1 ORIGINS OF THE INTERNATIONAL ECONOMY

Long before the age of the sovereign state, trade was as much a feature of relations between political units as was war. Indeed, sometimes there was little perceptible difference between them, as flotillas would sail into foreign ports – to trade, if they met resistance, to plunder if they did not.[1] And, of course, the earliest economic transactions were those of primitive barter in which people with a surplus of, say, salt, skins, shells, women or whatever would trade them for commodities they lacked. As the first Empires developed – in China, India and the Middle East – some of these exchanges were in the form of 'tribute' from conquered to conqueror. Later, the notion of a medium of exchange, of a store or measure of value, took hold – something generally in demand. For thousands of years the commonest medium of exchange in many countries was cattle – in Latin, *pecus*, from which we get the word pecuniary, pertaining to wealth, or impecunious, lacking in wealth, as in the phrase 'impecunious student'. Subsequently, in more sophisticated societies, as in ancient China, Egypt, Greece and Rome, the medium of exchange was to be more durable, more versatile and easier to handle – gold, silver, copper or some other precious metal, sometimes in the form of coins with the embossed heads of some of the more distinguished, though not necessarily the most handsome, leaders of the time.[2] There are several chilling reminders of the practice in the British Museum's Money Gallery, including a coin bearing the image of Caligula engaged in his favourite pastime – killing people.

16.2 MEDIEVAL TRADE AND COMMERCE

Later, in medieval Europe the Church, wielding secular as well as spiritual power, determined the ground rules for trade and commerce, but when its power declined, the guilds, which were medieval associations of skilled workers (rather like the 'white collar' trade unions of today) detailed the conditions. But given the mountain of regulation and regional customs barriers, the lack of sophisticated transport and the hazards of the highways, the level of international trade remained comparatively low until the end of the Middle Ages. However, as Europe's monarchs began to assert their new-found power, the situation changed. With the recently invented mariner's compass and the sextant, the seas could now be utilised as never before, and with the new rulers improving the highways, removing local tariffs and creating common currencies, the scene was set for a vast expansion of international commerce.[3]

16.3 SEVENTEENTH-CENTURY MERCANTILISM

The development of sea power brought a rapid increase in Europe's economic relations with the Orient and the Americas, and for much of the seventeenth century such trade exceeded, in volume and value, trade within Europe. Indeed, it profoundly affected national taste buds. For example, by the end of the seventeenth century tea from China had become virtually the English national drink, and of course the tomato, the potato and tobacco from the Americas and coffee from Arabia altered both diets and social manners. On the other hand, the Europeans tended to import more tea, coffee, sugar, spices, silks and slaves than they could pay for with the textiles and other manufactures sold in return, and as a result they had to export precious metals like gold and silver to make up the deficit. Yet, given that these were precisely the commodities needed to pay for their incessant wars, the European states were soon in financial crisis. In their anxiety to enlarge and consolidate their political domains while overcoming their economic problems, the new rulers imposed strict controls on trade.

First, to protect domestic enterprise, they severely restricted imports through quotas and tariffs, and excluded altogether certain goods directly competing with home industries. Though some commodities could still enter duty-free, these tended to comprise luxury items and foodstuffs which could not be produced in the home country or raw materials needed for a priority domestic industry such as shipbuilding. By the Navigation Acts of the seventeenth century, Britain insisted that the commodities it traded overseas were to be conveyed in ships which it owned and operated, and for the purpose encouraged the import of pitch, tar and stout timbers to speed development of a large mercantile marine. Secondly, the state began to take an increasing share in trade, helping to finance certain export and import substitution industries and to encourage the poaching of skilled craftsmen and inventors from other countries. Thirdly, to secure cheap raw materials, a ready market for manufactures and a trading surplus, the new rulers sought overseas colonies. Sir Francis Bernard, the governor of Massachusetts in the mid-eighteenth century, explained exactly what his royal employer had in mind. 'The two great objects of Great Britain in regard to the American trade must be to oblige her American subjects to take from Great Britain only, all the manufactures and European goods which she can supply them with; [and] to regulate the foreign trade of the Americans so that the profits thereof may finally centre in Great Britain'.⁴ Scarce wonder the Americans longed for independence! Fourthly, the international movement of precious metals was strictly monitored and controlled. Such, in brief, was the system to be known as 'mercantilism',[5] a system which has much in common with classical Realism, presupposing that one country's gain is another's loss, and which governed Europe's foreign economic relations for more than three centuries.

16.4 FREE TRADE VERSUS MERCANTILISM

By the eighteenth century, however, mercantilism was coming under attack from many different quarters. Abroad, its restrictive practices contributed greatly to the revolt of the American colonies, and their successful bid for independence in 1776. At home mercantilism was savaged in a treatise published in the year of the American rebellion and which was to revolutionise thinking about production and trade – *Wealth of Nations*.[6] In it, Adam Smith, a professor both of logic and of moral philosophy, put his ruthless logic in the service of those manufacturers, financiers and traders irritated by the restrictions, regulations and intrusive inspections of mercantilism and frustrated by the protectionist Corn Laws which kept the price of wheat artificially high.

To begin with, Smith ridiculed mercantilism's love affair with gold and silver. One could not eat, wear or live on precious metals and unless they were to be used to produce commodities which people could enjoy, their accumulation was more likely to depress rather than to raise living standards. Smith then made a powerful case for what we now call market forces. In the tradition of the then fashionable theories of balance as expounded by Newton in relation to the solar system and by Hume in relation to the power relations between states, Smith claimed that any trade imbalance would automatically correct itself, as if by an invisible hand. For any rapid influx of gold, as happened after the Spanish conquest of Mexico, Bolivia and Peru, would tend to produce inflation, raising a country's price level as currency increased relative to the supply of goods; such a situation would lead both to increased imports and to a drop in exports because of the comparatively high prices, but to pay for the excess of imports over exports it would be necessary to export gold, and in this way restore the balance of trade.

In arguing for a free market and the removal of trade restrictions, which, whether or not he understood the implications, could not have been achieved without a raft of legislation and administrative measures,[7] Smith propounded two principles still in wide circulation. First, that because countries differ in their natural resources, land values, technological competence and wage levels, a country with an absolute advantage over others in the supply of a particular commodity, resource or skill should specialise in developing it. Likewise, if it cost a country more than its foreign competitors to produce a particular commodity, then it should import it. This is what Smith called the doctrine of Absolute Advantage. Secondly, a country having an absolute advantage in the production of everything should nonetheless specialise where its comparative advantage in terms of costs measured in man-hours is greatest so that other countries could develop their least inefficient enterprises. This is what Smith's fellow liberal economist, David Ricardo, dubbed the doctrine of Comparative Advantage.[8] It was based on the belief that the division of labour – specialisation – was an indicator of efficiency and that a free and unfettered world market (i.e. free trade) would serve to maximise efficiency, adding greatly to the wealth of nations.

But Smith, who was a strong believer in natural liberty, condemned restrictive practices not just in economics, but in politics, too. In particular, he attacked the whole colonial system so essential to mercantilist thought, which had brought Britain to frequent blows with the Dutch in the seventeenth century and the French in the eighteenth, claiming that colonialism 'depresses the industry of all other countries but chiefly that of the colonies, without in the least increasing . . . that of the country in whose favour it is established'.[9]

While Smith's call to free the political economy may have delighted the enterprising and the educated in both mother country and colonies, not everyone stood to benefit equally from a free-trade policy. For the class of artisans and labourers just beginning to emerge, it introduced new uncertainties into their lives and had potentially ominous overtones for the women and children who were to be sucked into the workings of an economy increasingly justified by the principle of *laissez-faire*.[10] As Smith himself said: 'The workmen desire to get as much, the masters to give as little as possible. The former are disposed to combine in order to raise, the latter in order to lower, the wages of labour . . . It is not, however, difficult to foresee which of the two parties must, upon all ordinary occasions, have the advantage in the dispute . . . The masters being fewer in number, can combine far more easily . . . We have no acts of parliament against combining to lower the price of work: but many against combining to raise it'.[11] Here Smith was accurately depicting a balance between labour and capital which was to tilt to the disadvantage of the former in most of the fledgling industrialising societies of the late eighteenth and early nineteenth centuries.

The perception that the new urban workers were being dehumanised by the situation at the workplace led the young Karl Marx to forsake his early liberalism for communism. For having felt as well as studied the effects of the depression in the Moselle wine-growing industry in the 1820s and 1830s[12] and gone on to examine the sorry state of working conditions in Britain as revealed in a succession of Parliamentary Committee reports, Marx began to consider capitalism world wide as a conspiracy against labour. In *The Communist Manifesto* of 1848 he concluded that the class interests of workers were the same everywhere, and that only a transnationally organised global revolution to wrest political and economic power could free them from increasing misery.[13]

His analysis was, in fact, premature. For the anti-labour legislation and the inhuman working conditions of the early years of capitalism were to be greatly modified, even during Marx's lifetime. And as, contrary to Marx's predictions but possibly in part because of them, working-class life began to improve in western Europe in the mid- to late nineteenth century with the advent of trade unions, cooperatives, labour parties and social legislation at least in Western and Central Europe, the worker would tend increasingly to identify with nationalist aspirations rather than with the revolutionary cause of 'proletarian internationalism'.

Even so, how secure have the political and economic gains of labour been in the century or more since the death of Karl Marx? Given the recurrent recessions and slumps, the recent backlash against union power in many countries, the economic blight in the manufacturing towns of many developed countries and the fact that economic efficiency is increasingly equated with downsizing the workforce and inflating managerial pay packets, it is hardly surprising that organised labour never feels entirely secure. On the other hand, perhaps recent anti-union legislation stems from a perception that the pendulum had swung too far towards organised labour and that some sort of Adam Smith-style balance between capital and labour needs to be restored.

16.5 THE NINETEENTH CENTURY AND THE POLITICAL ECONOMY OF IMPERIALISM

Despite the forceful logic of Adam Smith's writings, and their appeal to all those who wanted greater freedom for the individual, mercantilism remained the predominant philosophy of international trade until well into the nineteenth century. Indeed, even when the system lost ground after the abolition of slavery and the slave trade, the termination of the monopoly powers of the East India Company and the other great trading organisations and the repeal of Britain's Corn Laws, it was never completely abandoned. Whether or not a country adopted free trade, ironically, tended to depend not so much on businessmen as on governments, and to a number of them free trade was simply not acceptable. In the leading industrialised countries which could produce a range of cheap goods for export, such as Britain, France, Belgium and Holland, the movement towards free trade went furthest. Free market conditions appeared to offer considerable economic benefit to countries which could undersell their rivals in open competition. However, in a country such as Russia where industrialisation was still in its infancy, high tariffs tended to be maintained, if only to protect new enterprises. And in the semi-industrialised countries of Central Europe and the US, the policy was generally to retain protectionist tariffs but at a comparatively low rate of duty. The argument was, and still is in many countries, that to abandon protection too soon would be to open the floodgates to a host of imports, thereby impeding the process of full industrialisation.

The powerful arguments of Smith and Ricardo demanded an equally incisive rebuttal and in his *National System of Political Economy* of 1841, the German economist Friedrich List provided one.[14] In a robust defence of protectionism derived, incidentally, from several years of work in the US, List suggested that, even if the economic benefits were considerable, the political and social costs of free trade for a country at an early stage of development would be too high. A free-trade policy could only perpetuate the economic dominance of a country such as Britain, given its almost unique comparative advantage in heavy industry, while the mainly agrarian German states, among others, would be permanently relegated to a position of economic inferiority and dependence. Further, such a policy would effectively deny to others the kinds of mechanisms – the Navigation Acts and the Corn Laws, for example – by which British industry had for centuries protected itself to boost its economic performance. As Bismarck was once pithily to observe: 'England abolished protection after she had benefited from it to the fullest extent . . . Free trade is the weapon of the strongest nation'[15] . . . a theme, incidentally, taken up by E.H. Carr in his *Twenty Years Crisis*.

However, as industrialised Western Europe moved towards free trade, official enthusiasm for empire began to dwindle, even if the fervour of missionaries, adventurers and certain trading concerns remained undimmed. In Britain, Benjamin Disraeli, ironically later to become an apostle of empire, summed up the case for retreat from it. In 1852 he dismissed Britain's overseas possessions as 'millstones round our necks', and fifteen years later queried the value of what he called these 'colonial deadweights'.[16] As for France, though it established itself in Algeria in the 1830s, it was too preoccupied with repeated revolutionary disturbances and changes in the European map to try to recover the vast areas of North America and India lost to Britain. Spain was in process of losing her vast dominions in the Americas, while Portugal and Holland had neither the will nor the means to further extend their control. And though the colonial powers would sometimes conflict over territories already claimed or occupied, by the early 1800s official encouragement for colonisation had virtually ended. During the time that international trade was bringing vast profits and prospects to Western and Central Europe, their governments had lost their appetite for further colonial acquisitions. There was no need for a trade monopoly in distant lands when vast populous markets were opening up in the teeming towns of Europe.

On the other hand, towards the mid-1870s, production throughout Europe and North America began to outstrip demand, in part, as Marx had predicted, because of the intensity of the competition between enterprises domestic and foreign. Markets were by now already well supplied, often near saturation point, and failing to find sales outlets, the goods piled up in the factories. As Europe's leading industrial powers came under mounting economic pressure, their enthusiasm for free trade began to evaporate. As profit margins dwindled, businessmen moved to restrict domestic competition through amalgamations and take-over bids. Soon the attempt to bring order out of competitive chaos resulted in a complex structure of price- and production-fixing trusts, syndicates, pools, combines, cartels and associations, with more and more workers employed in fewer and fewer enterprises and small business and handicrafts in decline. It was a far cry from Adam Smith's free enterprise, *laissez-faire* capitalism,[17] and as the shibboleth of economic efficiency began to lose its appeal the way was open for a return to protectionism.

In 1879 Bismarck exacted heavy duties on industrial and agricultural imports. Two years later France followed suit, raising tariffs at first modestly and then much more steeply. Across the Atlantic the very steep McKinley Tariff of 1890 marked the abandonment of America's customary low-tariff policy. Other states did likewise, Britain – once 'the workshop of the world' – almost alone clinging to the wreckage of free trade until 1931.

The return to protectionism at the end of the 1870s (ironically just as overseas transportation and communications were being revolutionised) surfaced at a time when Europe's governments were beginning to intervene in the domestic economy with welfare legislation to cushion workers against the baleful effects of recession. It also came in the wake of the apparent stabilisation of the European continent following the Franco-Prussian war, the Bismarckian system of alliances and the deliberations of the 1878 Congress of Berlin concerning the tangled affairs of the Balkans.

As before, with the return to protectionism came renewed interest in imperialism,[18] but the arrival of the railway which could open up the hinterland of continents never fully explored in the past ensured that the scramble for overseas possessions would be more rapid than and at least as extensive as the earlier phase. In thirty years Britain alone added over three million square miles to its existing possessions and by 1900 its Empire covered nearly one-fifth of the land surface of the globe. The French were to take even more terrain during this period, claiming an additional four million square miles, while the Germans, Belgians and

Italians, acquiring colonial territory for the first time, each secured around a million square miles. By the time of the First World War all of Africa save Liberia, Ethiopia and South Africa was controlled by seven European powers (Belgium, Britain, France, Germany, Italy, Portugal and Spain), thereby ending a process of colonisation of the continent that had begun with the Phoenicians three thousand years before. In the Far East and the Pacific only Siam (Thailand), China and Japan remained outside the direct control of Europe or the United States. But in fact China had been divided into spheres of influence by foreign powers, and Japan, having wrung certain concessions out of China, was also to emerge as an imperialist power – the first great oriental colonial power of modern times – having acquired Korea and Formosa (Taiwan). In the Western hemisphere the US expanded across its continent, acquired Puerto Rico from Spain, extended its colonial reach westwards to Hawaii and the Philippines (which God had expressly told President McKinley to annexe),[19] leased the Panama Canal 'in perpetuity' from the new state of Panama, also an American creation, and came to exercise considerable political leverage over Cuba and several other Caribbean islands. When the orgy of expansionism was exhausted shortly before the First World War, there was very little territory left to colonise.

Although imperial possessions had become important symbols of national power and prestige, a group of radical thinkers at the beginning of the twentieth century began to see the phenomenon in strictly economic terms, i.e. as an unequal relationship emanating from capitalism. For some, imperialism was the product of the malfunctioning of the capitalist system: for others it was an inevitable outcome of it. For some, imperialism served the capitalist system as a whole; for others it served the interests of particular groups within the system; yet others saw imperialism in terms not so much of interest as of ideology – an ideology of expansionism, as in the mercantilist age, to keep out competitors, control the investment, trade, currency, production and labour of the colonies, keeping them in a state of economic subjection.

16.6 ECONOMIC THEORIES OF IMPERIALISM

Hobson

Two such economic theories were especially influential in the first half of the twentieth century, the first being the pioneering study on *Imperialism* by J.A. Hobson, written in 1902.[20] Like E.H. Carr, whose persuasive ideas were also to mould the thinking of a generation or more, Hobson was multi-talented: economist, university lecturer, essayist and journalist – and all these gifts are on display in his riveting study. What makes his analysis all the more compelling is that he brings to it insights gained in South Africa where as a correspondent for the *Manchester Guardian* he reported on the course and consequences of the Boer War. Central to his study is the notion that the unequal distribution of income and wealth in capitalist countries leaves large sections of the population without the means to consume very much, forcing capitalists to invest abroad and to compete with others to control foreign markets, which is most easily achieved with the acquisition of colonies. So is imperialism an inevitable product of capitalism? Not according to Hobson. For if the surplus wealth of the richer capitalists were creamed off and redistributed among the poorer sections of the community, the greater domestic consumption that would result would make imperialism unnecessary.

Before Hobson's treatise, imperialism was popular with the masses in most of the Western European countries. They were encouraged by the mass media of the day to view it as an instrument by means of which backward peoples could learn to enjoy the fruits of civilisation: industrialisation, the spread of education, the rule of law, parliamentary institutions, rational administration and the like. But Hobson changed all that. It is a mark of the sheer force of his prose that he not only more or less originated the economic theory of imperialism, he also did much to create at least in the English-speaking world a feeling of revulsion against imperial rule. But for him it was not simply immoral, it was also irrational and generally economically disadvantageous for the country as a whole, even if some groups – shipbuilders, arms manufacturers, engineers and those filling the ranks of the colonial civil service – benefited. In short, the meagre results of imperialism in the form of increased trade and a modest return on capital were out of all proportion to the enormous risks and costs involved. And in an attack on capitalist profiteering, which had certain anti-Semitic overtones (later to be picked up by Hitler but not Lenin, whose intellectual debt to Hobson was considerable), Hobson claimed 'there is not a war, a revolution, an anarchist assassination or any other public shock which is not gainful to these men; they are harpies who suck their gains from every new forced expenditure and every sudden disturbance of public credit'.[21] What one hears in that passage is not the scholarly tone of the academic, which he was to become, but the moral outrage of a journalist/philosopher who like Lenin believed that something had to be done.

Lenin

In his analysis of *Imperialism: The Highest Stage of Capitalism*, of 1916, Lenin, seeking to explain why nationalism rather than world revolution had triumphed in 1914, drew heavily on Hobson's ideas, but reached a different conclusion. Imperialism was, in his view, the inevitable outcome of what he called monopoly capitalism, when the rate of return on domestic investment is low, when production is concentrated in combines and cartels and when financial and banking interests predominate over the commercial. For the monopoly capitalists, according to Lenin, in pursuit of massive profits seek to export surplus capital to backward countries where 'capital is scarce, the price of land is relatively low, wages are low, raw materials are cheap'.[22] The effect, according to Lenin, was the *de facto* division of the world into spheres of influence, making capitalism a world phenomenon, despite the uneven economic development of the various countries. In the process a wedge was drawn between the workers of the metropolitan countries and those of the colonies, the former benefiting at the expense of the latter, which is why they supported leaders who bribed them with the spoils of imperialism in return for their active support in war. If Hobson saw the answer in a redistribution of wealth under capitalism, Lenin saw it as lying in capitalism's overthrow, believing that as the tally of war dead mounted, the workers would realise they had been betrayed and in their fury turn to revolution.

16.7 CRITIQUES OF THE ECONOMIC THEORIES OF IMPERIALISM

As will be evident by now, theses tend to generate counter-theses and in fact such economic theories of imperialism were to come under intense criticism. Among the better-known critics were the Austrian economist Joseph Schumpeter, the American historian, William Langer and the former West German Chancellor Helmut Schmidt.[23] So what are their objections?

(1) That such theorists ignore the history of imperialism before the age of capitalism and err in identifying a single cause for a complex and recurrent phenomenon, and in neglecting the political, military and social dimensions of the problem;

(2) That their theories do not explain what they purport to explain since it is not businessmen but politicians who decide on imperial expansion, war and the like; and that in any case, as Marx himself pointed out, capitalism for all its alienating qualities requires order, predictability and rationality and therefore peace for profit maximisation;

(3) That their theories rest more on inflammatory and inflated rhetoric than on empirical evidence.

So what is the counter-evidence they suggest?

(1) That the idea that the most advanced capitalist countries would be the most expansionist was simply not valid. For instance, Sweden and Switzerland displayed no interest whatever in colonial ventures, while Portugal, one of the most under-capitalised states in Europe, was a leading colonialist;

(2) That far from being enslaved, many recipients of European capital, such as Japan, the US, Australia and Argentina profited handsomely and became independent powers of formidable proportions;

(3) That, contrary to the theorists, from the 1870s to 1914 more capital moved into most of the metropolitan countries than out of them;

(4) That much of the capital exported from the metropolitan countries came not from monopoly concerns but from governments and government-backed public utilities;

(5) That most colonies during this period were open to international trade on a more or less equal basis with the mother countries, and that therefore it was not necessary to have colonies to extend trade with the LDCs;

(6) That the colonies were not nearly as important in the trade and investment patterns of the capitalist countries as the theories suggested. Then as now most of the capital exported from the advanced economies went to other advanced economies. The bulk of German capital went to the United States and Latin America and only about three per cent to its African colonies, and while up to a half of British capital did indeed go to the Empire, almost all went to the white dominions – South Africa, Rhodesia, Canada, Australia and New Zealand – while the rest went to the advanced capitalist countries.[24] In fact both capital and trade, as if in accord with the law of comparative advantage, tended to be directed outside the colonies;

(7) That although the Boer War and the Chaco War between Bolivia and Paraguay in the early 1930s may have been fought almost entirely for economic reasons, it is hard to see economics as the major motive for most of the other wars of the past century or so. Where, for example, was the economic motivation in the two World Wars, the Arab–Israeli Wars, the Korean War, the several Indo-Chinese wars, the Indo-Pakistani wars over Kashmir and Bangladesh, the recent civil wars in Afghanistan, Somalia, Sudan, Rwanda, former Yugoslavia and so forth?

16.8 IMPERIALISM AND THE INTERNATIONAL ECONOMY PRE-1914

This is not to say that there is no connection between capitalism, imperialism and war. Clearly the transformation of the world map in little more than a generation was almost bound to create some instability, and, in consequence, many capitalists were indeed able to profit handsomely from the manufacture and trade in arms. As regards the conflict which Hobson covered for the *Manchester Guardian*, the Boer War, the economic motivations of the British, in particular, were only too evident. As a corrective, therefore, to what had been an excessive concentration on the political and strategic dimensions of imperialism and warfare, the economic theories are very useful. But for a phenomenon as complex as imperialism, a monocausal approach can only be partial and, no matter how sophisticated or plausible, must be open to the charge of oversimplification.

On the other hand, opening up the new colonies to international trade not only provided the imperialists with a regular supply of cheap foodstuffs and other primary products, it also had a tonic effect on the world economy as a whole, and had it not been for imperialism, the participation of the colonies in the world trading nexus might have been much slower. As it was, world trade leapt ahead in the years before the First World War: from a mere $4 billion in 1850 to $17.5 billion in 1890, $33.6 billion by 1910, and on the eve of war $40.4 billion.[25] Interestingly enough, throughout this period, despite high tariffs, the industrialised states continued to be one another's best customers; yet their increased trade with one another rested upon the bounty of raw materials which imperialism made possible.

16.9 THE INTERNATIONAL ECONOMY POST-1918

The First World War might or might not have resulted from imperialism, as Hobson and Lenin suggested, but certainly it shattered the previous structure of international trade, as governments once again imposed strict controls on imports and exports. Though the intention was to restore free trade after the war, further shocks to the international economy on the onset of peace made this a pious hope. First, the collapse of the continental empires – Ottoman, Austro-Hungarian and Russian – involved the disintegration of long-established integrated economies and the creation of new states, many, like Austria, barely economically viable and an easy prey to extremist ideologies. Indeed the pattern has been repeated recently following the break-ups of the Soviet Union and Yugoslavia. Secondly, the vast public debts incurred during the war distorted both domestic and international economies as the supply of money in circulation had increased to such an extent that after hostilities, their currencies had virtually lost their value. In any case with the US, the major creditor, imposing its highest ever tariffs on imports by the end of the decade, repayment of debt was made difficult, if not impossible. Thirdly, the excessive reparations levied on Germany – the equivalent of $33 billion – could not possibly be met, given that total world trade on the eve of war had been $40.4 billion.[26] In fact, of course, Germany's initial efforts to cope soon destroyed the value of the mark, and by the middle of August 1923 the mark stood at 20 million to the pound sterling. The effect of that massive inflation can in fact be seen in the postage stamps of the day when a 100-mark stamp might have superimposed on it a 10,000-mark imprint. Attempts to re-establish the German currency in the 1920s failed to pare down the debt to a realistic figure, obliging Germany to take out new short-term loans to pay off its older longer-term dues. Not until the Depression of the 1930s had punctured this fragile financial boom were the Americans forced to put a moratorium on debts and reparations.

Finally, the need to export gold to pay for debts led to a gross imbalance in stocks as by 1929 the US had 38 per cent of the world's gold, while the whole of Europe put together had only 41 per cent. This haemorrhage of precious metal from Europe stimulated economic nationalism and revived mercantilist ideas, so that by 1936 not a single state had a convertible currency. By this time, however, a number of banks had collapsed, stock markets had crashed, unemployment was soaring and many financiers had committed suicide (despite the old adage that 'old moneylenders never die, they just lose interest!').

This was the era of the Great Depression, an economic crisis compounded by the fact that governments were seeking salvation in the whole panoply of high tariffs, import quotas, trade preferences, exchange controls and managed currency. Such restrictive practices virtually eliminated export opportunities and reduced what international trade there was to the level of primitive barter; meanwhile the economic chaos of the inter-war period provided both the setting and the pretext for the rise of Fascism as the unemployed flocked to join the new parties of the Right.

Interestingly enough, this was for many on the Left a signal that capitalism was in its death throes and that the world was teetering on the edge of socialist revolution. But the Marxists were wrong. What was in prospect was not a world revolution but a world war. But the monetarists had also misjudged the situation. By standing firm against government expenditure on arms or indeed on anything else, they merely contributed to a climate of rising unemployment and appeasement of aggressors. Those who, arguably, did have their finger on the pulse of events were, first, the followers of John Maynard Keynes, whose *General Theory of Employment, Interest and Money* of 1936[27] contended that given falling demand the states should abandon classical economic theory and spend their way back into prosperity providing loans, price supports and public service jobs to reflate the economy – something that Roosevelt and Hitler in their different ways were already doing; and, secondly, those like E.H. Carr and Georg Schwarzenberger who were writing of the politics of not being overpowered, though, surprisingly, in his first edition of *The Twenty Years' Crisis*, Carr seemed too ready to appease Fascism, at any rate in the short term.

Just as the founders of the UN were determined to avoid the mistakes of the League, so those meeting in the American New Hampshire resort of Bretton Woods in 1944 to fashion a new international economic system were also keen to learn the lessons of the previous 30 years. The following chapter traces what they decided and the trials and tribulations of the system they fashioned.

NOTES

1. Brown, C., *Understanding International Relations*, Basingstoke, Macmillan, 1997, p. 147.
2. Bozeman, A.B., *Politics and Culture in International History*, Princeton, Princeton University Press, 1960, pp. 39–43, 152, and 167–71.
3. Trevelyan, G.M., *English Social History*, London, The Reprint Society, 1948, pp. 187–97.
4. Huberman, L., *Man's Worldly Goods*, London, Gollancz, 1937, pp. 133–4.
5. See for example Viner, J., 'Power versus plenty as objectives of foreign policy in the 17th and 18th centuries', *World Politics*, vol. 1, no. 1, 1949, pp. 1–29.
6. Strictly speaking, *An Inquiry into the Nature and Causes of the Wealth of Nations*, [1776], London, Methuen, 1930.
7. Karl Polanyi, in *The Great Transformation*, argues that 'there was nothing natural about *laissez-faire*', which had to be enforced by the state and which required 'not only an outburst of legislation repealing restrictive regulations but also . . . a central bureaucracy able to fulfil the task set by the adherents of (economic) liberalism', Boston, Beacon Books, 1944, p. 139.
8. [1817], *Principles of Political Economy and Taxation*, Harmondsworth, Penguin, 1971.
9. Op. cit., vol. II, p. 111.
10. The phrase *laissez-faire*, coined in France in the mid-eighteenth century, does not appear in either Smith or Ricardo, but was widely used to summarise the kind of liberalised economy they advocated.
11. Op. cit., vol. I, pp. 68–9.
12. See McLellan, D., *The Thought of Karl Marx*, 2nd edn, London, Macmillan, 1980, pp. 11–12.
13. [1848], Harmondsworth, Penguin, 1967.
14. London, Frank Cass, 1966.
15. Quoted in Culbertson, W.S., *International Economic Policies*, New York, Appleton, 1925, p. 13.
16. Quoted in Northedge, F.S. and Grieve, M., *One Hundred Years of International Relations*, London, Duckworth, 1971, pp. 49–50.

17. The measures to restrict competition are traced in Hodges, C., *The Background of International Relations*, New York, Wiley, 1931, pp. 333–9; Hobson, J., *The Evolution of Modern Capitalism*, London, Macmillan, 1914; and Moon, P., *Imperialism and World Politics*, London, Methuen, 1926.
18. The connection between protectionism and imperialism is detailed in Hobsbawm, E., *The Age of Empire, 1875–1914*, London, Weidenfeld & Nicolson, 1987.
19. Carr, E.H., *The Twenty Years Crisis*, London, Macmillan, 1962, p. 78.
20. London, Nisbet, 1902.
21. Ibid., p. 65.
22. London, Lawrence & Wishart, 1948, p. 76.
23. See for example Schumpeter, J., *Imperialism and Social Classes*, Oxford, Blackwell, 1951; Langer, W.L., *The Diplomacy of Imperialism*, 2nd edn., New York, 1951; Winslow, E., 'Marxian, Liberal and Sociological theories of imperialism', *The Journal of Political Economy*, vol. 39, no. 6, December 1931; and Koebner, R. and Schmidt, H. *Imperialism: The Story and Significance of a Political World*, Cambridge, Cambridge University Press, 1964.
24. Feis, H., *Europe, The World's Banker: 1870–1914*, Boston, Yale, 1930.
25. Hartmann, F.H., *The Relations of Nations*, 2nd edn, New York, Macmillan, 1964, p. 142.
26. Ibid., pp. 143–9.
27. London, Macmillan, 1936.

CHAPTER 17

UNDERDEVELOPMENT: CAUSES AND PROPOSED CURES

17.1 BRETTON WOODS

When in July 1944 officials from 44 mainly Western countries met at Bretton Woods – a secluded estate in America's New Hampshire – to plan the post-war economic shape of the world, their deliberations were to be complicated by divergencies in economic outlook between the US and the European countries – differences which, as it happens, mirror those between the developed North and the less developed South today.

Like Britain when it was economic 'top dog' a century before, the basic goal of Washington, whose post-war economy was in excellent shape, was to return to Adam Smith – to reduce and gradually eliminate tariff barriers and institute free trade. But for the Europeans who had imposed such barriers during the Depression and had kept them during the war, it was much too soon to set about removing them. In fact, John Maynard Keynes, Britain's chief negotiator at Bretton Woods, spoke for most Europeans when he maintained that rapid trade liberalisation could be de-stabilising. Cheap imports were all very well, but if they led to large-scale unemployment in particular regions and industries, the social costs could outweigh the economic benefits. And though he agreed that economic nationalism had been a cause of the Second World War, for the time being, he argued, tariffs and quotas were necessary safeguards against another possible slump.

In short, a balance had to be struck between the North American and the European view, but it was agreed that while trade liberalisation was the ultimate goal, for the moment international economic matters could not be left to the market. Some international regulation of currency and exchange rates was essential, at least in the short term.

Learning the lessons

Priority number one was to learn the lessons from the collapse of the international economy in the 1920s and 1930s.[1] By common consent, a major cause had been the failure of US leadership. Washington had returned to isolationism, apparently indifferent to world economic as well as world political developments. In the post-war world, however, it was felt the US would have to be involved. After all, while the war had devastated European, Asian and North African economies, mainland USA, shielded from the main theatres of conflict, had profited. Leaving the Depression swiftly behind, America's industrial advance during hostilities had been more rapid than at any time before or since. Moreover, in contrast to other combatants, American living standards had actually risen during this period. By 1945, according to Paul Kennedy, the US accounted for nearly a half of world industrial production and held about two-thirds of world gold reserves.[2] Scarce wonder, then, that the participants at Bretton Woods looked to the world's only economic superpower to manage the post-war international economy, and this time Washington had to agree.

The second lesson was the need to avoid the kind of reparations tangle that had led in the 1920s from the collapse of the German mark to the collapse of the inter-war economy. Admittedly, the Soviet Union, having lost some 27 million people – one in 9 of its population – as a result of the Nazi invasion, demanded sizeable reparations. But though Germany had in fact been much more responsible for the Second than for the First World War, the consensus at Bretton Woods was that for the sake of the world economy reparations would have to be much smaller than in the 1920s and be generally in kind rather than in cash.

The third lesson – the need to keep war debt within bounds – had been understood early in the war when the US made use of a device called Lend Lease. Accordingly, any credit or commodities Washington made available to its allies were to be regarded as 'Uncle Sam's' contribution towards winning the war and repayment was to be made only if it did not impede the revival of world trade.

The fourth lesson was to correct the monetary imbalances caused by the gold drain to the US. How? The Bretton Woods formula for financial prudence involved two main devices – first, fixed exchange rates among the major currencies; second, the use of gold as a reserve asset, which the US with its vast stocks promised to sell at a fixed price of $35 an ounce. And since Washington agreed to exchange gold for dollars at any time, the dollar became literally as good as gold. In return for Washington's pledge to maintain the value of the dollar, other countries agreed to keep fluctuations in their exchange rates within strict limits. Currencies were not, in other words, to be allowed go into free fall. For several years the West German mark and the Japanese yen were fixed at, respectively, 4 and 310 to the dollar – a rate low enough to tempt Americans into buying Volkswagens and Sonys. To control inflation and increase productivity, the central banks were when necessary to either buy or sell their country's own currency using the US dollar to raise or depress the currency value.

To manage and lubricate the Bretton Woods system the participants were to sign an accord – the General Agreement on Tariffs and Trade (GATT) pledging themselves where possible to reduce trade barriers, and created two institutions – the International Monetary Fund (IMF) and the World Bank – to keep international finances on track.

Institutions

The IMF would provide overdraft facilities and short-term credits to stabilise the currencies of countries with balance of payments problems. It would also advise on national exchange rates, and its approval was necessary before any devaluation or revaluation. The World Bank was to make longer-term investments to speed post-war reconstruction and development, and in particular to finance transportation needs and other infrastructure projects. The funding of both institutions was to be largely through quota contributions from its members in the form of gold and national currency; and there would be a system of weighted voting, clearly giving the US, the largest contributor, a dominant influence in both.

17.2 UNFORESEEN DIFFICULTIES

In practice, developments turned out to be very different from what had been envisaged.[3] In the first place, the goal of a single global economic community based on multilateral trade and currency convertibility was unrealisable as long as the world remained polarised between East and West and the developing countries were more concerned with matters of justice and equity than Western notions of economic efficiency. Secondly, within the Western world, the economic imbalance between Europe and North America was far greater than expected. Pre-war Europe's trade deficits with the US had always been offset by a surplus on what are called 'invisible' items in the balance of payments such as banking, insurance, shipping, freight services and so forth. After the war, however, it was different. The enormous carnage and devastation, the bombed-out housing, the clapped-out machinery, the need to resettle refugees, the lost markets and the like created enormous economic problems which could not easily be solved, and the consequent fall in consumer goods production greatly enlarged the export deficit. At the same time the pre-war surplus on 'invisibles' was also replaced by a deficit because of the sales of overseas investments to finance the war, the loss of shipping during hostilities and the need to maintain a high level of military spending even after the war. Before long, Europe's imports from the US were seven times its exports to that country, creating a massive 'dollar gap' with which neither the IMF nor the World Bank could cope.

By 1947 Washington decided it must act. Economically, a bankrupt Europe would hit US trade because the Europeans would not be able to afford to buy American. Politically, it was argued, Moscow would profit from Europe's economic plight, using it to augment the list of conscripts to the Communist system. Already it was pressurising Iran and Turkey for territorial concessions, in Greece Communist guerrillas were making significant advances, and the mass Communist parties of Italy and France were seen as potential threats to democracy. Washington's anxieties in this respect were probably greatly exaggerated, since Moscow's own economic problems of post-war recovery were massive and its control of world Communism far more tenuous than it appeared. Nonetheless, what matters in international relations is what people imagine – and because the Truman Administration perceived that the Kremlin was both promoting and waiting for the economic collapse of Western Europe, it feared that the US could be dangerously isolated. It was therefore up to Washington to fill the economic gap. How?

17.3 THE US RESPONSE

In March 1947 President Truman outlined to Congress what was to become known as the Truman Doctrine, offering aid to what he called 'free peoples who are resisting subjugation by armed minorities or by outside persons',[4] the first beneficiaries of which were Greece and Turkey. It was a watershed in American history which had stood aloof from entangling relations with Europe ever since the Monroe Doctrine. Within three months Washington was giving its new-found concern for the European balance much more extensive application when Secretary of State George Marshall announced his massive plan of assistance to, as he put it, 'permit the emergence of political and social conditions in which free institutions can exist'.[5] In theory Marshall aid was available to both Communist and non-Communist alike. The only stated condition was that the recipients should cooperate in an Organisation for European Economic Cooperation (OEEC) to reduce trade and monetary barriers between themselves, even if it meant their discrimination against US exports (a generous gesture!), but the free-market implications were enough to bring about a rebuff from Moscow – probably as intended. Though Communist leaders in Czechoslovakia and Poland might have accepted Marshall aid, Stalin objected on their behalf, and in economic terms Eastern and Western Europe went their separate ways.

17.4 ECONOMIC EFFECTS

By 1951 when the Marshall plan had run its course, Western Europe had benefited to the tune of $17,000 million dollars, only a fraction of it being repayable, and in part consequence was well on the way to recovery. With mounting economic success came the idea of closer economic integration along the lines suggested during the Second World War by David Mitrany in *A Working Peace System*. Mitrany had suggested that habits of functional cooperation – that is, cooperation in economic, technological and social areas – would have political effect, lessening economic disparities, dissolving political differences and ultimately eliminating any pretext for war.[6] This Functionalist idea was given its first practical application in the European Coal and Steel Community of 1951 whereby France, West Germany, Italy, Belgium, the Netherlands and Luxembourg were to eliminate restrictive practices in these industries, and its architects, Jean Monnet and Robert Schuman, saw in it a pilot project presaging a much more comprehensive association of European powers. In the European Economic Community (EEC), established in 1957, their hopes seemed fulfilled. It was an auspicious beginning as, thanks to continuing US military as well as economic assistance and the effects of technological advance, Western Europe was about to experience record growth rates in manufactures, exports, employment, investment capital and disposable income.[7] In the process several of the objectives of Bretton Woods were being realised in the Western European theatre. Trade liberalisation proceeded apace and with it monetary convertibility as the members of OEEC reduced or removed quotas and tariffs on trade with one another.

But Western Europe was not alone in its economic success. Eastern Europe was apparently prospering, too – though the extent of its progress is rather difficult to gauge because of the notorious unreliability of Communist statistics at the time. Certainly the official figures pointed to a massive growth in production, and even if they were only half true, that expansion will have been assisted in no small measure, ironically, by Western trade embargoes and boycotts. For Western sanctions imposed from 1948 onwards merely encouraged, as sanctions so often do, the target states to produce for themselves what they had formerly imported. So that by the perverse logic of history, we in the West – by curtailing our economic contacts with the European Communist countries once Marshall aid had been rejected – helped to create the Soviet bloc.

On the other hand the economic system developed in the East was too inflexible to reward innovation or efficiency, too uncompetitive, too centralised and wasteful in human and material resources, and so quality was continually being sacrificed for quantity. A plethora of totally unusable goods would pour from the Communist factories – leaky hot water bottles, fridges giving an electric shock as they were opened, spin-dryers that slopped water on to the floor, to say nothing of the tenements that had to be rebuilt within a few years because they were in danger of collapse.

Part of the problem was that the Eastern European Communist countries never developed any suitable mechanism for economic cooperation. True, there was an institution called COMECON, the Council for Mutual Economic Assistance, dating from 1949, but for many years it was no more than a forum for attacking the economic arrangements of the West and a cover for Soviet exploitation. When it did attempt in the late 1950s to develop joint investment projects, specialisation and the coordination of national plans, results rarely matched expectations, and, when cold war conditions eased, in their search for managerial skills, technology and foodstuffs, its members were increasingly drawn to the West.[8]

If there was rather less economic cooperation in Eastern Europe than was suggested by their common Communist ideology, Western Europe, too, remained somewhat divided. Though each country had experienced some kind of economic miracle up to 1970, collectively in institutional terms they were literally at 'sixes and sevens'. Reacting to the setting up of the EEC in 1957, seven non-Common Market countries had formed the European Free Trade Area (EFTA) which shared with its Common Market neighbours the objective of eliminating tariffs and quotas. Unlike them, however, it made no provision for a common external tariff. Led by Britain, EFTA was an experiment in balance-of-power economics. As a counterweight to the EEC it was able to accommodate Commonwealth economic interests in a way that the Community would not. Commonwealth preference, in a word, was maintained. Yet even though by 1959 there was an economic fault line dividing Western Europe and the OEEC had reached its 'sell-by' date, the region as a whole continued to prosper. Moreover, like Japan, whose economy had also flourished in part due to American generosity, it was able to benefit from the American market while being able to restrict US imports[9] (something which it has continued to do).

17.5 THE US ECONOMY IN TROUBLE

So how was the US economy faring during this time? In fact by about 1960 it was in trouble, as Washington's policy of providing enough dollars to facilitate international trade turned out to be only too successful. For as Western Europe and Japan completed their post-war recovery, the dollar came under pressure. Whereas in 1945 the world suffered from a shortage, by 1960 there was a glut, and for the first time there were more dollars in circulation than the US had gold to redeem them. If every foreign bank had then asked the US for an ounce of gold for every $35 in its possession, Washington could not have paid. Moreover, its continued assistance, foreign investments and overseas military expenditure were creating a balance-of-payments deficit that threatened to get out of control, and in November 1960 the US experienced its first ever run on the dollar as international speculators began to convert dollars into gold.

Soon the US needed the help of bankers and finance ministers from the leading Bretton Woods countries, as it could no longer manage the monetary system largely on its own. But then by this time no one state could, since sudden massive movements of capital from one country to another and the internationalisation of banking and production facilities through the MNCs were starting to make every currency, including the dollar, sensitive and vulnerable. At the same time, America's tendency to act as 'world policeman' was undermining the US economy. President Johnson's reluctance to raise taxes to finance the costly Vietnam conflict, or the country's huge burden of defence expenditure while the bills for his domestic anti-poverty programme were skyrocketing, generated serious inflation. Furthermore, by 1971 the US was suffering its first trade deficit this century, indicating the precariousness of its economic situation. In short, while the EC and Japan's share of world trade grew rapidly, that of the US was in decline.

17.6 WASHINGTON TAKES DRASTIC ACTION

Faced with a mounting economic crisis which had domestic political implications, President Nixon in August 1971 took drastic action. Reversing previous policy and without consulting his Bretton Woods partners he introduced wage and price controls, a surcharge on imports, the suspension of dollar convertibility and then devaluation, effected by increasing the price of an ounce of gold.[10] Though somewhat inconsistent with a world in which managed currencies were beginning to yield to market forces and major economic corrections were expected to be preceded by discussion, it was a foretaste of what was to come. With the price of gold and dollar convertibility no longer guaranteed, the financial and regulatory disciplines of Bretton Woods began to break down and by 1972 had virtually collapsed. But prospects of a new international monetary regime were to be checked as the international political economy was rocked by a series of additional shocks.

17.7 FURTHER SHOCKS

The food crisis

The first blow was the world food crisis of the early 1970s. Precipitated by the kinds of climatological calamity in the Soviet Union, China and much of Africa and Asia which we tend mistakenly to think of today as unprecedented – severe droughts in some regions, severe floods in others – it was compounded by the largest commercial transaction in foodstuffs ever, as the Soviet Union purchased 28 million tonnes of grain, mainly from the US. The effect was to drive up the world price, and the resulting crisis was made still worse by a sudden decrease in the world catch of fish, in part the result of over-fishing by countries such as the Soviet Union and Japan. The abrupt fall in the supply of staple foodstuffs could only further compound the problems of countries where the population growth was outstripping available food supplies – the LDCs.[11]

The oil-price shocks

Hard on the heels of the food crisis came an even bigger catastrophe – the first massive oil-price hike – a rise of some 400 per cent generated by the oil-exporting countries (OPEC) in the wake of the 1973 war between Israel and its Arab neighbours. With more countries switching to oil from coal, a resource they thought to be environmentally unfriendly (it had not yet occurred to a lot of people that oil might also be environmentally unsound!), the producers of petroleum had a golden opportunity to make money while putting Islamic and, in particular, Arab grievances on the map. The effect, however, was to destabilise the world economy, putting severe pressure on the non-oil-producers, and precipitating an inflationary spiral that ended in a world recession. Since oil is used in almost every sector of the economy – industry, agriculture, transport, domestic heating, etc. – many an LDC non-producer had to either forego industrialisation, search for alternative fuels or borrow heavily.

A further oil-price shock at the end of the 1970s following the fall of the Shah in Iran, and the widespread fear of a drop in oil-production in the Gulf merely compounded the problem, and into the vocabulary of economics entered a new word – 'stagflation' – when stagnation in output is combined with massive inflation. For in six years the price of petroleum had soared sixteenfold – from just over two and a half to forty dollars per barrel.[12]

The fall in oil prices

On the other hand, so traumatic were the oil shocks that consumers were forced to rethink their energy policies. Some developed new technologies for extracting oil from hostile environments such as Alaska and the North Sea. Some researched and exploited alternative energy sources, while most countries (the US excepted) went in for energy conservation. Not surprisingly, demand for OPEC's oil fell, and as its price plummeted in consequence, by the early 1980s even the oil-producers began to feel the pinch.

Meanwhile the oil crisis was seriously affecting the circulation of money. As payments had been much more than their economies could absorb, the oil-producers would tend to deposit their surpluses in the banks. Soon the whole banking system was awash with so-called 'petro-dollars' – dollars obtained from the sale of oil – and, naturally, the banks had been keen to dispose of them in the form of loans. As it happens, there had been no shortage of borrowers, especially among oil-importing countries unable to balance the books. In this way 'petro-dollars' had been recycled from oil-exporter to oil-importer, by far the biggest borrowers being the LDCs and the Eastern European Communist countries hoping to modernise their economies.[13]

The debt crisis

At first all had seemed well, because LDC and Eastern European exports grew along with the debt, but with the second oil shock the picture changed dramatically. For the debtor countries in particular this had been an unmitigated disaster since they faced soaring interest rates, spiralling costs of debt-servicing and a collapse in the value of their exports as they saturated the market with a narrow range of commodities for which there was only limited demand. Some, moreover, compounded the problem by mismanaging their debt, frittering away their credit on prestige projects, sophisticated weaponry and consumer durables for the wealthy elites. Yet the LDCs and Communist countries had continued to borrow and the banks to lend, expecting that imminent world recovery which the leading economists of the day, with their enormous talent for getting things wrong, were constantly predicting. But instead of recovery the world was in for a severe recession – in part due to increased international tension in several different areas simultaneously – the Iran/Iraq war, the Soviet intervention into Afghanistan, the introduction of martial law in Poland and the war between Britain and Argentina for the Falklands/Malvinas. As confidence ebbed on capital markets, many banks had called for immediate repayment on some short-term loans. But Mexico, one of the world's largest debtors, had been among the many countries unable to meet its financial obligations, and in 1982 triggered off what was to become known as the debt crisis.[14]

The Mexican experience

Mexico's economic problems had been in many ways typical of what was happening elsewhere. Like many a developing country, its economic growth from the 1940s to the 1960s had been impressive. But the cumulative impact of the various shocks of the 1970s had put the country, even though an oil-producer, into economic reverse, while the population growth and drift to the cities ended agricultural self-sufficiency. By August 1982 the Mexican government was facing a foreign debt of just over $80,000 million – making it second only to that of Brazil. How had it amassed such a huge deficit?

In the early 1970s the banks had been as eager to lend to Mexico as to any other country, and at negligible interest. But the rapid global rise of interest rates in the 1980s and the combined effects of corruption and inflation, a mounting imports bill, a fall in the value of exports, a flight from capital and dwindling foreign exchange reserves had brought Mexico to the point where it could scarcely afford to even service its debt. For a time there was talk, encouraged by Cuba's Fidel Castro, of a 'cartel' of Latin American debtors, which would refuse as a group to pay their arrears. If effected, such a course could have led to a collapse of confidence in the international banking system, driving even secure financial institutions to the verge of ruin. But since a collective default might have met collective punishment, doing harm to developed and underdeveloped alike, the idea was dropped.

Another suggestion favoured by Peru was to limit debt repayment to a percentage of export earnings. This too proved unpopular with the banks as did the proposal for reimbursing part of the debt either in local currency or in kind. The preferred alternative was for Mexico to reach an understanding with both the private foreign banks and the IMF. The banks, in turn, fearing a collective default, wrote off some debts, agreed to reschedule others and offered bridging loans in return for what is called a 'structural adjustment package' – an austerity programme developed in the West by Western economists largely for Western conditions involving massive cuts in government spending, privatisation of public enterprises and the removal of import restrictions.

Sadly, for many countries the remedy was often worse than the disease as it effectively prioritised debt-repayment over indigenous welfare, health and education and further penalised the domestic comsumer by skewing the economy in favour of the production of exported cash crops.

Since, moreover, interest rates were rocketing at the time, debtors such as Mexico would soon be obliged to repay the original debt several times over.[15] Demands for the outright cancellation of debts were met with claims that such a proceeding would be both morally iniquitous and economically counter-productive, in effect rewarding inefficiency and encouraging indigence and dependency. Yet debts had been waived before. The US had long since forgotten the billions of dollars owed it by Britain since the First World War, while the West Germans had been asked to pay only a fraction of its debts to the Western Allies.

It is, however, true that since the early 1990s, as interest rates have fallen and the IMF has provided a trust fund to help reduce the debts of the Heavily Indebted Poor Countries (HIPC) to what the creditors regard as sustainable levels, the economic problems of the very poorest have been eased. On the other hand, not even the Central American states devastated by Hurricane Mitch in October 1998 have been spared the burden of repayment. In the meantime, the economic strain had merely increased political instability, probably contributing to the rise of religious fundamentalism and the fall of several debt-ridden governments in the third world.

A volatile international monetary system

There were to be other crises in the financial markets. When the system of fixed exchanges gave way to one of floating rates in the early 1970s, the professional economists assumed, with their usual flair for beginning with an unwarranted assumption and ending with a preconceived conclusion, that the rate would be determined by the laws of supply and demand and a reflection of purchasing power. They were wrong. In practice, exchange rates can be so easily undermined by financial speculators like George Soros who on a whim or rumour can move vast sums across frontiers either physical or notional, as from one side of a computer screen to another. Alternatively currency values can be manipulated by governments, as policy priorities shift between devaluation, the Keynesian solution, which tends to stimulate exports but promotes inflation; or revaluation, the monetarists answer, which tends to cheapen imports but causes unemployment. This combination of speculative capital transfers and policy-induced shifts in exchange rates have together created a somewhat volatile and unstable international monetary system since the 1970s.

That it did not collapse into complete chaos, as in the period between the First and Second World Wars, is in part because of the financial institutions, such as the IMF, which remained in place, the development of what are called regimes, i.e. regularised patterns of cooperation in given financial, monetary and other issue areas,[16] the managerial capacity of the G7 – the so-called 'rich man's club' – and the growth of regional organisations in both North and South. Meanwhile in a supreme irony the world's biggest debtor – the US – has continued to flourish economically, largely escaping the consequences of its own extravagant behaviour.

For Robert Keohane and other proponents of the so-called 'theory of hegemonic stability',[17] it is America's leading role in the world economy, like that of Britain before the First World War, that largely accounts for the maintenance of what international economic order there is. For the US plays a key role in the institutions sustaining it, and even if America shows signs of relative economic decline, it still has what Susan Strange refers to as 'structural power ... the power to shape and determine the structures of the global political economy within which other states, their political institutions, their economic enterprises ... have to operate'.[18] And of the four components of structural power she identifies, 'control over security, control over production, control over credit and control over knowledge, beliefs and ideas', arguably only in the last of these has US structural power come under serious challenge. On the other hand if, as Robert Gilpin believes, there is 'an inevitable shift in the international distribution of economic and military power from the core to the rising nations in the periphery and elsewhere',[19] and the US is, in Paul Kennedy's words, in 'imperial overstretch', what happens to the 'stability' which 'the hegemon' has helped to fashion, maintain and enforce? The theory would appear to suggest that disorder must result if US military and economic dominance are seriously undermined. But how valid is the theory and, in any case, is not the perceived decline of US power more apparent than real?

As usual the theorists are divided in their answers;[20] nonetheless, the perceived decline in Washington's economic leadership, the repeated shocks to the international financial and political system and the impetus to enlarge the European Union, with its protectionist agricultural tariffs, encouraged those doing especially badly out of the system – i.e. the LDCs and the Communist countries – to put accepted economic orthodoxies – capitalist and socialist – under critical scrutiny.

17.8 CRITIQUE OF ECONOMIC ORTHODOXIES

Reformist

The reformist starting point was that the implementation of orthodox liberal theories concerning world trade had produced not balance but a kind of two-tier system whereby some countries were enriched and rather more were impoverished.[21] According to Raoul Prebisch, a left-wing Argentinian economist, the world was divided economically into what he called 'centre' countries – fully developed, industrialised and with power over the sources of capital and technology – and 'periphery' countries – non-industrialised and prey to a trading system whose terms seemed to be permanently loaded against them. For Prebisch the only way out of this structural vicious circle was for the periphery countries to undertake forced industrialisation so as to reduce dependence on imports and foreign credit. But how was this to be achieved? Domestically, by control-ling imports to speed the development of a domestic manufacturing base. Internationally, by pressurising the developed countries to show greater regard for the interests of the periphery.[22]

Prebisch's ideas were to provide the intellectual inspiration for the activities of the United Nations Conference on Trade and Development (UNCTAD), created in 1964, and the idea of a New International Economic Order (NIEO), adopted by the Group of 77 Less Developed Countries ten years later. In fact it represented a serious bid by the LDCs for the levers of 'structural power' and was designed to shift the economic order from a liberal market-oriented order, in whose creation they had played no part, in favour of a more state-based model. It called for (1) preferential treatment in trade for the LDCs with easy access to Western markets and the building of buffer stocks of and long-term contracts for commodities likely to change in price over time; (2) technological transfers, long-term development assistance and debt-relief programmes for the Third World; (3) greater controls over the activities of MNCs and other foreign investors in the LDCs, and (4) changes in international economic institutions to give the LDCs a greater voice.[23]

Radical

On the other hand, being proposals widely regarded as favourable only to the LDCs, they commanded scant support in the developed countries on whose goodwill they were dependent for implementation. But if the Group of 77 thought that their numerical strength in the UN and pos-session of valuable resources would give them added bargaining power and persuade the industrialised countries to look more favourably on the NIEO, they were to be sadly disappointed. But resistance from the developed countries and lack of support from the OPEC states were to give currency to more radical theories. The late former Prime Minister of Jamaica, Michael Manley, though in broad agreement with the Prebisch analysis, felt that it did not go far enough. For since the domestic market of most LDCs was too small to be economically efficient, there was a need for regional trading regimes such as the Caribbean Community and

Common Market (Caricom), Mercosur, the Southern African Development Community (SADC), the Economic Community of West African States (ECOWAS), etc.[24] It is a persuasive argument if those joining the relevant organisations have complementary economies. Where, however, they trade in similar products – bananas or rum, for instance – the benefits of association are likely to be meagre.

Another radical perspective is that of Thomas Weisskopf who, from his American campus, instructed the LDCs to selectively delink from the world economy and pursue a policy of self-reliant development. In essence it was a call to diversify overseas sources of supply and markets, ban luxury imports, stockpile essentials, disperse and diversify domestic production, increase the share of investment financed fron indigenous savings and replace foreign experts where possible.[25] The trouble with such a proposal is that it already assumes a position of financial power few LDCs can muster, and because it advocates import-substitution industrialisation and disregard of the law of comparative advantage, the commodities produced are likely to be expensive, of poor quality and incapable of competing on world markets. Thus Weisskopf's answer is in danger of compounding the very problem he sought to solve.

Revolutionaries

More politically extreme than the reformists and radicals were the revolutionaries who believed that the very people on which Prebisch and Co. were relying to rid the world of the structure of dominance and dependency were part of the problem. For the elites of each dependent economy represented the interests not of their peoples but of the 'centre' states, and the revolutionaries claimed that without their overthrow nothing would be fundamentally changed. Such revolutionary theorists divided into two schools – the neo-Marxists such as Samir Amin, who believed that through national revolution and selective or comprehensive delinking from the capitalist world economy, true national liberation could be achieved;[26] and the more orthodox Marxists such as Wallerstein, who believed that the internationalisation of capital was such that nothing short of world revolution would suffice.[27] For illustration of that internationalisation, reference might be made to the vessel called the Sea Empress that went aground off the Welsh coast in 1996; for it had been built in Spain, was owned by Norwegians, had been registered in Cyprus, was managed by a Scottish firm, had been chartered in France, and had an American cargo and a Russian crew. If capitalism is global, says Wallerstein, then revolution has to be global, too.

On the other hand, in emphasising structural forces to the exclusion of such factors as religious and cultural values, charismatic leadership and technological developments, the revolutionaries oversimplify and distort. And in largely ignoring the question as to whether there can be much economic development in the absence of a development ethos – the idea that things can be other than they are – they fail to address one of the critical problems affecting many of the LDCs.

17.9 MORE ORTHODOX SOLUTIONS AND THEIR EFFECTS

Throughout the 1970s and most of the 1980s reformist, radical and revolutionary ideas were in vogue in many an LDC, and several leaders, especially in Africa and Latin America, tried to put one or other of them into effect. However, the collapse of Eastern European Communism, China's successful move into the world market, and the enormous economic problems now experienced by Cuba and North Korea and the radical nationalist countries such as Myanmar (Burma) dampened LDC enthusiasm for the more radical solutions.

For devotees of neo-liberal or classical economics, Francis Fukayama's famous text of 1989 proclaiming *The End of History*[28] served as an inspiration. For a time, most of the post-Communist rulers of Eastern Europe, some of them former Communists, went in for 'shock therapy', administered largely by Western economists and involving selling off national assets to private and often foreign-owned enterprise, cutting state subsidies and freeing the market. In Taiwan, South Korea, Singapore, Hong Kong, Thailand, Indonesia and Malaysia, which had long 'bought into' the strategy of development associated with neo-liberals such as Walt Whitman Rostow,[29] market mechanisms helped turn their once struggling economies into Asian 'tigers', though as in China the process was largely government-led and therefore hardly along the lines of Adam Smith.

Meanwhile, in the developed countries environmentalists were elaborating a Green approach, as in the Brundtland Commission's report of 1987 on *Our Common Future* and which was meant to apply to developed and developing countries alike.[30] While not altogether repudiating the market, it rejects unlimited industrial growth in favour of 'sustainable development' which provides for the present 'without compromising the ability of future generations to meet their own needs', and measures development in terms of life-expectancy, adult literacy and purchasing power. And instead of large capital-intensive projects, it advocates small-scale labour-intensive enterprise and the use of local 'experts' rather than expensive jet-setting international 'whiz-kids'. It is a mode of thought that fits in with a perception, detailed in the next chapter, of a planet which will need to constrain industrialisation and rampant consumerism if it is to survive.

With investors fleeing tumbling share markets in parts of Asia and Latin America, and market mechanisms in crisis in many of the post-Communist countries of Eastern Europe, thanks to the foolhardiness of those economists who with a blithe disregard of history believed that a planned Socialist command economy could be transformed into a liberal free-enterprise economy without handing it to the Mafia, it may not be too long before more radical remedies are again in vogue. Already in Russia and some of its former Eastern European allies, former Communists are climbing back into power, this time by courtesy of the ballot not the bullet. For the post-Communist experience has been for many a disaster. For political freedom has often gone hand-in-hand with plummeting living standards, massive corruption, soaring crime rates, crumbling social services and the return of long-forgotten diseases. As George Soros who benefited from the market system has recently warned, democracy itself could be endangered by the very 'market values' supposed to promote it.

None of this necessarily suggests a return to full-blooded Socialism, complete with nationalisation, deficit financing and central direction of the economy. After all, while Communists reappear in Eastern Europe, Social Democrats return to Western Europe, and with policies far removed from the left-wing agendas of the 1940s and 1950s. On the other hand they do reflect disillusionment with Thatcherite/Reaganite free-market fundamentalism. They also indicate mounting dissatisfaction with the structural adjustment shibboleths of the World Bank, described by one disillusioned critic on its fiftieth anniversary in 1994 as '. . . an old temple of cold warriors; a highly centralised, secretive, undemocratic vestige of another time. Fifty years is enough'.[31] Whether or not the new mood exemplifies what both Professor Anthony Giddens and Britain's Prime Minister Tony Blair call 'The Third Way', it does look as if many Western governments are groping towards a kind of welfare capitalism in which economic criteria are tempered by social considerations – and since many Eastern European countries prepare to enter the EU they may be tempted to emulate this latest form of Social Democracy. At the same time, were the Euro to succeed in matching economic advance with political stability, it could well encourage other countries, especially in Asia, Africa and Latin America, to develop common currencies of their own.

17.10 THE FOLLY OF UNIFORMITY

On the other hand, if we have learned anything from recent history it is surely that what works in one country does not necessarily work in another; that to try to thrust capitalism on a country not geared to it is as foolish as the attempt to socialise a country that does not want it, or to enrol a country into a common market or currency to which it does not wish to belong. Perhaps what in the end succeeds is something that accords with experience as well as aspiration. In a complex world surely there can be no simple or uniform solutions to global problems, and the sooner the world's economists and politicians grasp that the better.

NOTES

1. See for example Hartmann, F.H., *The Relations of Nations*, 2nd edn, New York, Macmillan, 1964, pp. 149–54.
2. Kennedy, P., *The Rise and Fall of the Great Powers*, London, Fontana, 1989, p. 461.
3. For an introduction to the post-1945 economic order see Scammel, W., *The International Economy since 1945*, 2nd edn, London, Macmillan, 1983, and Spero, J., *The Politics of International Economic Relations*, 4th edn, London, Unwin Hyman, 1990.
4. 'The Truman Doctrine', in *Public Papers of the Presidents of the United States, Harry S Truman*, Washington, US Government Printing Office, 1947, pp. 178–9.
5. 'European initiative essential to economic recovery', in *Department of State Bulletin*, vol. 16, 15 June 1947, p. 1160.
6. London, Royal Institute of International Affairs, 1946.
7. Kennedy, P., op. cit., p. 543.
8. Stern, G., *The Rise and Decline of International Communism*, Aldershot, Elgar, 1990, pp. 209–12.
9. On Japan's 'economic miracle' see Kennedy, P., op. cit., pp. 537–40 and 591–608.
10. On Nixon's New Economic Policy see Spero, J., op. cit., pp. 4–5 and 109–11.
11. For an admirable survey of the problems involved see Kegley, C. and Wittkopf, E., *World Politics: Trend and Transformation*, New York, St Martin's Press, 1981, pp. 220–59.
12. Spero, J., op. cit., pp. 58–95 and 311–14.
13. Ibid., pp. 74–8.
14. Ibid., pp. 78–99.
15. See George, S., *A Fate Worse than Debt*, Harmondsworth, Penguin, 1988, and Nowzad, B., 'Lessons of the debt decade', *Finance and Development*, 27 March 1990.
16. On regimes see Krasner, S.D. (ed.) *International Regimes*, Ithaca, Cornell University Press, 1983, and Levy, M.A., Young, O. and Zurn, M., 'The study of international regimes', *European Journal of International Relations*, no. 1, 1995, pp. 267–330.
17. Keohane, R., *After Hegemony*, Princeton, Princeton University Press, 1984.
18. Strange, S., *States and Markets*, London, Pinter, 1988.
19. *The Political Economy of International Relations*, Princeton, Princeton University Press, 1987, pp. 77–8.
20. While Paul Kennedy, op. cit., claims that US hegemony is in decline, his thesis

is vigorousy denied by Nye, J., in *Bound to Lead: The Changing Nature of American Power*, New York, Basic Books, 1990, and by Strange, S. 'The persistent myth of lost hegemony', *International Organisation*, vol. 41, 1987, pp. 551–74. For Keohane, op. cit., the existence of regimes suggest that interstate cooperation would still continue without a single hegemon.

21. Kegley, C. and Wittkopf, E., op. cit., pp. 72–102 and 182–204.
22. *The Economic Development of Latin America and its Principal Problems*, New York, The United Nations, 1950.
23. Reubens, E., *The Challenge of the N.I.E.O.*, Boulder, Colorado, Westview, 1981, especially pp. 1–17.
24. Interview with Michael Manley in Stern, G., *Leaders and Leadership*, London, LSE/BBC World Service, 1993, p. 98.
25. 'Self-reliance and development strategy' in Manh-Lau, N. (ed.), *Unreal Growth*, Delhi, Hindustan Publishing Co., 1984, pp. 845–61.
26. See for example *Imperialism and Unequal Development*, New York, Monthly Review Press, 1977.
27. *The Politics of the World-Economy*, Cambridge, Cambridge University Press, 1984.
28. *The National Interest*, no. 16, Summer 1989, pp. 3–18.
29. His book, *The Stages of Economic Growth: A Non-Communist Manifesto*, Cambridge, Cambridge University Press, 1960, defines development in terms of economic growth and increase in Gross Domestic Product and industrialisation, and prescribes the same model of industrialisation for the LDCs as he claims was followed by the Western countries. To Rostow this meant adopting market mechanisms, opening up the country to foreign investment and minimising government control – a formula which would produce not merely impressive growth rates but an abundance of wealth which would 'trickle down' to benefit the whole population.
30. *World Commission on Environment and Development*, 1987.
31. Danaher, K. (ed.), *Fifty Years is Enough: The Case against the World Bank and the IMF*, Boston, South End Press, 1994.

PART VII

WORLD SOCIETY?

CHAPTER 18

PLANETARY DANGERS AND OPPORTUNITIES

As we moved into a new millennium many were glad to see the back of the twentieth century, with its world wars, weapons of mass destruction, totalitarian ideologies, genocidal massacres, concentration camps, mass deportations and the like. But some were clearly surprised that we ever survived 1999. For the year had presaged for some of the more deranged devotees of the Bible not just the *fin de siècle* but the *fin du monde*, as foretold in the Book of Revelation, following a cataclysmic war from whose ravages the devout claimed, with some relish, to be exempt. But they had not been the only prophets of doom. According to some of the more apocalyptic New Age sects, we faced planetary collisions, hostile visitations from outer space, alien abductions and a universe about to self-destruct, if not annihilated by nuclear meltdown then slowly poisoned by the baleful effects of genetically modified food. And even some secular sages seemed to believe that as a species we had little to look forward to: that we were becoming more unhealthy, unhappy, dishonest, cynical, insecure and (especially in the United States) overweight, that our computers were about to crash along with the stock market and that were we to reach the twenty-first century it would probably be even worse than the twentieth.

Even now, barely a day goes by without the prophets of doom adding some new catastrophe to the mounting tribulations apparently in store for us. And though as a species our lives are probably far less perilous than those of our grandparents and parents, as Frank Furedi reminds us in his book *The Culture of Fear*,[1] people today tend to worry far more than our ancestors did, and are less and less able to distinguish real dangers from media-induced scares.

18.1 NINETEENTH-CENTURY OPTIMISM

Yet the contrast with the nineteenth century – an age of unbridled optimism, at least in the West – could not be more striking. For the century of Hegel, Marx, Darwin and John Stuart Mill had seen growing literacy, prosperity and democratisation as well as rapid scientific and technological advance. Indeed, the scientists of the time had been revered as people of great learning with the potential for solving the world's problems and transforming the moral as well as the material conditions of life. And though the twentieth century also produced its optimists – people such as Woodrow Wilson, David Mitrany and Jean Monnet, for example, who envisioned new world orders – the prevailing mood at least among the creative and the intellectual was generally much more sombre. Why was the prospect of a science-based Utopia in which ideals are realised to be replaced by nightmare visions of dystopia in which ideals are shattered?

18.2 TWENTIETH-CENTURY PESSIMISM

The first hints of a change of attitude came around the turn of the century when a number of creative artists began to voice concern at the direction society was taking. For writers such as Joseph Conrad, composers such as Edward Elgar and artists such as Edward Munch, who produced that evocative painting *The Scream*, the social, economic and political structures that people had felt reasonably comfortable with were passing and humankind was plunging into the unknown. And, of course, their forebodings were merely reinforced in 1914 when the world was engulfed in war, at the end of which the German philosopher Osvald Spengler produced a text encapsulating their apprehensions. It was called, appropriately enough, *The Decline of the West*.

18.3 THEMES

Machines a threat to liberty

Ironically it was largely those elements that had made for such optimism in the nineteenth century that were beginning to generate a mood of despondency in the twentieth. First, the revolution in technology. Though new technologies were already beginning to add to the sum of human happiness, more thoughtful people realised that there was a price to be paid. The main danger seemed to lie in the potential threat machines posed to individual initiative. For while some might have liberating qualities, others seemed to dehumanise. After all, the negative side of technology was already to be seen in assembly-line production, where a whole day might be taken up with repetitive work involving merely tightening a screw, clamping a lid, affixing a label or stoking a fire – all totally soul-destroying! And, of course, the very technologies that were taking the drudgery out of life could also lead to its extinction, as in the Boer War and the First World War, and also, though in different vein, the sinking of the 'unsinkable' *Titanic*.

Science a threat to spiritual values

The second element to be re-evaluated at the turn of the century was the very 'scientism' of the previous half-century or so – the idea that science could solve all problems. Increasingly the scientific attitude was seen, possibly in error, as being in conflict with spiritual values – with religion, with metaphysics and with the kinds of irrational forces and drives which Freud and the psychoanalysts had indicated were of the very stuff of human existence. As an antidote to the very precision and logic of science, artists and intellectuals took to the mystical and the mythical, the instinctive and the intuitive, the ambiguous, the enigmatic and the downright bizarre.

Capitalism a threat to health and welfare

The third element for reassessment was the nature of the economic system – capitalism. True, in the nineteenth century the capitalist criteria of efficiency, market mechanisms and profit motives had been largely responsible for the phenomenal rise in the supply and distribution of consumer goods and the development of international communications. Nonetheless, the negative, alienating characteristics – which Marx had warned about – had largely gone unheeded, and it was becoming increasingly evident that capitalism could have adverse effects on health and welfare:

a) because of the toxic fumes, hazardous wastes and often insanitary working conditions;
b) because of the drudgery involved in much of the work; and
c) because of the even greater drudgery if one suddenly found oneself jobless and homeless as a result of one of capitalism's many recessions.

Hypocrisy and 'double standards'

A further element under critical scrutiny at the turn of the century was the moral certainty of the so-called Age of Progress. One of the dominant myths of the nineteenth century was that material advance had also brought moral progress and that science and technology had fostered a kind of higher ethic distinguishing Western from non-Western societies. From such notions both imperialism and racism derived their justification.

However, critics contrasting the rhetoric with the reality as regards, say, the Victorian family or the colonial experience, began to feel that the whole system was riddled with hypocrisy: that what was supposed to be happening often bore little relation to the real situation and that public virtue simply concealed private vice – respectable married men doing unspeakable things with and to their housekeepers, politicians and businessmen seducing their secretaries, public benefactors 'ripping off' their beneficiaries, pillars of the religious and military establishment engaging in the 'vice that dare not speak its name'. 'Double standards' railed the critics – and, as in our own day, they were right!

Symptoms of depression

With the unleashing of the ever more awesome destructive power of science, culminating in the second half of the century with the H-bomb, together with the ability of corrupt rulers to use such power in the service of totalitarian ideologies, what had begun as a concern of artists and intellectuals soon spread. But by this time there were additional reasons for collective gloom. The economic depression of the 1930s, the murderous antics of both Stalin and Hitler, in whom many had placed their trust, and the growing disillusionment with some of the religious and secular antidotes to nineteenth-century 'scientism', brilliantly satirised by Aldous Huxley in his novel *Brave New World* of 1932, produced in many the physical symptoms of depression.

Society under totalitarian control

Even after the end of the Depression and the horrors of the Second World War, the mood of doom and gloom became difficult to dispel. Cold war replaced hot war, and the images became darker and starker. George Orwell's *1984*, written in 1948, set the tone for the new pessimism, with its grim picture of a fully developed police state in which the individual's every word and action are kept under 24-hour television surveillance, and the thought police stand ready to stamp out any behaviour deemed subversive. With the pervasive message 'Big Brother is watching you', and its ominous slogans emblazoned on the white façade of the Ministry of Truth: 'War is Peace'; 'Freedom is Slavery'; 'Ignorance is Strength', it was an immensely powerful and influential text. And the representation of the boot trampling on a human face has served as a powerful metaphor for oppression ever since.

Nuclear war

By the 1950s, when CND was in its heyday and the slogan was 'disarm or perish', there was no shortage of events, in Berlin, Cuba and Vietnam, to terrify people throughout the globe. A few characteristic films of the period capture the mood. In *The Day of the Triffids*, lethal stinging plants inherit a world devastated by nuclear war; in *On the Beach*, people in Australia await death by fall-out following a nuclear holocaust; in the widely acclaimed *Dr Strangelove*, a power-crazed nuclear scientist, apparently based on a composite of Henry Kissinger and the strategist Herman Kahn, sets in train a catastrophic chain of events, as a cowboy-hatted American accidentally falls out of a B-52 together with an H-bomb, emblazoned with the words 'Nuclear warhead, handle with care, Hi there!' The effect is to detonate the Soviet doomsday machine and to destroy the world to the tune of 'We'll meet again'.

Abuse of power

By the late 1960s there was a return to themes exploring the many dimensions of oppression and abuse of power. In *Fahrenheit 451*, for example, firemen spend most of their time burning books; in *Barbarella*, there is much sexual ecstasy, but unfortunately not much fun since any erotic encounter has to be modulated by machine; and an even gloomier prospect is offered in the movie *Logan's Run* in which the most one can hope for is mandatory euthanasia at the age of 30.

The triumph of evil

In the late 1970s, 1980s and 1990s came a whole series of films in which technology is used to dramatise age-old issues of right and wrong and in which the power of evil often triumphs. This is the period of the space fantasy offering nightmarish examples of possible future worlds. The space odyssey, *2001* of 1968 portrays a world in which a computer can become a homicidal maniac. The menacing figure of Darth Vader, destroyer of planets, makes his debut in *Star Wars* of 1976. He reappears in *The Empire Strikes Back* and *The Return of the Jedi* and is anticipated in *The Phantom Menace*, and evil triumphs yet again in the shape of the boy Damien in *The Omen* I, II, III and IV, and in the succession of movies under the title *Terminator* in the second of which, *Judgement Day*, the final conflagration takes place in 1997. Clearly we are lucky to be alive!

18.3 ENVIRONMENT IN CRISIS

It was in the context of a world widely portrayed as facing either Armageddon or technological purgatory that another kind of doom-laden scenario began to surface in the 1970s. As before, it had been prompted by the convictions of those persuaded, in the words of the humorist Woody Allen, that there were only two choices open to us – either extinction or merely catastrophe – and it stemmed from the perception of a world in the throes of an ecological crisis with implications potentially no less devastating than those of nuclear war. And anyone bearing witness to the kind of environmental damage a single stricken oil-tanker can cause or the toll on public health of a few diseased cows or chickens, must have some sympathy for this view. On the other hand there is a danger of exaggeration, especially as the more extreme exponents of the global environmental predicament seem to exude not just pessimism but paranoia.

For example, in his *Enquiry into the Human Prospect* of 1975, Robert Heilbroner suggests that we live in a world of unparalleled violence and brutality, mass poverty, hunger and disease as well as of calamitous environmental degradation. Furthermore, that those who could stem the process show little sign of willingness to do so. The human prospect is, therefore, dim.[2] In an essay of 1979 called *A Choice of Catastrophes*, the science-fiction writer Isaac Asimov goes even further, suggesting that the dispersion of nuclear weapons and knowledge, the depletion of the world's resources, the wanton destruction of the ecosphere and the phenomenal growth of the world's population now impact on one another and are virtually impossible to reverse.[3] In short, such global trends constitute a time bomb that is ticking away, threatening to destroy what some call *Spaceship Earth*, and others *The Global Village*. And every time there is a man-made environmental disaster, usually summed up in one word – Windscale, Minimata, Seveso, Bhopal, Chernobyl – the doomsday scenario sounds particularly plausible. In a book *The Sixth Extinction*, conservationists Richard Leakey and Ronald Lewin take us to the ultimate, claiming that, as five times in the past, at least two-thirds of all species are in danger of being wiped out.[4] What then is the nature of the planetary crisis as depicted in the writings of those who are deeply or even mildly Green?[5]

Depletion of resources

The Greens' main contention is that on present form the human race will soon have exhausted the capacity of the planet's resources and environment to support it, and that it has reached this predicament as a belated consequence of the industrial revolution. Further, that in attempting to satisfy ever-expanding consumer demand, vigorously promoted by the devotees of free-market fundamentalism and bolstered by advertising slogans offering instant gratification and designed to persuade people 'to buy things they don't want in order to impress people they don't like',[6] industry has seriously depleted the fossil fuels and other non-renewable resources on which it depends. At the same time it has created the conditions for a population explosion especially in the less developed parts of the world which can least afford to sustain it. For the burgeoning population puts intolerable strains on already overburdened support systems, threatening both town and countryside with mass starvation and the collapse of social institutions. Nor can such social dislocations be confined to the LDCs. For their plight contributes to the production and export of potentially lethal commodities such as cocaine and heroin that fetch a high price on world markets, and while narcotics may keep Hollywood happy, they cause many of the less affluent in our cities to take to crime to feed the habit. The impoverishment of LDCs also creates growing pressure for international food assistance, in turn, placing ever more burdensome demands on the farmer and encouraging possibly dangerous experiments in the genetic engineering of corn and other staple foodstuffs.

Furthermore, since food-production increasingly relies on chemical fertilisers, pesticides, irrigation equipment and the like, each of which is dependent on oil and gas, such fuels are bound to become scarce, hence more expensive, in turn driving up the price of foodstuffs.

Destruction of the ecosphere

Meanwhile, the chemicals used in producing high crop yields are already taking their toll, destroying natural soil fertility and posing new chemical hazards to water supplies, producing health problems for livestock and humans alike and threatening the sperm count. At the same time, the pesticides are already proving counter-productive, encouraging the appearance of new insects immune to existing pesticides, but not before these have themselves destroyed natural biological control mechanisms, introducing further perils into the food chain and threatening the support systems that sustain life on the planet.

But, according to the environmentalists, our current habits threaten not only the land. We also pose daily hazards to the oceans, and presumably to the sailors and fishermen who navigate them. Already the harvesting of fish is in decline due to a mixture of overfishing and pollution – the product of the dumping into the seas of toxic wastes, sewage, refuse, and other kinds of effluent. And with salinisation as well as sewage, fresh water, pond and bird life are also at risk, with many species threatened with extinction. Meanwhile, our abuse of the oceans causes more and more mammals, such as whales and dolphins, to lose their sense of direction so that they end up as decaying corpses on our shores; and with high levels of oestrogen in the water supply, increasing numbers of male fish are beginning to produce eggs.

But we abuse not merely land and sea. We also degrade the atmosphere. We pollute the air and cause acid rain through releasing into the atmosphere fossil fuels and synthetic gases – so-called CFCs – and in turn these adversely affect our wildlife, crops, soils, oceans, lakes, buildings and, of course, our lungs. In addition there is the dangerous depletion of the protective ozone layer in the earth's atmosphere which increases the amount of cosmic radiation reaching the surface of the planet and in turn causes a 'greenhouse effect'. This can only do serious damage to our food crops, increase the incidence of skin cancer, interfere with our genetic programming, encourage the resurgence of traditional diseases such as TB and malaria and threaten Pacific coral islands and low-lying deltas from China to the Netherlands and from Egypt to Bangladesh.[7]

Although the main culprits here are the developed countries, the LDCs, so the Greens claim, create a serious problem of their own by their heavy dependence on firewood to supply much of their energy needs. For it means destroying large areas of forest – already imperilled by the rancher as well as the logger. But the process of deforestation not only destroys plant and wildlife; in countries such as Indonesia and Brazil it produces smoke-filled fogs that permeate the country and beyond, causing serious respiratory diseases and killing people in its wake; it also produces climatic changes. With tree cover gone, more heat is returned to the atmosphere, local moisture stocks are depleted and as a consequence wind and rainfall patterns and local temperatures are disturbed. Hence, Greens claim, the recent record droughts in Africa, the record floods in Bangladesh, China, California and the US Midwest, the disastrous ice storms in Canada, the avalanches in Austria, recent record temperatures in Britain and one of the most active hurricane seasons ever.

Overpopulation

To the Greens, the problems of the developing and the developed countries are intertwined – pollution, resource depletion and overpopulation adversely affecting the whole planet. Indeed, they claim that a burgeoning population not only puts pressure on resources well beyond a country's frontiers, it can also trigger war, imperialism or mass migration.

In the case of Japan in the 1930s, the population explosion clearly provided the stimulus for both war and imperialism. As for migration, there is no doubt that growing numbers from the Third and Second Worlds (i.e. the former European Communist countries) are making their way to the First World, hoping to build a new life for themselves and their families. During the last two decades of the twentieth century, for example, at least 12 million Mexicans and Central Americans migrated, legally or illegally, to the US. At the century's end there were more Mexicans in Los Angeles than in any other city except the Mexican capital, while in Miami Spanish seemed to have become the first language. And there are increasing migrations of South-east Asians to Australasia; of Kurds, Turks, North Africans, Sub-Saharan Africans, South Asians and Eastern Europeans to Western Europe; and a considerable influx of non-Europeans claiming some sort of Jewish ancestry to Israel – each migration producing significant socio-political changes, thereby testing tolerance of foreign immigration to almost breaking point, even though historically immigrants have often made an invaluable contribution to the economy. Sadly, the tendency of the developed countries, and particularly those of Western Europe, has been increasingly to erect new Iron Curtains – to try to exclude the people from the poorer countries on the grounds that they are economic migrants and not genuine refugees from persecution and thus qualifying for asylum.

The fetish for industrialisation

Finally, most environmentalists would claim that the widespread belief that the solution to underdevelopment and Third World poverty lies in industrialisation is profoundly mistaken. Those contributing to the famous team efforts known as *The Limits to Growth* of 1972,[8] and *The Global 2000 Report to the President* of 1980,[9] argued that as long as the poor nations seek to become rich and the rich continue on their profligate path, the total collapse of civilisation through the degradation of the environment is virtually inevitable. The main problem, they argue, lies in what is called 'exponential growth' – a steady growth whose ultimate outcome can only cause alarm. For example, even a comparatively modest growth rate such as a 2 per cent annual rise in population or of economic activity or of ozone depletion can mean that they double their volume in only 35 years. As the economist Kenneth Boulding observed, 'Anyone who believes that exponential growth can continue indefinitely in a finite world is either a madman or an economist'.

Not surprisingly, to many Third World leaders such an argument sounds like special pleading by those who have long had it all and want to keep it that way. It is the philosophy of the prostitute turned nun. But if the Greens have their way then many LDCs could be trapped between the unequal distribution of global wealth and the limits to growth which the Greens assert are imposed by the ecological crisis. Moreover, many of the LDCs would have no way of amassing sufficient capital to invest in industrialisation even if they wanted to. And if they remain importers of finished products they will find themselves having to pay higher and higher prices for the manufactures they need. But if the Green message is accepted, is there nothing the peoples of the Third World can do to rid themselves of the cycle of poverty and deprivation?

18.5 SOME GREEN ANSWERS

Those Greens who still see a long-term future for this planet – such as Johan Galtung, Kenneth Boulding, Herbert Girardet and the Gaia Movement – provide a number of different answers, but all based on the notion that to survive we all have to radically change our view of ourselves in relation to nature.[10] Beyond that, what are the LDCs to do? First, to sacrifice development of 'high-tech' industries in favour of more labour-intensive enterprise, using more modest intermediate and low technologies. Secondly, to curb population growth through family-planning advice and free contraceptives, even if it means defying the Mullahs and the Catholic priests.

But if the LDCs are to change their patterns of reproduction and development, then the developed countries have to reciprocate by providing food assistance, being prepared to import and pay more for the manufactures as well as the resources of the LDCs, and generally scaling down their consumption. Finally, it is argued, the solution to the environmental crisis cannot be achieved by traditional means. It can only be found in a global context and if the world is to have a future it requires international cooperation, planning and the creation of new and permanent global institutions. Periodic environmental summits – in Stockholm, Rio, Cairo, Beijing, Rome, Kyoto or wherever – will not suffice.

18.6 SOME CORRECTIVES

What we make of the environmentalists' case is likely to depend on our existing beliefs and presuppositions. It is, however, worth pointing out that prophets of doom are often mistaken and that those who specialise in trying to 'scare the pants off us' will often blithely ignore anything that is positive. It is clear that Greenpeace, which deserves credit for finding new ways of alerting us to many of the problems of the environment, has lost support since it pressurised Shell into dropping its plan to sink the Brent Spar oil rig and instead to favour Greenpeace's own and apparently ecologically unsound policy of towing the rig across miles of ocean to be broken up on land. Perhaps people are becoming a little more sceptical of nightmarish scenarios! For though clearly the world was never on the verge of the paradise which many nineteenth-century theorists envisaged, can it ever have been on the verge of destruction, as so many twentieth-century sages assumed?

Irreversible depletion of resources?

As against what CND was saying in the 1950s and 1960s, the world did not perish, though it failed to disarm. As against the political doom-mongers, 1984 came and went without the universal police state. And what many Greens have portrayed as irreversible depletion of resources may well have to be revised in the light of recent discoveries – first of precious metals, manganese nodules and other such mineral deposits which are constantly being renewed as volcanic activity spews them out on to the sea-bed, with modern technology enabling us to recover them; and secondly of fossil fuels which though not renewable are always turning up in unexpected places, even in the Queen's own 'back yard' in Windsor, so that the indices of available supplies are constantly being revised upwards. And, of course, we are finding novel ways of *conserving* fossil fuels.

Irreversible environmental degradation?

If we are slowly poisoning ourselves to death with contaminated or genetically engineered food, how is it that we in the West are living longer and the infant mortality rate is generally in decline? And what of the endangered flora and fauna? True, some are threatened with extinction or genetic modification. But then the rise and decline of species has always been part of our evolutionary history, and in any case today's endangered species can become tomorrow's infestation. For example, in Siberia as in Scotland the deer population, once regarded as in serious decline, is increasing alarmingly, while the once-threatened rabbit and hare have bounced back, straight into the cooking pot, and the otter has returned to our rivers. Further, as those nineteenth-century soothsayers who prophesied that by the turn of the century London would be waist-high in horse excrement discovered, 'irreversible' degradation can also be reversed.

Until the 1950s, London was known for its life-threatening 'pea-soupers', its 'smogs', its smoke-filled fogs, but these have faded into history, thanks to smokeless fuels and the development of electric or gas central heating. And just as certain aspects of London's environment have been altered to the good, so has its river. In T.S. Eliot's poem *The Wasteland* (another doom-laden diatribe!), 'The river sweats oil and tar'. When that was written, anyone who ventured to swim in the Thames was at risk, so polluted had it become. Indeed, little over 100 years ago the stench from the river was so pungent that the windows of the Houses of Parliament had to be permanently closed. But in the 1960s the Thames was cleaned up and salmon began to be discovered round about Richmond, Barnes and Hammersmith. Though the water may look fairly dirty, because of its high mud content, it is in fact largely pollution-free, and we have learnt that it is perfectly possible to clean virtually any river as long as someone is prepared to foot the bill. And if some of Britain's other rivers fail to meet European standards, the privatised water companies have it in their power to direct funds away from their directors and shareholders and do the job for which the consumer pays through the nose.

True, London suffers, as do Los Angeles, Athens, Istanbul, Cairo, Sydney and many other major cities from the carbon monoxide gases emitted, among other things, by the motor car. But, again, the situation is not irreversible. When the electric, solar-powered or compressed-air-driven cars become commonplace, the level of air pollution should fall, and already many cities have benefited from unleaded petrol and the catalytic converter, the return of the electric tram and trolleybus, the kind of public transport policy the government has refused to finance in Britain, the pedestrian precinct, heavy taxes and tolls on private motoring, a ban on day-time deliveries by heavy lorries, the mandatory introduction of school buses, generous provision for the humble bicycle and the fact that more and more people work at or from home.

A population out of control?

As with pollution, so with population, many of the doom-laden forecasts have turned out to be somewhat wide of the mark. A survey by Johns Hopkins University and recently confirmed by a British demographer indicates that though world population is indeed growing apace, it is at a lower rate than earlier predicted.[11] It points out that in the LDCs as cities grow, and with them the middle class, the family unit comprises some three to four children instead of the six or seven as in the mid-twentieth century. Most of us will probably find that our great-grandparents had far more children than our grandparents; our grandparents more than our parents, and so on – and this seems to be an almost universal experience in an increasingly urbanised world. Where population growth is not checked naturally, it can be induced by government regulation. In India, for example, Mrs Gandhi once promoted male vasectomy as a method of birth control; in Iran where the mullahs once encouraged large families, today's politicians encourage education in population restraint; and in China the government has used financial and other pressures more or less successfully to reduce the number of live births to one per family. In any case, if our sperm count is falling we will be having fewer children anyway.

A climatological time bomb?

Finally, the evidence of serious climatological disturbance caused supposedly by noxious emissions is somewhat suspect. For one thing from the 1940s to the 1970s while carbon dioxide, methane, nitrous oxide and other 'greenhouse gases' were pouring into the atmosphere, global temperatures actually fell, and some scientists were talking of the possibility of a new ice age. In any case much of the gaseous emissions are natural rather than man-made – the product of sun spot activity, volcanic eruptions, earthquakes and the like. In fact the 'greenhouse effect' is to a considerable extent a natural phenomenon coming from water vapour in the atmosphere which warms the earth by trapping some of the heat from the sun. Without it the average temperature would be far below zero and the earth would probably resemble the planet Mars. Although we could not survive cooking-pot temperatures and have to be concerned when a huge chunk of Antarctica about the size of Oxfordshire breaks away and floats towards Chile, some measure of 'global warming' is an absolute necessity.[12] If, moreover, this century sees the widely predicted rise in earth temperature of two degrees Celsius, this would be less than the warming occurring between AD 900 and AD 1300 which produced the kinds of conditions enabling cattle to pasture in what is now frozen tundra in Greenland, oats and barley[13] to grow abundantly in Iceland and the wine industry to flourish in England. The American egronomist Dennis Avery goes so far as to suggest that 'a modest degree of warming might help rather than hinder crops'. And as for the record droughts, record floods, record hurricanes, etc. of recent times, we tend to forget that we are struck by such meteorological disasters every seven years or so with the reappearance of the oceanic and climatological catalyst known as *El Niño*.

No hope of change?

As for the change of life-style the Greens seek, to some extent this is already beginning to happen. More and more people are becoming ecologically aware as environmental lobbies serve to, in the words of Gwyn Prins: 'make people altruistic for selfish reasons'.[14] Who dares wear a fox fur or a mink coat these days? What self-respecting middle-sized town does not have a bottle bank or a collection point for old newspapers? Who outside of the US and its near neighbours would think of buying a gas-guzzling car? Could the US Navy ever again use whales for target practice? Why does tuna have to be 'dolphin-free'? Why has the US constructed no nuclear plants in over twenty years? Who would advocate reopening the mines and going back to burning coal? Who would have thought it conceivable that an American administration would sue the giant American Tobacco Corporation for endangering the health of the nation? Who would have thought ten years ago that it would become politically correct to give up smoking and eat organically grown fruit and vegetables, generally at grossly inflated prices, from bio-degradable containers?

Only global solutions?

People such as Richard Falk who believe that to survive on this planet we need to dismantle the state system as at present constituted,[15] which rests on the basis of collective selfishness, have to face the fact that the system is unlikely to be replaced in the foreseeable future. The modest attempts to get a regime in international ecological cooperation have so far been rather disappointing, while the contribution of the United Nations Environmental Programme (UNEP), established in the wake of the 1972 Stockholm Conference on the Environment, has been more in conscious-ness-raising than in practical achievements. To date, international environmental law remains somewhat rudimentary and underdeveloped, and it is indicative that the world's biggest polluter, the US, having been lobbied by the well-heeled business concerns of the so-called 'carbon club', reneged at the environmental conference at Kyoto in 1997 on its pledges to curb CFC emissions made at Rio five years before.[16] On the other hand, there is much that can be done to improve the quality of life on earth without having to alter unduly the present nature of the world political system.

In the first place, though such matters as ozone depletion and global warming affect the planet, not all environmental problems are global in origin or in implication, and therefore do not necessarily require global solutions. Health hazards such as the contamination of a stream or the noxious emissions of a particular factory are local in scope and may therefore be removed by local legislation. Other problems, for example overfishing or deforestation, may have more national application, and national governments can help to improve the environment if their primary concern – security – is broadened to include an ecological dimension, and this already appears to be happening in Britain, Canada and the countries of Scandinavia. But it is not necessary to look only to governments, national or local, to make adjustments, since positive contributions to the environment can be made by business corporations, by bodies of concerned citizens, and by regional organisations. The EU, for example, is by and large very environmentally friendly, setting standards and contributing towards costs. And of course we humble individuals can also play our part. Since the writer believes that a 'bottom-up' approach to these matters is probably more realistic than a 'top-down' panacea, there follow some modest proposals for saving the universe.

18.7 TO 'SAVE' THE UNIVERSE

First, as individuals we can walk more, cycle more, make better use of our rivers, improve on insulation of our houses and invest more in solar energy. We can employ more energy-saving devices, recycle a great deal more, share cars and use our gardens and patios much more productively and get in the habit of picking up litter. And if we have shares in multinationals we can turn up at shareholders' meetings and hold the directors to account if their enterprises are less than friendly environmentally – something Shell and BP are having to get used to. But after all, as many an insurance company has discovered, eco-efficiency can be good for business as well as the environment. As a community we might as a matter of course bring an environmental dimension into our decisions, invest more in public transport, plant more trees and grasses, devote more land to organic farming, cut back on cattle that eat and excrete too much and pesticides and toxic sprays that also pollute too much, package less, conserve more water, possibly through a market approach, build smaller dams, give tax advantages to those who come up with schemes for conserving energy, develop fluids such as bio-diesel oil refined from rapeseed which can treat oil spills without harming the environment, make sure that the polluter always pays, decommission nuclear plants where they are in danger of emitting harmful rays, finance more small labour-intensive projects and, of course, encourage safe sex and family-planning. In addition we might propel into the stratosphere balloons filled with ozone, which while a pollutant in the lower atmosphere can offer protection from the sun's harmful ultra-violet radiation in the upper atmosphere – these balloons to burst in low pressure where the ozone layer is particularly thin. We might also use 16-inch naval rifles fired vertically to project dust into the atmosphere if we think we need added protection from the 'greenhouse effect'.

18.8 THE OPPORTUNITIES WE FACE

To summarise. Even if some Green fears may be exaggerated and over-dramatised, the basic theory concerning exponential growth is probably substantially valid and in this regard the rise of ecological awareness in the West and beyond is a positive development. For anything that helps to combat ignorance and carelessness and serves as an antidote to complacency can only do good. On the other hand, what is also needed is an appreciation of the opportunities as well as of the dangers the planet faces. The revolution in communications, for example, offers possibilities of mental, intellectual, emotional and spiritual growth we could never have even dreamed of even 15 to 20 years ago. If we can get the opportunities as well as the dangers into perspective, we will have got the balance about right, and begin to enjoy what the new millennium has to offer.

NOTES

1. London, Cassell, 1998.
2. London, Calder, 1975.
3. London, Hutchinson, 1980.
4. London, Phoenix, 1996.
5. The following analysis owes much to Myers, N., *The Gaia Atlas of Future Worlds*, London, Robertson McCarta, 1990.
6. The phrase was used by Israeli writer Amos Oz in a discussion programme on BBC Radio 4, 17 June 1999.
7. A detailed analysis of global warming is contained in Leggett, J. (ed.), *Global Warming: The Greenpeace Report*, Oxford, Oxford University Press, 1990.
8. Meadown, D. *et al.*, Washington, DC, Potomac Associates, 1972.
9. Barney, G.O., New York, Pergamon Press, 1980.
10. See Galtung, J., *Environment, Development and Military Activity*, Oslo, 1982; Boulding, K., *Three Faces of Power*, San Francisco, Sage, 1989; and Girardet, H., *Earthrise: How we can heal our injured planet*, London, Paladin, 1992.
11. Robey, B., Rotstein, S. and Morris, L., 'The fertility decline in developing countries', *Scientific American*, December 1993, pp. 30–7.
12. Salmon, J. 'Greenhouse anxiety', *Commentary*, 12 July 1993; and Kenny, A., 'The earth is fine: the problem is the Greens', *The Spectator*, 12 March 1994.
13. Avery, D., 'Welcome to the Garden of Eden', in the *Guardian*, 15 May 1999.
14. 'Politics and the Environment', *International Affairs*, no. 66, 1990, p. 729.
15. *This Endangered Planet: Prospects and Proposals for Human Survival*, New York, Random House, 1971.
16. On the vicissitudes of negotiations on the environment see for example Benedick, R.E., *Ozone Diplomacy: New Directions in Safeguarding the Planet*, Cambridge, Mass., Harvard University Press, 1998.

CHAPTER 19

PRESCRIPTIONS
FOR PEACE

On 4 November 1918, a young man was killed in the trenches barely a week before the Armistice ending the First World War. He was just 25 years old and was to become posthumously one of the most celebrated of Britain's war poets. His name was Wilfred Owen, and in a volume of poems written shortly before his death he speaks of war as 'the eternal reciprocity of tears' and in the preface explains that his book 'is not about heroes . . . Nor is it about deeds or lands, or anything about glory, honour, might, majesty, dominion or power . . . My subject is war and the pity of war . . . All that a poet can do is to warn'.[1] Though Owen's volume was to be widely read and admired, his warning, sadly, went unheeded. In the succession of wars, both inter-state and civil, during the twentieth century, upwards of 120 million are believed to have perished either as a direct result of hostilities or indirectly as a consequence of war-related famine and disease.[2] Increasingly, moreover, the casualties were to be innocent civilians rather than trained soldiers, as a new breed of strategists decided that anyone of any age, regardless of gender, capable of holding a gun was a legitimate target.

The problem is that though most people yearn for peace, they also have other objectives for which they may deem it necessary to fight. For many, the price of peace may be too high if it means submission to the bully, the tyrant, the oppressor, to those who threaten to kill our kith and kin and destroy our way of life; and, clearly, burning grievances can impel whole communities to resist and challenge what they see as the forces of injustice. It is this sense of outrage that fuelled the Kurdish revolt, for example, and the attempt of the Kosovars to free themselves from Serb control. Yet if the past is strewn with the corpses of the fallen, it is also, paradoxically, littered with the failed hopes of those who dreamed of turning 'swords into ploughshares and spears into pruning hooks'. So is it futile to attempt to limit the scope, scale and frequency of warfare?

Revolutionists like Marx and Lenin would be sceptical of anything dealing only with symptoms and not with fundamental causes, and would hold therefore that short of the ultimate revolutionary remedy, anti-war panaceas must fail. By contrast, Rationalists such as Grotius, J.S. Mill or Woodrow Wilson would have an array of answers. For they would see war as a kind of social disease for which there might be a number of antidotes, treatments or cures. Realists would be far less hopeful. From Thucydides, through Machiavelli down to Waltz, they have tended to see war as inherent in the international system, believing that even if we located its causes, an effective remedy might still prove elusive. On the other hand even though they are long-term pessimists, Realists can be short-term optimists, regarding particular wars – possibly a third World War – as avoidable. What is required are expedients to stabilise rather than transform the international system and to create the conditions for defusing the kinds of tension that can escalate into hostilities. Like the Rationalist, the Realist also seeks ways to limit the scope and effects of war.

19.1 REGULATING WARFARE THROUGH CODES OF CONDUCT

Since war is about achieving political purposes through violence, it would not appear to be an obvious subject for regulation. Yet, as Michael Ignatieff explains in The Warrior's Honour, many societies have, in fact, developed rules of armed combat.[3] As indicated in Chapter 4, hostilities in ancient China had to subside during planting and harvesting time and it was forbidden to strike the elderly or further injure an already wounded man. The ancient Greeks banned the destruction of olive groves during warfare and provided for periodic intervals of peace to enable combatants to bury their dead. In the Middle Ages codes of chivalry provided a measure of protection to Christian women and children as well as to knights, while even before Grotius natural-law theorists such as Vitoria and Suarez sought to construct rules that would apply to 'barbarian' as well as Christian[4] and defended the notion of proportionality in hostilities – an eye for an eye, but no more.[5] More recently there have been various conventions proscribing genocide and torture, prescribing the treatment of POWs and those wounded in civil and inter-state conflicts, and regarding the protection of civilians in occupied lands, the right of asylum and so forth.

True, to sign is not necessarily to implement such compacts, yet millions will have been the beneficiaries of such codes. For example, no matter how badly the Nazis treated civilians, their own included, Germany's treatment of uniformed POWs, despite notable exceptions, was on the whole correct. The prisoners could exercise and receive food parcels and letters and there was the occasional swap of prisoners through the good offices of the Swiss. And what of the right of asylum? In recent years as refugees flood into what they see as safe havens, governments worry about the implications; and yet millions of people will have attained citizenship of a particular country because their parents or grandparents were given asylum as escapees from a particular conflict. The extent to which governments have chosen to respect codes granting rights to strangers would no doubt have surprised the classical Realists, but whether those adhering to such standards do so because of moral principle, the thought of reciprocity or its potential propaganda value need not concern us here. The fact is that they can and do play a role in helping to mitigate the horrors of war.

19.2 LIMITING THE SCOPE OF WARFARE

'Neutrality' and 'neutralisation'

When two parties resort to violence, third parties can easily get sucked into their conflict, wittingly or unwittingly. For centuries countries in the vicinity wishing to stay neutral could do little to insist on their detachment unless they had sufficient strength or diplomatic skill to deter the warring sides or else, like Switzerland, enjoyed geographical protection. But in the seventeenth century, as international law was being developed, neutrality was given a legal status in which the non-belligerent would enjoy rights and duties concerning, among other things, trade, commerce and innocent passage for ships, as well as freedom from the fray.

In the nineteenth century another term entered the diplomatic vocabulary – 'neutralisation' – a status of permanent neutrality guaranteed by the Powers. Here, the law set limits on the belligerent activities of such neutralised states as Switzerland, Belgium and Luxembourg and, in the twentieth century, the Vatican, Austria and Laos. A neutralised state could have armed forces but could join no alliance or fight for any state other than itself.[6] Sadly, during the Second World War only five European states succeeded in retaining the neutrality that a dozen or more had declared in 1939; and the fact that today only Switzerland and Austria remain of the neutralised nations indicates the precariousness in practice of the legal status. Neutrality has probably been best preserved where wars are fought for limited objectives, as in the Italian city states system; where belligerents would be afraid of converting non-belligerents into enemies, as during the 1870 Franco-Prussian war; or when there existed a complex balance of several great powers, as in the period from 1815 to 1914.

'Neutralism' and 'non-alignment'

What, then, determines the success or otherwise of what is called 'neutralism' and 'non-alignment'? Once again, we must define our terms. In fact both concepts belong to the political vocabulary of the past fifty years or so. Unlike 'neutrality' and 'neutralisation', they are not about legal status; they have to do with policy options. The term 'neutralism' emerged in France in the late 1940s and indicated distrust of alliances in general and of membership of NATO in particular.[7] Though at the time its advocates had little effect on policy, their ideas eventually contributed to the development of the concept of 'non-alignment', taken up by a number of governments in the 1950s. Nowadays non-alignment has economic over-tones. It has become a movement of LDCs seeking a new international economic order. For some time, however, it meant dissociation, at least in theory, from the cold war, but whether or not it was sustainable depended largely on circumstance. Those most at risk were countries such as Laos, Afghanistan, Grenada and Nicaragua which happened to figure in what a Great Power claimed as its back yard; and at moments of extreme cold war tension, non-alignment was at its most vulnerable.

19.3 LIMITING THE INCIDENCE OF WAR

Given the evident lack of equality within and between states it is not at all clear that peace, even in the limited sense of an absence of war, has the same importance for all. Can it have the same salience, say, for the dispossessed and downtrodden as for the well-heeled and fulfilled? Thus, any suggestion for curbing the resort to arms has to rest on an analysis of the causes of war, and as Kenneth Waltz reminds us there are at least three broadly distinct modes of explanation – one relating to human nature, a second to socio-political systems, a third having to do with the system of states.[8] Those favouring the first method of explanation would try to change human beings; those of the second school would attempt to remove or transform certain sorts of governments or social systems; adherents of the third would attempt to tackle the thorny question of collective insecurity in a world lacking government or moral consensus.

19.4 COMBATING ANTI-SOCIAL DRIVES

As regards the first mode of explanation, favoured by many psychologists, biologists and theologians, if war ultimately stems from some defect in human nature, then it is to that same nature we have to look for the antidote. The remedy has to lie in overcoming, redirecting or suppressing such anti-social characteristics.

World government

For Thomas Hobbes, life was likely to prove 'nasty, solitary, poor, brutish and short' if the passions were unbridled, and his 'solution' was strong and uncontested government. But his concern was only with the domestic context.[9] Not only do such governments not solve the problem of international conflict, they may well exacerbate it, which is why some modern Realists, Hans Morgenthau for example, take the Hobbesian formula to its logical conclusion and advocate world government. But there are at least two problems with this formulation. First, how do you get it? The idea that states jealous of their sovereignty would willingly hand over their powers to a world authority would seem on present evidence to be highly implausible save in the wake of some unforeseen tragedy – a nuclear or environmental holocaust or an invasion from Mars. And if the world authority were to be the product of world conquest it would hardly be desirable. Furthermore, if we are talking of effective government, the world authority would presumably need a monopoly on weaponry and without proper accountability could become highly dictatorial, possibly instigating a world civil war.

Re-education

If not world government, then a world run more or less along lines prescribed by certain psychologists and behavioural scientists. People like John Burton and James Rosenau seem to believe that the best way to end the cycle of war is to re-educate, to change the human conceptual apparatus, to bring about, in the jargon, a 'paradigm shift'.[10] Exactly how such intellectual therapy would be administered and upon whom is not exactly clear, but the prospectus is. It would promote a greater understanding of the predicaments of others, discourage a zero-sum approach to disputes, encourage conflict-avoidance, conflict-management and -resolution and foster the use of non-confrontational language. It would also appeal to self-interest by suggesting that it is, in Norman Angell's words, 'a great illusion' to believe that anyone can profit from war, since, given its pernicious effects on national economies, even the victors lose. And it would offer a variety of techniques of non-violent resistance in the event of an invasion by a foreign power whose forces have not been so re-educated.

But who would foster and finance such intellectual therapy, who would choose and keep an eye on the therapists and what would be its value if taken up, say, in Sweden and Switzerland and not in Saddam Hussein's Iraq or Slobodan Milosevic's Serbia? And would it work anyway? Does greater familiarity with the predicaments of others necessarily increase either sympathy or willingness to compromise? Conceivably if Chamberlain had understood Hitler a bit better Britain might have declared war in 1938 instead of waiting till 1939. And was the Second World War or for that matter the cold war due to a lack of understanding or the very real understanding of the existence of a conflict of interest?

Redirection

The psychologist William James suggests a third approach for tackling potentially lethal anti-social impulses – to redirect them.[11] His idea was to harness an individual's basic energies into socially useful pursuits, exacting physical labour and feats of endurance. And James was also persuaded that spectator sports were a useful safety valve. The trouble is that the kinds of task James prescribes have long been a feature of societies both at war and at peace, and so there is no reason to suppose that a few more miners, boxers, Everest explorers and Everton supporters is likely to make any difference to the incidence of war. Indeed, to judge by the scale of football hooliganism and of brain-damaged boxers as well as their fans, it might be better for all concerned if there were fewer rather than more supporters.

19.5 TRANSFORMING SOCIO-POLITICAL STRUCTURES

Authoritarian regimes

Regarding the second mode of explanation, if war is an international manifestation of certain sorts of domestic structure, then such structures have either to be dissolved, radically transformed or destroyed. So what kinds of socio-political system deserve to be consigned to the rubbish heap of history? The most familiar theory is the Kantian view as reinterpreted by Woodrow Wilson that elitist or authoritarian governments put humankind most at risk, either because they seek national glory or because they need an activist foreign policy to direct attention away from domestic discontents.[12]

To their arguments there is a less familiar though no less formidable answer: that it is precisely the kind of internal discipline and order provided by authoritarian government that can check those popular passions that can lead to war; that a Stalin, for example, can make his peace with his arch-enemy Hitler precisely because he has no need to explain it to parliament, and that a Castro can far more easily make his peace with the US than the US government can with him because he does not have to face a contested election. Indeed, there is a tradition of thought from Plato onwards that holds that the tendency to war is greatest when established hierarchies decay through inept leadership or the agitation of popular demagogues as, say, in Serbia over the past decade.[13] In other words, that men such as Tito and Gorbachev are to be preferred to their successors because through their firm and responsible leadership they keep a better check on foreign adventurism.

Capitalism

While the controversy continues over political systems, it rages over economic systems too. Abolish capitalism, say the Marxists, and you abolish war. You do away with the class system which projects conflict from the domestic to the international stage and you also rid the world of all those with a vested interest in the production and distribution of weaponry.

Not so, say the free-marketeers such as Francis Fukayama[14] who have followed Adam Smith and Richard Cobden into the twenty-first century. In their pursuit of profit, capitalists have a vested interest in peace. It is through non-violent competition that they achieve social standing and status. Abolish capitalism and you lose the *Pax Economica*. At the same time you give governments far too much control over human affairs, ending up with the kinds of violent confrontation manifested between former Communist countries such as China and Vietnam, Vietnam and Kampuchea, the Soviet Union and China, and the kinds of military interventions Moscow staged in East Berlin, Hungary, Czechoslovakia and Afghanistan.

Many a non-Communist Marxist would regard such a critique as largely irrelevant since in their view no country has ever been truly socialist. Those more sympathetic to Communism would argue that the anti-Communist mistakes crisis behaviour in a Communist-ruled state for general policy, and that to criticise the Soviet Union or Cuba for aggressive behaviour is to obscure the extent to which they have themselves been constantly at risk in a hostile environment.[15] Finally, they would argue, the trend towards global capitalism is hardly consistent with an end-to-war thesis, given the competitive nature of capitalism and the political implications of the polarisation between rich and poor that globalisation tends to engender, especially within the LDCs. The debate continues . . .

Nationalism

The relations between the state and the nation give rise to a further controversy about the external implications of certain national systems. If the 'state' is a territorial entity of legal and diplomatic consequence, and the 'nation' a group of people with a shared sense of political or cultural kinship, then clearly state and nation frequently fail to coincide. For example, the Palestinians and the Kurds can be considered to be nations, yet have no state of their own. But does it serve the peace of the world if nation and state correspond? The nineteenth-century Italian theorist Mazzini believed that peace would come only when the nationally self-aware were permitted to give political expression to their sense of shared identity. Writing in the 1820s, he saw the nation as neither exclusive nor aggressive, nor did he regard love of one's own country as incompatible with service to humankind. Good liberal that he was, Mazzini believed in a harmony of interests between the nations[16] – concepts rooted in liberal democracy, middle-class cross-frontier solidarity and mutually advantageous international trade. Yet three decades later, the Italian statesman, Cavour, was taking a very different view. 'If only we did for ourselves what we do for our nation' he said, 'what rascals we should be.'[17] And in the twentieth century men such as Mussolini and Hitler manipulated the symbols of nationhood to destroy some of the liberal values nationalism had originally promoted. While it gave people a sense of belonging, all too often it sought the good of one society at the expense of another. A policy designed to unite within stable frontiers people sharing a sense of national solidarity could so easily develop into the most savage imperialism. Once again a noble ideal had been debased, and in the process the idea that the cause of peace is best served by the grant of national self-determination thrown in doubt.

Religion

In addition to the prescriptions already detailed there are the claims of those who would commend to us a world of states united by a common religious bond. But passionate conviction can easily become a prey to fanaticism and bigotry, and the record past and present of, say, Christians in Northern Ireland, the American South or South Africa; of Muslims in, say, Afghanistan, Somalia or Yemen; of Buddhists in Burma, Thailand or Sri Lanka is hardly more edifying than the record of Marxism–Leninism. In fact, the aspiration to universal brotherhood is all too often confounded by human frailty or political irresponsibility.

Selection

What of the idea of some behavioural scientists that peace would be better served by a selection process which would exclude the unintelligent and the irrational from leadership. On the surface this would appear an attractive idea, especially as it might rid us of about 75 per cent of the world's existing presidents and prime ministers. But, of course, it raises more questions than it answers. Who is to say whether any particular form of selection is better than any other? How and by whom would the processes of selection be introduced? And what if some of the leaders that some of the scrutineers regard as ill-chosen and ill-informed insist on clinging to office? Are they to be forcibly removed?

More women in power

What of the attendant notion propounded by some feminists that there would be greater harmony with more women among the political elites? Certainly it would make politics more colourful. On the other hand, it is based on a stereotypical idea of gender differences that associate men with competition and women with cooperation. Yet it is not blindingly obvious that there is a perceptible lessening of international tension when formidable ladies such as Eva Perón, Golda Meier, Indira Gandhi, Siri-mavo Bandaranaike, Margaret Thatcher, Benazir Bhutto, Khalida Zia, Sheikh Hassina, Eugenia Charles, Tansu Ciller and the like take the helm. And though women are less likely than men to see force as a legitimate instrument for resolving conflicts and are not generally prominent in warrior tribes or castes, they apparently played a notable role in the military activities of the ancient Scythians, have been leading players in guerrilla and terrorist organisations such as the Baader-Meinhof gang and the Red Brigades, and are not unknown in the swashbuckling world of seafaring and piracy.[18] Since power structures tend to be largely man-made, whether politics would be very different if largely in the hands of 'an old girls" rather than an 'old boys' network' is debatable. Arguably, the 'greying' of the population, as projected by demographers, could have more impact on the incidence of war than its feminisation.

19.6 TRANSFORMING THE INTERNATIONAL SYSTEM

But perhaps it is not a particular kind of decision-making structure but the whole structure of international society that is the problem. It is, after all, a society without government, in which power is dispersed among 186 or so heavily armed sovereign states with ambitions of their own, and in which, lacking any effective law-enforcing authority, the arbiter in disputes is often force. This brings us to the third mode of explanation. War occurs because there is basically nothing to prevent it, and if it is to be curbed then there must be some device, technique or stratagem to act as constraint or deterrent.

Once again, there is an array of pet schemes. But at this particular level of analysis, many of the antidotes are rooted in concepts of power, and what to do about it. One major difficulty, as has been repeatedly emphasised, is lack of agreement on the meaning of 'power'. Even if taken to mean, in Bertrand Russell's phrase, 'the capacity to produce intended effects' and, by implication, to deny to others whatever adverse effects they intend, what is to be done? The Revolutionists envision a day when the instrumentality of power politics, the state, withers away. Their solution, thus, involves the transcendance of power. At the other end of the spectrum there are the arch-Realists whose ultimate answer – a monopoly of power by a world government – was discussed above. In between there is a range of possible solutions for keeping power in check.

Liberal and Neo-liberal remedies

Erosion of power – disarmament

In the 1920s and 1930s, Soviet Foreign Commissar Litvinov repeatedly tabled at the League of Nations his proposal for general and complete disarmament – general, to embrace all states: complete, to include all weapons save those needed for internal order. Needless to say, it was a non-starter. His argument that a world without arms would be a world without war seemed, frankly, incredible. After all, long before modern weapons were invented there were organised hostilities, and clearly these were always possible as long as there were to hand sticks, stones, iron bars, knives, broken bottles, matches to make fire and, of course, bare fists. For example, the horrific injuries in the recent conflicts in Burundi, Rwanda and Algeria were largely inflicted by axes, hatchets and knives. In a disarmed world, war might conceivably become less frequent, destructive or extensive; yet in such a world some states would still in effect have a military advantage over others since a nation's war potential resides not just in its weapons but in a complex of economic, technological and demographic resources. Thus, with the requisite know-how, the military capacity that had been dis-established could be re-established, and discarded weaponry reinstated.

Yet all this is in any case beside the point. For the arms trade remains one of the world's most profitable, and there seems scant prospect of even the poorest state agreeing to sacrifice what it ultimately relies on to preserve its sovereignty. So what of less drastic proposals, such as partial, selective or unilateral disarmament? Though it would be gratifying if all governments answered the late Princess Diana's call to scrap landmines and signed up to the recent convention, Washington, Moscow and Beijing steadfastly refuse, and as mines are neither difficult nor costly to produce and lay, even those who have initialled the accord can easily renege. Nor are the historical precedents encouraging.[19] The 1920s and 1930s taught us that the world is not necessarily more secure when a few Powers agree to selective disarmament, especially when, following the Washington Conference of 1922, they merely scrap weapons that are already obsolete or, as in the Anglo-German Naval Treaty of 1935, freeze deployment of a particular weapon leaving them free to develop others. Nor is peace necessarily secured when the non-aggression pacts pile up (after all, the Soviet Union was to be at war with most of the countries with which it had signed non-aggression treaties in the 1930s), or when the weak lack the weapons that protect the strong – as many countries found to their cost in 1940. The danger is of creating disequilibrium in favour of the most advanced militarily and of leaving the weak virtually defenceless. On the other hand agreements between the US and what was the Soviet Union on strategic and intermediate nuclear arms reductions suggest that some meaningful disarmament may be possible but only after international tensions have been considerably eased.

Regulation of power – arms control

What of a much more modest ambition – arms control – where the emphasis is not on arms reductions as such but on perceived balance, equilibrium, equivalence or strategic sufficiency? Here the states are asked to limit the production, testing, deployment or use of certain weapons to keep in step with potential enemies. In the case of the Geneva Protocol on poison gas, the record has been none too bad. Though the Italians used gas in Abyssinia in 1935, the Japanese in China in 1937 and the Iraqis in the Gulf War against Iran, most other states have been comparatively restrained. And within the last 30 years or so of the twentieth century several more arms-control accords were initialled – including the partial nuclear test-ban treaty, the nuclear non-proliferation treaty, the ban on weapons in outer space and on the sea bed, and the anti-ballistic missile treaty. On the whole these, too, have been observed. But as the late twentieth-century nuclear escalation on the Indian sub-continent reminded us, not all states are parties to these agreements. The main obstacles to an accord relate to negotiation rather than to implementation. So what are the difficulties that usually have to be overcome?[20]

First, establishing a basis of trust is no easy matter, given that arms proliferation is itself a symptom of lack of trust among the nations. Yet even when a degree of confidence is acquired and substantive discussions begin, there is often a problem of definition. In the 1930s, for example, arms talks were constantly bedevilled by failure to agree on what constituted an offensive and what a defensive weapon. For many delegates an offensive weapon was one their enemy possessed and they did not –

hardly a promising basis for negotiations. And more recent discussions on nuclear disarmament tended to get bogged down on what constituted a strategic and what an intermediate weapon. To the West, anything that could hit Europe but not the US was intermediate. To Moscow anything that could hit it from any source was strategic. A third problem relates to the extremely complex arithmetic any such agreement must involve. After all, power inventories are never symmetrical. One side may have more ground-launched, another more sea-based missiles. One side more launchers, another more warheads. One may have more external adversaries, another more serious enemies within. So that the attempt to balance out such considerations in an appropriate package may take time. And if there is eventual accord, there then has to be some means of inspection and verification – again, not easy when lethal weapons have become miniaturised and thus easier to hide. Chemical weapons, for example, could be manufactured in a school laboratory, bacteriological weapons on a farm; but clearly it would be unfeasible to have arms inspectors combing through a country's academic and agricultural establishments. Finally, how is any arms-control arrangement to be enforced? And what sanctions for the cheats, given that any violation could confer an unfair political advantage?

Yet perhaps the impetus to reduce or scrap weapons rests on a misconception about the nature of arms. Many assume that weapons are the basic cause of war, but they are not. They are simply instruments in the hands of people who feel they have cause to fight. Without hostilities, the arms are immaterial. Another, related notion is that arms races cause war. Even though plausible, it has to be remembered that neither the Anglo-French arms race in the late nineteenth and early twentieth century, nor the Anglo-US naval race in the first third of the twentieth century, nor the Superpower arms build up from the 1940s to the 1990s ended in war. More than that, had there been an Anglo-German arms race in the 1930s instead of unilateral rearmament by Germany, Hitler might conceivably have been deterred by Britain's warning not to invade Poland. The fact is that arms races can be as much a guarantor of peace as a harbinger of war. Largely a reflection or symptom rather than a cause of international tension, arms races will tend to subside when tensions ease.[21] In this sense, it is perhaps the tensions rather than the weapons that should merit our urgent attention.

Community of power – collective security

As regards collective security, when all states join together to deter or defeat aggression, it has a number of flaws, some of which were rehearsed in Chapter 14. First, there is the difficulty of getting all states involved, especially when the theatre of conflict is remote; then there is the problem of getting agreement on whether an aggression has indeed occurred, and here states tend to be partisan – reluctant to admit that an ally might be an aggressor or a foe the victim of their ally's aggression. Further, even where it is agreed that an aggression has occurred, it is one thing to take action if the perpetrator is a small power, quite another when one or more Great Powers are involved. In any case, even when it is agreed that the aggressor is a relatively minor power and that something has to be done to stop it, there may still be genuine doubt as to what to do. Whether, for example, a military response would improve matters, as in Bosnia, or possibly make things worse, as in Vietnam.

Pooling of power – federalism

Given the evident persistence of people's attachment to their state, their nation, their tribe, their locality and so on, world federal union would appear to be on virtually nobody's agenda.[22] Meanwhile East Africa, the Caribbean and the Middle East are littered with failed attempts at regional integration. And though the EU is supposed to be a shining example of successful integration, unmistakable strains persisted at the end of the twentieth century, and as we saw from the machinations over British beef exports, fishing rights, a common currency, taxation, defence and foreign policy, national sentiment tends to reassert itself the more the exercise of sovereignty seems to be diminished. And even if regional integration proceeded apace in Europe and elsewhere, inter-state conflicts would hardly disappear in a world of fewer but larger sovereign units.

Pooling of power – functionalism

The pooling of power through functionalism would appear to be prey to similar kinds of problem.[23] For though governments may choose to hand over some of their sovereign powers to international bodies of technical experts, it does not follow that a transfer of loyalties away from the state or the national community must result. Nor does there appear to be any warrant for the suggestion that increased cooperation in trade and other non-political fields must diminish the arena for political conflict. After all, Germany and Britain, Japan and the US and the Soviet Union and Germany were close trading partners when they went to war with one another in 1939, 1940 and 1941, respectively, while the history of the cold war when the Soviet Union rather than Germany was Eastern Europe's main trading partner suggests that politics determines the scope and intensity of international trade and commerce and not the other way round. Furthermore, if modern technologies accentuate interdependence, they can also facilitate the extension of government power within the states. Admittedly, thanks to institutions such as CNN and the Internet we have become much more mutually aware internationally. Sadly, however, this does not necessarily engender mutual liking or respect, and there are undoubtedly those whose minds seem to have been narrowed rather than broadened by foreign travel and their exposure to cultures other than their own.

Sharing of economic power

A fairer share-out of economic power as advocated by Carr, Keynes and the proponents of a New International Economic Order might appear to offer a partial solution.[24] After all, the 'have nots' often have a multitude of grievances, which can escalate into violence. The difficulty here is first to persuade the more fortunate to part with some of their riches, and second to encourage often inept or corrupt governments to guarantee that any outside help is channelled to those most in need rather than to their own overseas bank accounts. All too often foreign assistance, when it is proffered, is misappropriated, and this merely fuels the kinds of resentment that, as in Congo (Zaire), Nicaragua or Guatemala, can lead to civil strife.

Realist and Neo-realist expedients

Balance of power

In respect of the balance of power as a proposed solution to the problem of war, the obvious question of course is what does one put into the equation? Is it merely a matter of megatonnages, throw weights and payloads, or does it include the non-measurable such as leadership skills, morale, cohesion, and non-military assets such as technological skill and diplomatic expertise? And if all or some of these factors are included, how exactly does one assess whether or not some sort of balance, equilibrium or equivalence has been struck? Who or what constitutes the countervailing force today to US military and economic power? How, if some rough parity is deemed to exist, are balances to be maintained in a world of rapid technological change? Do decisions relating to war and peace depend solely on power calculations? What about national or leadership attitudes and aspirations?

Power hierarchy

Whether power hierarchy is to take the form of either a Concert of Great Powers – as after the Napoleonic Wars – or a more subtle gradation of powers based on protection of the weak and deference to the strong, as in medieval times, two questions arise: first, how in a dynamic world is any such hierarchy to be sustained and, secondly, what of the demand of the less privileged for just change? For such hierarchies are likely to resist the claim of the subordinate to equal treatment, and it is difficult to imagine the underprivileged, who comprise a majority in international society, allowing their concerns to be indefinitely subordinated for the sake of world order. The argument that peace depends on the kind of power preponderance of the Roman Empire would be open to similar objections.

Power dispersal

Perhaps the most bizarre of these power-based theories is that of nuclear dispersal among those nations that want them, which would give each the capacity to inflict unacceptable damage on the others and hence, so the argument goes, to deter attack from every other state.[25] But is it clear that the nuclear-endowed nations would always be proof against attack – nuclear or conventional? What if there were a technological breakthrough leading one power to believe it could attack another and fend off all possible retaliation from any source? What if one Power were able to sabotage the nuclear installations of another? What if a less than rational leader of a government or terrorist group were prepared to risk retaliation and launch a war for the sake of a religious or some other principle? The possibilities and permutations in a world of general and complete nuclear proliferation are endless.

19.7 THAT ELUSIVE FORMULA!

What, then, are we to conclude from the above critique of some of the proffered prescriptions for perpetual peace? Is a formula for ending the all too frequent recourse to war as elusive as ever? And without a panacea can there be any hope for humankind? The following chapter attempts to furnish a few answers and draw some salutary lessons.

NOTES

1. Owen's 'Preface' is quoted in Giddings, R., *The War Poets*, London, Bloomsbury, 1988, p. 102.
2. I arrive at the figure from an extrapolation of the studies of Sivard, R., *World Military and Social Expenditures*, Washington, DC, World Priorities, 1996; Sollenberg, M. and Wallensteen, P., 'Major armed conflicts', in *SIPRI Yearbook 1998*, Oxford, Oxford University Press, 1998; Kane, H., *The Hour of Departure: Forces that Create Refugees and Migrants*, Washington, DC, Worldwatch Institute, 1995; Smith, D., *The State of War and Peace Atlas*, London, Penguin, 1997; and Kaldor, M., *New Wars and Old Wars*, Cambridge, Polity, 1998.
3. London, Chatto & Windus, 1998. See also Best, G., *Humanity in Warfare*, London, Methuen, 1983.
4. See for example Wight, M., *International Theory: The Three Traditions*, Leicester, Leicester University Press, 1991, pp. 22, 39, 70–2 and 137–8.
5. The 'just war' tradition stemming from the writings of St Augustine evolved into two separate sets of theories. One, *ius ad bellum*, has to do with the morality of going to war; the other, *ius in bello*, is concerned with the constraints on violence during hostilities. This is where the notion of proportionality arises.
6. See, for example, Karsh, E., *Neutrality and Small States*, London, Routledge, 1988; and Andren, N. 'On the meaning and uses of neutrality', *Cooperation and Conflict*, vol. 26, no. 2, 1991, pp. 67–83.
7. See Martin, L. (ed.), *Neutralism and Non-Alignment*, New York, Praeger, 1962.
8. *Man, the State and War*, New York, Columbia University Press, 1959.
9. Bull, H. in 'Hobbes and the International Anarchy', *Social Research*, vol. 48, no. 4, Winter 1981, points out that because Hobbes felt that states were less vulnerable than humans he saw no need for a world Leviathan.
10. Their arguments are analysed by Waltz, K., op. cit., pp. 42–79.
11. 'The moral equivalent of war', in *Memories and Studies*, New York, Longmans, 1912, pp. 262–72.
12. See Hurrell, A., 'Kant and the Kantian paradigm in International Relations', *Review of International Studies*, vol. 16, no. 3, July 1990.
13. See Kisker, G. (ed.), *World Tension*, New York, Prentice-Hall, 1951.
14. *The End of History and the Last Man*, Harmondsworth, Penguin, 1992.
15. See for example Garrison, J. and Shivpuri, P., *The Russian Threat: its myths and realities*, London, Gateway, 1983.
16. *Selected writings*, Gangulee, N., (ed.), London, Lindsay Drummond, 1945.
17. See Salvadori, M., *Cavour and the Unification of Italy*, Princeton, Princeton University Press, 1961.
18. See for example Klausmann, U. and Meinzerin, M., *Piratinnen*, Munich, Frauenoffensive, 1992, and also Creighten, M. and Nerling, L. (eds), *Iron Men, Wooden Women; Gender and seafaring in the Atlantic world, 1700–1900*, Baltimore, Johns Hopkins University Press, 1996.
19. See for example Bull, H., *The Control of the Arms Race*, London, Weidenfeld & Nicolson, 1961, especially pp. 30–64.
20. Ibid., pp. 65–76.

21. See for example Huntingdon, J.P., 'Arms races: prerequisites and results', *Public Policy*, Harvard University, 1958.

22. See Johnson, J. (ed.), *Federal World Government*, New York, H.W. Wilson, 1948.

23. For a penetrating analysis of the integration theories of which 'functionalism' is one, see Taylor, P., 'A conceptual typology of international organisation' in Groom, A.J.R. and Taylor, P., *Frameworks for International Cooperation*, London, Pinter, 1991, pp. 12–26.

24. See for example Carr, E.H., *Conditions of Peace*, London, Macmillan, 1944; and Keynes, J.M., *The General Theory of Employment, Interest and Money*, London, Macmillan, 1936.

25. See Waltz, K., *The Spread of Nuclear Weapons: More may be Better*, Adelphi Paper 171, London, International Institute for Strategic Studies, 1981.

CHAPTER 20

PREREQUISITES FOR PEACE

The previous chapter examined the various theories, stratagems, contrivances and devices designed to reduce the effects, scope, scale and incidence of what the poet Wilfred Owen called 'the pity of war'. It assessed the endeavours to regulate hostilities through codes of conduct from the early Chinese and Greek ordinances down to more recent conventions relating to the treatment of civilians, refugees, POWs, etc. It then explored the various attempts to limit the geographical scope of armed conflict through policies of neutrality, neutralism and non-alignment, but devoted the main body of the argument to a discussion of the several proposals for limiting the incidence of warfare suggested by the three distinctive theories of war-causation outlined by Waltz, the first presupposing flaws in human nature; the second presuming defects in socio-political organisation; the third locating its origin in the nature of the international system. Since each of the proffered remedies appeared to be flawed and in consequence inadequate as a prescription for perpetual peace, was all this talk of panaceas, nostrums and cure-alls a thorough waste of time?

Even if a prescription for perpetual peace remains as distant as ever, at least a critical analysis of the suggested remedies obliges us to formulate our own ideas in response. And, though this study has tried to refrain from policy recommendations and problem-solving, it can offer guidelines as to how, if not what to think about limiting the incidence and effects of warfare. Since, however, there is already a considerable body of literature on peace-enforcement – where force is employed to compel a ceasefire; peacemaking – in which mediators work to secure a ceasefire; peacekeeping – in which third parties monitor and resolve violations of a ceasefire; and peace building – in which third parties work for a final resolution of a conflict, such concepts will not be essayed here. Nor will the virtues of democracy be proclaimed here since, as indicated in Chapter 13, democratic systems are not necessarily immune from the kinds of motivations and pressures that can promote conflict and ultimately war. Nonetheless, those still searching for that elusive prescription for a peaceful world might care to consider the following:

1. that for any such formula to be viable, due regard for the feasible – what can be done – has to precede any contention regarding the desirable – what should be done; and that discussion of the viable has

to start from where we are, not where we should have been or where we would like to be;

2. that instead of trying to discover remedies, panaceas and cures, perhaps it would be more feasible to look for palliatives and coping strategies for living with conflict, as a pair of glasses might help the myopic to live with short-sightedness;

3. that concentration on arms, arms build-ups and arms races, so often taken to be the source of the problem, are somewhat misconceived. For weapons are symptoms rather than causes, and are used only when tensions escalate to the point where they cannot be contained without violence. What is required, therefore, is an understanding of the kinds of antagonisms, both domestic and international, that can escalate into war, for such a study might yield valuable insights into how they might be deflected or defused.[1]

For example, when in 1989 Serbia's Slobodan Milosevic revoked Yugoslavia's 1974 Constitution granting autonomy to Kosovo, he was virtually certain to radicalise the Albanian Kosovars and fuel their demand for outright independence. The bloodshed that has resulted was almost entirely predictable, save that it took far longer for the Kosovars to organise resistance than most of the pundits predicted. Again, Israel's decision to bulldoze land in East Jerusalem that the Palestinians claim is theirs, in order to construct Jewish settlements which could quite easily have been built in Israel proper, was bound to encourage violence and mistrust, thereby compounding the security problem the then Prime Minister Netenyahu was pledged to defuse. And NATO's decision to recruit states once allied to the Soviet Union and in violation of an understanding given to former Soviet leader Mikhail Gorbachev could only cause apprehension in Russia, raising doubts about the West's good faith, giving comfort to extreme nationalists and Communists and producing the potential for a new cold war. Such policies, which are unnecessarily provocative and run the risk of causing serious political, diplomatic, military and other problems outweighing any short-term advantages they may bring should be either discouraged before they materialise or opposed as soon as they are effected, but with some escape route, such as a UN mediation, to enable a climb-down without too much loss of face. Clearly, there should be a premium on preventive diplomacy, which involves recognising potential dangers and developing, where possible, appropriate strategies for non-violent alternatives;[2]

4. though differences between states are as common as differences between individuals or groups of people, many can be resolved without recourse to violence since between states, as between individuals and groups, cooperation is as much the norm as is contention. On the other

hand, the diplomatic bargaining, third-party mediation and arbitration that have been among the time-honoured techniques for defusing or deflecting international tensions can benefit from the addition of more novel procedures. And one technique to add to the inventory of negotiating routines, and much used by both Henry Kissinger and Eduard Shevardnadze when in charge of the foreign policies of their respective countries, is what is known as 'the pre-emptive concession'. Essentially, it involves giving away something prior to substantive discussions to sweeten the atmosphere and indicate seriousness of purpose, and was employed with considerable success in the pursuit of detente in the early 1970s and late 1980s.

Another and related procedure is what is called GRIT (Graduated Reciprocation in Tension-reduction) which involves unilateral and unambiguous initiatives of a confidence-building character – small at first, but of increasing import given a measure of reciprocity. If there are no reciprocal concessions, the process comes to an end, though it can be renewed at any time. The writer was himself involved in the process in early 1983 when he was approached by Soviet foreign office officials and asked to suggest ways by which Moscow might begin the GRIT process. My suggestion that the Kremlin might make a gesture by releasing several well-known dissidents was surprisingly well received. 'Since they are a nuisance and an embarrassment to us, we would love to release them', one of them replied. 'If you'd love to release them, why not let them go now?' was my rather obvious retort, to be countered by: 'Because you keep on telling us to. If you can stop lecturing us on how to behave for three months or so then we can release them, but we can't be seen to be pushed around by Washington and the West.' There, then, was the outline of a deal – the release of dissidents following a period of official silence on Moscow's conduct – and it was rejected by the West! There followed the airline disaster in which the Soviets shot down a Korean passenger plane which had strayed off course on to the USSR's most secret and most sensitive installations in the Far East, and the cold war escalated still further. Had the West been prepared to give GRIT a try, perhaps the Korean airliner might have been spared and those dissidents released much earlier. Indeed, perhaps the cold war might have ended several years earlier than it did;[3]

5. that the process of confidence-building does not have to be confined to diplomats and Foreign Office officials. A positive role as advisor or participant can be played by research institutes and think tanks, informed bodies of journalists, businessmen and bankers, special-interest groups and lobbies as well as concerned individuals. The work of the Rand Corporation or the Brookings Institution in the US and of

the Royal Institute of International Affairs in London are taken seriously by governments, and every so often the views of academics, including luminaries from the LSE, are canvassed by the Foreign and Commonwealth Office, by the media or by former students who are near the levers of power. In this way non-professionals of experience and expertise can have an influence on policy;

6. that confidence-building need not proceed on the basis of common ideals. After all, even the notion of peace can mean different things to different people, ranging from mere absence of war or an interlude between wars to a state of affairs in which justice or harmony in some sense prevail. It is sufficient, in a strategy to defuse or deflect tension, that the protagonists recognise common concerns, interests and perils. Indeed, there can even be what Coral Bell in her book *The Conventions of Crisis* calls an 'adversary partnership'[4] where two rival powers, say the US and the former Soviet Union, Israel and Egypt or India and Pakistan recognise their common interests in ensuring that grievances are not allowed to fester and their differences do not escalate into armed conflict. Moreover, from a study of how international crises such as the Berlin Blockade or the Cuban Missile Crisis have been successfully handled in the past, how potential crises have been deflected or defused or how 'the diplomacy of decline' was effectively managed in the Soviet Union by Gorbachev and in South Africa by de Klerk, there is much to be learned for the future;

7. since the communications revolution affects much of the world, and TV satellite transmission plays such a large part in our lives, they are almost bound to have an impact on the scope, scale and incidence of war.[5] In the 1970s, for instance, the relentless rise of the body-count as portrayed on TV intensified the popular pressure which led to the US pull-out from Vietnam; the Soviet Union's all too public tribulations in Afghanistan produced a similar pressure for a Red Army withdrawal from Kabul; while in the 1990s the Russians were obliged, for much the same reasons, to curtail their actions in Chechnya, which is not even a foreign country. Not that the effect of TV is always to spread defeatism. It can just as easily inflame – as when Iraqis, Israelis, Mexicans, Indonesians, Serbs or Hutus are seen to be gunning down innocent people. It is, however, interesting that nowadays inter-state wars are comparatively few, while intra-state wars, civil, ethnic or secessionist conflicts which can spill over into neighbouring territories, are on the rise, and it is not inconceivable that the communications revolution has played its part. After all, in the age of instant and graphic communication, inter-state war can lose and probably has lost, to some extent, its glamour;

8. although globalisation, i.e. the rise of global commerce and finance, does not make inter-state war impossible, it may affect its scope, scale

and incidence, particularly if the 'haves', if only in their own self-interest, become more sensitive to the demands and claims of the 'have nots'. Why might this be in their self-interest? In the first place, because there are rather more 'have nots' than 'haves'; secondly, and related to this, the political, social and economic cost of ignoring the frustrations of the underprivileged whether in Indonesia, Iraq, Serbia or Turkey can cumulate to boiling point, resulting in mutually ruinous conflicts to be followed by belated concessions from the 'haves' made at the point of a gun. One has only to consider, for example, the effects of Belgium's sudden retreat from the Congo in 1960, having previously resisted all attempts at fostering self-government.

Apart from considerations of the kinds outlined above, we may also be able to look forward to an era in which people interested and perhaps steeped in the study of IR play some part in the conduct of political, economic or diplomatic affairs. This might not usher in a new Utopia, but in a world which continues to see far too many decision-makers whose ignorance of international politics is only exceeded by their persuasive power, their replacement by graduates of IR would on balance have a positive effect. Certainly international society is not likely to be ill-served by scholars who could conceivably put to practical use the kinds of ideas imbibed from luminaries such as Bull, Krasner, Giddens or Burton. It is, of course, open to very few to make significant changes to the world we live in, but if former Professors of International Politics such as Henry Kissinger and Zbigniew Brzezinski can do it, then why not other students of the subject? And perhaps they could do it better!

NOTES

1. Two useful and remarkably prescient introductions to the study of escalating tensions and how they may be defused is to be found in Gross, F., *World Politics and Tension Areas*, London, University of London Press, 1966, and Gurr, T., *Why Men Rebel*, Princeton, Princeton University Press, 1970.
2. Two useful volumes in this regard are Galtung, J., *There are Alternatives! Four Roads to Peace and Security*, Nottingham, 1984, and Kriesberg, L. and Thorson, S.J., *Timing the De-escalation of International Conflicts*, Syracuse, Syracuse University Press, 1991.
3. Both Greece and Turkey may be said to have begun the GRIT process when, following their respective earthquakes in the summer of 1999, each responded with speed and generosity to the other's plea for assistance.
4. London, Oxford University Press, 1971.
5. See for example Shaw, M., *Civil Society and Media in Global Crises*, London, Pinter 1996.

PART VIII

POSTSCRIPT

CHAPTER 21

AGENDA FOR THE TWENTY-FIRST CENTURY

Common observation has it that the repercussions of any explosion grow weaker the further they are from the point of origin. However, in the light of what has been called the 'knowledge explosion', this may have to be revised. For futurologists such as John Platt suggest that if by the end of the eighteenth century the sum total of human knowledge was doubling roughly every fifty years, by 1950 the interval had been shortened to some ten years and by 1970 to five.[1] By this reasoning more than ninety per cent of our current scientific knowledge has accumulated since 1945. And while such analyses beg the question as to what one means by 'scientific knowledge' and how precisely the appropriate calculations can be made, it is nonetheless indisputable that we are living in an age of enormously accelerated innovation and discovery.

Anyone aged 55 and over will have been born before the age of nuclear fusion, of jet engines and space rockets, of solar power, fibre optics and lasers, of molecular biology and genetic engineering, of transistors, satellite communications, fax machines, word processors, smart cards and, of course, super-smart computers. But such innovations have had a profound effect on almost every aspect of contemporary life – economic, political, demographic, ecological and cultural – and it is against this background that the complex interlinkages that constitute international society have to be fashioned and understood.

Trying to make sense of such tumultuous developments and understand their implications must be a priority for the politicians, economists, financiers, ecologists, creative artists and other agenda-setters of the twenty-first century. Clearly that agenda is vastly different from that of a hundred years ago. For at the beginning of the twentieth century informed discussion in the world's major capitals centred around imperialism, monarchy, protectionism, European domination and national self-absorption expressed in the form of, for example, British 'jingoism', German naval expansion and American isolationism. But 'imperialism' is now a dirty word and 'protectionism', which has reappeared in the Balkans, is far more controversial than a century ago. As for monarchy, it has lost its mystique nearly everywhere and where it still exists, even its symbolic, ceremonial functions tend to be little more than nominal. And even if the performance and potential of the European Union are being studied with interest in different parts of the globe, Europe no longer dominates world politics. Yet, paradoxically, though much of the national self-assertiveness once so characteristic of the Western European state has been blunted, it has become one of the region's least attractive exports. At the same time, 'isolationism' now can have virtually no place in a world bound by such a complexity of political, economic, technological and cultural inter-linkages – formal and informal.

Yet, no matter how different the two agendas, they share at least one common thread. As was pointed out in Chapter 18, at about the turn of the twentieth century there was some reassessment of the role science was playing in our lives, and it seems that the matter is again under review. In the light of some of the more controversial developments in weapons technology, nuclear physics, genetic engineering and the like, people are asking: are the scientists as dispassionate in their enquiries as they would have us believe, do they know where they are taking us, will we want to go there and will the effects be generally beneficial or detrimental to the human race and the planet that has to sustain it?

Altogether, the twenty-first century agenda comprises a mixture of the novel and the well worn. But four major and interrelated themes dominate it. First, international security – a notion informed by the realisation that at the end of the twentieth century the typical armed conflict was based on religious or ethnic antagonism and occurred within rather than between societies. Furthermore, that instability, conflict and perceptions of threat in one country or part of the globe can have serious repercussions in another. After all, like a vortex, the bitter conflagrations in what was Yugoslavia sucked in NATO, the European Union, the Organisation for Security and Co-operation in Europe (OSCE), the Islamic Conference as well as the UN, and generated in turn a flood of refugees to and bankruptcies in countries both near and far. At the same time, with hopes of a 'new world order' confounded by the reality of a world seemingly in exceptional disorder as the familiar landscape of the cold war fades into history, the future role of the UN must be a key consideration. Is it to continue to be overstretched, underfunded and, in consequence, periodi-cally humiliated in its inability to cope adequately with the tasks it is required to perform; will it be properly financed or, alternatively, allowed like its predecessor the League to decline into impotence and insignifi-cance? Whatever the international community decides will affect the perception and treatment of other issues on the agenda, especially as regards economic and social welfare, the environment and human rights.

The international economy constitutes a second major item on the agenda. Almost entirely unregulated a century or so ago, it became, for reasons elaborated in Chapter 17, an arena for 'global management' at the end of the Second World War. However, the 'managers' have tended to come from the more affluent and industrialised countries, many of which practise a form of neo-mercantilism (how else could one characterise the European Union's Common External Tariff or Common Agricultural Policy?) while extolling the virtues of the market, and have been less than sympathetic to the pleas of the underprivileged for a New International Economic Order. And as the economic gulf between the increasingly interdependent developed countries and the increasingly dependent and debt-ridden LDCs tends to widen, the question of whether or not something can or should be done to close the gap preoccupies the pundits. Though the neo-liberals would leave it up to 'the market' to decide and the nationalists would argue that 'charity begins at home', yet others, possibly worried about the implications of allowing the resentment and anger of the world's poor to fester, advocate subsidised loans, government-to-government grants, most-favoured-nation trading agreements, technical assistance and/or the cancellation of debt, bi- or multi-laterally. On the other hand there must always be the fear of foreign assistance creating a dependency culture and the danger that without some check on population growth and bureaucratic corruption and incompetence, the proffered help will be wasted, with virtually no way out for those trapped in a vicious circle of poverty and deprivation.

But there are additional economic problems for the agenda-setters to deliberate. In particular, the opportunities and challenges presented by the relative decline of Washington's economic hegemony, the absorption of the US into NAFTA and the development of new centres of economic power, including Japan, the countries of ASEAN, which show signs of recovering the economic momentum they lost at the end of the 1990s and, of course, the European Union, expanding to include new members and with special trading arrangements with upwards of 60 countries in Asia, the Caribbean and the Pacific. Apart from anything else, the creation of regional blocs tends to fragment rather than integrate the world economy, often causing acute problems for states that by either choice or mischance belong to none of the regional trading associations. Moreover where, as in the EU, there are both discriminatory policies against certain imports and also subsidies for agricultural products, which create massive surpluses which are then released on to the world market, their effect is to seriously undermine the earning power of those countries especially dependent on the export of foodstuffs. Scarce wonder that so many Eastern European countries are clamouring for admission to the EU!

A further problem likely to preoccupy the framers of the economic agenda for decades to come relates to the growing power and all too frequent lack of accountability of many transnational enterprises. For the MNCs can often find ways of evading taxation in their countries of operation and of eluding official control in their pricing, marketing and employment policies. Moreover, for all their positive achievements on local economies, by being able suddenly to switch operations from one country to another, they are apt to leave trails of economic and political dissatisfaction as the credits, know-how, employment and export opportunities which they promise fail to be sustained.

The contest over economic systems constitutes an additional issue for deliberation. Though the virtual collapse of Communist rule and the transition from GATT to the WTO appeared to suggest that the debate between the 'free-marketeers' and the 'social engineers' had been settled in favour of the former, the collapse of the rouble, Eastern Europe's soaring crime and unemployment rates, the disintegration of much of the region's welfare, health and other social services, plummeting living standards and the spread of disillusion and despair in the wake of the attempt to turn a command economy into a free-market economy through 'shock therapy' are already occasioning much rethinking about the universal applicability or otherwise of the market approach. This is where the economic dimension ties in with other issues on the agenda. For political and demographic stability are increasingly dependent on the ability of governments to satisfy expectations, and if they fail to deliver there is always the danger of civil strife, rampant criminality and mass migration.

Of all the possible items on the agenda, the international environment constitutes the most novel, for until recently states, multinationals and even tribes tended to exploit and deplete the earth's resources with little consideration for their neighbours or, indeed, for future generations. In the process, land, sea and air became polluted, irradiated and toxified, posing dangers to health which, like the medieval plagues, are no respecters of frontiers. Yet since the first global initiative – the UN Environmental Programme established in Stockholm in 1972 – and the appearance of a variety of international, regional and transnational bodies specifically designed to tackle environmental issues, cross-frontier cooperation on the ecosphere has been all too slow and half-hearted, and it is often left to governments – national and local – business concerns and even individuals to make the requisite adjustments. On the other hand, at least the wider implications of environmental hazard are probably better understood today than hitherto, with notions of prevention, preservation, conservation and restoration much to the fore. And once again a leading item on the agenda is linked to the others – to the international economy insofar as environmental degradation is connected in part with the level and direction of economic development: to international security in so far as the threat of an ecological catastrophe in one country potentially jeopardises the security of all the others.

As with the international environment so with human rights, a comparatively recent concern has become a key item on the agenda. Certainly Iraq's treatment of the Kurds in the north of the country together with recent conflicts in Somalia, Rwanda and what was Yugoslavia have raised fundamental questions as to whether or not international society should legitimise 'humanitarian intervention' unambiguously where a total breakdown of civilised life or else gross violations of human rights are perceived to be occurring. One obvious problem is that such a conception challenges fundamental norms of sovereignty and non-intervention in the internal affairs of states. A further problem concerns the politicisation of the very concept of 'human rights', which for all the declarations and conventions on the subject remains a somewhat nebulous concept to be used frequently in a partisan way by governments wishing to expand their influence or to strengthen resistance to regimes to which they are already opposed.[2] In any case, armed humanitarian intervention, as in Vietnam, may prove counter-productive, or else inordinately costly in terms of lives and real estate, as in Kosovo. As, moreover, there are ways short of military intervention by which a country can put pressure on governments of whose actions it strongly disapproves – moral censure, diplomatic rupture, economic sanctions and political subversion among them – we can expect the international community to try these before taking military action as a last resort.

Nonetheless, the electronic media tend to sensitise people to the suffering of others, and ever since the Nuremberg and Tokyo trials after the Second World War, the gross abuse of human rights in the form of genocide, 'ethnic cleansing' or mass oppression has aroused international concern. Subsequently the notion of what constitutes a human right has been extended to include a social and economic dimension, including the 'right' to a job, a home, a decent standard of living and so forth. As such it ties in with other items on the international agenda, because the use of arbitrary power or the condition of mass and unalleviated poverty can lead, as in the case of former Yugoslavia, to mass migrations, affecting the security and economic well-being of other societies, and ultimately necessitating a colossal financial outlay in the work of rebuilding and resettlement.

So far we have considered the practical agenda for the twenty-first century. But, since this is a student text, what about the academic agenda? As indicated earlier, International Relations has been steeped in controversy ever since it was first taught. For much of the time the debate was between Realists, Pluralists and Structuralists, and no doubt that contention will continue until well into the twenty-first century. But like many other studies, IR is beginning to feel the influence of both post-modernism and critical theory. The post-modernist scepticism of universal values and its embrace of new social movements has already been expressed in the form of international studies stressing feminist, gay, environmental, ethnic and religious issues, and no doubt the new century will see additions to the list including, perhaps, the politics of age and of disability.[3] The future for critical theory is, however, less clear. Presaged on a particular conception of human emancipation, it is in danger, as one of its detractors recently pointed out, of being 'open to the charge of not being a "theory" at all, but a form of propaganda or persuasion masquerading as science'.[4] An even more serious objection is the opaque and sometimes well-nigh incomprehensible prose of some of its leading protagonists, whose penchant for quoting one another scarcely aids comprehension. Clearly, therefore, if critical theory is to have an academic future it has to acquire a more empirical base and, in our media-conscious age, a more congenial mode of exposition. More assured of a future are IR texts with a proven track record and with a foundation in international political economy, international law or strategic studies or some prescription for a better-ordered international society.

Is the discipline at a turning point? Those who believe that International Relations has to be restructured along the lines now fashionable in some of the other social and philosophical disciplines will say that it is. Those accepting the logic of this text may well feel that it is not. After all, throughout the centuries societies have been characterised by an encounter between elements of continuity and the forces of change, and, as indicated in Chapter 1, international society is no exception. Moreover, the dialectic between continuity and change has also informed the discipline. If, therefore, the state were to be pronounced clinically dead, and IR was to lose touch with its traditional subject matter and methods of enquiry, the study would indeed be at a turning point. In that event there would be little or no call for a text of this kind, save as an intellectual curiosity. But if this volume and others of a similar character continue to be on the academic agenda throughout the twenty-first century rather than being left to gather dust on the library shelves, it would suggest that the subject had not yet completely outgrown its original preoccupations and was not about to turn itself into an abstruse, arcane and mildly pretentious sub-branch of social science theory. Perhaps the solution is, as Mao once put it in a rather different context, to continue to 'let a hundred flowers bloom: let a hundred schools contend'.

NOTES

1. 'The acceleration of evolution', in *The Futurist*, 14 February 1981.
2. See for example Ignatieff, M., *The Warrior's Honour*, London, Chatto & Windus, 1998.

3. Post-modern approaches to the study are essayed in Booth, K. and Smith, S. (eds), *International Relations Theory Today*, Cambridge, Cambridge University Press, 1995; Derby, P. (ed.), *At The Edge of International Relations: Postcolonialism, Gender and Dependency*, London, Pinter, 1997; Neufeld, M., *The Restructuring of International Relations Theory*, Cambridge, Cambridge University Press, 1995; and Rosenau, P., *Postmodernism and the Social Sciences*, Princeton, Princeton University Press, 1992.

4. Moon, J.D. 'Political ethics and critical theory', in Sabia, D.R. and Wallulis, J. (eds), *Changing Social Science*, New York, State University of New York Press, 1983, p. 176.

SELECTED BIBLIOGRAPHY

General introductory texts

J. Baylis and N. Rengger (eds), *Dilemmas of World Politics*, Oxford, Clarendon Press, 1992.

C. Brown, *Understanding International Relations*, Basingstoke, Macmillan, 1997.

H. Bull, *The Anarchical Society*, London, Macmillan, 1977.

B. Hocking and M. Smith, *World Politics: An Introduction to International Relations*, Hemel Hempstead, Harvester Wheatsheaf, 1990.

B. Hollis and S. Smith, *Explaining and Understanding International Relations*, Oxford, Clarendon, 1990.

K.J. Holsti, *International Politics*, 6th edn, Englewood Cliffs, Prentice Hall, 1992.

C.W. Kegley and E. Wittkopf, *World Politics*, 7th edn, Basingstoke, Macmillan, 1999.

R. Little and M. Smith, *Perspectives on World Politics*, 2nd edn, London, Routledge, 1992.

E. Luard, *Basic Texts in International Relations*, London, Macmillan, 1992.

F.S. Northedge, *The International Political System*, London, Faber, 1976.

W. Olson and A.J.R. Groom, *International Relations: Then and Now*, London, HarperCollins, 1991.

R. Purnell, *The Society of States: An Introduction to International Politics*, London, Weidenfeld & Nicolson, 1973.

P.A. Reynolds, *An Introduction to International Relations*, 3rd edn, London, Longman, 1994.

B. White, R. Little and M. Smith, *Issues in World Politics*, Basingstoke, Macmillan, 1997.

M. Williams (ed.), *International Relations in the Twentieth Century: a Reader*, Macmillan, 1989.

A. Wolfers, *Discord and Collaboration*, Baltimore, Johns Hopkins University Press, 1966.

Contending theories

D. Baldwin (ed.), *Neorealism and Neoliberalism: The Contemporary Debate*, New York, Columbia University Press, 1983.

C. Beitz, *Political Theory and International Relations*, Princeton, Princeton University Press, 1979.

J. Burton, *World Society*, London, Cambridge University Press, 1972.

E.H. Carr, *The Twenty Years' Crisis*, London, Macmillan, 1939.

M. Donelan, *Elements of International Political Theory*, Oxford, Oxford University Press, 1990.

J. Dougherty and R. Pfaltzgraff, *Contending Theories in International Relations*, 3rd edn, New York, HarperCollins, 1990.

J.C. Garnett, *Commonsense and the Theory of International Politics*, London, Macmillan, 1984.

F. Halliday, *Rethinking International Relations*, London, Macmillan, 1994.

K.J. Holsti, *The Dividing Discipline*, London, Allen & Unwin, 1985.

S. Huntingdon, *The Clash of Civilisations and the Remaking of World Order*, London, Simon and Schuster, 1997.

R. Keohane and J. Nye, *Power and Interdependence*, Boston, Little, Brown, 1977.

M. Light and A.J.R. Groom (eds), *International Relations: A Handbook of Current Theory*, London, Pinter, 1985.

R. Little and M. Smith, *Perspectives on World Politics*, 2nd edn, London, Routledge, 1992.

H. Morgenthau, *Politics Among Nations*, New York, Knopf, 1948.

J. Rosenau, *The Scientific Study of Foreign Policy*, London, Pinter, 1980.

J. Rosenberg, *The Empire of Civil Society: A Critique of the Realist Theory of International Relations*, London, Verso, 1994.

G. Schwarzenberger, *Power Politics*, 3rd edn, London, Stevens, 1964.

I. Wallerstein, *The Capitalist World Economy*, London, Cambridge University Press, 1979.

K. Waltz, *A Theory of International Politics*, Reading, Mass., Addison-Wesley, 1979.

M. Wight, *International Theory: The Three Traditions*, London, Pinter, 1990.

The evolution of international society

G. Barraclough, *An Introduction to Contemporary History*, Harmondsworth, Penguin, 1967.

A. Bozeman, *Politics and Culture in International History*, Princeton, Princeton University Press, 1960.

H. Bull and A. Watson (eds), *The Expansion of International Society*, Oxford, Oxford University Press, 1984.

I. Clark, *The Hierarchy of States*, Cambridge, Cambridge University Press, 1989.

F.H. Hinsley, *Power and The Pursuit of Peace*, London, Cambridge University Press, 1963.

E. Luard, *Types of International Society*, New York, Macmillan, 1977.

R.N. Rosecrance, *Action and Reaction in World Politics*, Boston, Little, Brown, 1963.

A. Watson, *The Evolution of International Society*, London, Routledge, 1992.

M. Wight, *Systems of States*, Leicester, Leicester University Press, 1977.

The state

G. Allison, *Essence of Decision*, Boston, Little, Brown, 1971.

B. Anderson, *Imagined Communities*, London, Verso, 1991.

J. Barber and M. Smith, *The Nature of Foreign Policy: A Reader*, Edinburgh, Holmes McDougall, 1974.

M. Clarke and B. White (eds), *Understanding Foreign Policy*, Aldershot, Elgar, 1989.

M. Donelan (ed.), *Reason of States*, London, Allen & Unwin, 1978.

I. Duchacek, *Nations and Men*, 3rd edn, New York, University Press of America, 1975.

E. Gellner, *Nations and Nationalism*, Oxford, Blackwell, 1983.

F.H. Hinsley, *Sovereignty*, Cambridge, Cambridge University Press, 1986.

E. Hobsbawm, *Nations and Nationalism Since 1780*, Cambridge, Cambridge University Press, 1990.

E. Hobsbawm and T. Ranger (eds), *The Invention of Tradition*, Cambridge, Cambridge University Press, 1983.

M. Ignatieff, *Blood and Belonging*, London, Oxford University Press, 1995.

G. Ionescu (ed.), *Between Sovereignty and Integration*, New York, Wiley, 1974.

A. James, *Sovereign Statehood: The Basis of International Society*, London, Allen & Unwin, 1986.

E. Karsh, *Neutrality and Small States*, London, Routledge, 1988.

E. Kedourie, *Nationalism*, London, Hutchinson, 1960.

J. Mayall, *Nationalism and International Society*, Cambridge, Cambridge University Press, 1990.

A.D. Smith, *The Ethnic Revival in the Modern World*, Cambridge, Cambridge University Press, 1981.

G. Stern, *Leaders and Leadership*, London, LSE/BBC World Service, 1993.

Inter-state behaviour

G. Blainey, *The Causes of War*, 3rd edn, Basingstoke, Macmillan, 1988.

H. Bull, *The Anarchical Society*, London, Macmillan, 1977.

I. Claude, *Power and International Relations*, New York, Random House, 1962.

B.C. Cohen, *The Question of Imperialism*, London, Weidenfeld & Nicolson, 1980.

M. Doxey, *International Sanctions in Contemporary Perspective*, London, Macmillan, 1987.

J.C. Hare and C.B. Joynt, *Ethics and International Affairs*, London, Macmillan, 1982.

R. Higgins, *Problems and Process: International Law and How we Use it*, Oxford, Clarendon, 1994.

M. Howard (ed.), *Restraints on War*, Oxford, Oxford University Press, 1979.

A. James (ed.), *The Bases of International Order*, London, Oxford University Press, 1973.

M. Kaldor, *New Wars and Old Wars*, Cambridge, Polity Press, 1998.

H. Kissinger, *Diplomacy*, London, Simon & Schuster, 1995.

K. Nelson and S. Olin, *Why War?*, California, University of California Press, 1979.

H. Nicolson, *Diplomacy*, London, Oxford University Press, 1963.

R. Niebuhr, *Moral Man and Immoral Society*, New York, Scribner's, 1952.

R. Pettman, *Moral Claims in World Affairs*, London, Croom Helm, 1979.

R. Rothstein, *The Weak in the World of the Strong*, New York, Columbia University Press, 1977.

R.J. Vincent, *Non-Intervention and International Order*, Princeton, Princeton University Press, 1974.

J.M. Walt, *The Origins of Alliances*, Ithaca, Cornell University Press, 1987.

K. Waltz, *Man, the State and War*, New York, Columbia University Press, 1959.

A. Watson, *Diplomacy: The Dialogue between States*, London, Methuen, 1982.

M. Wight, *Power Politics*, Harmondsworth, Penguin, 1979.

Non-state actors

A.L. Bennett, *International Organisations*, 5th edn, Englewood Cliffs, Prentice Hall, 1989.

M.S. and L.S. Finkelstein (eds), *Collective Security*, San Francisco, Chandler, 1966.

A. James, *Peacekeeping in International Politics*, Basingstoke, Macmillan, 1990.

C. Kedley (ed.), *International Terrorism*, New York, St Martin's Press, 1990.

R. Keohane and J. Nye (eds), *Transnational Relations and World Politics*, London, Harvard University Press, 1971.

S. Krasner (ed.), *International Regimes*, New York, Cornell University Press, 1982.

E. Luard, *Conflict and Peace in the Modern International System*, Basingstoke, Macmillan, 1988.

R.W. Mansbach *et al.*, *The Web of World Politics*, Englewood Cliffs, Prentice Hall, 1976.

J. Piscatori, *Islam in a World of Nation States*, Cambridge, Cambridge University Press, 1986.

A. Roberts and B. Kingsbury (eds), *The U.N: Divided World*, 2nd edn, Oxford, Clarendon Press, 1993.

G. Stern, *The Rise and Decline of International Communism*, Aldershot, Elgar, 1990.

P. Taylor, *Non-State Actors in International Politics*, Boulder, Westview, 1984.

P. Taylor and A.J.R. Groom, *International Institutions at Work*, London, Pinter, 1988.

H. and W. Wallace (eds), *Policy-making in the European Union*, 3rd edn, Oxford, Oxford University Press, 1996.

The international political economy

P. Bauer, *Reality and Rhetoric*, London, Weidenfeld & Nicolson, 1984.

W. Brandt *et al.*, *North-South: A Programme for Survival*, London, Commonwealth Secretariat, 1981.

E. Brett, *The World Economy since the War: The Politics of Uneven Development*, London, Macmillan, 1985.

R. Cassen, *Does Aid Work?*, Oxford, Oxford University Press, 1985.

F. Fukayama, *The End of History and the Last Man*, Harmondsworth, Penguin, 1992.

S. George, *A Fate worse than Debt*, Harmondsworth, Penguin, 1988.

S. Gill and D. Law, *The Global Political Economy*, Hemel Hempstead, Harvester, 1988.

R. Gilpin, *The Political Economy of International Relations*, Princeton, Princeton University Press, 1987.

N. Harris, *The End of the Third World*, Harmondsworth, Penguin, 1986.

G.K. Helleiner, *International Economic Disorder*, London, Macmillan, 1980.

R. Keohane, *After Hegemony*, Princeton, Princeton University Press, 1984.

S. Krasner, *Structural Conflict: The Third World Against Global Liberalism* Berkeley, California, 1985.

R. Lipschutz, *When Nations Clash*, Ballinger, 1989.

J. Spero, *The Politics of International Economic Relations*, 4th edn, London, Hyman Unwin, 1990.

S. Strange (ed.), *Paths to International Political Economy*, London, Allen & Unwin, 1984.

S. Strange, *States and Markets*, London, Pinter, 1988.

I. Wallerstein, *The Politics of the World-Economy*, New York, Columbia University Press, 1984.

World society?

M. Banks (ed.), *Conflict and World Society*, Brighton, Wheatsheaf, 1984.

H. Bull, *The Control of the Arms Race*, London, Weidenfeld & Nicolson, 1961.

J. Burton, *World Society*, London, Cambridge University Press, 1972.

F. Cairncross, *Costing the Earth*, London, Economists Books, 1991.

R. Falk, *The Promise of World Order*, Brighton, Wheatsheaf, 1987.

Y.H. Ferguson and R. Mansbach, *The State, Conceptual Chaos and the Future of International Relations Theory*, Boulder, Lynne Rienner Publishers, 1989.

M. Finkelstein, *Collective Security*, San Francisco, Chandler, 1966.

J. Galtung, *There are Alternatives: Four Roads to Peace and Security*, Nottingham, Spokesman Books, 1984.

A. Hurrell and B. Kingsley, *The International Politics of the Environment*, Oxford, Oxford University Press, 1992.

M. Ignatieff, *The Warrior's Honour*, London, Chatto & Windus, 1998.

E. Luard, *The Globalisation of Politics*, London, Macmillan, 1990.

R.L. Mansbach *et al.*, *The Web of World Politics*, Englewood Cliffs, Prentice Hall, 1976.

J. Mueller, *Retreat from Doomsday: The Obsolescence of Major War*, New York, Basic Books, 1989.

R. Pettman, *Human Behavior and World Politics*, New York, St Martins, 1975.

J. Rosenau, *Turbulence in World Politics: A Theory of Change and Continuity*, Princeton, Princeton University Press, 1990.

T. Skocpol, *States and Social Revolutions*, London, Cambridge University Press, 1979.

J. Spanier and J. Nogee, *The Politics of Disarmament*, New York, Praeger, 1962.

C. Thomas, *The Environment in International Relations*, London, Royal Institute of International Affairs, 1992.

NAME INDEX

SUBJECT INDEX